100 Hikes / Travel Guide

Eastern Oregon

SECOND EDITION

William L. Sullivan

Navillus Press

The Hoffer Lakes in the Elkhorn Range (Hike #28).

Published by the Navillus Press
1958 Onyx Street
Eugene, Oregon 97403

www.oregonhiking.com
ISBN 0967783097
Printed in USA

Cover: Tombstone Lake (Hike #69). Inset: Mariposa lily. Spine: Painted Cove Trail (Hike #15). Back cover: Baker City. Frontispiece: Little Blitzen Gorge at Steens Mountain (Hike #93). This page: Frances Lake (Hike #61).

SAFETY CONSIDERATIONS: Many of the trails in this book pass through Wilderness and remote country where hikers are exposed to unavoidable risks. On any hike, the weather may change suddenly. The fact that a hike is included in this book, or that it may be rated as easy, does not necessarily mean it will be safe or easy for you. Prepare yourself with proper equipment and outdoor skills, and you will be able to enjoy these hikes with confidence.

Every effort has been made to assure the accuracy of the information in this book. The author has hiked all 100 of the featured trails, and the trails' administrative agencies have reviewed the maps and text. Nonetheless, construction, logging, and storm damage may cause changes. Corrections and updates are welcome, and often rewarded. They may be sent to the publisher or to *sullivan@efn.org*.

Contents

(Horse icon) - Horses OK (Bicycle icon) - Bicycles OK (Dog icon) - Dogs on leash (Crossed dog icon) - No pets

(Flower icon) - Wildflowers (count petals for peak month) *Parking fee

C - Crowded or restricted backpacking area

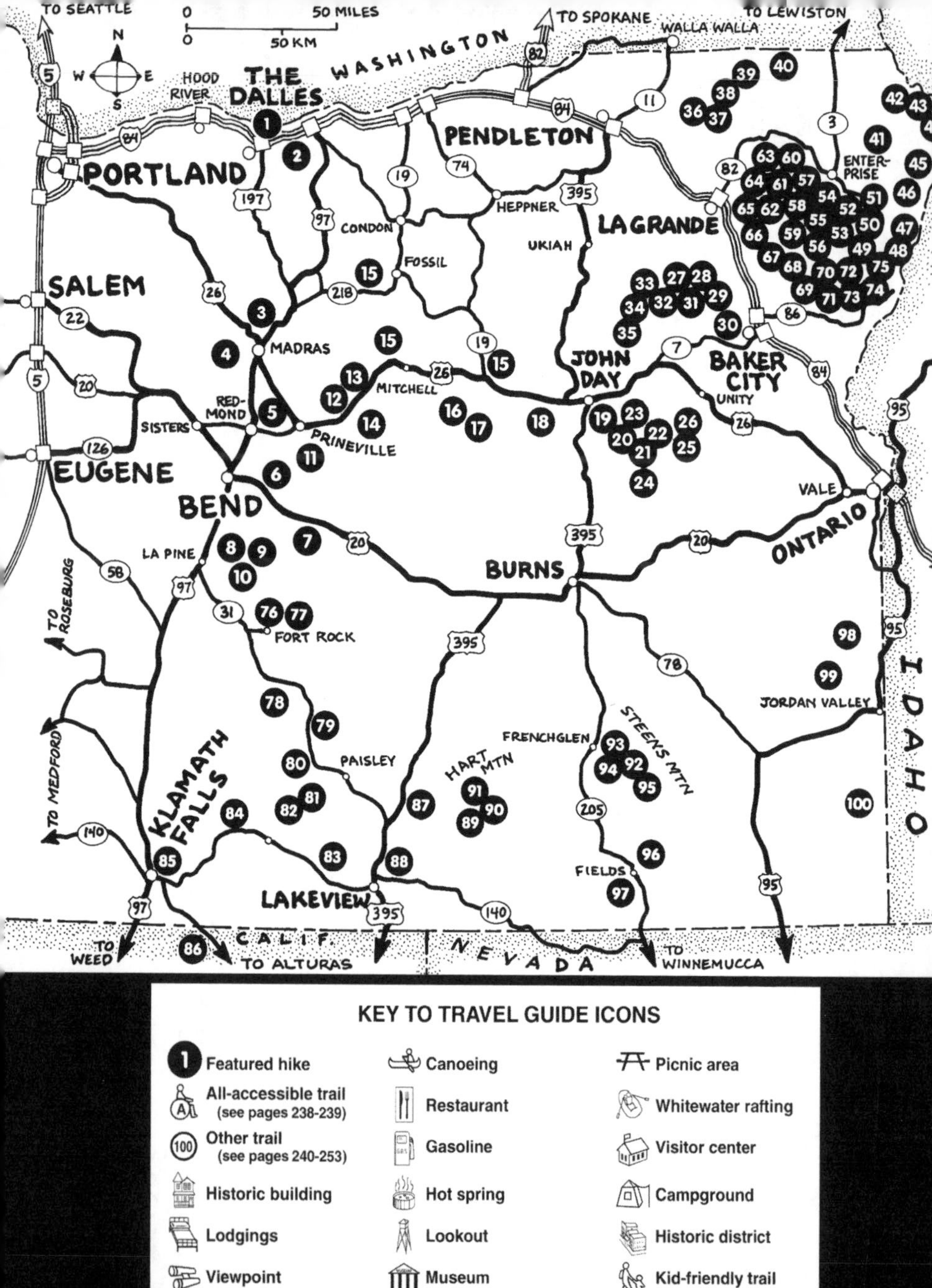

KEY TO TRAVEL GUIDE ICONS

- Featured hike
- All-accessible trail (see pages 238-239)
- Other trail (see pages 240-253)
- Historic building
- Lodgings
- Viewpoint
- Boat launch
- Canoeing
- Restaurant
- Gasoline
- Hot spring
- Lookout
- Museum
- Birdwatching
- Picnic area
- Whitewater rafting
- Visitor center
- Campground
- Historic district
- Kid-friendly trail
- Backpacking

[horse] - Horses OK [bicycle] - Bicycles OK [dog] - Dogs on leash [no dog] - No pets

[flower] - Wildflowers (count petals for peak month) *Parking fee

C - Crowded or restricted backpacking area

[Horse symbol] - Horses OK [Bicycle symbol] - Bicycles OK [Dog symbol] - Dogs on leash [No-dog symbol] - No pets
[Flower symbol] - Wildflowers (count petals for peak month) *Parking fee
C - Crowded or restricted backpacking area

Introduction

Welcome to the spectacular trails and byways of Eastern Oregon! This comprehensive guide has everything you need to plan a day hike, a weekend tour, or a weeks-long vacation, with tips on where to stay and what to see.

HOW TO USE THIS BOOK

The Travel Guide

The book divides Eastern Oregon into 11 regions, each identified by a geographic title (for example, *Strawberry Mountain*) and by the name of the nearest city (for example, *John Day*). For each region you'll find travel notes and an overview map featuring campgrounds, historic districts, bed and breakfast inns, interpretive centers, hot springs, birdwatching sites, and other attractions.

The Trail Guide

When you're ready to hit the trail, look through the book's 100 featured hikes. To quickly find an outing to match your tastes, look for the following special symbols in the upper right-hand corner of the hikes' headings:

 Children's favorites—walks popular with the 4- to 12-year-old crowd, but fun for hikers of all ages.

 All-year trails, hikable most or all of winter.

 Hikes suitable for backpackers as well as day hikers. Crowds unlikely.

Crowded or restricted backpacking areas.

The Information Blocks

Each hike is rated by difficulty. **Easy** hikes are between 1 and 7 miles round trip and gain less than 1000 feet in elevation. Never very steep, they make good warm-up trips for experienced hikers or first-time trips for novices.

Trips rated as **Moderate** range from 4 to 10 miles round trip. These routes may gain up to 2000 feet of elevation or may require some pathfinding skills. Hikers must be in good condition and will need to take several rest stops.

Difficult trails demand top physical condition, with a strong heart and strong knees. These challenging hikes are 6 to 20 miles round trip and may gain 3000 feet or more. Backpacking can break difficult hikes into manageable segments.

Distances are given in round-trip mileage, except for those trails where a car or bicycle shuttle is suggested and the mileage is specifically listed as one-way.

The **elevation gains** show the *cumulative* amount of climbing required, including uphill sections on the return trip. Those who puff climbing a few flights of stairs may consider even 500 feet of elevation a strenuous climb, and should watch this listing carefully.

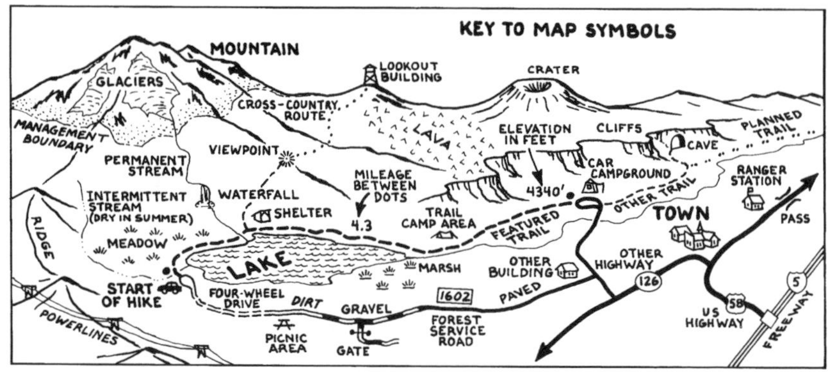

The **hiking season** of any trail varies with the weather. In a cold year, a trail described as "Open May through October" may not yet be clear of snow by May 1, and may be socked in by a blizzard before October 31. Similarly, a trail that is "Open all year" may close due to storms or may be inaccessible when wet weather makes dirt roads undrivable.

The **allowed use** of a trail may be limited to hikers, or may include bicyclists, equestrians, and motorcyclists. For a quick overview of paths recommended for horses and mountain bikes, look for the list of horse and bicycle symbols in the table of contents.

Dogs are allowed on 97 of the 100 featured hikes, and leashes are required on 8 trails. Restrictions are noted both in the text and in the table of contents.

TOPOGRAPHIC MAPS

All hikers in wilderness and other remote areas should carry a **topographic map,** with contour lines to show elevation. Topographic maps can be downloaded for free at *msrmaps.com* and many other Internet sites. Maps of Wilderness Areas can be purchased at outdoor stores or from Nature of the Northwest at *www.naturenw.org*. It's also handy to have a visitor map of the local National Forest or Bureau of Land Management District, available at ranger stations and information centers for about $10.

TRAILHEAD PARKING FEES

No fees are charged to use the majority of trails described in this book, but the Forest Service does require a **Northwest Forest Pass** for cars parking within a quarter mile of a few trailheads, primarily in the Wallowa Mountains. The text descriptions for these hikes mention whether parking permits are required, and if you can pay at the trailhead. You can also pick up a parking permit in advance at a ranger station or outdoor store. A Northwest Forest Pass costs $5 per car per day, or $30 per year, but this may change. A few state parks have their own trailhead parking fees, described in the appropriate entries.

WILDERNESS RESTRICTIONS

Sixty-one of the featured hikes enter designated Wilderness Areas—beautiful, isolated places protected by special restrictions. Advance permits are not required to enter Wilderness Areas in Eastern Oregon, although you may have to fill out a permit at the trailhead. Some rules vary, but in general you can expect certain limits in Wilderness Areas:

- Groups must be no larger than 12.
- Campfires are discouraged, and are banned within 100 feet of any water source or maintained trail.
- Bicycles and other vehicles (except wheelchairs) are banned.
- Horses and pack stock cannot be tethered within 200 feet of any water source or shelter.
- Motorized equipment, hang gliders, and fireworks are banned.
- Live trees and shrubs must not be cut or damaged.

In addition, some rules apply to all federal lands:

- Collecting arrowheads or other cultural artifacts is a federal crime.
- Permits are required to dig up plants.

SAFETY ON THE TRAIL

Wild Animals

Part of the fun of hiking is watching for wildlife. Lovers of wildness rue the demise of our most impressive species. Grizzly bears were hunted to extinction in Oregon by 1891. Wolves, once also extinct in the area, have been reintroduced to Idaho and have recently established a few small packs in the mountains of northeast Oregon, although they do not interact with people. The black bears and cougars in Oregon are so profoundly shy you probably won't see one in years of hiking. No one has ever been killed by any of these animals in the history of Oregon.

Rattlesnakes, too, have become extremely rare. The State Health Division reports that only one Oregonian died from a rattlesnake in the most recent decade. Statistically, this makes rattlesnakes less of a threat than horses, bees, dogs, or even cows. Nonetheless, if you hear a rattle or recognize the snake's diamondback pattern, it's your cue to give this reclusive animal some space.

Ticks have received some publicity as carriers of Lyme disease, which begins with flu-like symptoms and an often circular rash. While this is a problem in other states, only a couple of cases have been reported in Oregon. Nonetheless, ticks can be a nuisance, particularly in dry grass or open woods during May and June. Brush off your clothes after a hike, and check the skin at your collar and pant cuffs. If a tick has attached itself, do not break it loose. Instead untwist its body like a screw for several complete rotations and it will let go.

Mosquitoes can be a problem for a few weeks each year. To avoid them, remember that these insects hatch about ten days after the snow melts from the trails and that they remain in force about two weeks. Thus, if a given trail is listed as "Open mid-June," you might expect mosquitoes there in early July.

Drinking Water

Day hikers should bring all the water they will need—at least a quart per person. A microscopic parasite, *Giardia,* has forever changed the old custom of dipping a drink from every brook. The symptoms of "beaver fever," debilitating nausea and diarrhea, commence a week or two after ingesting *Giardia.*

Many hikers and most backpackers now carry a water filter that has been certified to remove *Giardia.* The filters are generally attached to a small pump or a bottle lid, making it easy to draw water directly from lakes and streams. Alternative methods of removing *Giardia* include adding approved water purification tablets (which can make the water unpalatable) and boiling the water for five minutes (which requires both fuel and time).

Proper Equipment

Even on the tamest hike a surprise storm or a wrong turn can suddenly make the gear you carry very important. Always bring a pack with the ten essentials: a warm, waterproof coat, drinking water, extra food, knife, matches in a waterproof container, fire starter (butane lighter or candle), first aid kit, flashlight, topographic map, and compass. Before leaving on a hike, tell someone where you are going so they can alert the county sheriff to begin a search if you do not return on time. If you're lost, stay put and keep warm. The number one killer in the woods is *hypothermia*—being cold and wet too long. Food is not nearly so important as water. For day hikes, carry a quart per person. For overnight desert trips, carry a gallon per person per day.

Global Positioning System (GPS) Devices

Some of the hikes in this book include GPS notations, such as *N43°45.554' W122°37.147'*. This optional information may be used to pinpoint your location using a handheld, battery-operated GPS device that tracks satellite signals. Though handy, GPS devices are no substitute for a map and compass, because the devices do not always work in dense forest and because their batteries can fail.

COURTESY ON THE TRAIL

As our trails become more heavily used, rules of trail etiquette become stricter:

- Pick no flowers.
- Leave no litter. Eggshells and orange peels can last for decades.
- Avoid bringing pets into wilderness areas. Dogs can frighten wildlife and disturb other hikers.
- Step off the trail on the downhill side to let horses pass. Speak to them quietly to help keep them from spooking.
- Do not shortcut switchbacks.

For overnight trail trips, low-impact camping was once merely a courtesy, but is on the verge of becoming a requirement, both to protect the landscape and to preserve a sense of solitude for others. The most important rules:

- Camp out of sight of lakes and trails.
- Build no campfire. Cook on a backpacking stove.
- Wash 100 feet from any lake or stream.
- Camp on duff, rock, or sand—never on meadow vegetation.
- Pack out garbage—don't burn or bury it.

FOR MORE INFORMATION

Visitor Bureaus

The Travel Guide portion of this book features a selection of the most interesting things to do and see in Eastern Oregon. Local visitor bureaus are glad to provide information about additional restaurants, motels, and commercial attractions. Here are the telephone numbers and websites for this free service:

Baker City, 888-523-5855, *www.visitbaker.com*
Bend, 877-245-8484, *www.visitbend.com*
Boardman, 541-481-9252, *www.visitboardman.com*
Burns, 541-573-2636, *www.harneycounty.com/thingstodo.html*

Elgin, 541-786-1770, *elginoregonchamber.com*
Enterprise, 800-585-4121, *www.wallowacountychamber.com*
Hermiston, 541-567-6151, *www.hermistonchamber.com*
John Day, 800-769-5664, *www.gcoregonlive.com*
Klamath Falls, 800-445-6728, *www.discoverklamath.com*
La Grande, 800-848-9969, *www.unioncountychamber.com*
La Pine, 541-536-9771, *www.lapine.com*
Lakeview, 877-947-6040, *www.lakecountychamber.org*
Madras, 800-967-3564, *www.madraschamber.com*
Maupin, 541-993-1708, *www.maupinoregon.com*
Nyssa, 541-372-3091, *www.nyssachamber.com*
Ontario, 866-989-8012, *www.ontariochamber.com*
Pendleton, 800-547-8911, *pendletonchamber.com*
Prineville, 541-447-6304, *visitprineville.org*
Redmond, 541-923-5191, *www.visitredmondoregon.com*
Sisters, 866-549-0252, *www.sisterschamber.com*
Sunriver, 541-593-8149, *www.sunriverchamber.com*
The Dalles, 541-296-2231, *thedalleschamber.com*
Umatilla, 800-922-4825, *www.umatillaoregonchamber.org*
Vale, 541-473-3800, *valechamber.com*

Trail Management Agencies

If you'd like to check trail conditions or restrictions, call directly to the trail's administrative agencies, listed below with the trails they manage. Ranger districts also have trail reports and rental information for cabins and lookouts at *www.fs.fed.us/r6.*

Hike	Managing Agency
7-10	Bend - Fort Rock Ranger District—541-383-4000
18-21	Blue Mountain Ranger District—541-575-3000
82	Bly Ranger District—541-353-2427
92-95, 97	Burns District BLM—541-573-4400
1	Columbia Hills State Park—360-902-8844
5	Crooked River National Grassland—541-416-6640
49-75	Eagle Cap Ranger District—541-426-5509
15	John Day Fossil Beds Nat'l Mon—541-987-2333
89-91	Hart Mountain Antelope Refuge—541-947-2731
42-48	Hells Canyon Nat'l Recreation Area—541-523-6391
85	Klamath County Dept of Tourism—800-445-6728
77, 87	Lakeview District BLM—541-947-2177
83, 88	Lakeview Ranger District—541-947-3334
86	Lava Beds National Monument—530-667-8113
12-14	Lookout Mountain Ranger District—541-416-6500
41, 96	Nature Conservancy—541-426-3458
33-35	North Fork John Day Ranger District—541-427-3231
2, 4, 76, 84	Oregon State Parks—800-551-6949
16, 17	Paulina Ranger District—541-477-6900
80, 81	Paisley Ranger District—541-943-3114
39, 40	Pomeroy Ranger District—509-843-1891
22-26	Prairie City Ranger District—541-820-3800
3, 6, 11	Prineville District BLM—541-416-6700
78	Silver Lake Ranger District—541-576-2107
79	Summer Lake Wildlife Area—541-943-3152
36-38	Walla Walla Ranger District—509-522-6290
27-32, 72-75	Whitman Ranger District—541-523-4476
98-100	Vale District BLM—541-473-3144

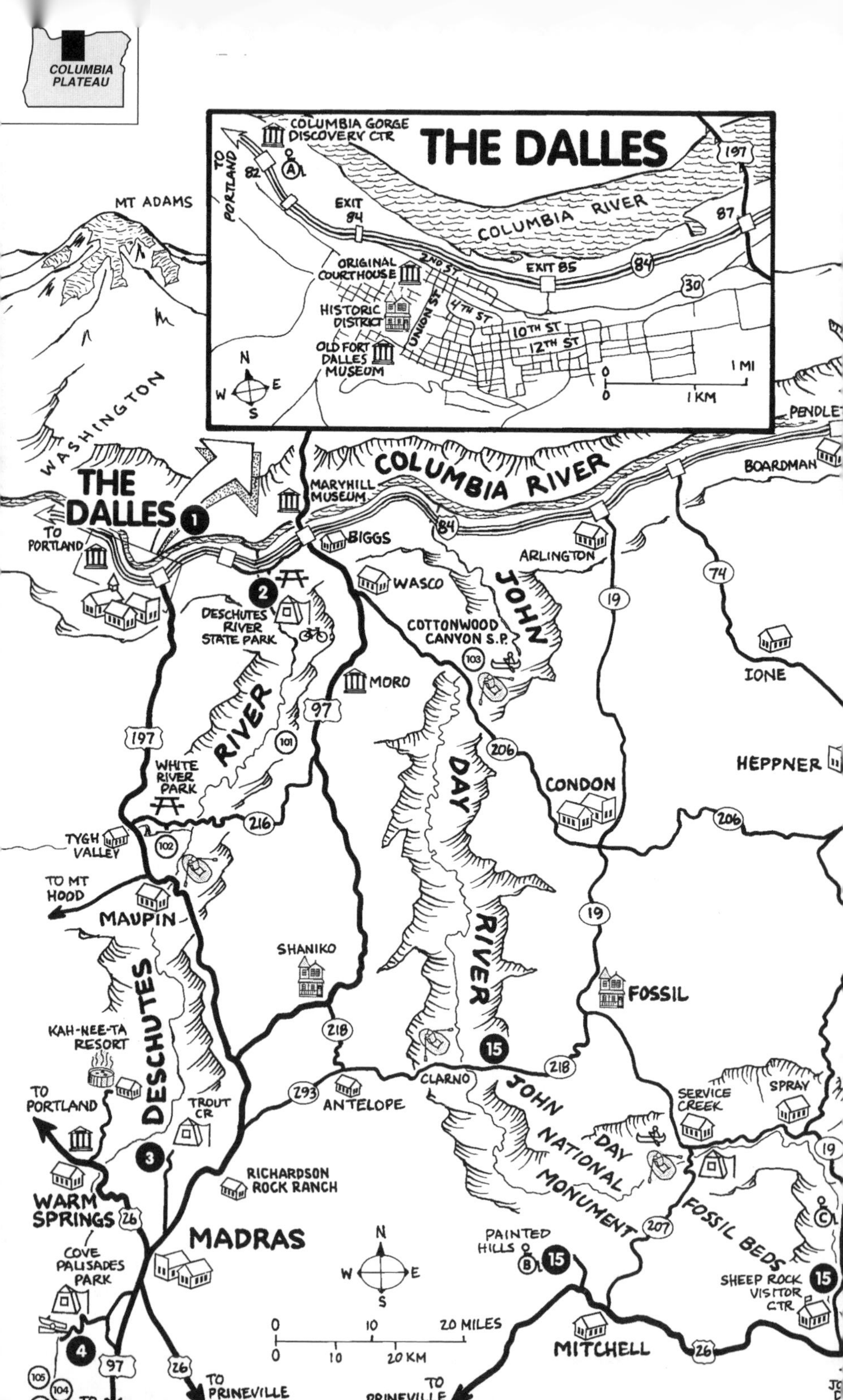
COLUMBIA PLATEAU
THE DALLES
COLUMBIA GORGE DISCOVERY CTR
TO PORTLAND
82
A
EXIT 84
COLUMBIA RIVER
197
87
ORIGINAL COURTHOUSE
2ND ST
EXIT 85
84
30
HISTORIC DISTRICT
UNION ST
4TH ST
10TH ST
12TH ST
OLD FORT DALLES MUSEUM
N
W
E
S
0
1 MI
0
1 KM
PENDLETON
MT ADAMS
WASHINGTON
THE DALLES
1
TO PORTLAND
MARYHILL MUSEUM
COLUMBIA RIVER
BOARDMAN
BIGGS
84
ARLINGTON
2
WASCO
JOHN
74
DESCHUTES RIVER STATE PARK
19
COTTONWOOD CANYON S.P.
IONE
103
MORO
97
RIVER
DAY
197
101
206
HEPPNER
WHITE RIVER PARK
CONDON
216
206
TYGH VALLEY
102
TO MT HOOD
MAUPIN
19
SHANIKO
RIVER
FOSSIL
DESCHUTES
KAH-NEE-TA RESORT
218
15
218
CLARNO
JOHN
SERVICE CREEK
SPRAY
TO PORTLAND
293
ANTELOPE
TROUT CR
DAY
3
NATIONAL
19
RICHARDSON ROCK RANCH
WARM SPRINGS
26
MONUMENT
C
MADRAS
207
FOSSIL BEDS
COVE PALISADES PARK
N
W
E
S
PAINTED HILLS
B
15
SHEEP ROCK VISITOR CTR
15
0
10
20 MILES
4
0
10
20 KM
MITCHELL
26
97
26
105
104
TO PRINEVILLE
TO PRINEVILLE

Mural in The Dalles of Celilo Falls, a Columbia River cataract that is now submerged.

THE DALLES

The Columbia River's narrows at The Dalles has always squeezed traffic at the east end of the Columbia Gorge—first the salmon that leapt upstream past Indian spearfishers, then the wagons of Oregon Trail pioneers, and now travelers exploring east from Portland in search of Eastern Oregon's wide open spaces. Museums and interpretive centers cluster about The Dalles.

Columbia Gorge Discovery Center

This first-class interpretive center in The Dalles features an outdoor collection of pioneer log cabins and Indian dwellings, as well as the displays of the Wasco County Historical Museum. Take I-84 exit 82 at the west end of The Dalles and follow signs. Admission is about $9 for adults, $7 for seniors, and $5 for kids age 6-16. Open 9-5 daily except major holidays *(www.gorgediscovery.org)*.

Fort Dalles Museum

Artifacts and displays recall a US Army garrison based here in the 1860s. Located at 15th and Garrison in The Dalles, hours are 10-5 daily from May 15 to September and 11-4 on weekends from March 1 to May 15. Adults pay $5, kids $1.

Original Wasco County Courthouse

Once The Dalles was the seat of the largest county in the US, stretching to Montana. Today Wasco County is smaller, but artifacts and displays of the pioneer era are preserved in the original wooden courthouse at 410 W. Second Place. The free museum is open Wed-Sat 11-4pm from June through August.

The Dalles Historic Walking Tours

Maps and brochures available at The Dalles Chamber of Commerce *(thedalles-chamber.com)* describe walking tours through downtown (47 historic buildings and many murals) and the Trevitt Historical Area (54 homes). Nearby is a bed & breakfast inn, the **Columbia House** at 525 East 7th Street (541-298-4686).

Maryhill Museum

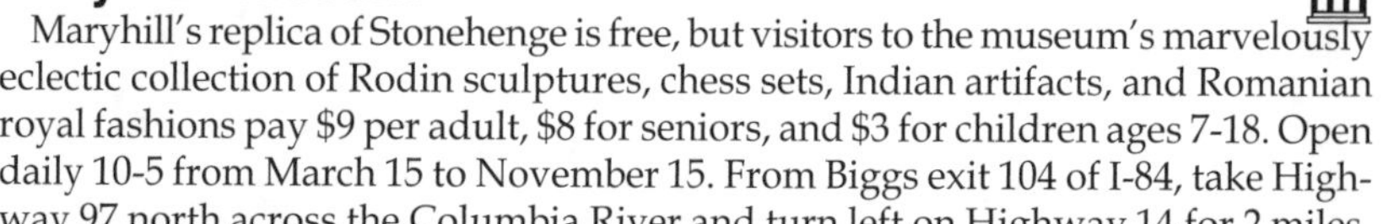

Maryhill's replica of Stonehenge is free, but visitors to the museum's marvelously eclectic collection of Rodin sculptures, chess sets, Indian artifacts, and Romanian royal fashions pay $9 per adult, $8 for seniors, and $3 for children ages 7-18. Open daily 10-5 from March 15 to November 15. From Biggs exit 104 of I-84, take Highway 97 north across the Columbia River and turn left on Highway 14 for 2 miles.

Warm Springs

This beautifully designed **Museum at Warm Springs** features the artifacts, songs, and culture of the five tribes on the Warm Springs Reservation. On Highway 26 in Warm Springs, the museum is open 9-5 daily May through October. Adults are $7, seniors $6, and children 5-12 are $3.50. Closed Mondays in winter. Next door is the tribe's **Indian Head Casino**, open 24 hours a day.

Kah-Nee-Tah Resort

On the Warm Springs Indian Reservation, this sunny resort 11 miles off Highway 26 features a warm springs swimming pool, hotel, tepees, golf, salmon bakes on summer Saturdays, and a trail to a nearby butte. Call 1-800-554-4786.

Deschutes River

Each year thousands of rubber rafts and whitewater dories drift a popular 51-mile stretch of the rimrock-lined Deschutes River from Maupin to the Columbia River. The 2- or 3-day run includes four thrilling and dangerous rapids, countless lesser riffles, and one mandatory portage, at Sherar Falls. Boaters must bring a Deschutes River pass, available at local sporting goods stores. Fishing is banned from boats or floating devices. Campfires are banned, except in enclosed pans in winter.

Cottonwood Canyon State Park

A lazier river than the turbulent Deschutes, the John Day River wends through a deeper, wilder canyon of desert rimrock. A 8114-acre state park with a campground, rental cabins, hike-in campsites, and an extensive trail network opens along the John Day River in 2013. Hikers can visit the site during construction. Drive Highway 206 east of Wasco 15 miles (or west of Condon 26 miles) to Cottonwood Bridge. Rubber rafts, drift boats, and even canoes float the John Day River from April to July; water levels are too low by late summer. It's usually a 2- to 3-day trip from the bridge at Service Creek to the bridge at Clarno, and another four days downstream to the Cottonwood Bridge at Highway 206. Clarno Rapids, the most dangerous whitewater, lurks 4.4 miles below the Clarno Bridge.

Shaniko

This "ghost town" 30 miles north of Madras on Highway 97 counts 26 live residents, several spooks, and a historic hotel. Founded by August Scherneckau in the 1870s, the town became an important wool-shipping railhead in 1904, with 600 residents and five saloons, but faded when a competing railroad opened in 1911.

Richardson's Rock Ranch

Rockhounds can dig for their own geodes and thundereggs on this private ranch for $1 a pound from May-October. Drive Highway 97 north of Madras 11 miles to milepost 81 and follow signs 3 miles. A shop on the ranch also sells and cuts stones.

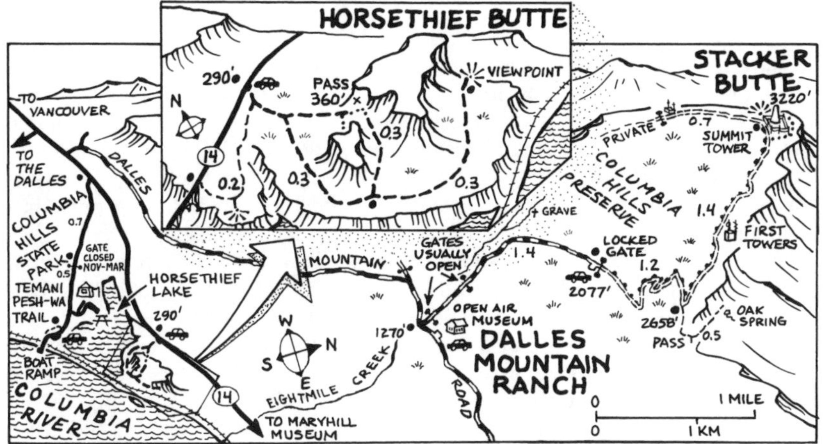

1 Columbia Hills

Easy (3 short walks)
1.5 miles total
200 feet elevation gain
Open all year
Use: hikers

Moderate (to Stacker Butte)
5.2 miles round trip
1140 feet elevation gain
Use: hikers, bicycles

Right: Petroglyph at the park.

The Dalles Dam silenced the thunder of Celilo Falls in 1957, but the magic of that Columbia River spiritual center still echoes. At Columbia Hills you'll find relocated petroglyphs, trails, rock climbing, and a historic ranch.

Start your voyage in The Dalles. Before crossing the Columbia River, pause at the Oregon end of The Dalles Bridge. Water roars from the spillways of the dam that drowned Celilo Falls. A few rickety fishing platforms and unpainted shacks recall the Indian salmon-fishing metropolis that once was the Northwest's economic hub. Petroglyph Canyon lies two miles upstream—and a hundred feet underwater. Thousands of painted images of owls, mountain goats, lizards, hunters, and spirit creatures made this 10-acre basalt gorge the richest rock art site in the Northwest. Just before the dam's waters rose, the Army Corps of Engineers chiseled a few dozen of those petroglyphs loose. In 2003 the petroglyphs returned to a site with dignity—the Temani Pesh-wa ("Written on Rock") Trail, not far from their original location.

To see the rock art, drive 3 miles north of The Dalles Bridge, turn right on Washington Highway 14 for 1.6 miles, and then turn right into Columbia Hills State Park for 1.2 miles to a big gravel parking area on the left. From November through March, when a gate closes the end of this road, you'll have to walk the last 0.5 mile. A 100-yard paved walkway tours the petroglyphs.

Guard cables and surveillance cameras protect the rock art from those who might be tempted to touch. The most impressive of the local petroglyphs, a table-sized spirit face called "She Who Watches," is out of sight around a corner, visitable only on 90-minute tours guided by rangers. Call 509-767-1159 for reservations.

If wind announces spirits, then this is the right place for such art. Gale-force winds blast the rock badlands almost constantly. The nearby campground has plank fences beside each site to help keep tents from blowing away.

For a more substantial hike—and a chance to see the petroglpyhs' original home—drive back to Highway 14 and turn east for 1.2 miles to a sign on the right for the Horsethief Butte Trail. Parking is tight on the shoulder.

Horsethief Butte is a mesa of columnar basalt that's popular with beginning rock climbers. Dogs must be on leash. The hiking trail forks twice in the first 150 yards. Go left and then right to take a tour around the butte's base. Big yellow balsamroot flowers bloom among the sagebrush here in April. The path ends after 0.6 mile at a panoramic cliff overlooking the Columbia River. The final 50 feet of the trail are crowded with poison oak, so long pants are best.

After taking in the view, turn back for 0.3 mile to a trail junction. If you don't mind a little scrambling, turn uphill to the right on an alternate return route that climbs to a miniature version of Petroglyph Canyon. The original basalt gorge is downhill to the south, now drowned by the reservoir. You'll need to use your hands to scramble over a rocky pass to return to your car.

Next visit a historic ranch and a higher viewpoint. For this trip, drive Highway 14 back toward The Dalles 1.8 miles. Between mileposts 84 and 85, turn north on Dalles Mountain Road. Ignore a paved left-hand spur toward a winery and keep right on a wide, bumpy gravel road. After 2.5 miles you'll reach a fork. The hiking route is up to the left, but first turn right for 100 yards to the Dalles Mountain Ranch. Park and walk 100 feet to the porch of a locked farmhouse. Then amble around the fields above the barn to see an exhibit of farm machinery dating to the late 1800s.

Then drive back 100 yards to the road fork at the Dalles Mountain Ranch and drive uphill 1.4 miles to small parking area beside a locked gate. This final stretch of road is rough and passes two gates that can be closed. From the final gate (which is always locked), hike on up the road 2.6 miles to a spectacular view at the summit of 3220-foot Stacker Butte. Along the way you'll pass a set of ordinary radio towers. The summit, however, has an eerily fenced array with an air control wigwam. The panorama here adds Mt. Adams to views of Mt. Hood and the great, snaking Columbia River.

Mt. Hood and the Columbia River from Horsethief Butte.

2 Lower Deschutes River

Easy (to Ferry Springs)
4.2-mile loop
600 feet elevation gain
Open all year
Use: hikers, bicycles

Moderate (to Gordon Canyon)
7.5-mile loop
800 feet elevation gain

Right: Bicyclists on the railroad trail.

The charms of a desert river are many: bright blue skies, the pungent smell of sage, birdsong across glassy water, and the cool grass of an oasis-like riverbank. You'll find it all on a loop hike from the state park at the mouth of the Deschutes River. Part of the loop follows the abandoned grade of the 1909 DesChutes Railroad, now a hiker/biker trail. The trip's prettiest if it's timed to see the wildflowers of spring or the colors of fall. Just avoid the heat of July and August.

From The Dalles, take Interstate 84 east 10 miles to Deschutes Park exit 97. Follow park signs 2.9 miles. On the far side of the Deschutes River turn right and drive straight through the park to the far end of the last parking area. Dogs are allowed on leash only.

Start by walking upriver through a picnic lawn 250 yards to a trail sign. Bicyclists must turn left here to the railroad grade, but hikers can keep right along the riverbank. As you hike amid the tall sagebrush of the riverside path, listen for the melodious call of the western meadowlark, Oregon's state bird. This is also a good place to spot a long-tailed, black-and-white magpie—or even a bald eagle.

After 1.2 miles along the river, the path passes an outhouse, a footbridge, and then Moody Rapids, a mild riffle. A few hundred yards later reach a trail junction. If you've brought young children, you may want to continue just another 0.2 mile along the river to a good sandy beach, let them romp there awhile, and then simply return the way you came.

If you're interested in the 4.2-mile loop hike to Ferry Springs, however, turn left at the junction near Moody Rapids and switchback up away from the river. After

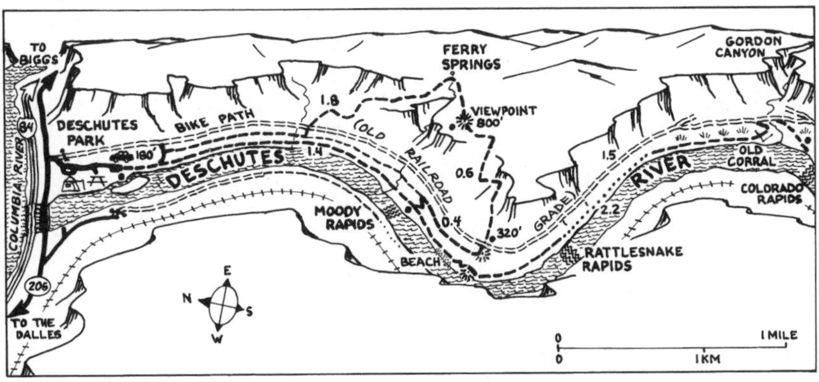

a few hundred yards keep right at another junction and continue 0.3 mile along a tableland to a cliff-edge viewpoint overlooking Rattlesnake Rapids. Here the trail reaches a gravel bike path. Cross the bike path, climb over a stile in a fence, and follow a path up past a viewpoint to Ferry Springs' creeklet. Next the trail descends along a remnant of an 1860s stagecoach road that connected The Dalles with the Canyon City gold mines. Recross the bike path and 50 yards later turn right at a junction beside a bench. Follow this path 0.9 mile back to your car.

Be sure to wear long pants if you're tackling the 7.5-mile loop to Gordon Canyon. This hike starts out the same along the river trail, but then goes straight at the junction near Moody Rapids. Continue along the riverbank 2 miles, although the trail peters out after Rattlesnake Rapids. Then go through a wooden corral gate and follow a road 150 yards up to the gravel bike path. Briefly turn right on the bike path, cross Gordon Creek, and walk down through a meadow to a beach overlooking Colorado Rapids. If you're backpacking, remember that campfires are banned. To return, follow the bike path 1.5 mile back along the cliffs. When you reach the state park boundary post, backtrack 30 feet to find the loop trail heading uphill to Ferry Springs—the prettiest route back to the car.

3 Central Deschutes River

Easy (to footbridge)
4.8 miles round trip
50 feet elevation gain
Open all year
Use: hikers, bicycles

Moderate (entire trail)
7.6 miles one way
100 feet elevation gain

The Deschutes River winds like a great blue-green snake through a dry rimrock canyon bordering the Warm Springs Indian Reservation. In 1910, when two rival railroad tycoons were racing to build competing lines from The Dalles to Bend, locomotives steamed along the riverbank. Now this portion of the old train route has been converted to a path where you can watch the glassy river glide past.

Both ends of the 7.6-mile river trail are at campgrounds that serve as popular launch sites for whitewater boaters. If you have a shuttle car, you can walk the entire trail one-way. If you don't have a shuttle, start downstream at the Trout Creek Recreation Area, in a scenic, twisty part of the canyon full of birdsong.

From Madras (43 miles north of Bend), drive Highway 97 north toward The Dalles 3.5 miles. Between mileposts 89 and 90, turn left on Cora Drive for 8.3 miles to the hamlet of Gateway. Along the way this paved road changes names to Clark Drive and then Bulkley Lane. Cross the train tracks in Gateway, turn right onto Clemens Drive, and stick to this gravel road for 5 miles to the campground, following "Trout Creek" pointers. In the campground itself, drive left past two large parking lots to a day-use parking area at the far left end of the campground loop.

Railroad trail along the Deschutes River. Opposite: Raft on the river.

At a signboard, set out on the broad railroad grade, a route lined with tall sagebrush, some juniper trees, bitterbrush, rabbitbrush, mulleins, and teasels. Ignore small side paths where fly fishermen have made their way down to the river's grassy bank. Listen for the squawk of ring-necked pheasants, the melodious warble of meadowlarks, and the chatter of long-tailed, black-and-white magpies. You may even hear a rattle, as rattlesnakes are not uncommon here.

For an easy hike, make your goal the 80-foot Frog Springs bridge at the 2.4-mile mark. Avoid stinging nettles along the side creek here, but do explore a spur trail that leads to a lunch spot by the river with shade trees and a small sandy beach.

If you want to hike the entire trail one-way, you'll need to leave a shuttle car at the far end, at Mecca Flat. To find that trailhead, drive back to Madras and turn right onto Highway 26 toward Mt. Hood for 12.5 miles. Near milepost 105—and just 100 feet before the Deschutes River bridge—turn right at an abandoned gas station on an unmarked gravel road, following the largest track. After 1.6 bumpy miles you'll enter the Mecca Flat Recreation Area, a shadeless campground with a boat ramp. Park in the trailhead day-use lot.

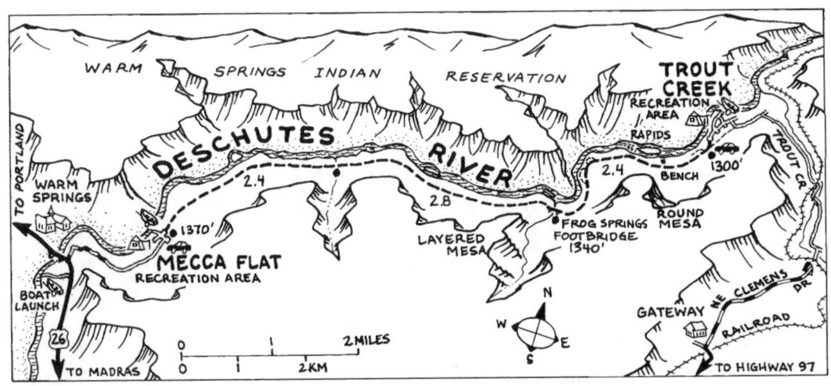

4 Cove Palisades

Easy (to The Peninsula)
3.6 miles round trip
550 feet elevation gain
Open all year
Use: hikers only

Moderate (to Peninsula tip)
7.2-mile loop
640 feet elevation gain

The Peninsula, an eerie desert plateau, resembles a gigantic aircraft carrier moored in the midst of the vast Billy Chinook reservoir. From the Tam-a-lau Trail atop the mesa's rim you can watch tiny ski boats from the Cove Palisades State Park cutting white V-shaped wakes into the sunny green waters far below. *Tam-a-lau,* a Sahaptin word meaning "place of big rocks on the ground," hints at the unusual geologic formations along the path. Summer can bring intense heat to this canyonland, but if you start your hike in the morning, most of the climb is still in shade. Dogs are allowed on leash only.

To drive here, turn off Highway 97 at a sign for Cove Palisades (either 15 miles north of Redmond or in the town of Madras) and follow similar signs on a zigzagging route west to the park's breathtaking canyon. Follow the main road down into the canyon, past a boat launch, across a suspension bridge, and up to a pass with a pullout for the Crooked River Petroglyph, a stone moved here when the reservoir drowned its original site. Drive 200 yards beyond the pass, keep left at a fork in the road, drive straight past the campground half a mile, and turn right at a sign for "Deschutes River Day Use." Here you'll have to pay a $5 parking fee at an automat. Then drive on, keeping left to a large, paved boat trailer parking lot at road's end.

The Tam-a-lau Trail starts by a sign at the left edge of the parking lot and winds through a juniper steppe with sagebrush, bunchgrass, and sunflower-like balsamroot blooms. You'll also pass truck-sized boulders that fell here from the canyon's rimrock long ago. Grasshoppers leap out of the trail before you. Western fence lizards do push-ups on trailside rocks.

The Island from The Peninsula. Above: View of bridge from the trail.

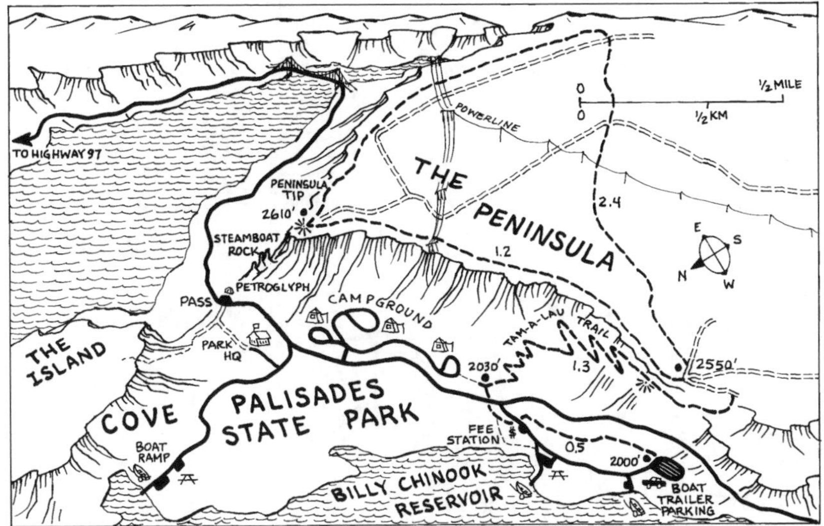

In the first half mile you'll cross a road, turn right on a paved path, and cross another road before reaching a large signboard with trail brochures. Campers at the park's campground can start the hike here simply by walking to the end of the rightmost campground loop.

Beyond the signboard the Tam-a-lau Trail begins switchbacking up through the basalt lava layers of the canyon wall. Most of these basalt terraces are part of the Deschutes Formation, 5- to 25-million-year-old lava flows from the Cascade Range. Halfway up the wall, however, you'll pass remnants of Intracanyon Basalt, a more recent flow that began 60 miles away at the Newberry Volcanic National Monument. That flow surged down the river canyon, puddled up here, and created The Island, a lonely plateau to the north surrounded by cliffs on all sides. If you look between the lava flows you'll see light-colored layers of ash, sand, and cobbles—riverbed deposits that built up during the long intervals between eruptions.

After climbing 1.3 miles you'll follow an old road up to a junction atop The Peninsula. Here the view opens up to the Cascade's snowpeaks. Mt. Jefferson dominates the view, but ghostly Mt. Hood haunts the horizon to its right, and to the left march a parade of lesser summits. If you're tired, or if sun's too hot, plan to turn back here.

For the 3.6-mile loop along The Peninsula's rim, however, keep left on a dirt path. Notice how the surface of this plateau has accumulated tan volcanic ash and cinder rocks, the fallout from millennia of Cascade eruptions. A fragile crust of dark lichens and moss holds the dusty soil in place. Unfortunately, because cattle grazing has been allowed on The Peninsula, hoofprints have largely destroyed the ground cover here. Scientists studying the area's native plants focus instead on The Island across the canyon, inaccessible to cattle.

Follow the path 1.2 miles to the tip of The Peninsula, where you can peer down at the colored pinnacles of Steamboat Rock, a weathered formation of volcanic ash. Then the trail continues along the rim another mile before looping back across The Peninsula's flat top to the junction with the path down to your car.

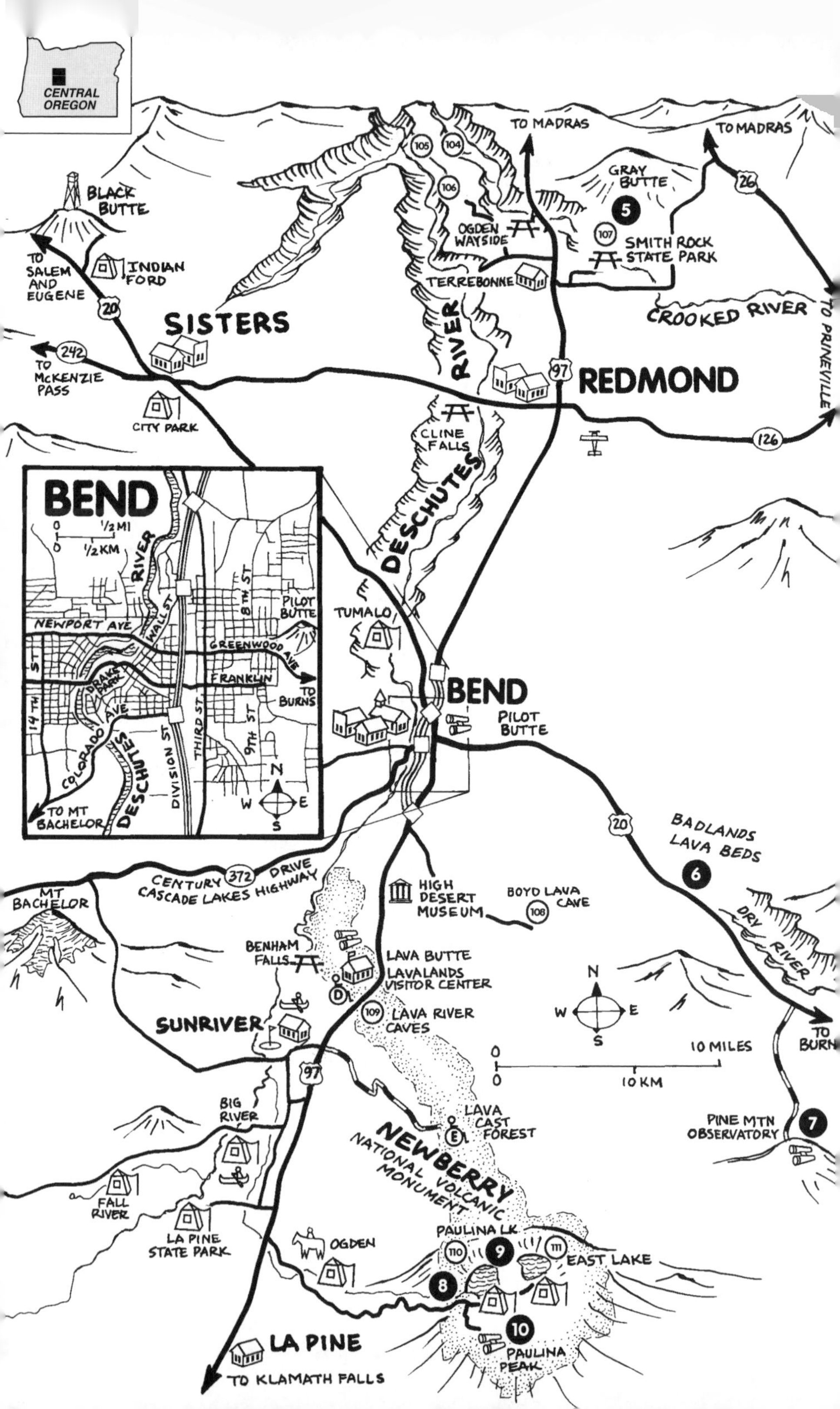
CENTRAL OREGON
TO MADRAS
TO MADRAS
GRAY BUTTE
BLACK BUTTE
OGDEN WAYSIDE
SMITH ROCK STATE PARK
TO SALEM AND EUGENE
INDIAN FORD
TERREBONNE
CROOKED RIVER
SISTERS
TO PRINEVILLE
TO McKENZIE PASS
RIVER
REDMOND
CITY PARK
CLINE FALLS
DESCHUTES
BEND
0 1/2 MI
0 1/2 KM
RIVER
8TH ST
PILOT BUTTE
NEWPORT AVE
WALL ST
GREENWOOD AVE
14TH ST
DRAKE PARK
FRANKLIN
TO BURNS
AVE
COLORADO
DESCHUTES
DIVISION ST
THIRD ST
9TH ST
TO MT BACHELOR
TUMALO
BEND
PILOT BUTTE
BADLANDS LAVA BEDS
CENTURY DRIVE
CASCADE LAKES HIGHWAY
MT BACHELOR
HIGH DESERT MUSEUM
BOYD LAVA CAVE
DRY RIVER
BENHAM FALLS
LAVA BUTTE
LAVALANDS VISITOR CENTER
LAVA RIVER CAVES
SUNRIVER
TO BURNS
10 MILES
10 KM
BIG RIVER
LAVA CAST FOREST
NEWBERRY NATIONAL VOLCANIC MONUMENT
PINE MTN OBSERVATORY
FALL RIVER
LA PINE STATE PARK
OGDEN
PAULINA LK
EAST LAKE
LA PINE
PAULINA PEAK
TO KLAMATH FALLS

The Crooked River at Smith Rock State Park.

BEND

Bend has boomed as the recreation mecca of sunny Central Oregon, but it's also the gateway to the less crowded recreation lands of Eastern Oregon beyond.

High Desert Museum

Plan to spend half a day here touring world-class exhibits of Native American culture, river otters, porcupines, a working sawmill, birds of prey, and more. Admission is $15 for adults ($10 in winter), $12 for seniors, and $9 for children age 5-12. Open 9am-5pm daily except major holidays (10am-4pm in winter), the museum is located 3.5 miles south of Bend on Highway 97 *(www.highdesertmuseum.org).*

Newberry National Volcanic Monument

South of Bend, the giant Newberry volcano has sputtered, collapsed, and leaked lava for half a million years, leaving a vast outdoor museum of geologic oddities. Start at the **Lava Lands Visitor Center** (open 9-5, May-October), 8 miles south of Bend on Highway 97 near milepost 150. A $5-per-car NW Forest Pass buys entrance to an interpretive center and cinder cone viewpoint. Then drive one mile south to **Lava River Cave**, a tube-shaped tunnel that's hikable for 1.1 mile underground. Cave admission is $5 if you don't have a NW Forest Pass, and lantern rentals run $4.

Next drive another 2 miles south on Highway 97 to milepost 153 and turn left for 9 gravel miles to the **Lava Cast Forest**, where a paved 1-mile loop trail explores a lava flow that inundated a forest, leaving trunk-shaped molds in the rock. Finally drive another 9 miles south on Highway 97 (between mileposts 161 and 162) and turn left on a paved 13-mile road into the heart of the old volcano, where two large mountain lakes fill a 6-mile-wide caldera. Winter snows close the five popular campgrounds at **Paulina and East Lakes** until July. See Hikes #8-10.

Sisters 

A charming Western-theme town packed with upscale shops and art galleries, Sisters slows traffic on Highway 20 to a crawl. Crowds are perhaps biggest for the outdoor show of nearly 1000 quilts, on a Saturday in early July. A smaller event in September, the Sisters Folk Festival, ranges from blues to bluegrass. The Western theme is perhaps overplayed at Bronco Billy's Ranch Grill & Saloon, especially considering that this touristy restaurant is housed in the former Hotel Sisters, an authentic 1912 relic of the Old West.

Smith Rock State Park 

Smith Rock juts from the Central Oregon lava plains like an orange-sailed ship in the desert. Oregon's most popular rock-climbing area, this park has 3 miles of rhyolite cliffs and Monkey Face, a 300-foot-tall pillar. A 4-mile hiking loop follows the river downstream, climbs past Monkey Face, and descends Misery Ridge on on staircases (see Hike #107). Drive Highway 97 to Terrebonne (6 miles north of Redmond) and follow park signs east 3.3 zigzagging miles. Expect a $5 parking fee.

Pine Mountain Observatory 

Atop a 6300-foot desert peak where the stars shine bright, this University of Oregon observatory uses its 32-inch telescope for research, but lets visitors peek through a 24-inch telescope for a $5 donation on Friday and Saturday summer nights at about 9pm. Check out the observatory's interesting Web site at *pmo-sun.uoregon.edu*. See Hike #7.

The Cove Palisades State Park 

Where the Billy Chinook reservoir backs up three rivers into a dramatic cliff-edged desert canyonland, this popular park packs a sunny peninsula with 174 campsites, three ramps for launching powerboats, and a marina. The park even rents log cabins and houseboats that sleep 10. See Hike #4.

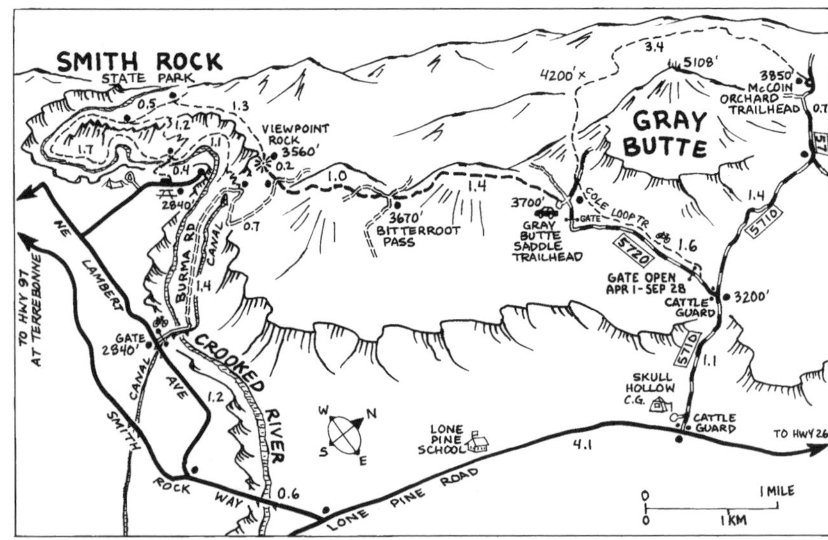

5 Gray Butte

Easy (to Viewpoint Rock)
5.2 miles round trip
160 feet elevation gain
Open all year
Use: hikers, horses, bicycles

Difficult (around Gray Butte)
16.1-mile loop
2050 feet elevation gain
Use: bicycles

Refer to map on previous page.
Right: Gray Butte from the trail.

The little-known path around Gray Butte serves as a secret back-door entrance to Central Oregon's immensely popular Smith Rock State Park—avoiding the park's crowds and parking fees. An easy hike from Gray Butte Saddle traverses sagebrush slopes with views to a string of Cascade snowpeaks. Mountain bikers can turn the trip into a challenging 16.1-mile loop. Avoid the heat of July and August.

To find the Gray Butte Saddle trailhead, turn off Highway 97 at a "Smith Rock State Park" sign in Terrebonne (6 miles north of Redmond or 20 miles south of Madras). This first park sign will head you east along paved Smith Rock Way, but later you'll pass other park signs that would have you turn left. Ignore these, continuing straight on Smith Rock Way for a total of 4.8 miles to its end at a T-shaped junction. Turn left on paved Lone Pine Road for 4.1 miles. At a "Gray Butte Trailhead" sign, turn left across a cattle guard onto gravel Road 5710 for 1.1 mile. Then turn left across another cattle guard onto Road 5720. In winter this road is gated after 200 yards; if it's locked, park and hike up the Cole Loop Trail. When the gate's unlocked (from April 1 to September 28), drive up 1.4 rough miles, open a wire gate, and continue up 100 yards to a saddle with a 4-way junction. The main road turns right, but go left 100 feet and park by the trailhead signpost (possibly missing its sign) on the right *(GPS location N44°23.963′ W121°05.894′).*

The path begins in a juniper forest but soon emerges onto a hillside of sagebrush. In May and June look among the bushes for lavender cushions of phlox, blue stalks of lupine, white tubes of locoweed, and the big yellow flowers of balsamroot and Oregon sunshine. After 1.4 miles you'll cross a dirt road in a saddle decorated with the pink, many-petaled, 2-inch-wide blooms of bitterroot—named *Lewisia rediviva* for Meriwether Lewis who discovered it on his 1804-06 expedition.

Beyond Bitterroot Pass keep straight on the trail, ignoring a dirt road that first forks to the right and then crosses the path. After a total of 2.4 miles the path officially ends at the crest of Burma Road. But for the best view (and a more satisfying turnaround point), continue across the road. Hike straight down the ridgecrest on an unofficial path 300 yards to a cluster of knobby orange rock outcroppings that overlook the Crooked River, Smith Rock, and a distant line of Cascade peaks.

Other Options

Hikers can extend the trip by continuing along the ridgecrest into Smith Rock State Park (see Hike #107). Mountain bikers aren't allowed on park trails, but back roads allow bikers to turn the trip into a scenic 16.1-mile loop. In this case it's best to start at a different trailhead and ride the path in the other direction. Park your car along NE Lambert Avenue where it bridges a large canal (see map). Then bike the gated, dirt Burma Road north alongside the canal and across a Crooked River bridge. After 1.4 miles Burma Road leaves the canal and climbs steeply 0.7 mile. At the road's crest, turn right onto the Gray Butte Trail for 2.4 miles to the Gray Butte Saddle trailhead. From there, follow a dirt road straight across an X-shaped intersection 200 yards toward Gray Butte to find a trail crossing. Turn right on this path for 1.6 miles to the bottom of Road 5720, turn left on gravel Road 5710 for 1.4 miles, turn left on Road 57 for 0.7 mile to the McCoin Orchard trailhead parking area, turn left on the Gray Butte Trail 3.4 miles back to Gray Butte Saddle, and then continue on the trail to Burma Road and your starting point.

6 Badlands

Dry River channel.

Easy (Ancient Juniper Trail)
3.3-mile loop
200 feet elevation gain
Open all year
Use: hikers, horses, bicycles

Moderate (to Flatiron Rock)
6.5 miles round trip
160 feet elevation gain

Easy (to Dry River channel)
3 miles round trip
60 feet elevation gain

The badlands just east of Bend are a lonely desert labyrinth of jumbled rock and sandy openings. Among the surprises in this maze are passageways atop fortress-shaped Flatiron Rock and a cave in the dry channel of a prehistoric river.

The fresh-looking lava here erupted 10,000 years ago, puddled up in a prairie, and then buckled into thousands of ten-foot-tall pressure ridges—in much the same way that paint can wrinkle when it dries. The low spots filled with volcanic sand after Mt. Mazama's cataclysmic eruption powdered the area 7700 years ago.

Bring lots of water, avoid midday heat, wear a big sun hat, and choose loose, long-sleeved clothing. If you stray from the old roads that serve as trails in this area, it's easy to be disoriented, so pack a compass or GPS device.

Start by driving 16 miles east of Bend on Highway 20 toward Burns. At milepost 16 turn left across a yellow cattle guard to the Flatiron Trailhead, a rough dirt parking turnaround *(GPS location N43°57.454′ W121°03.086′)*.

From the right-hand edge of the parking area, walk past some boulders 30 feet to a fork in the trail. To the left is the return route of the optional loop. So turn right on an ancient sandy roadbed that veers near the highway before heading north.

The desert here is dominated by sagebrush and gnarled, 20-foot juniper trees that can be thousands of years old. Spring brings clumps of yellow, daisy-like Oregon sunshine and the tiny, pea-sized purple blooms of miniature monkeyflower.

After 1.3 miles, veer left at the start of a large triangle where trails meet. A hundred steps farther you'll reach another junction, and you'll face a decision *(GPS*

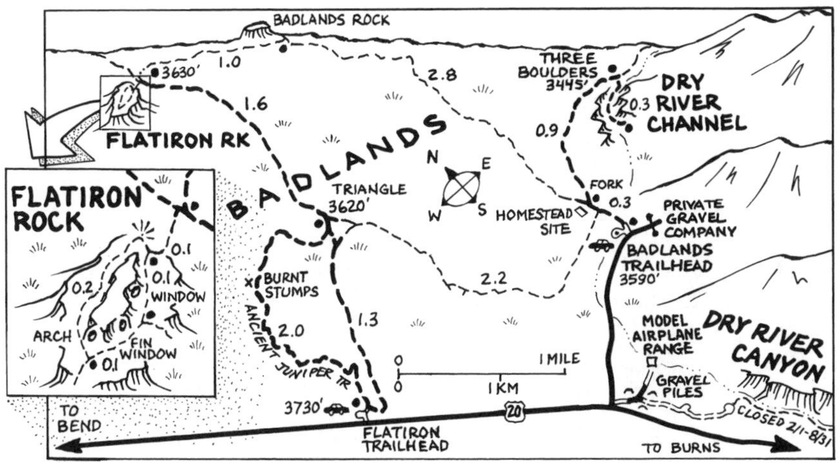

location N43°58.209' W121°02.398'). If you're ready to head back, turn sharply left on the Ancient Juniper Trail, an old roadbed that winds 2 miles back to your car.

If you're headed for Flatiron Rock, however, go straight. Beyond the triangle 1.6 miles you'll reach the 30-foot outcrop of Flatiron Rock *(GPS location N43°59.362' W121°02.748').* Turn left on a steep sandy path that climbs to the rock castle's parapet, where 10-foot walls line a maze of paths. For a loop, keep right to a viewpoint of distant Mt. Jefferson. Then continue 0.2 mile to a natural arch in a 20-foot pillar. Just beyond, where two slots join, keep left for 0.2 mile to return to Flatiron Rock's entrance. Then turn right to hike back to your car.

The next recommended hike visits a channel of the vanished Dry River. During the Ice Age a tributary of the Deschutes River drained a vast lake on the present site of Millican. The stream cut through Dry River Canyon and snaked across this lava landscape. Dry River Canyon is now closed to visitors most of the year (February 1 to August 31) to protect nesting falcons. Out in the badlands, however, you can hike to a different part of the old river's channel, where petroglyphs in caves remain from the people who fished here thousands of years ago.

Drive Highway 20 east of the Flatiron Trailhead 1.5 miles (or east of Bend 18 miles). At the bottom of a hill, turn left on an unmarked paved road for one mile. Then turn left into the dirt Badlands Rock Trailhead *(GPS location N43°57.216' W121°00.883').*

The trail starts as an ungated dirt road that's closed to motor vehicles. Walk 0.3 mile to a fork in the road. You'll want to go right here, but first explore the sagebrush area to the left, a homestead from the early 1900s. A wire fence protects an old cistern. All artifacts are federally protected.

Then take the right-hand fork at the homestead and continue 0.9 mile. Leave the road when you reach three large boulders on the right *(GPS location N43°57.788' W121°00.286').* Take a downhill track sharply to the right 150 yards and keep to the right to a pole fence at the mouth of the Dry River's channel. Beyond is a narrow canyon with 40-foot rock walls. An overhang to the right served as a cave campsite when the river ran with fish, perhaps 6000 years ago. The faint red ochre petroglyphs here can be damaged even by the oil of fingerprints, so don't touch! The canyon peters out after a few hundred more yards, where circular pits in the rocks remind of the vanished river's swirling waters.

7 Pine Mountain

Moderate (to crags viewpoint)
5.6 miles round trip
1060 feet elevation gain
Open May to mid-November

This desert summit has a visitable University of Oregon observatory, but the mountain itself is also a star attraction. With a bit of easy bushwhacking you can hike 2.8 miles along the open crest of a rolling ridgeline, discovering rock formations, ponderosa pine groves, wildflowers, and views across Eastern Oregon.

Start by drving Highway 20 east of Bend towards Burns for 26 miles. At milepost 26 you'll pass Millican's closed store. Continue another quarter mile to a big green sign for the Pine Mountain Observatory and turn right on a wide red cinder road. After crossing a cattle guard in another 3.3 miles, veer to the right on one-lane gravel Road 2017, climb 4.7 miles to a saddle, and pull into the observatory parking area on the left *(GPS location N43°47.503' W120°56.471')*. On weekends, volunteers are usually on hand to give observatory tours. Fundraising is underway to build a Science Education Center with interpretive displays.

Across the road is a free, primitive campground with picnic tables and an outhouse, but no water. The camp comes in handy if you're planning to stay for nighttime stargazing. The public is allowed to use a 24-inch reflector telescope to view the moons of Jupiter, the ring nebula of Lyra, and other wonders every Friday and Saturday night at 9pm from late May through September. Be sure to dress warmly, show up about an hour before sunset, and bring $5 per person. White-light flashlights are not allowed. Large groups should call 541-382-8331 to confirm a visit.

From the parking area, walk up past a locked green gate marked "Quiet Zone". A ten-foot dome to the right houses a 14-inch telescope that's robotically controlled for the use of remote researchers via the Internet. Continue up the road to a larger silver dome on a white concrete block base. This houses the 24-inch scope. Behind is another large dome with a 32-inch research telescope. All the telescopes have been placed a little below Pine Mountain's summit to avoid high winds.

For the hike, start beside the white concrete-block observatory and climb a 200-yard trail to the mountaintop. A low stone shelter here serves as a windscreen. Views extend to the Three Sisters and Mt. Jefferson. Twelve-petaled, cream-colored bitterroot flowers bloom among the sagebrush in June.

Long pants, boots, and a sense of adventure are required to bushwhack beyond this point. If you're game, continue straight past a smaller stone circle (due east), descend a steepish sagebrush slope 0.3 mile to a road, and keep left along the road half a mile. Leave the road at a broad forested saddle where the road turns sharply to the right *(GPS location N43°47.523' W120°55.537')*. Go straight and level

Rock knoll on Pine Mountain. *Opposite: The University of Oregon observatory.*

on a faint cattle trail amid ponderosa pines. After 200 yards, scramble up to the right around a big rock outcrop. Regain the ridgecrest beyond the rock outcrop, and continue along the crest a mile to a summit that is actually the highest point of Pine Mountain, marked only with a broken wooden post.

This is a possible turnaround point, but there's a better view in another 0.7 mile. Continue along the ridgecrest, bushwhacking northeast down through a forest. Cross a semi-open saddle and follow an old cat track left around some rock crags to a viewpoint summit with a post marked "H 530". Although the ridge continues another 1.6 miles to a cluster of radio towers, the route loses a lot of elevation, so this is the place to declare victory and turn back.

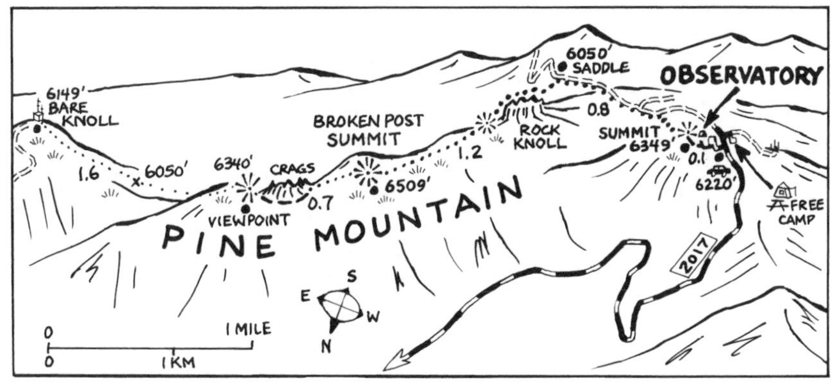

8 Paulina Creek Falls

Easy (to falls viewpoints)
1.6 miles round trip
300 feet elevation gain
Open late June to late October

Easy (to McKay Crossing)
5.6 miles round trip
500 feet elevation gain
Open except after winter storms
Use: hikers, horses, bicycles

Difficult (entire trail)
16.6-mile loop
2050 feet elevation gain

Paulina Creek spills from a caldera lake high in the Newberry National Volcanic Monument, tumbles down the volcano's slopes in a series of waterfalls, and meanders across the high desert. The 8.5-mile trail tracing the stream is a bit long for a day hike, so most hikers focus on shorter segments—either exploring the spectacular summer viewpoints up at Paulina Creek Falls, or strolling along the lower creek where trails are usually snow-free even in winter.

To start, drive south of Bend 22 miles on Highway 97 (or drive north of La Pine 7 miles). At a "Newberry Caldera" sign between mileposts 161 and 162, turn east on a paved road for 11.3 uphill miles to a fee booth where rangers will check that your car has a Northwest Forest Pass. Then continue 1 mile up this paved road and turn left into the Paulina Creek Falls picnic area.

The trail begins beside a restroom. Walk straight for 100 yards to a railed clifftop viewpoint of two massive, side-by-side 60-foot waterfalls. Most tourists turn back here, but paths lead to two other excellent viewpoints nearby. To find the first, head upstream past the picnic area. You'll discover a lovely trail that follows the creek 0.2 mile up to Paulina Lake's outlet. Horses and bicycles are banned on this path. Turn left across a road bridge, immediately turn left on a spur road, and 50 feet

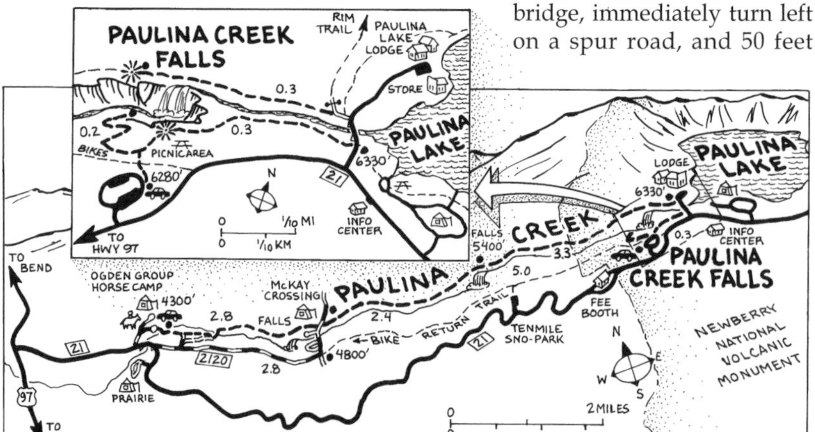

Paulina Creek Falls. *Opposite: Waterfall at McKay Crossing.*

later veer left on a creekside trail that descends 0.3 mile to a railed viewpoint on the far side of Paulina Creek Falls.

To find the third viewpoint, head back to your car, but turn right 50 feet before the parking lot. This trail switchbacks down through the woods 0.2 mile to its end at a decked platform wedged between creek boulders below the falls.

If you'd prefer a longer hike (or if the trail at Paulina Creek Falls is closed by winter snow) try the lower end of the creek's trail instead. To find this route, turn off Highway 97 at the Newberry Caldera exit, drive 2.8 paved miles, turn left at Ogden Group Camp, and follow "Trailhead" pointers to a large gravel parking area for the Peter Skene Ogden Trail.

This path crosses glassy, swift Paulina Creek on a bridge and heads upstream. The creek's meadowed banks form a narrow oasis here, with the dry flora of the high desert on either hand. The sagebrush-like brush is bitterbrush (*Purshia tridentata*)—a member of the rose family, as its tiny blooms reveal. The prominent trailside bunchgrass is known as "needles and thread" because of its needle-like, seed-bearing stalks and curly, thread-like basal leaves.

After a footbridge, half a mile of the path follows the level bed of an abandoned railroad grade, used for logging in the early 1900s. Since then, lodgepole pines have returned in force and ponderosa pines are already a proud 100 feet tall, but occasional 3-foot-thick stumps recall the earlier Central Oregon woods.

At the 2.8-mile mark you'll reach a twisting rock gorge and a 15-foot waterfall just before McKay Crossing Campground. This makes a good turnaround point for an easy hike. If you're out for a challenge, however, continue 5.7 miles upstream to Paulina Lake. Horses and mountain bikes share this route, but bicyclists aren't allowed to zoom back down the same way. Instead they have to ride back on paved Road 21 for 0.2 mile and then veer to the right on a well-marked return trail that follows a powerline 5 miles down to McKay Crossing.

Other Options

Perhaps the best shuttle option for this hike is to drive to Paulina Lake, lock a bicycle at the top of the trail, drive back to the bottom, hike 8.5 miles up to your bike, and then zoom down the paved road to your car.

9 Paulina Lake

Easy (to Warm Springs)
2.4 miles round trip
No elevation gain
Open mid-July through October

Moderate (around lake via Little Crater)
8.6-mile loop
500 feet elevation gain

Paulina Lake has the feel of an exotic sea. Deep, azure waters lap against rocky shores. Seagulls cry. Hidden beaches beckon. But this remarkable lake is actually well over a mile above sea level, and the forested rim that walls it from the outside world is in fact the collapsed caldera of the enormous Newberry Volcano. If all this fails to pique your curiosity, how about a lakeshore hot springs, a gigantic flow of obsidian glass, and a miniature cinder cone crater?

To start, drive south of Bend 22 miles on Highway 97 (or drive north of La Pine 7 miles). At a "Newberry Caldera" sign between mileposts 161 and 162, turn east on a paved road for 11.3 uphill miles to a fee booth where rangers will check that your car has a Northwest Forest Pass. Then continue 1.5 miles to a small information center on the right. If you plan on hiking the entire 8.6-mile loop around the lake, it's best to start here, at the Paulina Day Use Area and boat ramp opposite the information center.

Paulina Peak from the lake. Above: Paulina Lake in winter from Paulina Peak.

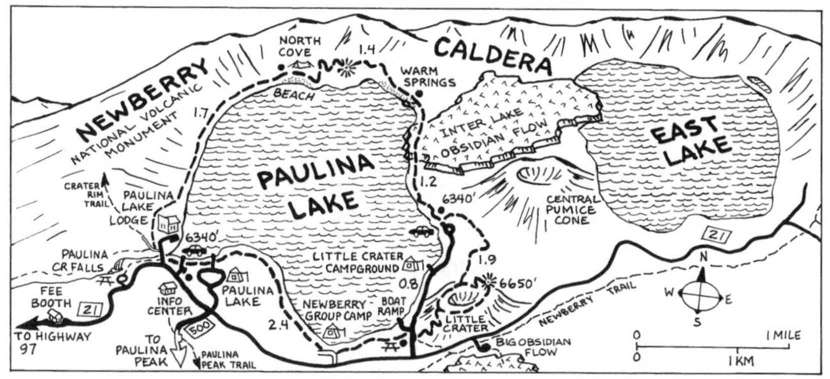

Walk to the right on a lakeshore trail that skirts campgrounds and summer cabins. The sparse forest here is an odd mix of lowland ponderosa pine and highland firs. Note that the older trees are flocked with glowing green letharia lichen, a sure sign of clean mountain air.

After 2.4 miles you'll reach the Little Crater Campground entrance road. At this point the quickest way around the lake is simply to follow the paved road left 0.8 mile. But if you've got the energy for a prettier route, turn right on the road for a few yards to a sign for the Little Crater Trail. This path climbs 0.3 mile to a tiny volcano's crater. Turn right along the rim to a spectacular viewpoint overlooking both Paulina and East Lakes. Then continue around the rim to a junction on the far side, turn right, and descend 0.6 mile to a parking area at the far end of Little Crater Campground.

If you're hiking with kids, this is where you should have started in the first place. To find this trailhead by car, drive 1.5 miles on the main road past the information center, turn left into the Little Crater Campground entrance, and keep right for 0.9 mile to a gravel trailhead parking spur at the far end of the campground *(GPS location N43°43.035' W121°14.492')*.

From this trailhead, the path continues along a dramatic, rock-lined part of the lakeshore. The jagged face of Paulina Peak looms across the lake. After 0.7 mile the trail skirts the Inter Lake Flow, passing glassy boulders of banded volcanic obsidian. Then you'll reach a Warm Springs' long, meadowed beach, a good turnaround point. Watch for mallards, mule deer, gray jays, and Stellar's jays. A 50-foot spur trail leads left to a hot springs on the beach. The hot carbon dioxide gas of this spring bubbles too far out in the lake to be usable until mid-July, but as the lake's level drops it exposes a 6-foot driftwood-and-rock-framed pool in the sand that's just barely large enough for two *(GPS location N43°43.767' W121°14.809')*. Tents and campfires are not permitted here.

If you're continuing on the loop, you'll climb to a viewpoint with a glimpse of distant, spire-topped Mt. Thielsen and cone-shaped Mt. McLoughlin. Then hike onward to primitive North Cove Campground, with picnic tables and a fine pebble beach suitable for (chilly!) swimming.

Another 1.7 miles brings you to the lake's outlet and the conclusion of the lakeshore loop. Here you can detour left, if you like, to visit Paulina Lake Lodge's boat rental dock and rustic general store.

10 Obsidian Flow & Paulina Peak

Easy (Big Obsidian Trail)
0.8-mile loop
450 feet elevation gain
Open late June through October

Difficult (to Paulina Peak)
9.6 miles one way (with shuttle)
2260 feet elevation gain
Open mid-July through October

In the ruined shell of Mt. Newberry, an easy nature trail tours the freshest lava flow in Central Oregon, a hill of shiny black obsidian glass. If you'd like to leave the tourists behind, hike a tougher trail around the obsidian flow to the desert of Pumice Flat, and up to the views atop cliff-edged Paulina Peak.

The Newberry Volcano is probably Oregon's strangest peak. It's the latest protrusion of a geologic "hot spot" that's been moving westward from Idaho for 10 million years, leaving a string of lava flows and volcanic buttes in its wake. Geologists theorize that North America's shearing collision with the Pacific plate has been stretching Eastern Oregon diagonally all this time, and lava has been leaking through the shifting cracks.

All that lava has made Newberry the state's most massive volcano, measured by volume. Countless thin basalt lava flows have built up its 25-mile-wide shield-shaped bulk over the past half million years. Like many aging volcanoes, Mt. Newberry's eruptions gradually contained more silica, making the lava thicker, glassier, and more explosive. The entire mountaintop has collapsed in Crater Lake fashion at least twice, leaving a gaping, 6-mile-wide caldera. The giant lake that once filled that caldera has since been split in two by lava flows. The largest of these flows, the Big Obsidian Flow, poured more than a square

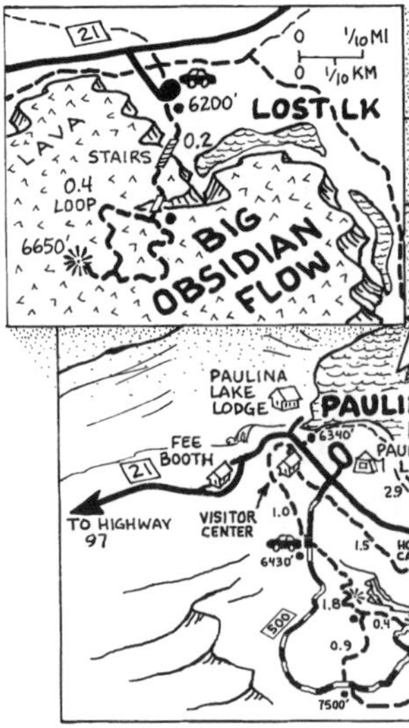

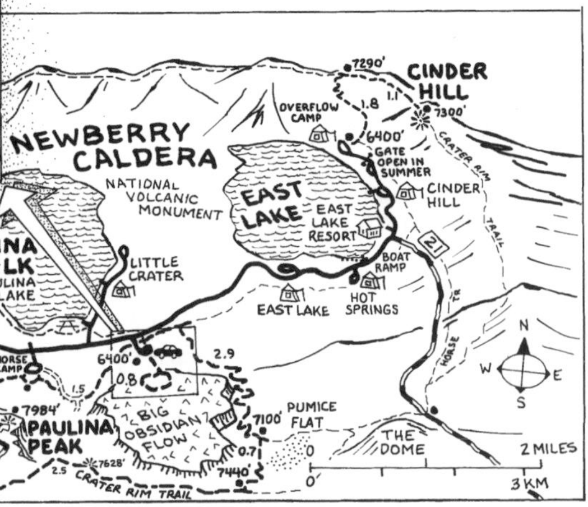

The Big Obsidian Flow. Opposite: Pumice Flat.

mile of black glass into the caldera just 1300 years ago.

Start by driving south of Bend 22 miles on Highway 97 (or north of La Pine 7 miles). At a "Newberry Caldera" sign between mileposts 161 and 162, turn east on a paved road for 11.3 uphill miles to a fee booth. Rangers here will check that your car has a Northwest Forest Pass, and sell you one if need be. Then continue 3.5 miles on paved Road 21 and turn right into the Big Obsidian Trail's huge parking area. Do not feed the cute, golden-mantled ground squirrels that beg for handouts here, because human food is dangerously unhealthy for them.

Hike a paved path through a picnic area 150 yards and then climb metal stairs up the glinting face of the lava flow. The trail skirts a jagged pressure crack in the lava. Much of the rock surface is gray pumice—the flow's frothy scum. Underneath, the silica-rich lava cooled without bubbles to leave shiny obsidian, colored black by a trace of iron oxide. Hike a final 0.4-mile loop to a viewpoint overlooking Paulina Peak (and the distant tips of snowy Mt. Bachelor and South Sister) before returning to your car.

The longer hike to Paulina Peak begins at the opposite side of the same trailhead, by a sign for the Silica Trail. Follow this faint path 0.1 mile back toward the highway, turn right at an X-shaped junction, follow the Newberry Crater Trail half a mile, and then turn right at a sign for the Lost Lake Trail.

After half a mile this path passes near Lost Lake, where you can smell volcanic sulfur. Then the trail switchbacks up through hemlock woods beside the Big Obsidian Flow. At the 2.9-mile mark, after cresting a pumice knoll, bear right at a fork marked "Crater Rim Trail ½". This path bypasses Pumice Flat, but you can see the clearing through the trees to the left, and it's worth a short detour. Then continue 0.7 mile up to the caldera's forested rim and turn right on the Crater Rim Trail. After another 2.5 scenic miles, cross gravel Road 500 (the path jogs 100 feet to the left), continue 0.9 mile up to a T-shaped junction, and turn right for 0.4 mile to a parking area at Paulina Peak's summit. The panorama here includes the entire caldera and all of Oregon's Cascade peaks.

You could leave a shuttle car at this summit, but the next 2.2 miles of trail are wonderful. Head back downhill (keeping right) past viewpoints to a big trailhead pullout beside Road 500. To shuttle a car here from the Big Obsidian Trailhead, drive 2 miles west on Road 21 (or a quarter mile east of the visitor center) and turn south on Road 500 for a mile. If you don't have a shuttle, cross Road 500 and continue on the trail a mile to the visitor center. A dusty horse path behind the visitor center leads 3 miles back to the Big Obsidian Flow, but hikers can cross Road 21 and take a prettier route along Paulina Lake (see Hike #9).

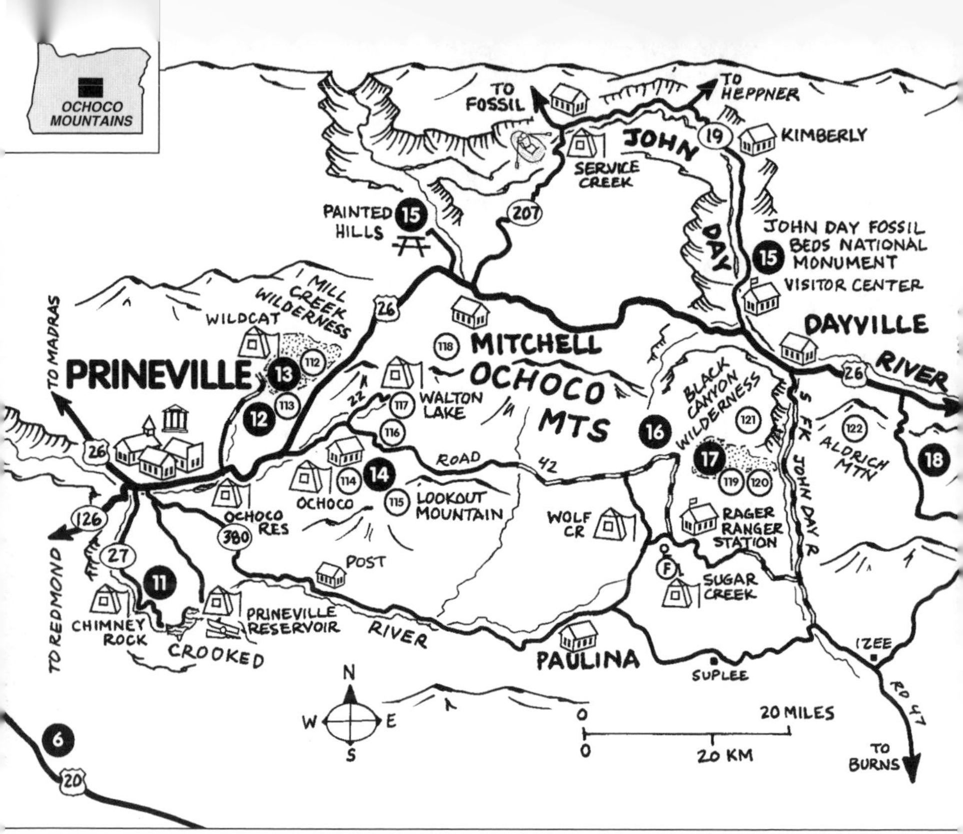

PRINEVILLE

Smack in the geographic center of Oregon, the forested Ochoco Mountains remain so surprisingly underrated and undiscovered that many Oregonians can't even pronounce their name (*OH-chuh-co*). The range's high, rounded crest is perhaps prettiest in June, after the snow melts and the wildflowers bloom. To the south, the Crooked River twists through a narrow desert canyon. In the west, Prineville marks the edge of Central Oregon, with its booming cities, pleasure ranches, and increasing sprawl. Founded in 1868 when Barney Prine opened a blacksmith shop, store, saloon, and hotel in a single building, Prineville today boasts a historic county courthouse (along Highway 26 in downtown), a modern library, a city-owned railroad line, and the headquarters of Les Schwab's tire store empire.

Bowman Museum

In a stone 1910 bank building, this downtown Prineville museum of local history preserves the original bank's vault room and marble countertops. Exhibits include artifacts from local Indians and pioneers, but the best displays are upstairs, where curators have reconstructed a tack room (complete with old saddles) and a small general store from the early 1900s. Located at the corner of Main and Highway 26, the museum is free, but donations are welcomed. Hours are 10-5 Mon-Fri and 11-4 Sat-Sun from June through August, otherwise Tue-Fri 10-5 and Sat 11-4. Closed January and major holidays *(www.bowmanmuseum.org)*.

The Crook County Courthouse in downtown Prineville.

Ochoco Reservoir

Conveniently located along Highway 26 east of Prineville 10 miles, this smallish reservoir on Ochoco Creek has a 22-site county park campground and a variety of private cafes and lodges. In dry years, expect low water levels.

Walton Lake

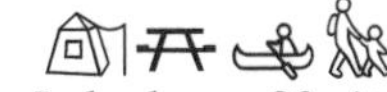

Set in the Ochoco Mountains' pine forests, 25-acre Walton Lake has a 30-site campground ($15 fee) with a small swimming beach and a 1-mile shoreline loop trail (see Hike #117). The dam creating the lake was funded by the Prineville chapter of the Izaak Walton League. Snow blocks the area from December to April. Each spring the lake is stocked with legal rainbow trout that can be caught with flies, lures, or bait. Only rowboats or boats with electric motors are allowed. From Prineville drive Highway 26 east toward John Day 17 miles. Near milepost 35, fork to the right at a sign for Ochoco Creek for 8.3 miles, and then veer left onto paved Road 22 at a sign for Walton Lake 7 miles.

Prineville Reservoir State Park

A dam has backed the Crooked River up into a desert canyonland, creating a lake popular with powerboaters. At the boat ramp, a 67-site state campground, complete with hot showers, charges $16-26 a site. Five rental cabins are available for $60-82. Take Highway 26 east of Prineville 2 miles and turn right, following "Prineville Reservoir" signs 15 paved miles.

Chimney Rock from the Crooked River. *Opposite: Steins Pillar.*

11 Chimney Rock

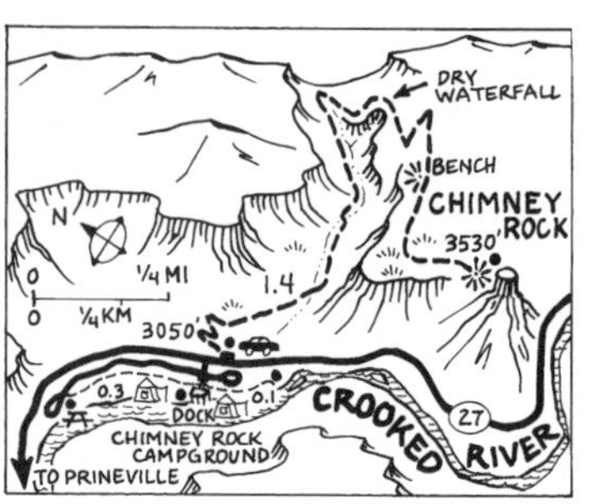

Easy
2.8 miles round trip
500 feet elevation gain
Open all year
Use: hikers, horses, bicycles

In one of the crookedest parts of the Crooked River's cliff-rimmed canyon, an easy trail climbs a dry side gulch to a viewpoint beside the thumb-shaped knob of Chimney Rock. Although it's open all year, this nearly shadeless hike can be too hot for comfort in July and August. After the hike, cross the road to a lovely riverside picnic area and campground, where a short path ambles along the glassy river's cool, grassy bank.

Take Highway 26 to the center of downtown Prineville. At a "Fairgrounds" pointer, turn south on Main Street, which soon passes the fairgrounds and becomes Road 27. After 16.6 miles on this quiet, paved, two-lane road you'll pass a sign for the Chimney Rock Recreation Site on the right. Immediately after the sign, park on the *left* side of the road in a grassy gravel flat with a messageboard marked "Rim Trail Trailhead."

The trail heads uphill to the left from the parking area, but soon switchbacks across a rocky sagebrush slope to a dry wash. Gnarled old junipers and scurrying lizards inhabit this gulch. In spring look for tiny, bright blue penstemon, purple aster, and white yarrow. After 0.7 mile the path switchbacks up to the rock lip of a 50-foot dry waterfall. Then the trail climbs to a canyon viewpoint with a bench. If you're here in June, notice how this bunchgrass mesa is dotted with bitterroot—giant pink blooms that appear to sprout from the ground without leaves or stalks. Named *Lewisia rediviva* for explorer Meriwether Lewis, the flowers have large, starchy roots once prized by Indians for food.

The trail ends at a second bench beside Chimney Rock, a 40-foot rimrock tower festooned with cliff swallow nests and bright yellow and green lichen. The view extends across the sinuous chasm of the Crooked River to the distant snowy cones of the Three Sisters.

From this arid perch, the lush green riverbank far below looks like an inviting oasis. To take up that invitation, hike back down the way you came and cross the road to the Chimney Rock Recreation Site. Campsites here cost a mere $8. From a large fishing pier by the entrance signboard, a riverbank path extends both directions. To the left the path leads past campsites 300 yards to the grassy tip of an island. To the right the path extends 0.3 mile to a picnic area with restrooms. Watch for yellow tanagers, redwing blackbirds, and zooming swallows against the dramatic backdrop of the far shore's gigantic cliffs.

12 Steins Pillar

Easy
4 miles round trip
680 feet elevation gain
Open April to mid-December
Use: hikers, horses, bicycles

Like a misplaced skyscraper, 350-foot Steins Pillar towers above the forested valley of Mill Creek. This odd pink spire remained unscaled until 1950. Skilled climbers still require at least six hours of dangerous work to reach the top. Hikers, on the other hand, can set their sights on a much easier goal: walking the 2-mile trail to the pillar's scenic base.

Start by driving Highway 26 east of Prineville 10 miles to the far end of Ochoco Reservoir. Just beyond milepost 28, at a sign for Wildcat Camp, turn left onto Mill Creek Road. Follow this road for 5.1 paved miles and an additional 1.6 miles of gravel. Then, at a pointer for Steins Pillar Trailhead, turn right across a bridge on

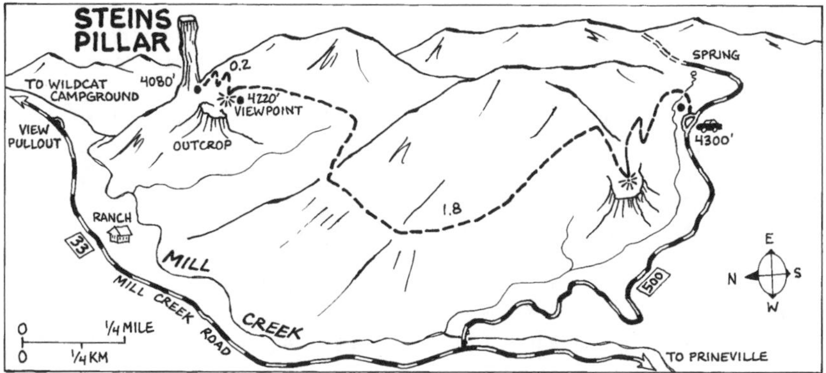

Road 500. After exactly 2 miles, turn left into a well-marked gravel turnaround. If you miss this trailhead you'll soon notice, because Road 500 becomes undrivable in less than 0.2 mile.

Start hiking at the far end of the gravel pullout loop and contour 100 yards to a crossing of a small spring-fed creek in a glen. From here the trail is obvious, climbing up through open woods of small Douglas firs, large ponderosa pines, and some junipers. In spring the slopes are brightened with yellow sunflower-like balsamroot, cushions of lavender phlox, and white death camas.

The path climbs to a viewpoint of the Three Sisters and then ambles gradually up and down along a wooded slope. At the 1.8-mile mark the official trail ends at a viewpoint of Steins Pillar. Much like Monkey Face at Smith Rock (Hike #107), this pink tower is made of rhyolite ash that erupted from the Old Cascades some 25 million years ago, settled in an inland sea, and compacted to stone.

To continue to the Steins Pillar itself, turn sharply right on a smaller path that leads downhill 0.2 mile to the tower's base. Technical gear is required to climb here. But if you walk back up to the viewpoint you'll find a fun rock outcrop nearby where sure-footed scramblers can vent their pent-up mountaineering urges in relative safety, exploring small knolls, caves, and rock windows.

13 Mill Creek and Twin Pillars

Twin Pillars.

Easy (to Ford #4)
2.6 miles round trip
150 feet elevation gain
Open mid-April to early December
Use: hikers, horses

Moderate (to Belknap Trail)
5.8 miles round trip
340 feet elevation gain

Difficult (to Twin Pillars)
11.6 miles round trip
1900 feet elevation gain
Open mid-May to mid-November

Little more than an hour's drive from Bend, the Mill Creek Wilderness is an uncrowded retreat. For an easy walk, hike up Mill Creek to a meadow. For a longer trip, climb to a viewpoint beside Twin Pillars, a pair of 200-foot volcanic plugs. Almost the entire route is through burned woods recovering from a 2000 fire.

Start by driving Highway 26 east of Prineville 10 miles to the far end of Ochoco Reservoir. Just beyond milepost 28, at a sign for Wildcat Camp, turn left onto Mill Creek Road for 5.1 paved miles and an additional 5.6 miles of gravel. Then fork to the right at an entrance sign for Wildcat Campground and 200 yards later turn right into a large gravel parking lot for the trailhead and picnic area.

At the parking lot ignore a footbridge to the picnic area and instead take the Twin Pillars Trail upstream. In 250 yards you'll meet the campground entrance road at a bridge. If you're on horseback, don't cross this bridge; simply cross the road, continue on the main trail a quarter mile, and then splash through the creek at the first ford. If you're on foot, however, cross the bridge into the campground, and keep left 0.1 mile to a "Trail" sign at the far end of the campground loop. This path skips the first and deepest ford of the hike.

The two routes rejoin just beyond ford #1. Then the trail continues upstream through a burned forest with snowberry, bunchgrass, and blue lupine. In early summer, red columbine and purple larkspur bloom in creekside meadows along the way. Butterflies seem to love these meadows too: yellow-and-black swallowtails, blues, coppers, and admirals.

At the 1-mile mark the official trail fords the creek again at the tip of an island. But because the trail recrosses a few hundred feet later, most people simply keep right on an obvious detour that avoids fords #2 and #3. Not far ahead, however, is ford #4. This crossing serves as a turnaround point for less adventurous hikers because the unofficial scramble trail that continues along the south bank is rough and steep, traversing an exposed rock slope over to ford #5. Beyond this, an even rougher detour avoids fords #6 and #7.

Just before ford #8 the trail forks. Keep right on an official trail that bypasses fords #8 and #9 in style. The trails rejoin in a grassy glade with big ponderosa pine trees near a sign for the faint Belknap Trail. The little side creek in this glen is another possible turnaround point. A nice campsite is nearby.

If you're headed for Twin Pillars, keep left on the Twin Pillars Trail. The path soon crosses Mill Creek for the tenth and final time and then launches uphill, gaining 1400 feet of elevation in 2.6 miles. Now watch for a steep side trail to the right with a sign for Twin Pillars. If you keep to the right on this scrambly side path 300 yards you'll reach a viewpoint at the base of Twin Pillars. Brightly colored lichens encrust the lava towers. The view across Mill Creek's forests extends to snowy Mt. Bachelor and South Sister.

Most hikers will want to return as they came, but explorers can follow a faint path clockwise halfway around Twin Pillars 0.3 mile to an even better viewpoint.

Other Options

A 2.6-mile route to Twin Pillars begins on Road 27. This trailhead is also the place for a shuttle car if you want to traverse the Mill Creek Wilderness one way. From Highway 26 in downtown Prineville, turn north on Main Street, which becomes NE McKay Road and then Road 27. Keep right at forks, especially at the 22-mile mark, where Road 27 makes a right-hand turn. In another 6 miles, pavement ends at a fork. Keep right on a dirt road 0.8 mile to the Twin Pillars trailhead.

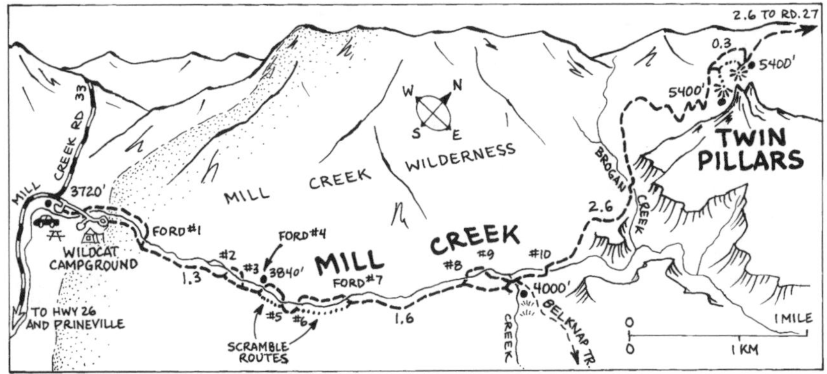

14 Lookout Mountain

Moderate
7-mile loop
1220 feet elevation gain
Open June to late November
Use: hikers, horses, bicycles

From the wildflower-spangled sagebrush meadows of Lookout Mountain's plateau, views stretch beyond the forested Ochoco Mountains to a string of Cascade snowpeaks. A loop trail not only visits the summit's old lookout site, but also a rustic shelter and an interesting abandoned mine.

From Prineville, drive Highway 26 east toward John Day 16 miles. Near milepost 35, fork to the right at a large highway sign for Ochoco Creek. Follow this paved road 8.2 miles to the rentable Ochoco Ranger Station on the left ($90 for 8 people, *www.recreation.gov*). A campground behind the building offers campsites for $13.

When you drive 200 yards beyond the rental ranger station, you'll notice a "Lookout Mountain Trail" sign on the right. This is a much longer, less interesting route to the mountain, so drive on another 0.2 mile to a junction, keep right on paved Road 42 toward Paulina, and continue on this charming, two-lane road 6.6 miles to a pass. Here turn right on Road 4205 at a large sign for the Independent Mine.

Just 100 yards up Road 4205 you'll see a giant parking area on the left. If you've brought a horse trailer or a low-slung Ferrari, it's safest to park here at the Round Mountain Trailhead, hike up the road another 50 feet, and take the 0.9-mile trail

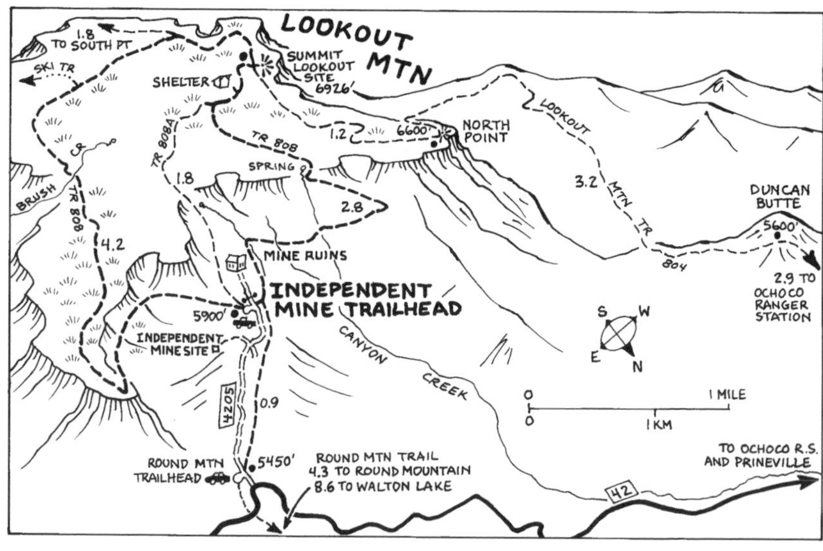

Lookout Mountain. Opposite: Abandoned Motherlode Mine buildings near the trailhead.

that angles up to the right to the upper trailhead. Most people, however, choose to shorten the hike by driving up the road a mile. The dirt road is rough and steep, so passenger cars have to take it slow. After 0.7 mile go straight at a junction, ignoring a sign to the old Independent Mine on the left.

At the Independent Mine Trailhead, a dirt berm blocks an abandoned road to an old mine. Three trails also begin here. Avoid the dusty, steep Trail 808a that charges straight uphill. Instead angle up to the left on the gentler loop Trail 808. This path climbs gradually through forests that shift from park-like groves of ponderosa pines to thickets of grand fir and finally to storm-stunted subalpine fir.

After a mile the path crests the rocky lip of Lookout Mountain's vast summit mesa. The rimrock is a basalt lava flow that oozed from vents north of the John Day River 25 million years ago, smothering most of the Ochoco Mountains. Today the sagebrush flats atop the old lava bloom each June with yellow desert parsley, mountain bluebells, sunflower-like balsamroot, and wild peony (with reddish bells on a lush bush). Look for yellowbell lilies where snow patches have just melted.

Continue up and down across the rolling plateau 3 miles, ignoring two side trails to the left, to reach a junction at an old stone corral on a summit's cliff edge. For the loop, you'll turn right on Trail 808, but first inspect the corral, where the mountain's namesake lookout building once stood.

Then return to the loop trail, following a "Snow Shelter" pointer. You'll have to follow Trail 808 downhill 0.2 miles and take a 100-yard side path to the right to find this 3-sided log hut, built primarily for Nordic skiers and snowmobilers.

Beyond the shelter turnoff 0.3 mile, the loop trail forks. If you're tired you can save a mile by bearing right on Trail 808a, an old road. It's more interesting, however, to turn left on Trail 808, which descends gently through woods. Just before your car, this path passes a derelict 3-story mine building and a collapsed shaft with ore cart rails. Don't explore off the trail because the red cinnabar ore mined here was processed into poisonous mercury, and the mine may still be contaminated.

15 John Day Fossil Beds

Moderate (Blue Basin overlook)
4-mile loop
800 feet elevation gain
Open all year
Use: hikers only

Easy (4 Painted Hills Unit trails)
2.6 miles round trip
360 feet elevation gain

Easy (2 Clarno Unit trails)
0.6 miles round trip
280 feet elevation gain

Nearly 100 miles of highway separate the three parts of the John Day Fossil Beds National Monument. Stop at each to take some short hikes. Collecting fossils is banned in the national monument, but from April to October you can hunt in the shale beds behind the high school in the city of Fossil (expect a small fee).

Consider planning a two-day trip so you'll have time to explore. For a place to stay, try the Wilson Ranches Retreat, 2 miles west of Fossil on a 9000-acre cattle ranch, where rooms run $79-129 (call 866-763-2227). In Fossil, the Bridge Creek Flora Inn is a B&B in a 1905 house at 828 Main Street with 9 rooms that run $60-75 (541-763-2355). In Mitchell, head for the historic Oregon Hotel (541-462-3027, open March-November). A night there ranges from a mere $15 for a bunk to $89 for a suite that sleeps 8. Camping is free at Mitchell's city park, while sites run about $5 at the BLM camp on the John Day River at Service Creek.

To start your tour, drive Highway 26 east of Prineville 83 miles (or west of John Day 38 miles) to Picture Gorge's canyon and turn north on Highway 19 for 2 miles to a free, modern visitor center on the left (open daily 9am-4pm, or 9am-5:30pm in summer). Here you can watch a short movie, tour dioramas of the fossil beds' history, and see some of the best fossils. It's also worth driving across the highway to the monument's old headquarters. Here you'll find a historic farmhouse, a picnic area, and short interpretive walks to a barn, a riverbank, and a valley view.

For the first recommended hike, drive north of the visitor center 3 miles and turn right into the Blue Basin trailhead. If you're pressed for time, head to the right on the Island in Time Trail, which ambles 0.6 mile up a green creekbed to trail's end in an eerie badlands canyon of volcanic ash. If you have more time, start by keeping left on the Blue Basin Overlook Trail. This 3.2-mile loop path climbs, steeply at times, around the scenic canyon's rim. Then it descends in 21 switchbacks.

After visiting Blue Basin, drive back 5 miles south on Highway 19 and turn right on Highway 26 for 38 miles. Beyond Mitchell 4 miles (between mileposts 62 and 63), turn north on Burnt Ranch Road at a sign for the Painted Hills. After 6 miles, turn left on Bear Creek Road for 1.2 miles, mostly on gravel, and then turn left 0.2 mile to the Painted Hills Overlook parking area.

The rounded, colorfully striped Painted Hills began as ash that erupted from the ancestral Cascades 33 million years ago and settled in a vast lake here. The resulting yellow claystone was colored by trace minerals—red from iron and black from manganese. Footprints last for years in the soft soil, so stay on designated paths.

Sheep Rock from the visitor center.   Opposite: The Painted Cove Trail.

Four trails explore the Painted Hills (see map). First stroll out the 0.3-mile path to the Painted Hills Overlook. Then drive another 1.2 miles to the Painted Cove Trail, a 0.2-mile loop with a boardwalk that crosses the colorful claystone. If you have more time, don't miss the 0.8-mile climb to a viewpoint atop Carroll Rim's lava rimrock. The fourth path, the 0.2-mile Leaf Hill Loop, circles a 30-foot hill.

The third unit of the national monument at Clarno is more than 60 miles away. To find it, drive back to Mitchell or the visitor center, follow signs north to Fossil, and turn left on Highway 218 for 19 miles to a paved parking pullout on the right marked "Picnic Area Restrooms ½ mile." If you reach the John Day River bridge you've driven 3 miles too far.

First hike uphill to the right on the Trail of the Fossils, a 0.2-mile loop lined with boulders that fell from the rimrock. The rock began as a volcanic mud flow 44 million years ago, and is riddled with leaf fossils from a subtropical forest inundated by the eruption. The other short trail climbs uphill to the left from the message board for 0.2 mile to the rimrock itself, where water erosion has carved a tall hollow into the cliff, topped with a dainty 10-foot arch. At this desert viewpoint, crickets chirp, crows squawk, and peregrine falcons swoop past, hunting cliff swallows.

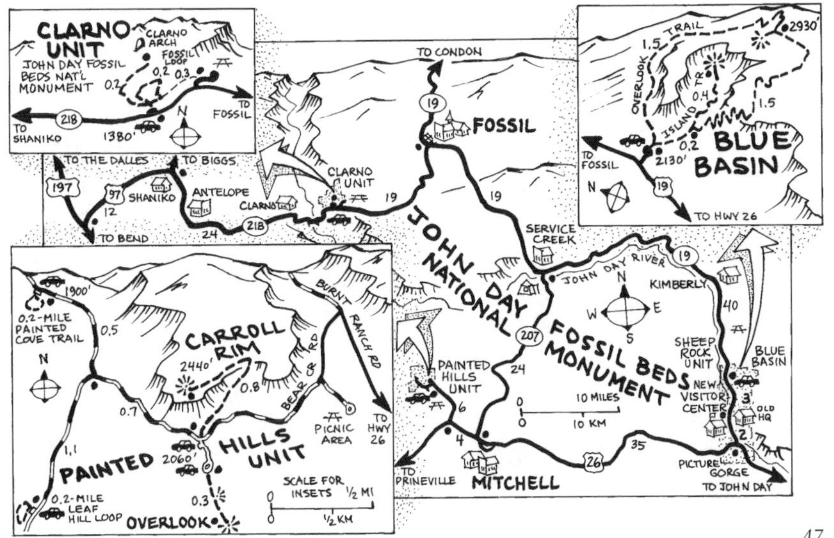

16 Rock Creek and Spanish Peak

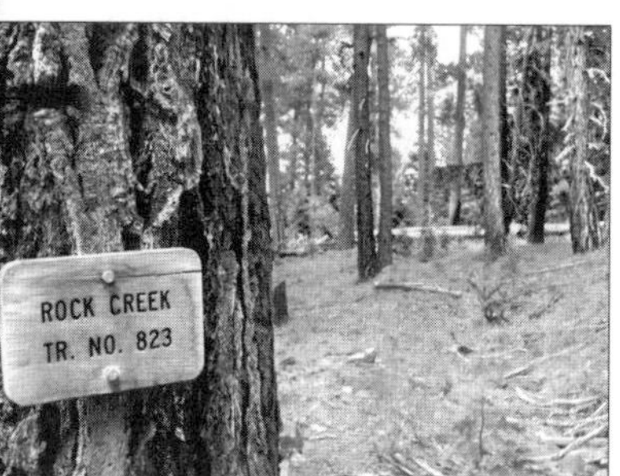

Moderate (Rock Creek to Fir Tree Creek)
7.6 miles round trip
620 feet elevation **loss**
Open late May to mid-November
Use: hikers, horses, bicycles

Moderate (to rim cairn and Spanish Peak)
7.9-mile loop
1000 feet elevation gain
Open early June to mid-November

A new trail on the crest of the Ochoco Mountains connects the views and wildflowers at Spanish Peak with a historic mining ditch along forested Rock Creek. For a day hike, try either end of this trail system. If you have a shuttle car, you can hike the entire route one way, mostly downhill.

Drive Highway 26 east of Prineville 48 miles to Mitchell and continue 13 miles toward John Day. At a sign for Forest Road 12, turn right on a paved road that passes Barnhouse Campground and turns to gravel. Stick to Road 12 for 15.4 miles. At a crossroads, turn left onto gravel Road 1250 for 3.9 miles. At another 4-way junction turn left onto gravel Road 38 for 1.7 miles to the Rock Creek Trailhead parking area on the left *(GPS location N44°21.322′ W119°46.957′)*.

The trail that starts here ambles across a meadow of blue lupine and scattered pines, descends 0.4 mile to a footbridge across 15-foot-wide Rock Creek, and then follows the creek down through lovely meadows and stands of lodgepole pine.

At the 2.4-mile mark, the trail drops to the Waterman Ditch, a flume begun in the late 1800s by E. O. Waterman to supply the Spanish Gulch Gold Mining District to the north. When you reach Fir Tree Creek, in a swale of larkspur and coltsfoot, continue 100 feet to the ruin of the ditch-builders' log cabin, a good turnaround point.

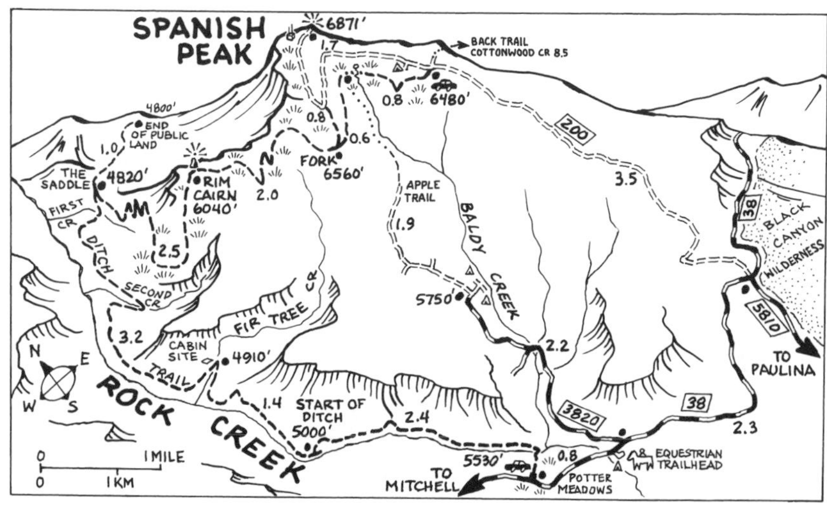

Spanish Peak from the rim cairn. Opposite: Rock Creek's ditch trail.

For the hike on Spanish Peak, you'll need to drive to a high trailhead on a much rougher road. Passenger cars can accomplish this if they're driven slowly.

Drive east on gravel Road 38 past the Rock Creek Trailhead 3.1 miles to a 4-way junction and turn uphill to the left on rough, rocky Road 200 for 3.5 slow miles. Where a Jeep road joins from the right, look for rock cairns marking the Spanish Peak trail on the left *(GPS location N44°23.985' W119°45.511')*. Road 200 does continue to Spanish Peak's summit, but it becomes too rough for cars.

From the trailhead hike a faint, level trail across a lupine meadow, following rock cairns. After 0.8 mile a lush growth of hellebore (corn lily) obscures the tread near the headwater spring of Baldy Creek, but keep traversing. At the 1.4-mile-mark, cairns mark a junction with the spur trail to the summit. Continue straight, traversing around Spanish Peak and down a rim 2 miles to a big clifftop cairn *(GPS location N44°24.440' W119°47.926')*. Views include most of the Ochoco Range and the John Day Fossil Beds canyonlands.

If you were to leave a shuttle car at the lower Rock Creek Trailhead, you could simply hike onward 2.5 miles down to the ditch trail and then hike up Rock Creek 7 miles to your car. If you don't have a shuttle, hike back from the rimrock cairn 2 miles to the trail fork on Spanish Peak's flank *(GPS location N44°23.961' W119°46.613')*. For a loop to the summit, turn uphill to the left, follow cairns 0.4 mile to Road 200, and turn left for 0.4 mile to the summit itself, where four concrete lookout tower foundations remain amidst wind-mown grass, lupine, and sagebrush. After absorbing the view, follow Road 200 back downhill 1.7 miles to your car.

17 Black Canyon

Moderate (to Black Canyon Creek)
5 miles round trip
1020 feet elevation **loss**
Open late May to mid-November
Use: hikers, horses

Difficult (to Second Crossing)
7.8 miles round trip
2300 feet elevation **loss**

The Black Canyon Wilderness stretches from the Ochoco Mountains' high forests to the South Fork John Day River's sagebrush canyonlands. There's room here for a weekend backpacking trek or horse trip, but hikers have trouble accessing the lower, eastern end of the Wilderness, where an iffy river ford is passable only in late summer's low water. So here's an easier, backdoor route to the high country. Just remember to save some energy for the return climb back out of the canyon.

Start by driving to the Rock Creek Trailhead described in Hike #16. Then drive east on gravel Road 38 for 3.1 miles to a 4-way junction and turn right on gravel Road 5810 for 1.2 miles to a high meadow with a parking pullout on the right and a sign for the Boeing Field Trail on the left *(GPS location N44°20.560′ W119°43.872′).*

The field's name recalls a B-18 bomber that crashed a mile away on Wolf Mountain during a World War II transit flight, killing all four crewmembers. Each June the field blazes with wildflowers—yellow balsamroot, desert parsley, purple larkspur, pink owls clover, and wild onion.

From the pullout, cross the road and walk across the field to a big "Black Canyon Wilderness" signboard, where the trail begins. The path descends half a mile, hops across Owl Creek, and climbs briefly to a junction. Turn left on the Black Canyon Trail. In the next 2 miles you'll descend through Douglas fir woods with blue huckleberries (ripe in August), elderberry, lupine, and gooseberry. The path recrosses Owl Creek and then reaches the confluence of Owl Creek and Black Canyon Creek—a good turnaround point.

If you'd like a longer hike, hop across Black Canyon Creek and continue down-

Boeing Field from the trailhead. Above: Balsamroot. Opposite: Phlox.

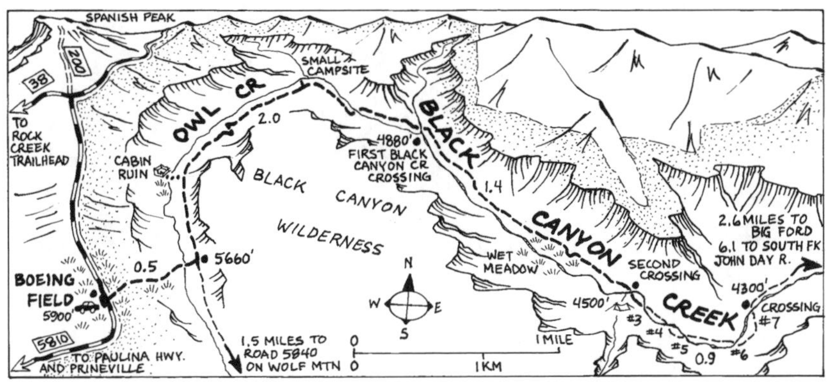

stream 1.4 miles to the second of this creek's many bridgeless crossings. Seven-inch trout watch as you balance across the stream on logs and rocks to the far shore. A campsite here makes another good turnaround spot.

Other Options

Off-trail adventurers with a global positioning device can look for the ruins of a log cabin beside Owl Creek Meadow *(GPS location N44°21.116′ W119°43.529′).*

If you continue downstream from Black Creek's second crossing, you can probably keep your feet dry even though the trail crosses the creek five more times in the next 0.9 mile. Then the path stays on the north side of the stream for 4.3 miles. Prepare to wade beyond that, however, because the path fords the deepening creek ten times in the final 1.8 miles before reaching the South Fork John Day River's awkward ford. To shuttle a car here, drive back to Highway 26, head east to Dayville, and turn right on the rough South Fork John Day Road 12.7 miles to the trailhead sign on the right *(GPS location N44°20.023′ W119°33.909′).*

18 Fields Peak

Moderate (to Fields Peak)
4.6 miles round trip
1850 feet elevation gain
Open mid-June through November
Use: hikers, horses, bikes, ATVs

Difficult (to McClellan Mtn.)
9.8 miles round trip
2400 feet elevation gain
Use: hikers, horses

Highest point between the Strawberry Mountains and the Cascades, the brown pyramid of Fields Peak commands a panoramic view of the John Day Valley. Although all-terrain vehicles are allowed on the summit trail, they are rare. And the delightful path to McClellan Mountain is blocked to motor vehicles altogether. Bring a hat, because the route has little shade on hot summer days.

Fields Peak's summit.

Drive Highway 26 east of Dayville 13 miles (or west of John Day 18 miles), and turn south on Fields Creek Road at a sign for the Murderers Creek Guard Station. Follow this paved, one-lane road 8.6 miles to a pointer for Fields Peak, turn left on gravel Road 115 for 0.4 mile to a T-shaped junction, turn right on Road 2160 for 200 yards, and fork left on Road 041—which is steep and a little rough, but OK for passenger cars—for 1.2 miles to its end at the McClellan Trailhead's parking turnaround *(GPS location N44°19.305′ W119°15.958′)*.

The wide trail starts uphill through sparse woods of ponderosa pine, Douglas fir, and juniper, but soon enters slopes of sagebrush. June wildflowers include short purple larkspur, red paintbrush, and the 3-inch yellow blooms of balsamroot.

After climbing 0.7 mile you'll round a ridge-end with your first view of McClellan Mountain. If you have time, you might amble cross-country out the ridge 0.2 mile to a viewpoint where pink bitterroot flowers bloom. Then continue up the main trail 0.8 mile to a fork in a forested saddle. Keep left on a wide trail that spirals 0.8 mile to Fields Peak's gravelly summit. Melted glass and concrete foundations remain from an old lookout. The view includes the distant snowy brown hump of Strawberry Mountain to the east, the glinting roofs of John Day Valley ranches to the north, and the snowy Aldrich Mountain to the west.

If you'd like a longer hike, return from Fields Peak to the saddle junction and turn left on the narrower McClellan Mountain Trail. This well-graded path weaves through four scenic passes as it traverses east along the crest of the range. After 2.2 miles, in the fourth pass, the tread vanishes in a sagebrush meadow *(GPS location N44°19.982′ W119°13.469′)*. This meadow is also a good place to head cross-country toward McClellan Mountain's summit. Simply climb a sagebrush slope to the left 0.2 mile to a knoll, and then follow the broad, treeless ridgecrest east a mile.

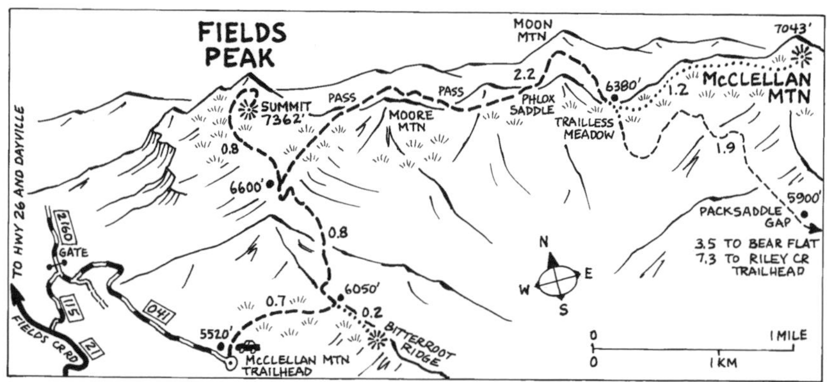

The Kam Wah Chung Museum, a Chinese gold rush store in John Day.

JOHN DAY

With snowy peaks and mountain lakes, the Strawberry Range seems like a chunk of the Canadian Rockies dropped in the midst of Eastern Oregon's ranchlands. One of the prettiest drives in Oregon traces the John Day River from the lava canyon of Picture Gorge through John Day to the base of the range. In downtown John Day, stop for a look at the **John Day Historic Church,** with its white wooden steeple and Carpenter Gothic frills. On the west edge of town, the City Park has the county's only **public swimming pool** (an inexpensive treat on a hot summer day) and the Kam Wah Chung Museum (see below).

Kam Wah Chung Museum

Chinese gold miners built this two-story stone structure in the late 1860s as a combination pharmacy, cultural center, temple, opium den, and fortress. Now the oldest building in John Day, the museum is filled with artifacts from the fascinating culture of pioneer Chinese immigrants. Open daily 9am-5pm from May through October. Tours start hourly 9am-4pm.Adults pay $3, seniors and kids over 5 $2.50.

Canyon City

Gold was discovered along Canyon Creek on June 8, 1862, and soon a boomtown of 10,000 sprang up. In two years, $26 million of gold was removed. The young C.H. Miller, later famous as Joaquin Miller, the "Poet of the Sierras," practiced law and wrote poems here 1863-69. A flash flood destroyed much of the town in 1896. Today the town is still the county seat, but its population has declined to about 700, while neighboring John Day has grown nearly three times that large.

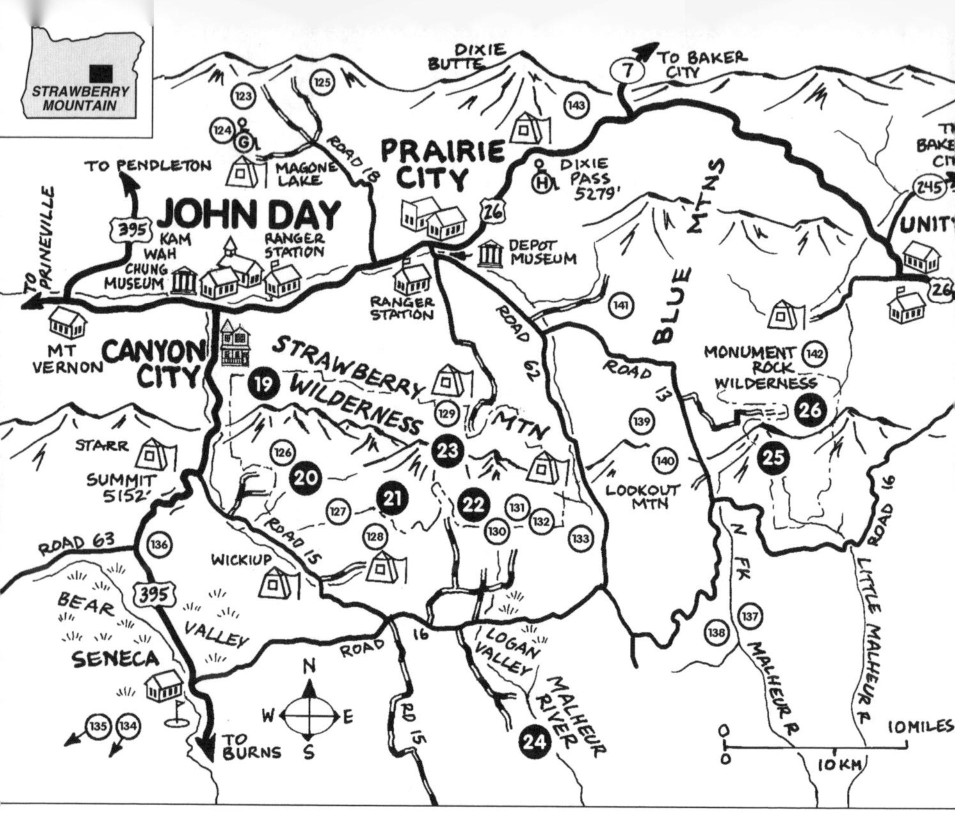

Walk a few blocks around **Canyon City's downtown** to see the old stone buildings, the city park's historic murals, and the **Grant County Historical Museum,** where Joaquin Miller's 1865 plank cabin has been moved. The museum is open 9-4:30 Mon-Sat from May 1 to Sept 30. Admission runs $4 for adults, $3.50 for seniors, and $2 for kids 7-17. Then drive up Main Street 0.8 mile and turn left toward the Canyon City Cemetery to see the white crosses of **Boot Hill.** Here, just outside the official cemetery, the gold rush boomtown laid its horse thieves and prostitutes to rest. Each year in early June, Canyon City toasts its heritage at **'62 Days,** a festival featuring a chorus line of can-can girls, a mock hanging, a beard contest, gold-panning demonstrations, and a sawdust-floored saloon.

Prairie City

Stop on Highway 26 to walk along a block of Front Street's original stone and board storefronts from the early 1900s. The elegant 1905 **Hotel Prairie** at 112 Front Street has 9 restored period rooms for $75-135 (check *www.prairiecityoregon.com* or call 541-820-4800). The **Oxbow Restaurant and Saloon** at 128 Front Street features a fabulous wooden saloon bar, steaks, prawns, and a "big game museum" of gigantic stuffed elk heads. Step into **Prairie Drug and Hardware** at 124 Front Street to see a store that really does have everything. The **Prairiewinkle Inn** at 134 Front Street offers nice rooms for $70-125 (call 888-820-4369 or ask at the dentist office next door). Then cross the street to check out an inexpensive **antique shop**.

Prairie City's restored 1910 **Sumpter Valley Railway Depot** houses the DeWitt Museum, featuring the small-gauge railroad that connected this town to Sumpter and Baker City until 1947. Several miles of the old railroad line near Sumpter have

Mural of gold rush days in Canyon City.

been reopened for a steam-powered excursion train, and Prairie City boosters envision extending the tracks 40 miles across the Blue Mountains to the original railhead here. Meanwhile the depot museum also exhibits pioneer artifacts and minerals. In downtown Prairie City, turn south 4 blocks on Main Street to Depot Park. Hours are 10am-5pm Wednesday-Saturday from May 15 to October 15.

Bed & Breakfast Inns

For a break from camping, spoil yourself at one of the area's bed & breakfast inns. Just half a mile east of Prairie City on Highway 26, the 1906 vintage **Strawberry Mountain Inn** (800-545-6913, *www.strawberrymountaininn.com)* has four elegant rooms from $95-125. A few miles southeast of Prairie City on Road 61, the **Riverside School House Bed & Breakfast** (541-820-4731, *www.riversideschoolhouse.com*) rents an entire century-old schoolhouse on a working cattle ranch for $135.

If you're in John Day, look across the street from the Kam Wah Chung Museum to find the **Sonshine Bed & Breakfast** (open May-September at 210 NW Canton Street, 541-575-1827, *www.sonshinebedand breakfast.com*), where rooms run $85-95. In Dayville, the **Fish House Inn** (541-987-2124, *www.fishhouseinn.com*) has rooms for $50-125.

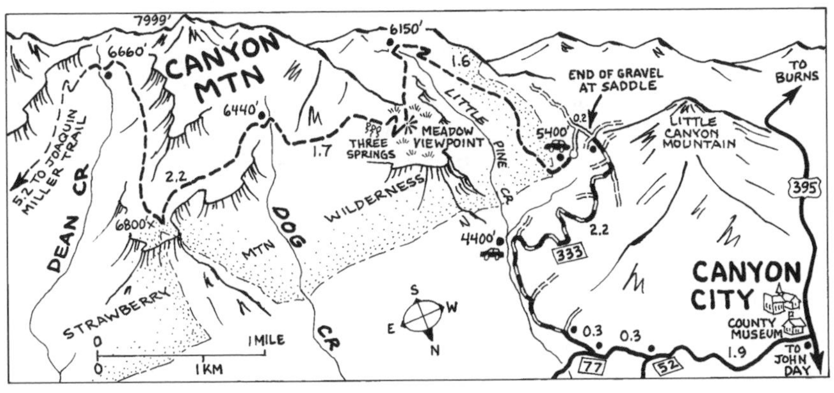

19 Canyon Mountain

Meadow on Canyon Mountain.

Moderate (to Dog Creek)
6.6 miles round trip
1200 feet elevation gain
Open June to mid-November
Use: hikers, horses

Difficult (to Dean Creek)
11 miles round trip
1700 feet elevation gain

Refer to map on previous page.

Gold drew 10,000 miners to Canyon City and Canyon Mountain in 1862. Today this craggy peak is part of the Strawberry Mountain Wilderness, with a scenic, well-graded trail zigzagging along the mountain's forested flanks.

Start in Canyon City, 2 miles south of John Day on Highway 395. At the Grant County Historical Museum turn east on Main Street (which becomes Road 52) for 1.9 miles. Then turn right onto paved Gardner Road 77 for 0.3 mile, and curve to the right onto a one-lane oiled road for 0.3 mile. At a fork, go straight onto a gravel road for 2.2 miles. This road is very steep at times! Ignore dirt spurs. When gravel ends in a saddle at a junction at the 2.2-mile mark, go straight on a dirt road 200 feet to a blazed pine tree, and then turn left for 300 yards to road's end at the trailhead parking area *(GPS location N44°21.75' W118°55.565')*.

The Canyon Mountain Trail sets off through an open forest of scattered ponderosa pines and Douglas firs. Little Pine Creek, at the 1.6-mile mark, splashes through a grotto with ferns, red columbine, paintbrush, and purple monkshood. The path climbs another 0.6 mile to an arid meadow with a bird's-eye view of the enormous, trough-shaped John Day Valley.

Continue to Dog Creek, a good turnaround point for a moderate hike. The bed of the tumbling stream shows off the colorful rock that attracted miners to this mountain: contorted green serpentinite and rough red peridotite, streaked with veins of white quartz and marble. Flecked with faint traces of gold, this rock was originally under the Pacific seafloor, but the advancing North American continent dredged it up like a plow 200-250 million years ago.

If you'd like a longer hike, continue another 2.2 miles to Dean Creek's miniature waterfall, another good goal. A rounded granite ridge above the path here harbors a few small tent sites—the first of the trip. Backpackers can continue up to a total of 37.1 miles along the crest of the Strawberry Range (see Hikes #20-23 and #126) to the Skyline Trailhead on Road 101 (Hike #133).

20 East Fork Canyon Creek

Easy (to Brookling Creek)
5.8 miles round trip
580 feet elevation gain
Open June through November
Use: hikers, horses

Difficult (Around Indian Creek Butte)
20.3-mile loop
3240 feet elevation gain
Open mid-July to early November

Left: East Fork Canyon Creek Trail.

One of the quietest forest canyons of Eastern Oregon slices along the southern edge of the Strawberry Range. A day hike up the East Fork of Canyon Creek offers only humble goals—a few creek views and a couple of park-like groves of big ponderosa pines—but if you're backpacking or riding a horse you can climb to Indian Creek Butte, where alpine meadows and viewpoints await. Expect to see mule deer and elk along the way. In the fall, dogwood and cottonwood trees fire the canyon with color.

Take Highway 395 south from John Day toward Burns 9.7 miles to a signpost pointing left toward "USFS Rt. 15; Wickiup CG 8". Turn left here on paved, two-lane County Road 65 for 2.9 miles. Then turn left onto gravel Road 6510 at a sign for "Alder Gulch; Fawn Spring". Keep left on this road for 1.6 miles, and then turn right on Road 812 for 2.8 miles to a large gravel parking lot at road's end. Equestrians will find a loading ramp and hitching posts here.

The trail sets off downhill through a grove of big orange-trunked ponderosa pines. After descending past a rockslide the path joins the creek and heads upstream. Wildflowers brighten the canyon floor: golden currant, purple aster, red paintbrush, blue lupine, and the white strawberries that gave this range its name.

After 2.2 miles a faint fork to the right leads across a grassy flat 100 yards to Yokum Corrals Camp, a possible campsite amid the ponderosas near the creek. In another 0.3 mile you'll cross Tamarack Creek (usually dry) and the junction with the Tamarack Creek Trail. Keep straight for another 0.4 mile and you'll reach 10-foot

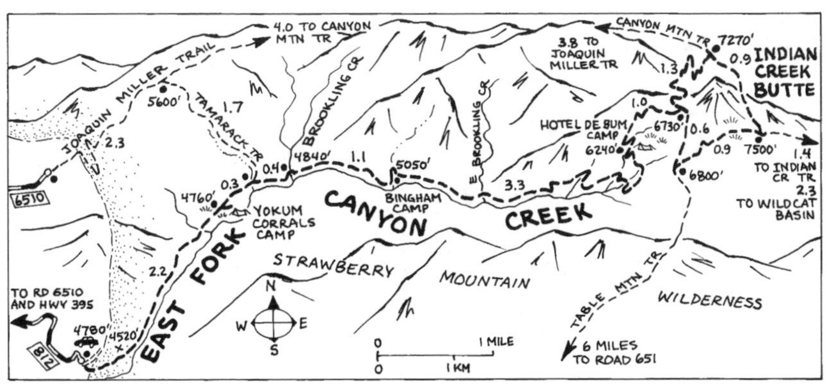

wide Brookling Creek. This shallow stream isn't an obstacle to serious hikers, but there is no bridge, so you might choose this as a turnaround point for a day hike.

Backpackers and adventurers who continue up the East Fork of Canyon Creek face a relatively uninteresting 4.4-mile climb to the wonderfully-named Hotel De Bum Camp, a small campsite at the creek's headwaters. A subalpine marsh here offers a view of Indian Creek Butte. Yet another mile up the trail is a junction for the 3.7-mile loop around Indian Creek Butte. At the high point of that circuit, a 7500-foot saddle, adventurers can strike out cross-country up a rocky ridge 0.3 mile to the summit itself, and a panoramic view of the upper John Day Valley.

21 Wildcat Basin

Moderate
6.9-mile loop
1330 feet elevation gain
Open late July through October
Use: hikers, horses

Trailside wildflower gardens and pinnacled ash badlands highlight the trail to Wildcat Basin. Lava flows built this part of the Strawberry Range 15 million years ago. Erosion has since cut through the lava layers, exposing the soft volcanic ash sandwiched between them. Seeps emerge between the old rock layers too, watering the wildflowers. About half of the hike's route burned in a 1996 forest fire, opening new views and letting in more light for the flowers.

From John Day, take Highway 395 south toward Burns 9.7 miles to a signpost pointing left toward "USFS Rt. 15; Wickiup CG 8". Turn left here on paved, two-lane County Road 65 (which becomes Road 15). After 13.6 miles, at a 4-way intersection with a stop sign, turn left on paved Road 16 toward Logan Valley. Drive 2.5 miles, and then turn left again (at a "Strawberry Wilderness" pointer)

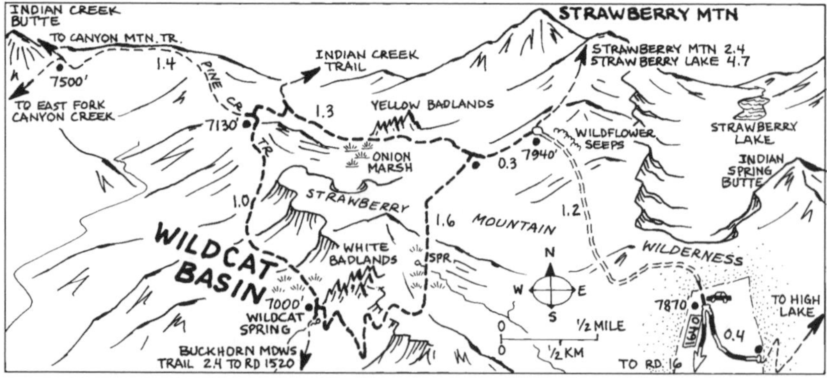

Wildcat Basin's ash badlands. Opposite: Asters.

onto gravel Road 1640. After 9.6 miles, where the road makes a switchback to the right, park in a pullout on the left marked "Roads End Trail 201A."

At 7870 feet elevation, this trailhead is higher than many Oregon mountaintops, so it's not surprising that the whitebark pines and noble firs here have been dwarfed by storms. The trail itself is actually an old roadbed, now strewn with white phlox, purple aster, and yellow composites. After a mile, when you enter the burned part of the forest, huge bushy clumps of wildflowers drape the old roadcut. The display features pink monkeyflower, white cow parsnip, purple penstemon, and delicate parrots beak.

When the old road ends at the 1.2-mile mark, you'll get a glimpse ahead to the brown pyramid of 9038-foot Strawberry Mountain. Turn left on a trail that descends across a wooded saddle to a fork. Keep left again for 1.6 miles to Wildcat Basin. When the trail finally switchbacks down into the basin you'll pass a white badlands of knobby pinnacles and striped volcanic ash.

In Wildcat Basin itself, a dry meadow below the badlands, you'll reach a T-shaped junction. Here you might detour briefly left 50 feet to see Wildcat Spring, a horse-hoof-damaged font with a few campsites back in the trees. Then take the T-junction's right-hand path to continue the loop. After another mile, turn right at a saddle and follow the Indian Creek Trail into a burned forest of standing snags. In 0.2 mile, the trail crosses a small creek to another junction. Turn right on a path that climbs steeply half a mile to a surprising marsh of wild onions—an entire meadow of blue, spherical, aromatic wildflowers on tall stalks. The path grows faint but continue to complete the loop and find the road/trail back to your car.

Other Options

The easiest route to the top of Strawberry Mountain also begins at this trailhead. Hike the old roadbed 1.2 miles to its end, turn right on the Onion Creek Trail, and then keep left at junctions. The route gains 1200 feet in a total of 3.6 miles.

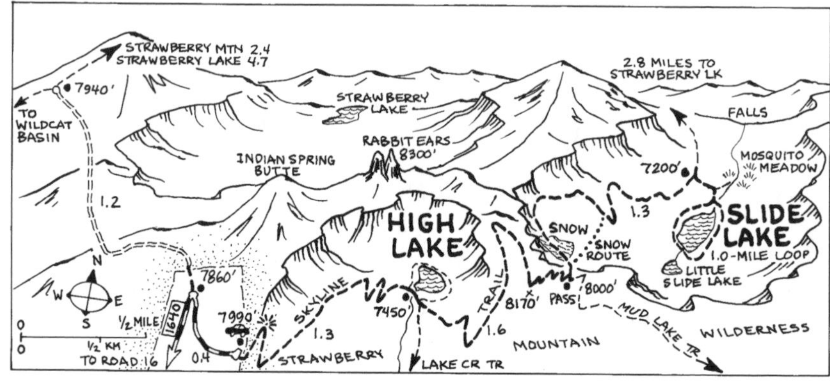

22 High Lake

Easy (to High Lake)
2.6 miles round trip
540 feet elevation loss
Open late July through October
Use: hikers, horses

Difficult (to Slide Lake)
9.4 miles round trip
2250 feet elevation gain
Open August through October

It's hard to imagine a better place for a first backpacking trip with kids than High Lake. An easy, 1.3-mile path leads past wildflowers and woods to a picturesque lake swarming with small trout. Both High Lake and its neighbor, Slide Lake, are set in giant rock-walled bowls carved into the crest of the Strawberry Range by Ice Age glaciers. The glaciers are gone, but snow lingers until late summer in the scenic pass between the two lakes.

To find the trailhead from John Day, take Highway 395 south toward Burns 9.7 miles to a signpost pointing left toward "USFS Rt. 15; Wickiup CG 8". Turn left here on paved, two-lane County Road 65 (which becomes Road 15). After 13.6 miles, at a 4-way intersection with a stop sign, turn left on Road 16 toward Logan Valley. Drive 2.5 miles on this paved road, and then follow a "Strawberry Wilderness" pointer left onto gravel Road 1640 for 10 miles to the road's end.

The Skyline Trail sets off toward High Lake by switchbacking down a slope of wildflowers, including blue lupine, pearly everlasting, yellow Oregon sunshine, and pink fireweed. Particularly notice the paintbrush, which usually blooms red, but here is a yellow species.

At High Lake the view extends across the fish-jump rings of the lake to a huge, rounded cliff face topped with the dark crags of Rabbit Ears, a pair of rock spires. The trail forks just before a driftwood logjam that marks the lake's outlet. The left-hand path circles the lake and leads to the quietest campsites. If you're continuing onward, however, keep right across the outlet creek.

At the far end of the footbridge, note that two different trails lead to the right. Don't take the far right path marked "Lake Creek Trail." Instead veer gently to the right on the Skyline Trail. This path climbs more than a mile to a high ridge-end, and then drops to a junction in a rocky pass. Go left across the pass.

For the next few hundred yards the Skyline Trail traverses a high slope where a dangerously steep snowfield may remain across the trail until August. If snow is still blocking the route, and if you're determined to continue, the safest choice is to head downhill and pick up the trail at its next switchback 0.3 mile below. Once past the snowy slope, follow the trail down a mile to a junction in the woods. Keep right for the loop around Slide Lake. Remarkable cliffs back the lake on three sides. Ice Age glaciers here sliced through ten lava flows, each 50 feet thick, leaving a massive cliff striped like a layer cake.

Other Options

If you're backpacking, consider continuing on a spectacular 13.3-mile loop past Slide Lake to Strawberry Lake and Strawberry Mountain (see Hike #23). The circuit ends at a trailhead on Road 1640 just 0.4 mile from your car. Total elevation gain is 2930 feet.

High Lake. Opposite: Slide Lake.

23 Strawberry Lake

Easy (around Strawberry Lake)
4-mile loop
550 feet elevation gain
Open July to mid-November
Use: hikers, horses

Moderate (to Little Strawberry Lake)
6.6 miles round trip
1200 feet elevation gain

Difficult (to Strawberry Mountain)
12.6 miles round trip
3320 feet elevation gain
Open August through October

With alpine lakes, snowy crags, and waterfalls, the Strawberry Range seems like a chunk of the Canadian Rockies dropped onto the sagebrush plains of Eastern Oregon. For a picture-postcard view of this surprising range, hike 1.3 miles to Strawberry Lake, a mountain pool backed by a palisade of cliffs. For an even better view, continue past Strawberry Falls to Little Strawberry Lake. And for the best view of all, take a well-graded trail all the way to the panoramic summit of 9038-foot Strawberry Mountain.

Start by driving Highway 26 to Prairie City (13 miles east of John Day). Turn south in the middle of Prairie City, following a pointer for Depot Park and Strawberry Lake. After 0.4 mile you'll reach a stop sign at a T-shaped junction. Turn left for two blocks, and then turn right at a "Strawberry Campground" arrow onto Bridge Street, which becomes County Road 60 and eventually Forest Road 6001. Continue a total of 10.7 miles (the last 7.6 on gravel) to road's end at Strawberry

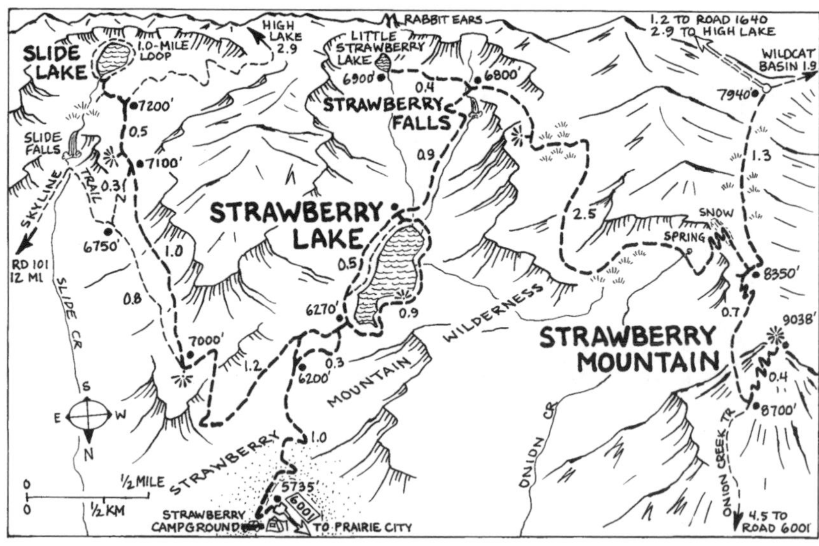

Strawberry Lake. Opposite: Strawberry Falls.

Campground. A campsite here costs about $8, but hikers park free.

The trail begins by a message board at the far end of the parking area and climbs up through a grand fir forest where huckleberries ripen in August.

Keep right at all junctions to the edge of Strawberry Lake at the 1.3-mile mark. Although the main trail turns left here, you'll get better views if you turn right on a smaller path around the quieter, west side of the lake. This path crosses a footbridge over the lake's outlet, a creek that usually flows underground.

Strawberry Lake formed about a thousand years ago when giant landslides dammed the valley. During the Ice Age a glacier filled the valley from wall to wall. When the ice melted, the unsupported cliffs on either hand collapsed. The most recent slide left a red-striped scarp that's still visible on the canyon wall. The lake now drains most of its extra water down a whirlpool, leaving the outlet "creek" gurgling beneath the landslide's rocks.

If you're strapped for time, you can simply loop counterclockwise around the lake and head back to your car. But a longer trip here is definitely worthwhile. To continue, follow the trail around to the far end of Strawberry Lake. After crossing several creeks, turn uphill on a steep, unmarked side path 50 yards and then turn right on a larger trail. This path climbs to Strawberry Falls, a 60-foot fan splashing onto mossy boulders. At the top of the falls you'll reach a junction—and face a choice. You can either turn left for 0.4 mile to Little Strawberry Lake, a dramatic turnaround point for a moderate hike. Or you can keep right for the longer, challenging climb to Strawberry Mountain itself.

The path up Strawberry Mountain climbs through several surprisingly diverse wildflower meadows, where sagebrush mingles with lush pink monkeyflower and red paintbrush. Beyond Strawberry Falls 2.5 miles the path switchbacks up to a windswept pass, where a steep snow cornice often lingers across the trail until August.

Keep taking the uphill fork at junctions and you'll end up on top Strawberry

Mountain, a pyramid of shaley, tilted rock strata where only yellow sulfur flowers and alpine butterflies seem able to survive. The fire lookout cabin that stood here until the 1950s, anchored to the rock by roof cables, blew out from under its roof in a winter storm. Years later the roof blew away too, leaving only the cables visible today.

From this lofty perch, the creekside forests at the foot of the Strawberry Range look like great green snakes crawling out into the brown desert. To the north, look for the gridiron of Prairie City. To the west, the Strawberry Range humps off toward the crags of Canyon Mountain. To the southeast, above Rabbit Ears' spires, shimmers the distant white stripe of Steens Mountain.

Other Options

Slide Lake is another popular day-hike goal from the Strawberry Campground trailhead. It's 4 miles away and 1500 feet up. Better still, plan a backpack trip to visit three lakes on a grand 15.6-mile circuit of the high Strawberries. Start by hiking past Strawberry Lake to the 8350-foot saddle on Strawberry Mountain's shoulder. If you keep left at all junctions from there on, you'll walk along Road 1640 for 0.4 mile, drop down to High Lake (see Hike #22), and cross a pass to Slide Lake before returning to Strawberry Lake and the trail down to your car. Total elevation gain for the loop is 3470 feet.

24 Malheur River

Easy (to gorge viewpoint)
3.8-miles round trip
200 feet elevation gain
Open May to early December
Use: hikers, horses, bicycles

Moderate (with shuttle)
7.6 miles one-way
800 feet elevation gain

The glassy, 30-foot-wide Malheur River gathers its strength at the base of the Strawberry Range to bluster through a rimrock canyon of ponderosa pines before striking off into the desert. The path through this canyon is a delight.

From John Day, take Highway 395 south toward Burns 9.7 miles to a signpost pointing left toward "USFS Rt. 15; Wickiup CG 8". Turn left here on paved, two-lane County Road 65 (which becomes Road 15). After 13.6 miles, at a 4-way intersection with a stop sign, turn left on paved Road 16 toward Logan Valley. After 5.3 miles, just before Logan Valley, turn right on gravel Road 1643. Following "Malheur River" pointers, drive 9 miles on Road 1643 to a fork and veer left on Road 1651 for 1.3 miles to Malheur Ford's riverside parking area *(GPS location N44°05.142′ W118°34.937′).*

Malheur Ford really does have a ford—a frightening 50-foot crossing where high-clearance rigs sometimes plow across the river to continue on Road 1651. Fortunately, there's no need to try it because the trail starts on the near side.

The Malheur River. Opposite: Porcupine.

The near side of the Malheur River has a lovely meadow with a picnic table, free campsites, and an all-accessible restroom. The well-maintained trail starts here and heads downstream through an open forest with big ponderosa pine, small lodgepole pines, and scattered Douglas firs. Wildflowers include blue lupine, white yarrow, and red columbine. Watch for stinging nettles by the trail in wet spots. Chipmunks are everywhere.

After 1.9 miles the trail climbs to a clifftop viewpoint in the most rugged part of the Malheur River's gorge. This makes a good turnaround point for an easy hike. You might also look along the trail near here for wild raspberry bushes, with tiny but intensely delicious red fruit in summer.

Beyond this gorge the trail follows the river another 4.5 miles downstream, passing several campable flats and small meadows along the way. Then the path switchbacks uphill for 1.2 miles to the far trailhead at Hog Flat *(GPS location N44°00.759' W118°32.187')*. If you've ridden the trail on a mountain bike, you can return from Hog Flat to Malheur Ford on a pleasant 16.8-mile backroad loop, simply by following the gravel road and keeping right at all junctions. If you want to hike the entire trail, it's best to plan on leaving a shuttle car at Hog Flat. To drive there from Malheur Ford, backtrack 1.3 miles on Road 1651 to a junction, turn left on Road 1643 for 6.5 miles, and turn left on Road 142 for 1.4 miles to its end. Antelope are frequently sighted along the way.

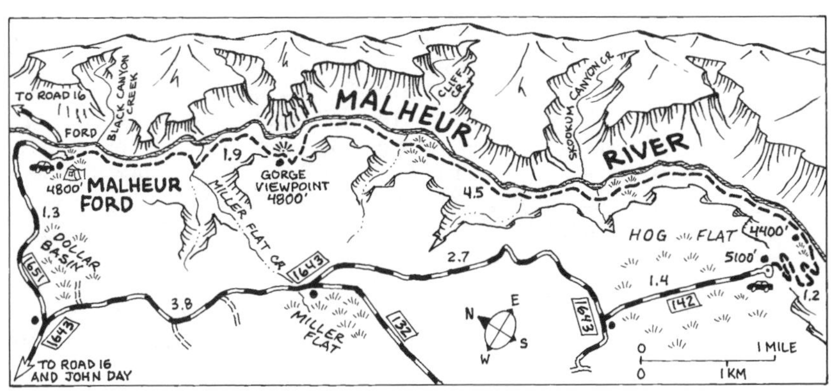

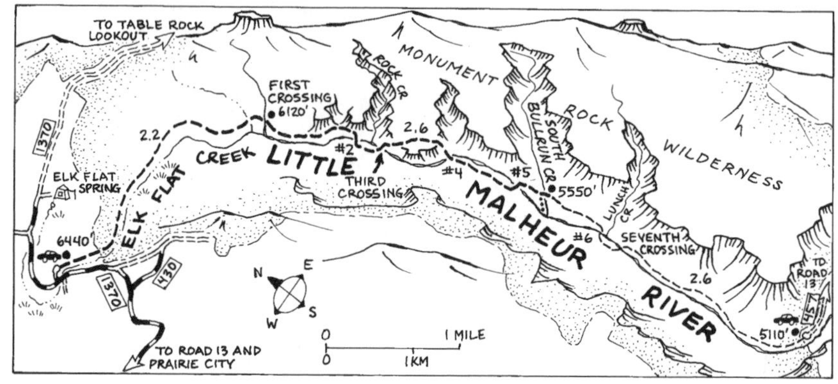

25 Little Malheur River

Moderate (to South Bullrun Creek)
9.6 miles round trip
890 feet elevation **loss**
Open late June through November
Use: hikers, horses

Difficult (entire trail)
14.8 miles round trip
1330 feet elevation **loss**

Left: Little Malheur River.

The Little Malheur River begins as a small creek tumbling through a densely forested valley high in the Blue Mountains. Even as you follow the river trail down into a canyon of ponderosa pines, the Little Malheur remains little enough that it's easy to negotiate the seven bridgeless crossings on fallen logs or rocks without getting your feet wet. This corner of the Monument Rock Wilderness is so rarely visited that elk, deer, and even shy black bears look up curiously before galumphing away.

Start by driving Highway 26 to Prairie City (13 miles east of John Day). Turn south in the middle of Prairie City, following a sign for Depot Park. After 0.4 mile, turn left at a stop sign. Then keep straight on what becomes County Road 62. Drive 8 miles on this paved highway, turn left on paved Road 13 following a "Short Creek" pointer for 11.7 miles, turn left onto gravel Road 1370 at a sign for the Little Malheur River, and keep left on this road for 5 miles to the trailhead's well-marked parking area *(GPS location N44°19.224' W118°22.554')*.

The path heads down to the right, following the grassy swale of Elk Flat Creek. The streambed itself is usually dry for the first mile. As you gradually descend, the trailside thickets of lodgepole pine give way to fir and a few gigantic 5-foot-thick larch, with an understory of low red huckleberry bushes. After 2 miles the trail hops a tiny side creek, and then reaches the first crossing of the rocky, 8-foot-wide Little Malheur River.

Downstream the canyon narrows between outcroppings of shaley lava rock. The trail begins switching from one side of the river to the other. The fifth river crossing has a mini-meadow with columbine, gooseberry, and alder brush. In another 0.2 mile the trail crosses brushy, 5-foot-wide South Bullrun Creek. At this point you've come 4.8 miles. If you're looking for a campsite, or a nice lunch spot where you can declare victory before heading home, bushwhack down the creek 100 yards to its confluence with the Little Malheur River *(GPS location N44°16.925' W118°19.306')*. Here you'll find small grassy flats along the river, where cheery cascades splash past boulders as big and flat as dinner tables.

If you decide to continue downriver, the trail continues 2.6 miles to its end at Road 457. To find this lower trailhead from the upper trailhead, drive 5 miles back down to Road 13, turn left on this paved road for 4.5 miles, turn left on gravel Road 16 for 11 miles, turn left on Road 1672 for 1 mile, and go straight on Road 457 for 3 very rough miles to its end.

26 Monument Rock

Easy (to Bullrun Rock)
4.4 miles round trip
380 feet elevation gain
Open July through November
Use: hikers, horses

Moderate (to Monument Rock)
5.6 miles round trip
550 feet elevation gain

Right: Monument Rock.

On this sagebrush mountaintop, white and orange butterflies swarm about the mysterious 8-foot circular rock cairn that gives the Monument Rock Wilderness its name. No trail climbs to this lithic landmark, visible from far across the wilderness area's alpine mesa. For easier viewpoint goals, hike to Bullrun Rock or drive to the Table Rock lookout, on the two other corners of this scenic triangular plateau.

From John Day, drive Highway 26 east 13 miles to downtown Prairie City and turn right at a sign for Depot Park. After 0.4 mile, turn left at a stop sign, and then keep straight on what becomes County Road 62. Continue 8 miles on this paved highway, turn left on paved Road 13 following a "Short Creek" pointer for 11.7 miles, and then turn left onto gravel Road 1370 at a sign for the Little Malheur River. After 4.4 miles, fork to the left to stay on Road 1370. At a junction in another 1.5 miles, turn right following a "Table Rock L.O." sign, still sticking to Road 1370. After just 0.2 mile the road forks. The right-hand branch is the entrance to the primitive Elk Flat Spring Campground, with six excellent, free campsites. For the hike, however, take the left-hand fork, This road quickly deteriorates to a rocky dirt track. Take it slow for 3.8 miles to a switchback with a message board and parking for three cars.

Although the hike begins at this switchback, first consider driving up the road

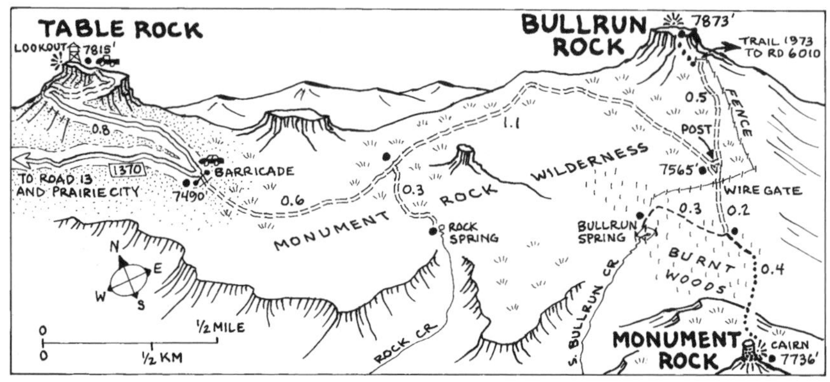

another 0.8 mile to say hello to the Table Rock Lookout staffer. The final 300 yards of Road 1370 are so steep and rocky that you'll need to use first gear and drive very slowly. At the top, the 14-foot-square, 1936-vintage fire lookout building has a view sweeping from Strawberry Mountain to the Wallowas. A snowfield lingers here until August. In 1989 the staffer had to evacuate when a forest fire swept over the ridge.

After paying your respects at Table Rock, drive back down to the switchback trailhead and hike out an old road that's closed to motor vehicles by a dirt berm. This nearly level road/trail crosses a sagebrush meadow with blue lupine, red paintbrush, purple aster, and patches of struggling subalpine fir. It's a pleasant stroll across a remote mountaintop prairie.

After 1.7 miles the old road grows faint at a signless, 7-foot post. For the easier hike to Bullrun Rock, walk past the left side of the post 100 feet to find a track that curves left toward Bullrun Rock, the highest rock outcrop on the sagebrush horizon. Follow this old road track 0.4 mile to a pass where a fenceline crosses at a wire gate. Leave the road here and scramble left up a steep rock hill 200 yards to the summit of Bullrun Rock *(GPS location N44°19.478' W118°17.017')*. To the north, the view extends past the distant town of Unity to the craggy Elkhorn Range and the hazy Wallowa Mountains.

Then hike back 0.5 mile to the faint road fork marked by a post. If you're ready for the trickier hike to Monument Rock, continue straight through a fenceline's wire gate 0.2 mile to a small cairn marking a faint junction in a burned forest of snags. Turn left on a dusty elk trail 100 feet to the broad crest of a pass, where the trail peters out. Then bushwhack to the right along the broad ridgecrest, up a steep slope, and across a mountaintop to Monument Rock *(GPS location N44°18.698' W118°17.276')*.

Lichens encrust only small parts of the shaley andesite in this mysterious cylindrical stack, suggesting that it was built about a century ago. Certainly the region's Paiute Indians did not use this kind of stonework. Perhaps the cairn dates to the gold miners who began prospecting north of Bullrun Rock in 1865. More likely, however, bored Basque shepherds assembled the cairn when they began grazing their flocks across these high meadows in the early 1900s.

If you're backpacking, bring water or a good filter pump, because the summit plateau's two water sources, Rock Spring and Bullrun Spring, have both been badly trampled by cattle and elk.

STRAWBERRY LAKE (Hike #23) lies between 9038-foot Strawberry Mountain and the snowy crags of Rabbit Ears.

A COVERED WAGON marks the original ruts at the Oregon Trail Interpretive Center near Baker City (see page 79).

PAINTED COVE'S boardwalk (Hike #15) loops through the John Day Fossil Beds National Monument.

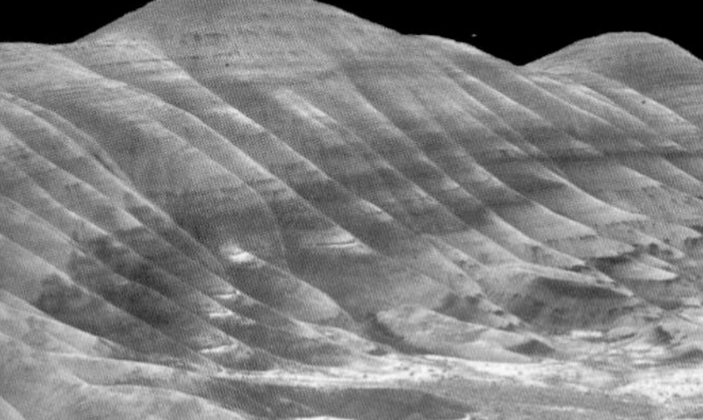

PAINTED HILLS (Hike #15) are composed of volcanic ash in the John Day Fossil Beds National Monument.

ANTHONY LAKE (Hike #28) mirrors Gunsight Butte.

THE SNAKE RIVER roars through Hells Canyon below Hat Point (Hike #45).

THE KAM WAH CHUNG MUSEUM in John Day is an 1869 Chinese gold miners' store (see page 53).

BAKER CITY's downtown features over 100 restored buildings from gold rush days (see page 77).

THE "STUMP DODGER," the Sumpter Valley Railroad, now serves as an excursion stream train (see page 79).

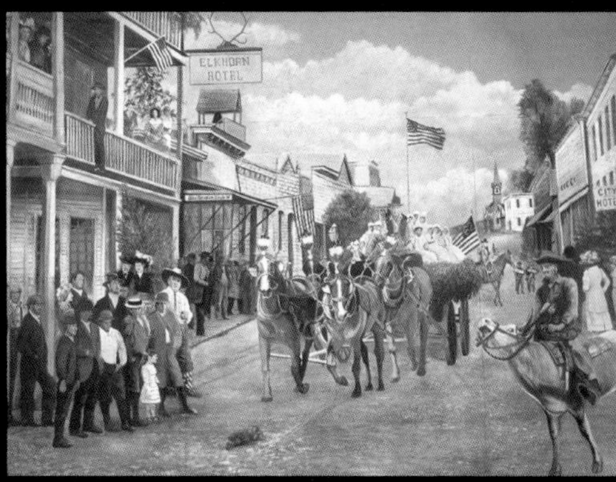

CANYON CITY'S 1860s gold rush lives again in a mural on a building in downtown Canyon City (see page 53).

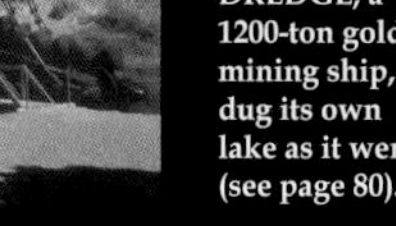

SUMPTER'S DREDGE, a 1200-ton gold mining ship, dug its own lake as it went (see page 80).

WHITNEY is a ghost town south of Sumpter, toward John Day 9 miles on Highway 7.

GRANITE'S city hall was once a schoolhouse.

Ghost Towns

The population of most of Eastern Oregon was larger a century ago than it is today, so ghost towns dot the map. The oldest date to the 1860s gold rush. Of these, **Granite** (see page 80) and **Sumpter** (page 80) are now growing. Ghost towns from the 1910s recall the failed homesteads of farmers at **Fort Rock** (page 177) and **Blitzen** (map, page 214). The logging town of **Whitney** (right) faded when the Sumpter Valley Railroad closed its Prairie City line in 1947.

Canyon Wildflowers

HONEYSUCKLE *(Lonicera ciliosa)*. This fragrant, viney shrub blooms in canyons early in summer.

PRINCE'S PINE *(Chimaphila umbellata)*. Also known as pipsissewa, this blooms in shade.

COLUMBINE *(Aquilegia formosa)*. In wet woodlands, this bloom has nectar lobes for hummingbirds.

TWINFLOWER *(Linnaea borealis)*. This double bloom grows in the far North around the globe.

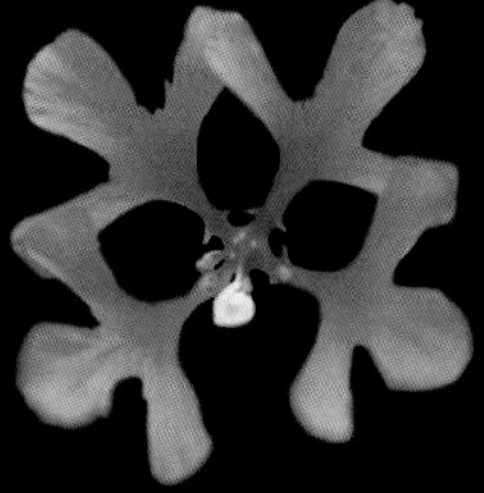

CLARKIA *(Clarkia pulchella)*. Named for Lewis and Clark, this bloom covers canyonsides in June.

STONECROP *(Sedum oreganum)*. This plant survives in bare, rocky ground by storing water in fat leaves.

BLEEDING HEART *(Dicentra formosa)*. Look near woodland creeks for these pink hearts.

OREGON GRAPE *(Berberis aquifolium)*. Oregon's state flower has holly-like leaves and blue berries.

FOXGLOVE *(Digitalis purpurea)*. Showy 5-foot foxglove stalks spangle sunny summer hillsides.

SOURGRASS *(Oxalis oregana)*. The shamrock-shaped leaves carpet forests and taste tart when chewed.

SHOOTING STAR *(Dodecatheon jeffreyi)*. Early in summer, shooting stars carpet wet fields and slopes.

CANDYFLOWER *(Claytonia sibirica)*. Common by woodland creeks and trails, candyflower is edible.

Alpine Wildflowers

GENTIAN *(Gentiana calycosa)*. These thumb-sized blooms near alpine lakes open only in full sun.

PHLOX *(Phlox diffusa)*. Like a colorful cushion, phlox hugs arid rock outcrops with a mat of blooms.

BEARGRASS *(Xerophyllum tenax)* resembles a giant bunchgrass until it blooms with a tall, lilied plume.

ELEPHANTS HEAD *(Pedicularis groenlandica)*. You'll see pink elephants like this in alpine bogs.

MARSH MARIGOLD *(Caltha biflora)*. This early bloomer likes high marshes full of snowmelt.

LUPINE *(Lupinus* spp.*)* has fragrant blooms in early summer and pea-pod-shaped fruit in fall.

GLACIER LILY *(Erythronium grandiflorum)*. These blooms erupt a week after the snow melts.

BROAD-LEAVED FIREWEED *(Epilobium latifolium)*, just inches tall, likes sandy alpine creekbanks.

PENSTEMON *(Penstemon* spp.*)*. Look for these red, purple, or blue trumpets in high, rocky areas.

ASTER *(Aster* spp.*)*. This purple daisy-like flower blooms late in summer, from July to September.

PAINTBRUSH *(Castilleja* spp.*)* has showy red-orange sepals, but the actual flowers are green tubes.

MOUNTAIN BLUEBELL *(Mertensia* spp.*)*. A favorite browse for elk, these plants fill subalpine meadows.

Prairie Wildflowers

SAGEBRUSH ***(Artemisia*** **spp.). Dominant shrub of the high desert steppe, sagebrush has lobed leaves.**

GRASS OF PARNASSUS ***(Parnassia fimbriata*****). Look for this saxifrage on grassy streambanks.**

YELLOW BELL ***(Fritillaria pudica).*** **Just 6 inches tall, this lily blooms in sagebrush grasslands in spring.**

SCARLET GILIA or SKYROCKET ***(Gilia aggregata)*** **blooms on dry, open slopes all summer.**

BALSAMROOT ***(Balsamorhiza spp.).*** **In spring this bloom turns entire hillsides yellow.**

LARKSPUR ***(Delphinium*** **spp.). Stalks of larkspur stand 3 feet tall in wet meadows, 3 inches in dry.**

BACHELOR BUTTON ***(Centaurea cyanus).*** **One of many showy blue composite flowers with this name.**

RABBIT BRUSH ***(Chrysothamnus spp.).*** **Fall's brightest wildflower turns the high desert yellow.**

PRAIRIE STAR ***(Lithophragma parviflora)*** **blooms in May amid sagebrush and pine.**

SALSIFY ***(Tragopogon dubius).*** **This dry June roadside flower turns to a giant dandelion-like seed puffball.**

WILD ONION ***(Allium*** **spp.). This pungent bloom hugs the ground in dry, rocky areas.**

BLANKETFLOWER ***(Gaillardia aristata)*****, alias brown-eyed Susan, blooms in grassy foothills all summer.**

High Desert Wildflowers

DESERT BUCKWHEAT (*Eriogonum spp.*). White, pink, and yellow varieties of this plant like dry areas.

OREGON SUNSHINE (*Eriophyllum lanatum*). The woolly stalks of this common bloom conserve water.

BITTERROOT (*Lewisia rediviva*). Noted by Lewis and Clark, these 3-inch blooms have edible roots.

PRICKLY PEAR (*Opuntia polyacantha*). Most cacti find Oregon's desert too cold. This one's rare too.

PENSTEMON (*Penstemon* spp.). The desert varieties of this showy flower often grow two feet tall.

DEATH CAMAS (*Zigadenus* spp.). This poisonous lily can be fatal if you mistake it for edible camas.

MARIPOSA LILY (*Calochortus* spp.) These showy lilies vary by area. Clockwise from upper left are blooms from Steens Mountain, the Wenaha River, the Wallowa Mountains, and Hells Canyon.

EVENING PRIMROSE (*Oenothera tanacetifolia*) forms a golden carpet on a Hart Mountain lakeshore.

FREEZEOUT SADDLE (Hike #46) offers a view west across the Imnaha River Canyon to the snowy Wallowa Mountains.

Covered wagon at the Oregon Trail Interpretive Center outside Baker City.

BAKER CITY

The craggy, granite Elkhorn Range that once drew miners to an 1860s gold rush now attracts hikers and skiers. The range also serves as a dramatic backdrop to several Old West ghost towns and the historic downtown of charming Baker City.

Geiser Grand Hotel

Restored in 1998 at a cost of $7 million, this elaborate, turreted 1889 hotel in downtown Baker City is worth a visit even if you don't book a room. At least take a table beneath the stained glass ceiling of the Palm Court, where liveried waiters serve steaks, pasta, or chicken for the reasonable rate of $10-$20. Champagne runs $15-$155. Overnight guests report a variety of benign ghosts, such as a smiling, 1930s-era "Lady in Blue," and several haunted rooms, including the "train room," where sleepers awake to the rumble of a nonexistent locomotive, and the "rain room," where an empty bath emits showering noises. Rooms run $79-249. Address: 1996 Main Street. Phone: 888-GEISERG (434-7374), *www.geisergrand.com.*

Baker City's historic downtown

Over 100 restored buildings line the streets of Baker City's turn-of-the-19th-century downtown. Pick up a free brochure describing a 1-mile walking tour at **Bettys Books** (1813 Main Street), one of Eastern Oregon's largest bookstores. For breakfast, lunch, or a cuppa, walk up the street a block to 1917 Main to **Mad Matilda's Coffee,** in an 1879 building with a stamped tin ceiling. A Belgian waffle breakfast costs less than a latte.

It's hard to miss the imposing **Geiser Grand Hotel** (see above), but make sure you cross the street to the humdrum-looking US Bank (2000 Main Street), to see its astonishing **gold display,** a glass case filled with gold pebbles, gold dust, and a monstrous 5-pound, fist-sized gold nugget.

Walk on to **Barley Brown's Brew Pub,** 2190 Main Street. Dare to order the

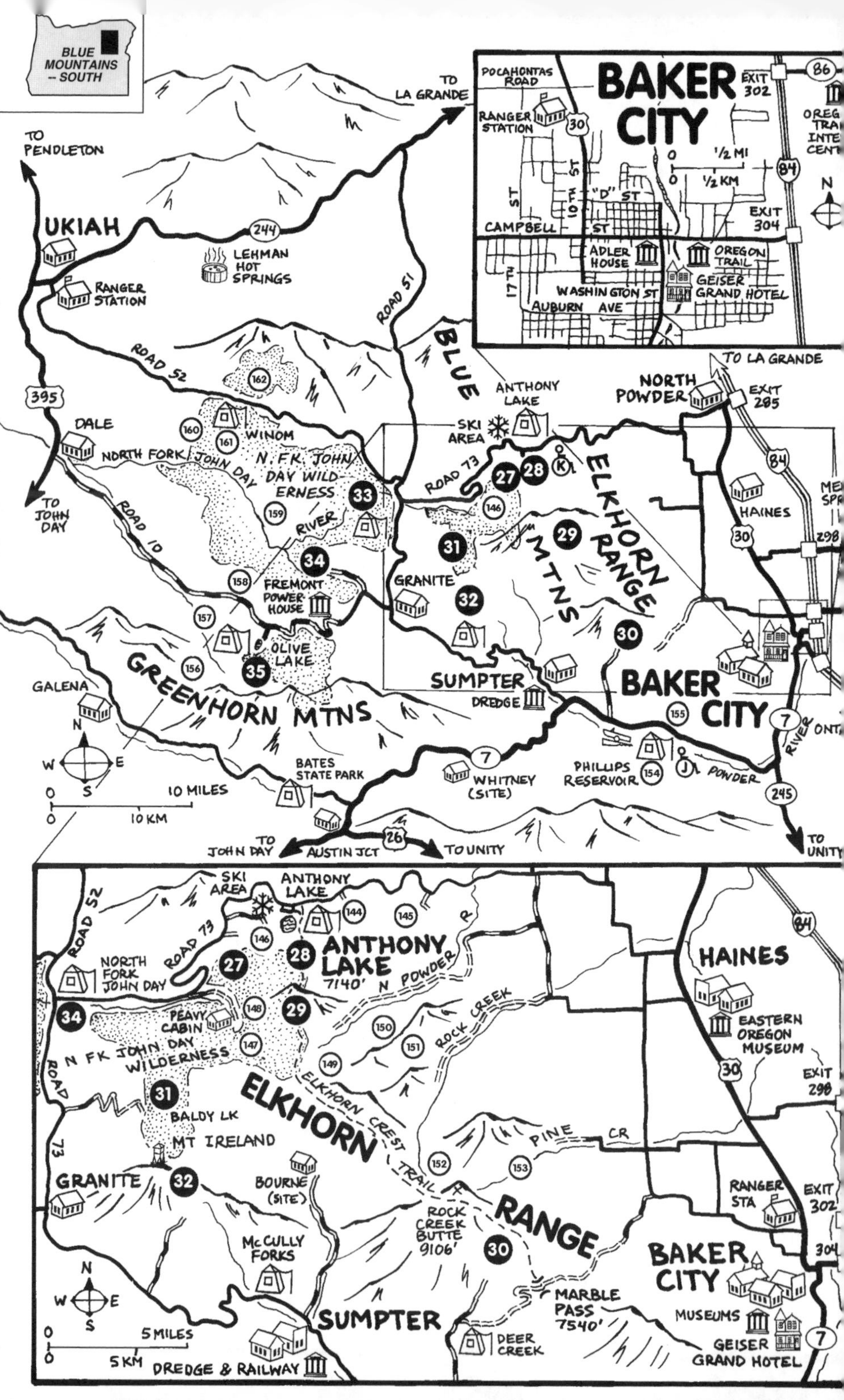

BLUE MOUNTAINS -- SOUTH
BAKER CITY
TO PENDLETON
UKIAH
RANGER STATION
LEHMAN HOT SPRINGS
TO LA GRANDE
ROAD 51
ROAD 52
DALE
NORTH FORK JOHN DAY RIVER
WINOM
N. FK. JOHN DAY WILDERNESS
ROAD 10
TO JOHN DAY
FREMONT POWER HOUSE
OLIVE LAKE
GREENHORN MTNS
GALENA
BATES STATE PARK
BLUE
ANTHONY LAKE
SKI AREA
ROAD 73
ELKHORN RANGE
MTNS
GRANITE
SUMPTER
DREDGE
WHITNEY (SITE)
PHILLIPS RESERVOIR
POWDER RIVER
NORTH POWDER
EXIT 285
HAINES
TO LA GRANDE
TO JOHN DAY
AUSTIN JCT
TO UNITY
10 MILES
10 KM
POCAHONTAS ROAD
RANGER STATION
EXIT 302
EXIT 304
10TH ST
"D" ST
CAMPBELL ST
ADLER HOUSE
OREGON TRAIL
GEISER GRAND HOTEL
WASHINGTON ST
AUBURN AVE
17TH
1/2 MI
1/2 KM
ANTHONY LAKE 7140'
N POWDER R
NORTH FORK JOHN DAY
PEAVY CABIN
N FK JOHN DAY WILDERNESS
ROCK CREEK
ELKHORN CREST TRAIL
ELKHORN RANGE
BALDY LK
MT IRELAND
BOURNE (SITE)
McCULLY FORKS
ROCK CREEK BUTTE 9106'
PINE CR
MARBLE PASS 7540'
DEER CREEK
DREDGE & RAILWAY
EASTERN OREGON MUSEUM
EXIT 298
RANGER STA
MUSEUMS
GEISER GRAND HOTEL
5 MILES
5 KM

The Geiser Grand Hotel in Baker City.

gigantic Death Burger, or go with some chicken nachos and a pint of the excellent Jubilee Golden Ale, brewed in honor of Baker City's annual **Miners Jubilee,** held each year in late July. Another block down Main Street is the **Adler House Museum,** a restored 1889 home at 2305 Main, packed with original antiques. It's open Friday through Monday 10am-2pm from late May to early September. Adults are $6 and kids under 12 are free. Then walk back to **Bella Main Street Market** (2023 Main, open 7am-7pm, 7 days a week), a wine shop with an upscale grocery and strange kitchen gadgets.

Oregon Trail Interpretive Center

The Conestoga wagons of the Oregon Trail crossed Flagstaff Hill to a dramatic view of the rugged Blue Mountains ahead. Today a world-class interpretive center perches atop the panoramic hill, with walk-through dioramas, a covered wagon camp, a gold mine replica, and outdoor hiking trails. Hike a 2.9-mile loop to visit a mine, a viewpoint, and the Oregon Trail's original wagon ruts. Open 9-6 daily Apr-Oct, 9-4 Nov-Mar. Hiking trails are free, but museum admission is $8 for adults and $4.50 for seniors, with kids under 15 free. From I-84 exit 302 near Baker City, drive 5 miles east on Highway 86. *Www.or.blm.gov/oregontrail.*

Oregon Trail Regional Museum

Folksier than the better known Oregon Trail Interpretive Center, this Baker City museum has collections of rocks, gems, and pioneer artifacts. A remodeled 1920 natatorium houses the museum at 2480 Grove Street beside the city's Geiser Pollman Park. Admission is $5 for adults and $4.50 for seniors, but children under 16 are free. Hours are 9-5 daily from late March through October.

Sumpter Valley Railroad

Nicknamed the "Stump Dodger" because it helped log the area's ponderosa pine forests in the 1890s, the narrow-gauge Sumpter Valley Railroad has reopened as a steam train on 5 miles of restored track between Sumpter and McEwen Station, 22 miles east of Baker City on Highway 7. Trains leave McEwen Station at 10am and 1:15pm (more often on holidays) from Memorial Day through September. The return train leaves Sumpter at 12noon and 3:15pm. Expect to pay $15 per adult ($9 for kids age 6-16) for the round trip (866-894-2268 or *www.svry.com*).

Sumpter

Founded by gold miners in 1862, Sumpter boomed to 3500 after the railroad line from Baker City reached here in 1896, but dwindled after a 1917 fire burned nearly every building and even the planked Main Street. Start your visit at the **Sumpter Dredge,** a 1200-ton, 60-foot-tall gold mill floating in a lake of its own making. The odd ship dug up $4.5 million in gold 1935-1954, but left miles of farmland churned to a moonscape of rock tailings. Now restored as a state heritage site, the dredge is open 7am-7pm May-Oct for free.

Walking from the dredge through town you'll pass the **Scoop & Steamer** (where 2-person log cabins rent for about $80; call 541-894-2236 or check *www.scoop-n-steamer.com*), the **Sumpter Municipal Museum** (open Thursday-Tuesday 11am-3pm and Wednesday 4-7pm), several antique shops, the **Depot Inn** (with 14 rooms for about $80; call 800-390-2522 or check *http://thedepotinn-sumpter.com/*), and the remains of a bank vault—one of the few relics from the 1917 fire.

Bates State Park

The lumber mill and company town of Bates closed in the 1970s, but a state park opened on the site in 2011 with 28 campsites ($10 per site, open May 15 to October 31). For a 2.7-mile loop, hike 0.6 mile around the old mill pond, continue 0.5 mile down Bridge Creek, and then keep right at junctions, crossing a wooded hill. To find the park, drive a mile north of Austin Junction toward Sumpter on Highway 7 and turn left on Upper Middle Fork Road half a mile.

Granite

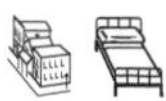

This 1862 gold boomtown shrank to a population of one in the 1960s, and although it has rebounded to 35, a smattering of weathered, abandoned buildings gives it a delightful ghost-town ambiance. Tasteful additions include a grocery/cafe/tavern with gas pumps and a modern log cabin-style lodge where a room with a light breakfast runs about $75 (541-755-5200).

Fremont Powerhouse

This historic stone building and a neighboring white frame Operators Cottage have been restored by volunteers to their original 1907 glory. To power the area's gold mines, engineers diverted water from Olive Lake (see Hike #35) through a 6-mile redwood pipeline and blasted it through turbines here. The plant generated electricity until 1967. From Granite, drive 5 miles west on Road 10.

Anthony Lake

In summer, this picturesque lake high in the Elkhorn Range is a popular spot to hike (see Hike #28), picnic, set up camp (37 sites with $8 fee), and paddle (no boat motors allowed). A **1930s guard station** by the lake is available for rental from May 5 through October ($80 per night; maximum 8 people). The historic log cabin has a kitchen, bathroom with shower, and three bedrooms. For reservations call 877-444-6777 or visit *www.recreation.gov.*

In winter, **Eastern Oregon's largest ski resort** opens beside Anthony Lake, with a triple chairlift (day pass: about $35), 13 kilometers of groomed Nordic trails, and equipment rentals, but no overnight lodging. At 7100 feet, the resort has the highest base elevation of all Northwest ski areas, and perhaps the best powder snow. For ski resort information, call (541) 856-3277 or check *www.anthonylakes.com.*

27 Crawfish Lake

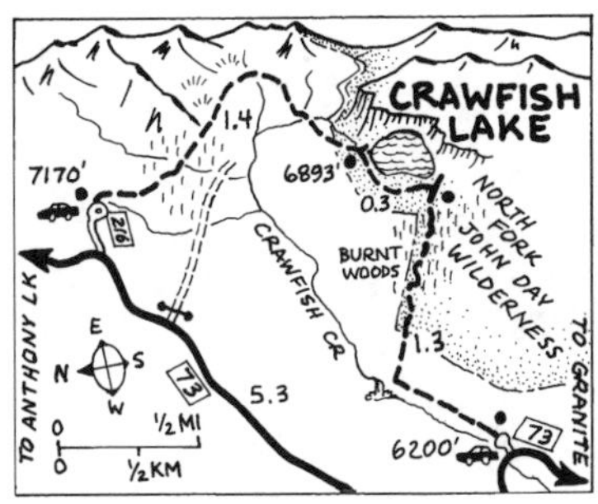

Easy
2.8 miles round trip
350 feet elevation gain
Open July through October
Use: hikers, horses

Easy enough for children, this hike traverses high alpine slopes of wildflowers and forest to a pretty mountain lake suitable for swimming.

From North Powder exit 285 of Interstate 84, follow "Anthony Lakes" signs 25 paved miles west on what becomes Road 73. Beyond the Anthony Lake Campground 4.8 miles (and 0.8 mile beyond a pass) turn left on Road 216 at a pointer for the Crawfish Lake Trail. Follow the gravel road a quarter mile to its end at a turnaround and parking area. Trailhead parking permits are required.

The trail sets off through sparse lodgepole pine woods, crossing several small creeks lined with pink monkeyflower. At times the trail traverses woods recovering from a 1989 fire, but elsewhere the route crosses unburnt forest or sagebrush meadows laced with mountain wildflowers. At the 0.9-mile mark you'll cross a narrow clearcut originally intended as a ski run for a never-completed expansion of the Anthony Lake ski resort.

After 1.4 miles the path climbs to Crawfish Lake. The deep water here invites swimming, while a 15-foot bedrock granite outcrop to the left seems designed for sunbathing. Fish jump and dragonflies zoom along the piney shore. If you like, continue on a trail to the right 0.3 mile to the lake's shallower end, where a grassy bank has a view of Lees Peak and The Lakes Lookout (Hike #146).

Other Options

If you can arrange a car shuttle, you don't have to hike back the way you came. At the far end of Crawfish Lake, keep right at a fork to find a continuation of the trail that dives steeply down through a burned forest 1.3 miles to a lower trailhead. To shuttle a car here from the upper trailhead, drive Road 73 downhill 5.3 miles to a switchback loop and a sign for the Crawfish Lake Trail.

The Lakes Lookout from Crawfish Lake.

28 Anthony Lake

Easy (to Hoffer Lakes)
2.9-mile loop
460 feet elevation gain
Open July through October
Use: hikers

Easy (to Black Lake)
2.4 miles round trip
200 feet elevation gain

Moderate (to Dutch Flat Saddle)
8.2-mile loop
1330 feet elevation gain

A glacier scoured out Anthony Lake's granite basin from the crest of the Elkhorn Range during the Ice Age. Today subalpine firs and wildflower meadows ring the lake, framing its reflection of craggy peaks. Several hikes explore the area from a picnic area beside the popular Anthony Lake Campground.

Drive Interstate 84 north of Baker City 19 miles (or south of La Grande 24 miles) to North Powder exit 285 and follow "Anthony Lakes" signs 21 paved miles west on what becomes Road 73. If you're hauling a horse trailer or backpacking equipment, plan to park in the well-marked Elkhorn Crest Trailhead lot on the left (see Hike #29).

If you're just out for a day hike, however, drive on past this trailhead 0.3 mile and turn left at a Anthony Lake Campground sign. After 100 yards fork to the right toward a picnic area, and in another 100 yards park on the left at a lakeshore picnic gazebo. The gazebo was built in the 1930s by the Civilian Conservation Corps, and so was the guard station across the street, a rentable log cabin (see page 80). A concessionaire charges a $4-per-car fee for day use here. Dogs must be on leash.

For all of the loop hikes, start by walking down past the gazebo and turning left along Anthony Lake's shoreline trail. Flowers here include blue gentians, purple

Gunsight Mountain from Anthony Lake. Above: The rentable guard station.

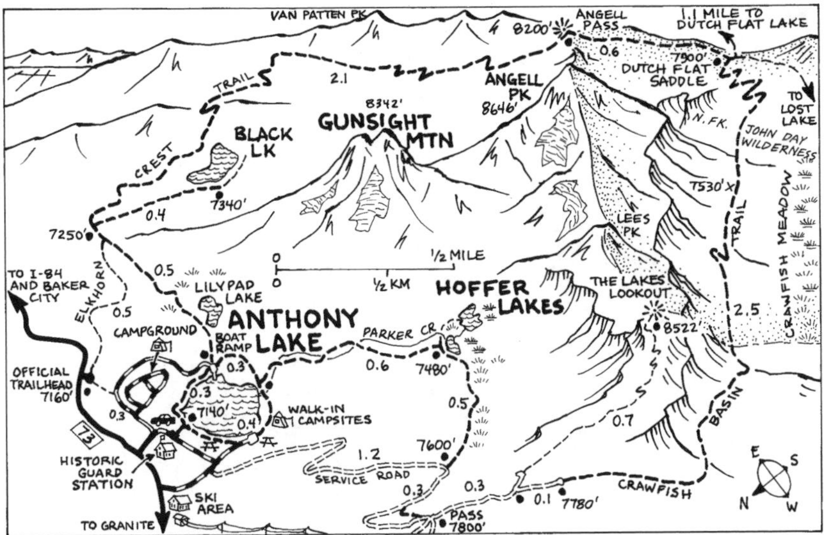

asters, and pink heather. After strolling 0.3 mile you'll reach a boat ramp and face a decision. Two trails set off from the far right-hand side of the boat ramp—the Black Lake Trail on the left and the Hoffer Lake Trail on the right.

For a very easy, 1-mile loop hike, take the right-hand trail and keep right around Anthony Lake to return to your car. On this route you'll pass walk-in campsites built by the Civilian Conservation Corps (CCC)in the 1930s. If you have time, detour up to the Hoffer Lakes. Just 0.3 mile beyond the boat ramp you'll see a message board on the left with a box of brochures. Turn left here on a nature trail that climbs 0.6 mile to the first Hoffer Lake, an alpine pool backed by the gigantic granite slab of Lees Peak. Most hikers turn back at the first Hoffer Lake, but the best scenery is actually to the right, on a 0.5-mile path through glorious alpine wildflower meadows. The path ends at a gravel service road. If you don't want to backtrack, simply turn right on the road for 1.2 miles to your car.

The hike to Black Lake is just as easy. From the Anthony Lake picnic gazebo, start by hiking 0.3 mile left around the lake to the boat ramp. Then take the Black Lake Trail (on the left) past Lilypad Lake and several lovely meadows. Keep right at junctions to climb 0.4 mile to Black Lake, a pool with a view of Van Patten Peak.

The most spectacular hike from Anthony Lake, however, loops 8.2 miles around a cluster of high Elkhorn peaks. After walking 0.3 mile to the boat ramp, veer left toward Black Lake for 0.5 mile, but then keep straight on the Elkhorn Crest Trail. This well-graded path climbs 950 feet in 2.1 miles to a breathtaking view at Angell Pass. Continue downhill 0.6 mile to a junction in Dutch Flat Saddle, a good lunch stop *(GPS location N44°55.793' W118°13.590')*. Detour 100 feet left for a view of Dutch Flat Lake, a mile below. Then return to the saddle and take the Crawfish Basin Trail downhill.

This path skirts high above Crawfish Meadow before ending at a dirt road. Go straight along this road 0.4 mile to a pass with a 4-way junction. Look to the right at this pass to find an unmarked trail angling downhill. Take this path to cut off the service road's first switchback. At the road's second switchback, turn right on the Hoffer Lakes Trail for the prettiest route back to your car.

29 Elkhorn Crest

Moderate (to Dutch Flat Lake)
8.6 miles round trip
1910 feet elevation gain
Open July through October
Use: hikers, horses

Difficult (to Lost Lake)
12.8 miles round trip
1860 feet elevation gain

Difficult (to Summit Lake)
20 miles round trip
2600 feet elevation gain

Difficult (to Marble Pass)
22.8 miles one-way
2820 feet elevation gain

One of Oregon's most beautiful backpacking routes, the 22.8-mile Elkhorn Crest Trail contours from pass to pass along the granite spine of the Elkhorn Range. Views from this timberline path stretch from the Wallowas to the John Day country. The trail itself passes almost no water sources or flat campsites, so plan to detour to Dutch Flat Lake, Lost Lake, Summit Lake, or Twin Lakes along the way.

Start by driving Interstate 84 north of Baker City 19 miles (or south of La Grande 24 miles) to North Powder exit 285. Then follow "Anthony Lakes" signs 21 paved miles west on what becomes Road 73. Just before the Anthony Lake Campground, turn left into the well-marked Elkhorn Crest Trailhead parking lot.

The trail begins beside a horse-loading ramp on the left side of the parking lot. After 0.5 mile, keep left at junctions with side trails to Anthony Lake and Black

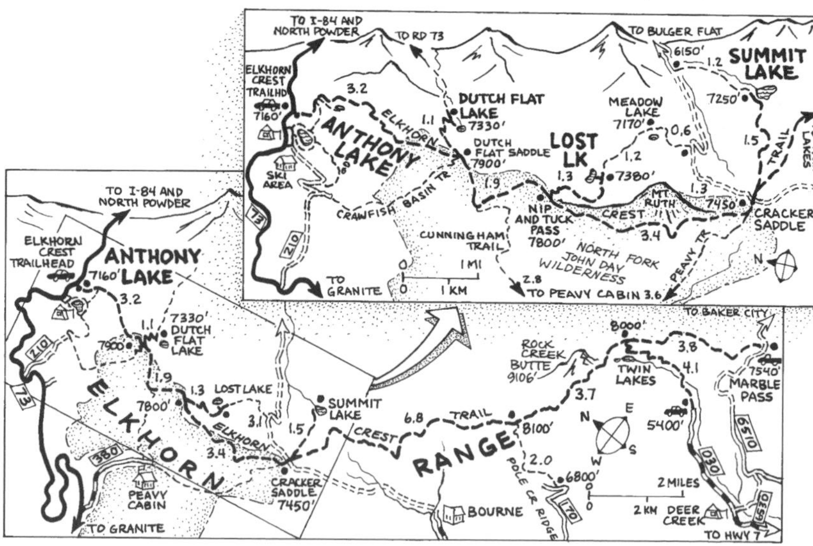

Summit Lake.   Opposite: Nip and Tuck Pass on the Elkhorn Crest Trail.

Lake (Hike #28). Beyond this the Elkhorn Crest climbs 1400 feet in 2.1 miles to scenic Angell Pass, and then descends 0.6 mile to a 4-way trail junction in Dutch Flat Saddle. If you detour 100 feet to the left, you'll get a birds-eye view of Dutch Flat Lake and its small island. Decide here whether you want to hike down another mile to the lake itself.

If you choose to continue on the Elkhorn Crest Trail you'll contour along an open slope 1.9 miles to Nip and Tuck Pass, where the trail slips through a crack in the granite ridgecrest. A few yards beyond the pass, a side path switchbacks down to the left toward Lost Lake (1.3 miles) and Meadow Lake (2.5 miles). Both are shallow and set among lodgepole pines, but Lost Lake is prettier, with a flowing inlet, while Meadow Lake is stagnant.

If you skip Lost Lake and instead continue on the Elkhorn Crest Trail beyond Nip and Tuck Pass, you'll contour 3.4 miles around Mt. Ruth to Cracker Saddle, where you leave the North Fork John Day Wilderness. Beyond this point motorcycles are permitted, but rare. In the saddle you'll cross a steep, rugged road from the ghost town of Bourne. In another 300 yards, a left-hand fork of the trail heads off 1.5 miles to Summit Lake. As large as Anthony Lake, but rarely visited, this beautiful pool borders a 1990s fire zone that left half the shore lined with white snags.

South of the Summit Lake turnoff, the Elkhorn Crest Trail traverses a slope with occasional old mining prospects. After 9.5 miles the route skirts 9106-foot Rock Creek Butte, the range's highest peak. Detour half a mile up to the summit, if you like, with a non-technical scramble.

Then hike onward a mile to a saddle junction, with Twin Lakes sparkling in the cliff-rimmed valley far below. To the right, the Twin Lakes Trail dives down a mile to the lakes and continues 3.1 miles to a trailhead on Road 030 that's accessible by passenger cars. If you go straight at the saddle junction, you'll follow the gentler Elkhorn Crest Trail 3.8 miles to its end at Marble Pass—a trailhead that can be reached only by rugged, high-clearance vehicles. To leave a shuttle car at one of these trailheads, drive to Baker City and follow the directions in Hike #30.

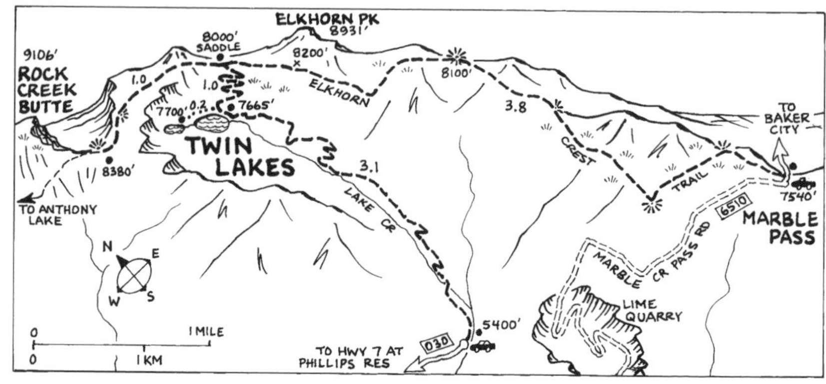

30 Twin Lakes

Difficult (from Marble Pass)
9.6 miles round trip
1200 feet elevation gain
Open mid-July through October
Use: hikers, horses, bicycles, motorcycles

Difficult (from Road 030)
6.2 miles round trip
2265 feet elevation gain

Expect mountain goats and wildflowers in the high meadows at Twin Lakes, in a cliff-rimmed cirque at the southern end of the Elkhorn Crest Trail. Take your choice of two trailheads. Start at Marble Pass if you prefer a gentler trail and don't mind a grueling drive. Start at Road 030 for an easier drive but a steeper hike.

Only high-clearance vehicles can negotiate the rugged road to the Marble Pass trailhead. From Interstate 84, take Baker City exit 304, drive west into town on Campbell Street for a mile to a traffic light at Main Street, continue straight another 0.5 mile to another light, and turn right on 10th Street for 1.1 mile to a flashing yellow light. Following a pointer for the Marble Creek Picnic Area, turn left on paved Pocahontas Road and follow this road through several zigzags 7.6 miles. Where Pocahontas Road turns right for the third time, go straight on gravel Marble Creek Road. In another 0.3 mile, turn left to keep on Marble Creek Road, and then follow it 7.8 miles to the trailhead in a high pass *(GPS location N44°46.407' W118°02.606')*.

The last 4 miles of the road to Marble Pass are agonizingly slow, with rocks and frequent drainage ditches. Ordinary passenger cars may not survive the trip intact. If your vehicle can handle this, park at the road's summit. The well-graded Elkhorn Crest Trail sets off across an alpine grassland of sagebrush, blue lupine, white yarrow, and a few whitebark pines. Every mile or so the path visits passes on the range's crest. Each pass has better views—east across the patchwork of ranches surrounding Baker City to the Wallowas, and west across Sumpter's valley to distant Strawberry Mountain. After 3.8 miles you'll reach a saddle with a junction. Turn left to switchback down a rocky wildflower slope a mile to Lower Twin Lake. The trail misses this lake by a hundred yards, and there's no sign, but it's easy to bushwhack over to the shore *(GPS location N44°48.525' W118°05.144')*. The deep blue pool has a backdrop of huge red cliffs, snowfields, and rockslides. Delightful denizens of those rocky slopes are pikas, the little round-eared "rock rabbits" who cheep to each other like a chorus of lost smoke alarms with rundown batteries.

From the lower lake, stroll 0.2 mile to the right to find the upper lake, whose meadowed shore hosts purple wild onions, blue gentians, and probably a mountain goat or two. The goats have become so fond of salt that they sometimes nibble on backpackers' tents. Wildlife specialists have taken the matter in hand by putting out salt blocks.

If you don't want to risk your car on the road to Marble Pass, drive east from downtown Baker City on Main Street (which becomes Highway 7 toward Sumpter) for a total of 23.3 miles. A mile beyond the end of Phillips Lake, between mileposts 29 and 28, turn right on gravel Deer Creek Road. After 4.2 miles, ignore a turnoff for the Deer Creek Campground to the right, and continue straight on Road 030 for 3.8 miles to its end. The final 0.4 mile is a bit rough, but passable for passenger cars and horse trailers. From this trailhead, a broad trail along a tumbling creek climbs through the woods. Blue huckleberries ripen along the path in late summer. After 3.1 steepish miles, look for Lower Twin Lake on the left.

Other Options

Whichever way you hike to Twin Lakes, consider adding an extra mile along the Elkhorn Crest Trail to the shoulder of Rock Creek Butte, the highest peak in the Blue Mountains. This part of the path has been blasted out of the cliffs so the trail can duck between two spectacular high passes. Backpackers can continue on the Elkhorn Crest Trail 18 miles to Anthony Lake (see Hike #28).

Twin Lakes and Rock Creek Butte. Opposite: Mountain goat.

31 Baldy Lake

Easy (from Road 7345)
2.4 miles round trip
400 feet elevation gain
Open July through October
Use: hikers, horses

Difficult (from Road 73)
12.6 miles round trip
1600 feet elevation gain

In an amphitheater of granite cliffs below Mount Ireland, blue-green Baldy Lake is deep enough both for swimmers and for large brook trout. Spire-topped firs circle the lake, while the shore itself sports a grassy fringe of wildflowers. Campsites abound at this scenic wilderness lake, but they're rarely full, and here's why: To reach the lake you have to choose between a short trail with very poor road access, or a very long trail with good road access.

For the easy drive but the longer hike, start by driving Interstate 84 north of Baker City 19 miles (or south of La Grande 24 miles) to North Powder exit 285. Follow "Anthony Lakes" signs 21 paved miles west to the Anthony Lake area, continue straight on Road 73 another 12.4 paved miles to a large sign for the Baldy Creek Trail, and turn left on gravel Road 380 for 200 yards to its end at a parking turnaround. Parking permits are required only at this lower trailhead.

The trail starts by crossing the swift, 20-foot-wide North Fork John Day River on a log footbridge. The forest here is a shady mix of lodgepole pine, grand fir, Engelmann spruce, and subalpine fir. After another 1.1 mile the path crosses Baldy Creek on a log—a possible turnaround point, if you're not really aiming for Baldy Lake.

Next the trail crosses Bull Creek and briefly traverses a fire zone where the lodgepole pines went up flames, but larch trees survived. Beyond this, the next viewpoint is at the 5-mile mark where the path switchbacks up through a grassy swath cleared for an ancient powerline. Built in the early 1900s, the line brought

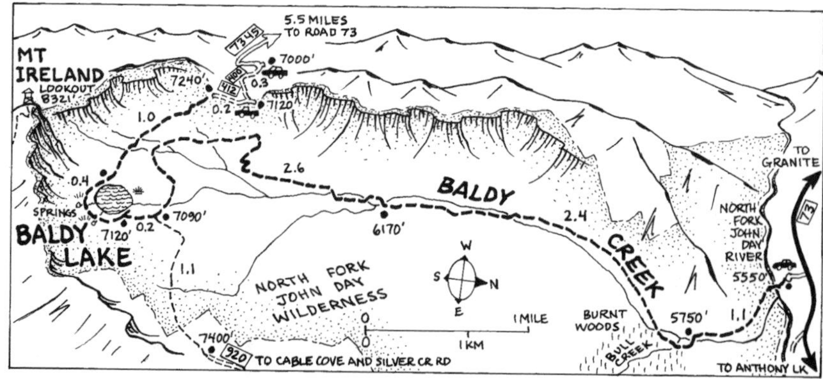

Mt. Ireland from Baldy Lake. Opposite: Baldy Lake from Mt. Ireland.

electricity from the Fremont Powerhouse (see page 80) to the gold mines of Cable Cove. Giant rock cairns along the route once held power poles.

After 6.1 miles, keep right at a junction for 0.2 mile to Baldy Lake *(GPS location N44°50.783′ W118°18.792′)*. Notice the Mt. Ireland lookout building (Hike #32) atop the cliffs across the lake. A shoreline trail continues left 0.4 mile, passing several springs that spill into the lake through small meadows. Look here for pink heather, purple aster, red paintbrush, and blue gentians.

A much shorter trail to Baldy Lake begins on a rough dirt road. Only high-clearance vehicles can reach this upper trailhead, but passenger cars can park half a mile away if they're driven slowly and carefully. To drive there from the lower trailhead, go back to paved Road 73, continue west on it 4.5 miles to a 4-way junction, turn left to keep on Road 73 for another 4.9 miles toward Granite, and turn left onto Road 7345 at a large sign for the Baldy Lake Trail. (If you're coming from Granite, take paved Road 73 north 4.2 miles to this turnoff.)

Road 7345 is strewn with such large gravel that it has to be driven very slowly and carefully. After 2.3 miles, fork left to keep on Road 7345. Passenger cars should park at the 5.5-mile mark, where the road switchbacks steeply up to the right and becomes Road 400. This steep dirt track has large rocks and ruts. In another 0.3 mile you'll reach a fork in a pass, where even high-clearance vehicles should park. Walk up the right-hand fork (Road 412) for 0.2 mile to its end at the Baldy Lake Trailhead *(GPS location N44°51.199′ W118°19.752′)*.

Although the upper trail to Baldy Lake is only a mile long it is poorly designed, diving down and scrambling up slopes for no apparent reason. When you reach the lake follow the shoreline trail to the right for the best views and campsites.

32 Mount Ireland

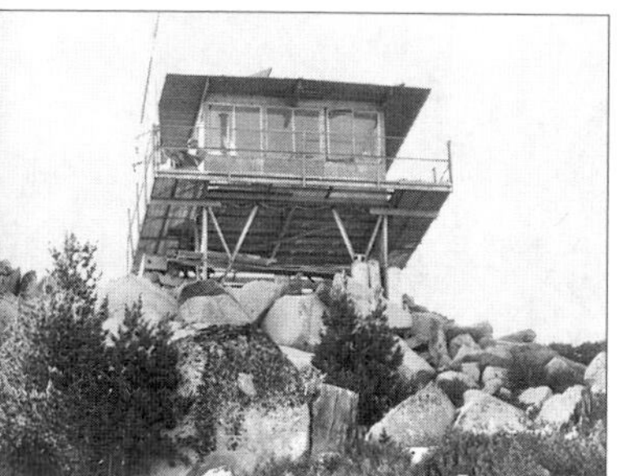

Difficult (to Mt. Ireland)
6.6 miles round trip
2320 feet elevation gain
Open July through October
Use: hikers, horses, bicycles

Difficult (to Downie Lake)
7 miles round trip
2350 feet elevation gain

The lookout tower atop 8321-foot Mt. Ireland not only has a terrific view of Baldy Lake and the Blue Mountains, but the tower is actually staffed each summer. A spur of the Mt. Ireland trail descends through the forest to silent Downie Lake. These are beautiful destinations, and just remote enough that the only person you're likely to meet is the lonely lookout staffer.

From downtown Baker City, drive south on Main Street (which becomes Highway 7) for 25 miles, turn right at a sign for Sumpter, drive 3 miles to this rustic gold rush boomtown, and continue toward Granite on the main paved road for 12.2 miles. Five miles beyond a sign marking the Grant County line, look carefully down one-lane gravel Road 7370 on the right to spot the sign, "Mt. Ireland L.O." Slowly follow this bumpy, rough road for 0.6 mile, fork left to keep on Road 7370 for another slow 1.8 miles to an unmarked fork, and veer steeply up to the left to stick to Road 7370. In another 0.6 mile, fork to the right on gravel Road 100. After 0.3 mile, park at a large "Mt. Ireland LO Trail" sign on the left *(GPS location N44°48.758′ W118°19.715′).*

From the trailhead sign walk up spur Road 130 (closed to cars by a large dirt berm). After climbing steeply 240 yards you'll reach a confusing road junction at the edge of a clearcut. Walk 30 feet left on Road 132 to find an old sign for the Mt. Ireland Trail. Following this sign, take an old road that climbs up the ridgecrest woods to the right. This ugly track steepens for 0.3 mile, but then suddenly becomes a lovely footpath traversing left into a shady, uncut forest of 3-foot-thick grand firs.

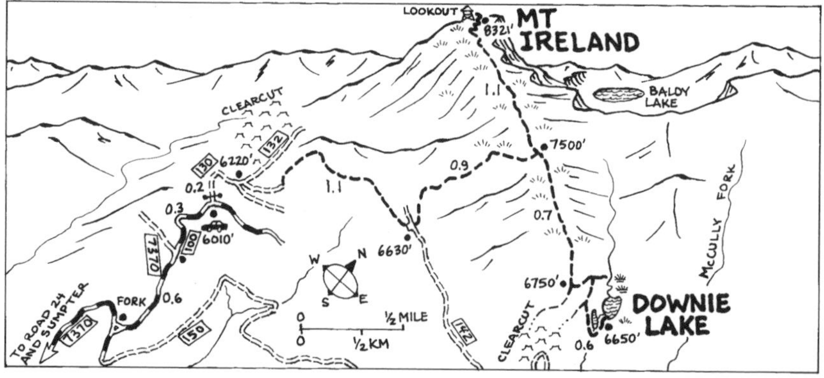

The trail crests a plateau with a lodgepole pine forest, crosses a small dirt road, and climbs 0.9 mile to a signpost marking a trail junction in a ridgecrest meadow *(GPS location N44°49.767′ W118°18.377′).*

At this signpost you'll have to decide whether you want to visit Mt. Ireland's lookout (up to the left), or Downie Lake (down to the right), or both. If you choose the lookout you'll climb up through meadows on a rocky, gullied path that's confused in places by all-terrain vehicle tracks. Look for cushions of white phlox, yellow sulfur flower, and purple penstemon among the white granite boulders. At the summit *(GPS location N44°50.216′ W118°19.235′)* you'll find a 13-foot-square metal lookout building, brought here by helicopter in 1957 to replace an earlier wooden structure. The staffers who live here from late June until late September report that only about 50 visitors make the climb each year. Almost directly below, Baldy Lake (Hike #31) looks like a giant sapphire at the head of a vanished glacier's long U-shaped valley. To the east, the distant, snowy Wallowas peer through a notch in the jagged Elkhorn Range.

To visit Downie Lake, return to the signpost marking the trail junction. To find the correct path down this ridgecrest meadow, face downhill from the signpost and then walk to your left, perfectly level, for 100 feet to a gap in the trees, where the tread becomes clear. After the trail enters the forest at the 0.7-mile mark and becomes an old road, turn downhill to the left at a "Downie Lake" pointer on a wide trail for 200 yards, and then turn right at another sign on a pleasant foot-path for 0.6 mile. After passing two large ponds the trail ends at broad, shallow Downie Lake. Frogs leap from boulders along the shore. Mt. Ireland resembles a slouching giant, asleep on the horizon. The lakeside forest of lodgepole pines and pointy subalpine fires is too thick for a campsite, but if you bushwhack to the right along the shore 200 yards and head uphill, you'll find a campable grassy knoll with mariposa lilies and views.

Mt. Ireland from Downie Lake. *Opposite: Mt. Ireland's lookout.*

33 North Fork John Day River

Easy (to Bigfoot Hilton)
5.2 miles round trip
350 feet elevation gain
Open May through November
Use: hikers, horses

Difficult (to Crane Creek)
13.5-mile loop
1280 feet elevation gain

Deep in the Blue Mountain's gold rush country, the 24.6-mile North Fork John Day River Trail traces a wilderness river through a rimrock canyon dotted with the decaying log cabins of ancient prospects. To sample the scenery, hike 2.6 miles downriver from the North Fork John Day Campground to the "Bigfoot Hilton," a cabin featured in William L. Sullivan's adventure narrative, *Listening for Coyote.* If you're on horseback, or if you don't mind wading across the chilly river, continue on a 13.5-mile loop that follows a side canyon back to your starting point.

To drive here from Interstate 84, take North Powder exit 285 (north of Baker City 19 miles or south of La Grande 24 miles), follow "Anthony Lakes" signs 21 paved miles west to the Anthony Lake area, and continue straight on Road 73 another 17 paved miles to a stop sign at a 4-way junction. Go straight into the entrance of the North Fork John Day Campground and drive to the far end (beyond an equestrian camping area) to the trailhead parking lot on the left. Parking permits are required.

If you'd rather drive here from Granite, take paved Road 73 north 9 miles to the stop sign and turn left into the campground. Campers should note that the

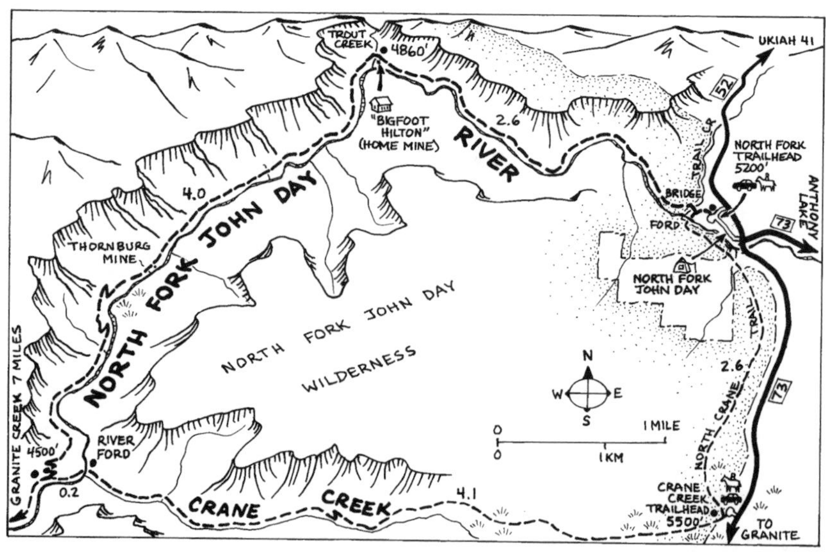

The North Fork John Day River. *Opposite: The Bigfoot Hilton.*

campground lacks drinking water and garbage service, and charges $8 per site.

The trail sets off through a rocky meadow regrowing with lodgepole pines. The area looks as though it has been damaged by floods, and that's almost true. Years ago, the high-pressure water hoses of a hydraulic mining operation washed the riverbank gravels through sluices to separate out gold, and the wounds are still raw. After 200 yards, turn right to cross Trail Creek on a footbridge. Then the trail follows the North Fork John Day River into the Wilderness, where the scenery hasn't changed much since the 1860s gold rush. The forest of Douglas fir and larch is open enough for sunny wildflowers, including purple aster, red fireweed, goldenrod, and blue gentians. Watch for tobacco tins or baby food jars nailed to tree trunks along the way. These have been left by prospectors to hold claim registration papers. No new claims have been permitted since the area was designated Wilderness in 1984.

The North Fork John Day Wilderness shelters the largest share of the Blue Mountains' 52,000 elk and 150,000 mule deer. Each fall, 800-pound elk bulls with 5-foot-wide antlers bugle challenges to rival males. Twice as large as mule deer, elk bulls assemble harems of as many as 60 female elk during the August-to-October mating season. In those months, listen at dawn and dusk for the bull's bugle, a weirdly musical snort that rises to a clarinet-like whistle and ends with several low grunts.

After 2.6 miles, just before a footbridge over Trout Creek, look for a log cabin to the left, known as the "Bigfoot Hilton" because it is often open as an emergency shelter. This small, publicly owned cabin makes a good turnaround point for a day hike.

Backpackers or equestrians interested in a loop trip can continue downstream another 4 miles to the Crane Creek Trail junction. Turn left 0.2 mile to a 30-foot-wide, knee-deep river ford, and hike up Crane Creek 4.1 miles to a parking area on Road 73. If you haven't left a shuttle car here, turn left on the North Crane Trail for 2.6 miles to the North Fork John Day River, where you'll have to cross a 20-foot-wide ford to return to your car.

Other Options

For a longer trip, continue down the North Fork John Day River Trail 3.4 miles to a river ford and another 3.6 miles to the bridge at Granite Creek (see Hike #34). Part of the route follows a historic mining water flume that has been converted to a perfectly level trail.

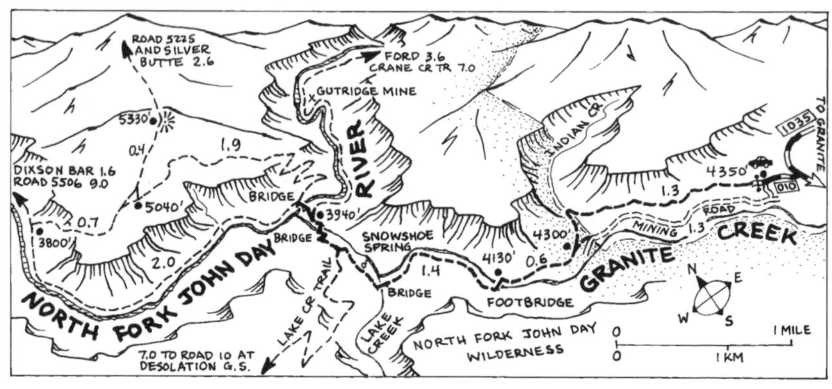

34 Granite Creek

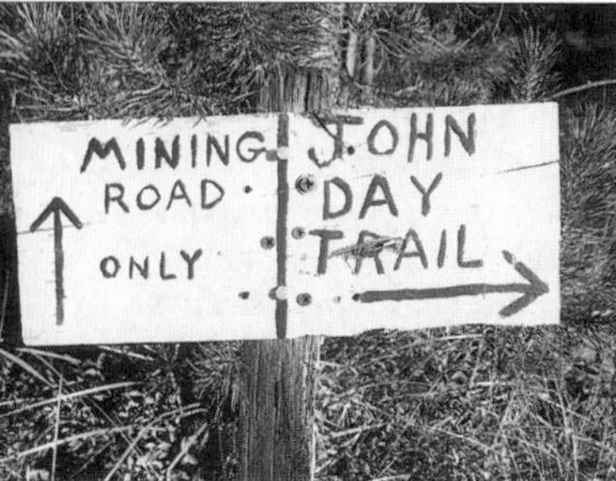

Easy
6.6-mile loop
500 feet elevation gain
Open April to December
Use: hikers, horses

The Blue Mountains' 1860s gold rush ended long ago, but a few miners still work their claims in the spectacular canyonlands where Granite Creek and the North Fork John Day River collide. Footbridges allow the trail to cross from one side to another of the cliff-edged canyon, passing huckleberry patches and old-growth ponderosa pines. To tour the area on a easy loop, hike an upper trail into the heart of the North Fork John Day Wilderness and return on an old mining road past the miners' rustic cabins. Angling is banned in Granite Creek.

To drive here from downtown Baker City, head south on Main Street (which becomes Highway 7) toward John Day a total of 25 miles, turn right at a sign for Sumpter, drive 3 miles to this rustic gold rush boomtown, continue on the main paved road 17 miles to a stop sign at Granite, turn left on paved Road 10 toward Olive Lake for 1.5 miles, turn right on gravel Road 1035 for 4.6 miles, and fork left on Road 010 for 0.2 mile to a trailhead parking area, where parking permits are required. Don't try to drive down the rough dirt mining road to the left (the return route for the loop hike). Instead start hiking on the trail straight ahead, by a message board at a pole fence gateway *(GPS location N44°50.776' W118°31.089').*

The Granite Creek Trail contours 300 feet above the creek, traversing a grassy slope with big, orange-trunked ponderosa pines. After 1.3 miles an unmarked trail joins from the left. On your way back this will be the path to take for the mining

The North Fork John Day River at Granite Creek. Opposite: Trailhead sign.

road loop. For now, continue straight 0.6 mile and cross 15-foot-wide Granite Creek on a large footbridge. The bridge is planked with redwood staves salvaged from the historic pipeline that once brought Olive Lake's water to the Fremont Powerhouse (see page 80). Beyond this bridge the trail follows the shore of Granite Creek through a Douglas fir forest where blue huckleberries hang heavy on trailside bushes from late July to mid-August. The narrow canyon twists between cliffs of contorted dark rock.

At the 2.7-mile mark, 200 yards beyond the Lake Creek footbridge, note Snowshoe Spring's box to the right, where a pipe delivers cold clear water. In another 0.6 mile the trail bridges Granite Creek again and enters a meadow alongside the North Fork John Day River. Go straight across the meadow to find a metal bridge spanning the 60-foot-wide river. Greenish boulders break the stream into whitewater. Flakes of mica shimmer like gold dust in the sandy riverbank. Explore the far right-hand end of the meadow to find a collapsed log cabin and campsites.

When you're ready to return, hike back 2 miles, take the trail's right-hand fork, and follow the old mining road 1.3 miles to your car. On this route you'll pass cobble wastelands where a gold mining dredge once churned up the creek. Pits in the hillside were washed out by high-powered hydraulic hoses to find more gold. Little treasure remains for the modern miners whose shacks you'll see. Stay on the road, because trespassing and unauthorized gold panning are not allowed on these private claims.

Other Options

For a longer trip, continue on one of three trails from the riverside meadow. At the start of the meadow, an uphill path to the right follows the river 3.6 miles to a bridgeless crossing and another 10 miles to the North Fork John Day Campground (Hike #33). A second option is to cross the river bridge at the meadow and turn left on the downstream portion of the North Fork John Day River Trail, which continues 11 miles to rough dirt Road 5506. A third choice is to cross the river bridge and turn right. On this route you can make a loop by switchbacking up past canyon viewpoints on the Silver Butte Trail for 1.9 miles, keeping left on a very steep 0.7-mile trail down to the river, and turning left on the North Fork John Day River Trail 2 miles back to the bridge.

35 Olive Lake

Easy (around Olive Lake)
2.7-mile loop
50 feet elevation gain
Open June through November
Use: hikers, horses, bicycles

Difficult (to Lost Creek)
11.9-mile loop
1860 feet elevation gain
Open July through October
Use: hikers, horses

Campers at this popular lake in the Greenhorn Mountains often hike around the shoreline trail, but relatively few have discovered the longer, more difficult loop to the alpine viewpoints on Saddle Ridge and the meadows of Lost Creek.

From downtown Baker City, drive south on Main Street (which becomes Highway 7) for 25 miles, turn right for 3 miles to Sumpter, continue on the paved road 17 miles to a stop sign at Granite, turn left on paved Road 10 for 3.6 miles, and fork to the right to keep on Road 10, which now becomes gravel. After another 1.4 miles, stop to visit the historic Fremont Powerhouse (see page 80), which operated 1907-1967. Later, on your hike, you'll see the 6-mile redwood pipeline that brought water here from Olive Lake and Lost Creek.

After inspecting the Fremont Powerhouse, drive another 6.7 gravel miles on Road 10 to a pullout on the right for the Lost Creek Trail *(GPS location N44°47.338' W118°34.749')*. Parking permits are required. If you've brought horses or backpacking gear, this is the place to start your trip. Cross the road to a message board, go 0.2 mile to a junction by the old pipeline, and turn right on the Saddle Camp Trail for 1.5 miles to join the path from Olive Lake.

If you're just out for a day hike, however, it's more fun to start at Olive Lake instead. Drive 0.8 mile past the Lost Creek Trailhead to a sign for Olive Lake, turn left on Road 480 for 0.4 mile, and then fork to the right at a "Boat Ramp" pointer for 0.2 mile through the campground to a lakeshore parking lot, picnic area, and dock. Campsites are $12, but day use parking is free.

Start at the far left end of the boat ramp parking area and walk left around the lake through lodgepole pine woods. Ignore numerous left-hand trails that lead up to campsites—until you've hiked 0.5 mile and the trail climbs away from the shore 50 feet to an old log walkway across a boggy spring.

Here you'll face a choice. For the easy loop, simply continue around the lake 1.8 mile, cross the 50-foot-tall earthen dam that created the lake, and keep right on a campground road 0.4 mile back to your car. For the much longer loop to Saddle Ridge and Lost Creek, however, turn sharply left on an upper trail that skirts campsite #27 to the campground road turnaround *(GPS location N44°46.770' W118°35.971')*. As soon as you reach this road, turn uphill to the right past a tree with a sign marking the boundary of the Indian Rock - Vinegar Hill Scenic Area. This path climbs for most of a mile to a small pond at the outlet of the Upper Reservoir. Early 20th-century engineers built a dam here to add water to their powerhouse pipeline, but the pool has almost entirely filled in to become a vast

Upper Reservoir marsh. *Opposite: Redwood pipeline at Lost Creek.*

marshy meadow. Mosquitoes are a problem in July.

Beyond the Upper Reservoir's marsh, the path climbs 1.9 miles to Saddle Camp, a dry ridgetop meadow *(GPS location N44°45.403′ W118°37.569′)*. The tread peters out in the grass, but angle left past a cut log to find a clear ridgecrest trail. Follow this path left 2 miles along the picturesque spine of Saddle Ridge.

Finally the ridgecrest trail descends through lodgepole pine woods to a faint junction at broad, grassy Dupratt Spring Pass *(GPS location N44°44.165′ W118°36.340′)*. Ahead is a dirt mining road, but don't take it. Look for a rock cairn on the left by a tree with a "Lost Cr. Trail" sign. No trail is visible here, but turn left and walk straight past this tree 50 feet to the cryptic sign, "3002". Now look left to see a tree blaze and an old roadbed. Follow this track.

After 2.3 miles, when the road/trail reaches a T-shaped junction in a forested pass, turn left on the Lost Creek Trail. In the next 2.7 miles this path crosses five meadows where the tread vanishes. At the first grassy swale, look for a tree blaze on the far lower end of the meadow, on the opposite side. At the second meadow, hop across Lost Creek and follow cairns. When the trail grows faint in the next three grassy openings, simply keep to the meadows' left-hand edge. Finally the path follows the old wooden pipeline down to a junction. Two routes return to Olive Lake from this point. Either turn left on a trail that climbs over a wooded hill, or simply go straight to Road 10 and save 0.6 mile by following the gravel road back to the lake.

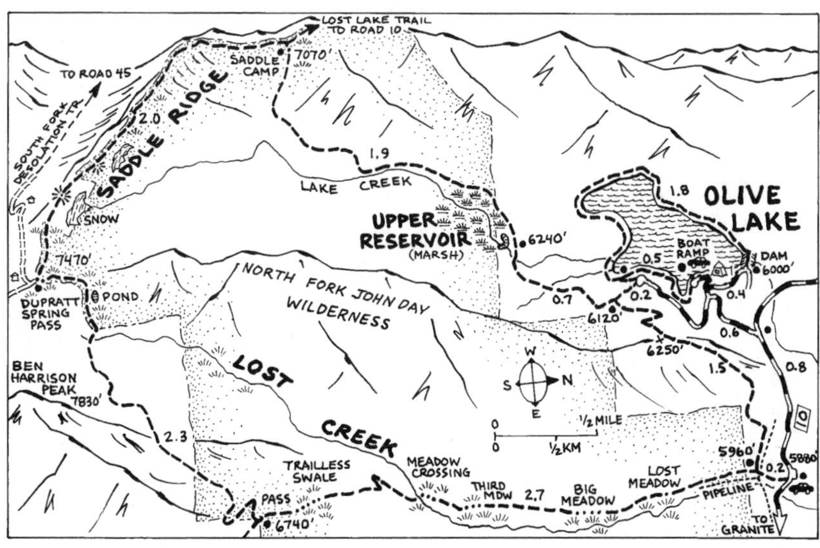

BLUE MOUNTAINS -- NORTH
PENDLETON
EXIT 207
37
WOOLEN MILL
11
AVE
UMATILLA RIVER
COURT
ROUND-UP GROUNDS
MAIN
EMIGRANT
209
MISSION RD
N
0 1 MI
0 1 KM
395
EXIT 210
84
30
EXIT 213
WALLA WALLA
12
WHITMAN MISSION
WASHINGTON
OREGON
TO LEWISTON
WENAHA-TUCANNON WILDERNESS
RD 65
ROAD 64
WENAHA R
MILTON-FREEWATER
11
MOUNTAINS
TROY
GRANDE RONDE R
FLORA
6413
62
RD
TOLLGATE
64
PENDLETON
204
WESTON
11
SPOUT SPRINGS SKI AREA
JUBILEE LAKE
3
163
TO THE DALLES
WILDHORSE CASINO
NORTH FORK UMATILLA WILDERNESS
WALLOWA
204
WALLOWA
RIVER
EXIT 216
84
MEACHAM
ELGIN
RD 62
395
0 10 MILES
0 10 KM
82
TO UKIAH
OREGON TRAIL INTERPRETIVE PARK
BLUE
N
W
E
S
LA GRANDE
ENTERPRISE
EXIT 248
HILGARD JUNCTION
WALLOWA MTNS
COVE
232
EXIT 261
HOT LAKE SPR
MOSS SPRINGS
244
RED BRIDGE
LEHMAN HOT SPRING
203
UNION
EAGLE CAP WILDERNESS
TO UKIAH
CATHERINE CREEK
LA GRANDE
EXIT 259
30
"Y" AVE
PIONEER PARK
82
EXIT 261
AVE
ISLAND
ADAMS
WALNUT ST
COVE AVE
84
HISTORIC HOMES WALKING TOUR
AVE
"N" AVE
N
2ND ST
4TH ST
SUNSET DR
EASTERN OREGON UNIV
0 1/2 MI
0 1/2 KM
12TH ST
30
"C" AVE
BIRNIE PARK
GEKELER LN
232
RD 77
NORTH POWDER
ROAD 67
MEDICAL SPRING
203
84
RD 70
EXIT 298
OREGON TRAIL INTERP CTR
86
BAKER CITY
TO ONTARIO

Store window display in Pendleton.

PENDLETON

Oregon Trail pioneers once dreaded the northern Blue Mountains' forested canyons, surprise snowstorms, and unpredictable Indian tribes. Although Interstate 84 now spans the range from Pendleton to La Grande, there's still plenty of adventure and wild beauty along the mountains' rarely visited back trails.

Downtown Pendleton

Get your bearings in this well-preserved downtown at the **railroad station** at the end of Main Street. Next door is the **Heritage Station Museum** (108 SW Frazier) with exhibits on the Oregon Trail and local history. Hours are 10-4 Tue-Sat and admission runs $2-$5. Just down the street, don't miss the **Pendleton Underground Tours,** where you can explore tunnels and opium dens built by Chinese railroad laborers beneath Pendleton's old town in the 1880s. The 90-minute tours cost $15 (no children under 6) and begin at 31 SW Emigrant Street (reservations 541-276-0730). Then walk Main Street four blocks north to **Hamley's Steakhouse**, a posh Wild West eatery that opened in 2007. Next door is the original Hamley business, a fascinating **leather goods store** that's occupied the same building since 1904.

The **Pendleton Woolen Mills** factory, founded 1909, still weaves Indian-inspired robes and shawls. At 1307 SE Court Place, the factory offers free tours Mon-Fri year-round; call 541-276-6911 for an appointment.

Pendleton Bed & Breakfast Inns

For a cozy overnight stay in town, try the **Pendleton House** (311 N Main Street, $100-135), a 1917 Italian Renaissance inn with original Chinese wallpaper. For reservations call 541-276-8581 or visit *www.pendletonhousebnb.com.* If you have a horse, head for **NEIGH-bors Horse Motel and Bed & Breakfast**, 543 NW 21st Street (541-276-6737, *www.neigh-bors.com*), within riding distance of the round-up, with a modern apartment in a barn loft for $85.

Pendleton Round-Up

Pendleton puts on its spurs each year for the **Pendleton Round-Up,** during the second full week of September, when contestants gather from across North America for a professional rodeo competition (tickets $15-25 at 800-457-6336 or *www.pendletonroundup.com/tickets*). The pageantry includes a parade, dance contests, and a Native American beauty contest. If you miss it, check out the **Round-Up Hall of Fame**, a museum of historic photographs, saddles, beadwork, and memorabilia under the rodeo arena's south grandstand at 1114 SW Court Avenue, Mon-Sat 10-4 in summer. Adults are $5, kids $2.

La Grande

The Old Oregon Trail runs through the south edge of La Grande (on B Street), but this city isn't stuck in the past. Catch a play at the McKenzie Theatre on the campus of **Eastern Oregon University** or drop by the **Farmers' Market** for local arts and crafts, open 9am-noon on Saturdays and Tuesdays 4-6pm from the end of May to the third week of October at 4th and Adams. At the **visitor center** (4th and Adams) you can pick up a brochure of a 2-mile walking tour of 33 historic homes. For dinner, try **Foley Station** (at 1114 Adams) or **Ten Depot Street,** a restaurant at 10 Depot Street, of course.

Wildhorse Casino and Tamastslikt Museum

The Cayuse, Umatilla, and Walla Walla tribes built this elaborate casino (hotel, RV park, golf course, restaurant, slots, gaming tables) and the neighboring Tamastslikt Cultural Institute, a museum with walk-through exhibits describing the tribes' past and present. The museum is open 9-6 daily from April through September, and 9-5 except Sundays October through March. Adults are $8. seniors $6, and kids $6.Drive Interstate 84 east of Pendleton 4 miles to exit 216.

Emigrant Springs State Heritage Area

See Oregon Trail wagon ruts and excellent outdoor interpretive displays on a paved 0.5-mile loop in the Blue Mountain forest. Between La Grande and Pendleton, take I-84 exit 248, follow signs 3.3 miles. Open April to October, with a $5 parking fee.

Hot Lake Springs

This sprawling 1908 sanitorium resort beside a hot spring-fed lake is being restored by renowned Western sculptor David Manuel. The artist's impressive bronze foundry moved here from Joseph in 2007. One-hour foundry tours start at 10am and 2pm Monday through Saturday, and cost about $10 (541-963-4685, *hotlakesprings.com)*. A trip to the spa's hot mineral pools costs about $25 an hour. Bed-and-breakfast rooms in the restored hotel building run $145-395, but include a spa visit, breakfast, and a $10 dinner credit. The complex also includes a history center, artists' marketplace, chapel, and gardens. It's located just east of La Grande. Take Interstate 5 exit 265 and drive east 6 miles toward Union.

Hat Rock State Park

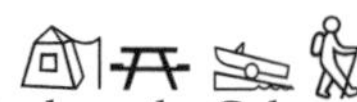

Lewis and Clark described the hat-shaped monolith in this park along the Columbia River. Today visitors flock here to cool off on hot summer days by picnicking on the shady lawns or launching boats onto the river. A hiker/biker path from the boat ramp follows an abandoned railroad grade along the river 4.8 miles to McNary Beach Park. From Interstate 82 in Umatilla, take Hwy 730 east 9 miles.

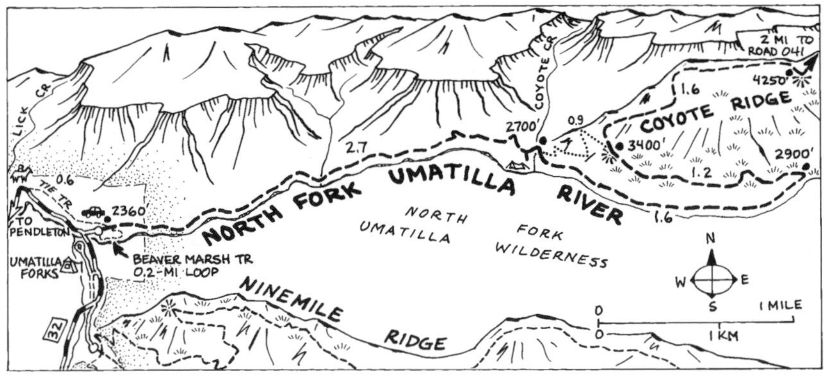

36 North Fork Umatilla River

Easy (to Coyote Creek)
5.4 miles round trip
350 feet elevation gain
Open except in winter storms
Use: hikers, horses

Moderate (to Coyote Ridge)
11 miles round trip
1050 feet elevation gain
Open April through November

Right: View from Coyote Ridge.

In Pendleton's backyard, the North Fork Umatilla Wilderness resembles a one-third-scale version of Hells Canyon, with jagged canyons carved into tablelands of Columbia River basalt lava. The smaller scale of this canyon makes it better suited for day trips. Even hikers with children can handle the 2.7-mile walk to Coyote Creek. And by adding a 2.8-mile climb you gain a viewpoint.

Start by driving Interstate 84 east of Pendleton 7 miles to the Wildhorse casino at exit 216. Head north toward Walla Walla for 2.1 miles to a flashing red light, turn right on Mission Road for 1.7 miles, and turn left on paved, two-lane Cayuse Road for 11.2 miles. Between mileposts 15 and 16, turn right across railroad tracks onto Bingham Road. Follow this road for 12.4 paved miles and an additional 3.3 miles on good gravel. Half a mile after entering the national forest (where the road changes names to Road 32), fork left to a parking turnaround.

Put on your boots, because the trail has a few small boggy spots. Then set off straight ahead on the main path, ignoring two spurs. The first of these side paths, the Tie Trail, heads left for 0.6-mile to a horse-loading area. The second side path, the Beaver Marsh Trail on the right, loops back 0.2 mile along the river.

The main trail follows the 30-foot-wide North Fork Umatilla River up through a forested canyon. Amid the riverside cottonwoods and red alders you'll find six-foot-tall cow parsnip plants, the 12-inch leaves of waterleaf, the orange clustered tubes of honeysuckle, and the red/yellow glow of columbine flowers. Elsewhere, beneath Douglas fir and grand fir, look for purple Oregon grape, white snowberry, and wild strawberry.

After 2.7 miles a large side trail to the right leads 200 yards to several big campsites by the river. The main trail curves left to the bank of 15-foot-wide Coyote Creek. This makes a good turnaround point for an easy hike.

If you're continuing onward, cross Coyote Creek on a log. The trail follows the river another 1.6 miles and makes a switchback at a small meadow with several nice campsites. Then the trail climbs up Coyote Ridge, traversing a grassy slope of sparse ponderosa pine, yellow lupine, pink clarkia, red paintbrush, and increasingly spectacular canyon views.

After a mile of climbing across these meadows, the trail forks near the tip of Coyote Ridge. This makes a good turnaround point. The official trail continues up to the right 3.6 miles to a gravel logging road atop the tablelands. The fainter trail fork that heads downhill to the left is a rough, steep, unofficial shortcut back to Coyote Creek. Because this old 0.9-mile trail is no longer maintained, it's sufficiently overgrown that it's easier to hike back to your car the way you came.

37 Ninemile Ridge

Difficult (to summit cairn)
7.2 miles round trip
2150 feet elevation gain
Open May to late November
Use: hikers, horses

One of the nicest hikes near Pendleton climbs up, up, and up grassy Ninemile Ridge to increasingly beautiful wildflower fields and viewpoints in the heart of the North Fork Umatilla Wilderness.

Start by driving Interstate 84 east of Pendleton 7 miles to the Wildhorse casino at exit 216. Then turn north toward Walla Walla for 2.1 miles to a flashing red light, turn right on Mission Road for 1.7 miles, and turn left on paved, two-lane Cayuse Road for 11.2 miles. Between mileposts 15 and 16, turn right across a set of railroad tracks onto paved Bingham Road. Follow this road (which becomes Forest Road 32) for a total of 16.1 miles. The final 3.7 miles are on good gravel. A quarter mile past the Umatilla Forks Campground, turn left at a sign for "Buck Creek Trail No. 3075" and follow a rocky side road 0.2 mile to a parking area at road's end.

Walk past several boulders on a broad path for 200 feet to a 4-way trail junction. The sign may be missing, but for the route up Ninemile Ridge you need to *turn left* here. This path heads uphill through a Douglas fir forest with a surprising diversity of woodland flowers: wild rose, strawberry, white fairy bells, purple larkspur, orange honeysuckle, and yellow Oregon grape.

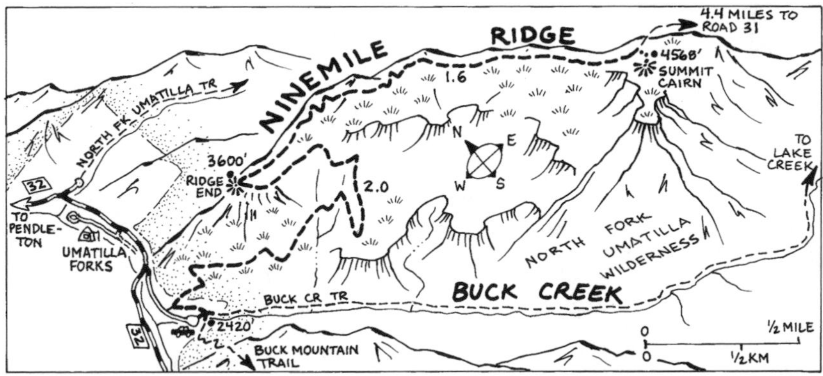

After just 0.1 mile you'll reach a T-shaped trail junction. Turn right past a Wilderness boundary sign on a steeper path that starts climbing up Ninemile Ridge in earnest. Almost immediately you leave the lush fir forest behind and climb through a drier band of big ponderosa pines. Then the trees give out altogether and you enter a steep grassland brightened with early summer wildflowers. Views across the canyonlands improve with every step.

At the 2-mile mark the trail reaches a crest and turns east, marching up the back of Ninemile Ridge's spine. At times the path levels out across saddles with sagebrush and elk sign. At other times the trail switchbacks up past rock outcrops.

When the trail finally crosses the broad, grassy summit of Ninemile Ridge at the 3.6-mile mark, leave the path and walk 100 yards across a field to a 4-foot-tall rockpile, the summit cairn. From here the panorama encompasses the entire North Fork Umatilla Wilderness. Far down the river canyon, the distant plains of the Umatilla Indian Reservation spread into the haze toward Pendleton.

Turn back here. Although the trail continues along Ninemile Ridge 3.6 miles, the tread becomes faint and the ridgecrest rollercoasters down and up. The final 0.7 mile traces an abandoned road (the Umatilla Rim Trail) to the Ninemile Ridge Trailhead on paved Road 31.

Ninemile Ridge. *Opposite: Clarkia.*

38 Jubilee Lake

Jubilee Lake.

Easy (around lake)
2.6-mile loop
No elevation gain
Open early June to late November
Use: hikers

Moderate (to South Fork Walla Walla River)
6.6 miles round trip
1880 feet elevation **loss**
Open mid-June to early November
Use: hikers, horses, bicycles, motorcycles

A dam created Jubilee Lake in 1968 to provide a recreation goal in the high, rolling forests of the Blue Mountain crest. For an easy walk, stroll around the lakeshore loop. For a tougher trail, hike to the South Fork Walla Walla River nearby.

From Interstate 84 in Pendleton, take exit 210 and follow "Milton-Freewater" signs through town and onto Highway 11 for 20.5 miles. Between mileposts 20 and 21, turn right at a sign for Elgin, and in another 0.8 mile fork left to keep heading toward Elgin on Tollgate Road (Highway 204). After 19.9 miles (beyond the Tollgate Store 1.2 miles) turn left onto Road 64 at a sign for Jubilee Lake. Then follow wide, graveled Road 64 north for 11.5 miles, turn right on the paved Jubilee Lake Campground entrance road for 0.6 mile to a fee booth (campsites $17, day use $3), and continue 0.2 mile to the boat ramp parking lot on the left.

Start your hike at the far left end of the parking lot, take a paved path through a picnic area to the shore, and head counter-clockwise around the lake. The high-elevation forest includes lodgepole pine, subalpine fir, and Engelmann spruce. After 0.5 mile you'll cross the lake's earth dam and trade pavement for a dirt path.

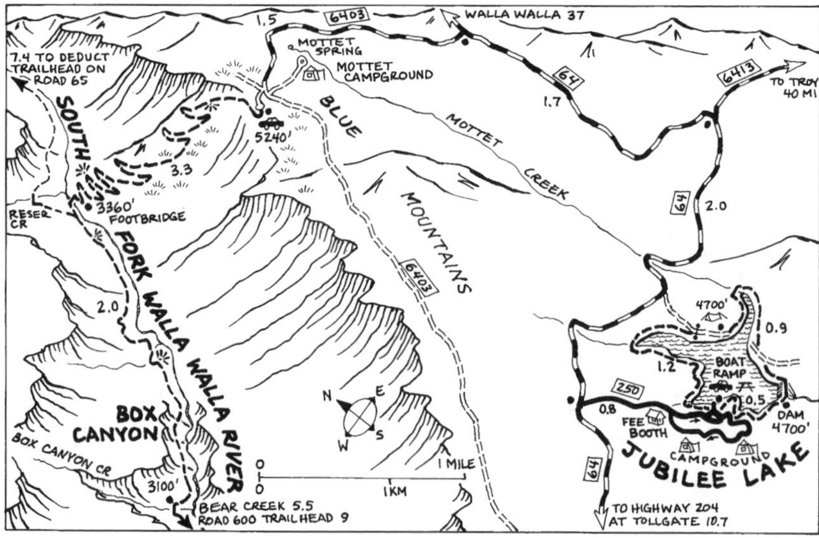

In another 0.9 mile the path briefly joins a closed road at a free campsite. Continue around the lakeshore 1.2 miles to return to your car.

For the tougher hike to the South Fork Walla Walla River, drive out of the campground, turn north on gravel Road 64 for 2 miles to a fork, veer left toward "Walla Walla" to keep on Road 64 for another 1.7 miles, and turn left on dirt Road 6403 for 1.5 miles to a meadow with a junction. Don't go straight ahead into Mottet Campground, but rather fork slightly to the right on an unmarked road 200 yards to a large gravel parking lot *(GPS location N45°52.138′ W117°58.041′).*

Set off down "Rough Fork Trail No. 3227," a well-graded path that ducks into a grand fir forest. Before long you'll descend across meadow openings with sagebrush, purple larkspur, blue lupine, and scarlet gilia. Views extend across the sharply crenelated South Fork Walla Walla canyon. After 3.3 miles the trail enters a lush, low-elevation forest, passes a campsite, and crosses the river on a bridge.

39 Upper Wenaha River

Moderate (to river ford)
4.6 miles round trip
850 feet elevation **loss**
Open mid-June to early November
Use: hikers, horses

Difficult (to Milk Creek ford)
9 miles round trip
1300 feet elevation **loss**

Right: Timothy Springs Guard Station.

The 31.4-mile Wenaha River Trail traces a gigantic canyon through the Wenaha-Tucannon Wilderness along the Oregon-Washington border. Here at the trail's upper end you can see the river begin at a high mountain spring in an old-growth larch forest. After just 2.3 miles the river has grown so large that hikers can't cross it with dry feet. If you don't mind fording you can continue 2.2 miles into an open rimrock canyon typical of the lower valley beyond.

To drive here from Interstate 84 in Pendleton, take exit 210 and follow "Milton-Freewater" signs through Pendleton and onto Highway 11 for 20.5 miles. Between mileposts 20 and 21, turn right at a sign for Elgin, and in another 0.8 mile fork left to keep heading toward Elgin on Tollgate Road (Highway 204). After 19.9 miles (beyond the Tollgate Store 1.2 miles), turn left at a sign for Jubilee Lake onto Road 64. (If you're coming from La Grande, take Highway 82 north 20 miles to Elgin and turn left on Highway 204 for 22 miles to this junction.)

Follow gravel Road 64 north of Highway 204 for 13.5 miles. At a fork 2 miles past Jubilee Lake, veer right onto Road 6413, following a sign for Troy. Continue 11.8 miles to a T-shaped junction, turn left to keep on Road 6413 another 1.8 miles, and then turn left onto Road 6415. The sign here may be missing, but follow Road 6415 for 2.2 miles of good gravel and another 4.7 miles of roughish dirt road to a sign for the Timothy Springs Campground on the right. Take the middle road through a meadow, ignoring spurs to a historic guard station on the left and to the primitive campground's three picnic tables on the right. After 0.2 mile, park by

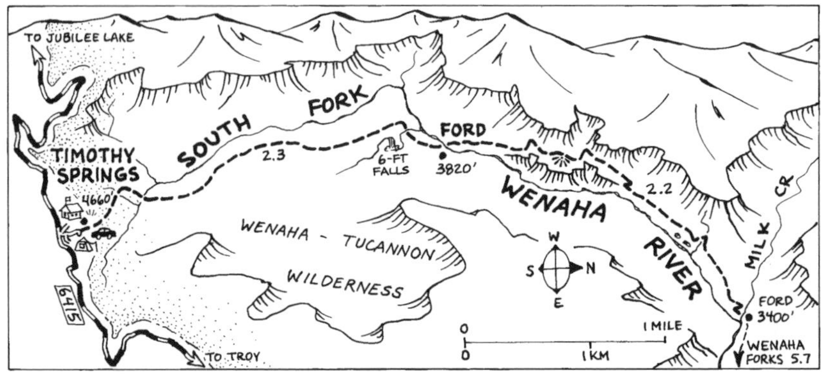

posts marking the Wilderness boundary *(GPS location N45°51.960' W117°53.535').*

Start at a message board and follow the trail past a "Wenaha-Tucannon Wilderness" sign into an open larch forest carpeted with yellow buttercups and yellow violets. Look here for morels, a strange mushroom resembling a pointy brown brain on a squat white stalk. The trail crosses two creeks, descends 2 miles through the woods, and then hops on rocks across a 7-foot-wide creek. Look upstream 50 feet to find a little waterfall in a fern grotto. Then continue down the trail 0.3 mile to the South Fork Wenaha River. Equestrians can simply splash across this 20-foot-wide, foot-deep ford. Hikers who want to continue, however, will have to wade.

On the far side of the river, the trail traverses to a viewpoint on a cliff overlooking the river canyon. Then the path descends to a small bouldery gravel bar at the confluence of Milk Creek and the South Fork Wenaha River. Save some time to laze on the rocks here, watching the rivers collide. Giant cottonwood trees tower above the canyon bottom's thimbleberry thickets. Because there is no bridge across Milk Creek, day-hikers generally declare victory here and turn around for the climb back to their cars. Backpackers and equestrians, on the other hand, can continue down the Wenaha River Trail for two or three days to Troy (Hike #40).

40 Lower Wenaha River

Easy (to National Forest)
4.6 miles round trip
350 feet elevation gain
Open all year
Use: hikers, horses

Difficult (to Crooked Creek)
12.8 miles round trip
580 feet elevation gain

Left: Wenaha River.

Like a jagged crack in the planet's crust, the Wenaha River canyon zigzags from the remote village of Troy into the Wenaha-Tucannon Wilderness. A 31.4-mile trail follows the river from the start of its desert canyon to its source high in the

Blue Mountains. For an easy day trip, explore the first few miles of the path. For a longer trip, continue to a campsite near the Crooked Creek footbridge.

From Interstate 84 in La Grande, take exit 261 and follow signs for Wallowa Lake 65 miles to Enterprise. At a pointer for Lewiston in the middle of Enterprise, turn left on First Street (alias Highway 3) for 35 miles to a sign for Flora. Turn left 3 miles to this interesting ghost town, which peaked as a wheat farming center in the 1910s. The town's schoolhouse has been restored as a cultural center.

Next drive on past Flora for 4.1 paved miles and an additional 7.2 miles of steep, winding, 1-lane gravel road down to a bridge across the Grande Ronde River. On the far side of the bridge, turn left on a paved road for 2 miles to the edge of Troy. A block before "downtown," (a cafe, store, laundry, gas station, and inn), turn right toward Pomeroy on Bartlett Road. Up this road 0.4 mile, where the road switchbacks to the right, park at a pullout straight ahead beside a trailhead message board *(GPS location N45°56.846′ W117°27.263).*

The Wenaha River Trail sets out through sparse ponderosa pine woods with teasels, elderberries, and salsify. In spring look for the sunflower-like blooms of balsamroot. After 0.7 mile you'll reach the first access to the river itself, a 60-foot current of boulder-strewn whitewater. After this the trail climbs past the first of several patches of poison oak. Beware these triple-leafletted shrubs!

After 1.8 miles you'll climb to a viewpoint above a riverbend pool where you can watch giant fish idling far below. Then the trail crosses a crude, private roadbed and climbs around a scenic cliff between layers of rimrock. White mariposa lilies dot the slope, along with Oregon sunshine and wild clematis.

In another 0.4 mile you'll pass a sign marking the National Forest boundary—a turnaround point for casual hikers. Beyond this, the trail continues upriver 4.1 miles, occasionally ducking under cliffs, to a rock cairn at a possibly unmarked junction. Ahead the trail passes a meadow with campsites along Crooked Creek. To the left, the Wenaha River Trail dips to a 100-foot bridge spanning Crooked Creek, another good turnaround goal *(GPS location 45°58.648′ W117°33.316′).*

Other Options

Backpackers and equestrians can continue upriver two or three days to trail's end at Timothy Spring (Hike #39). To drive a shuttle car there from Troy, go south through downtown past the cafe, go straight toward "Long Meadows Ranger Station" for 0.3 mile, fork right toward Elgin on what becomes Road 62 for 27 miles, and turn right on Road 6415 for 6.9 miles.

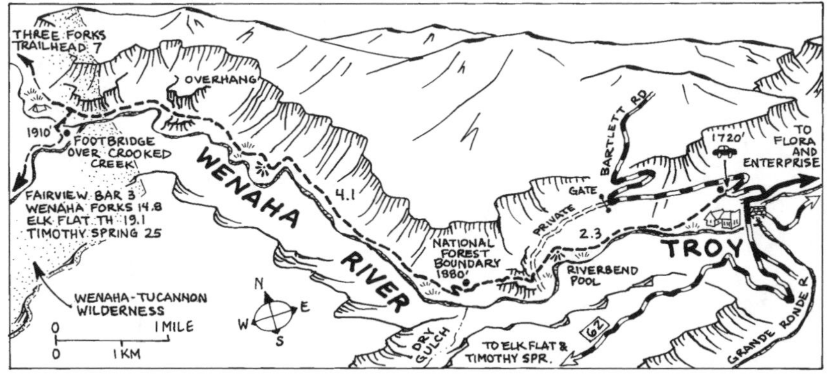

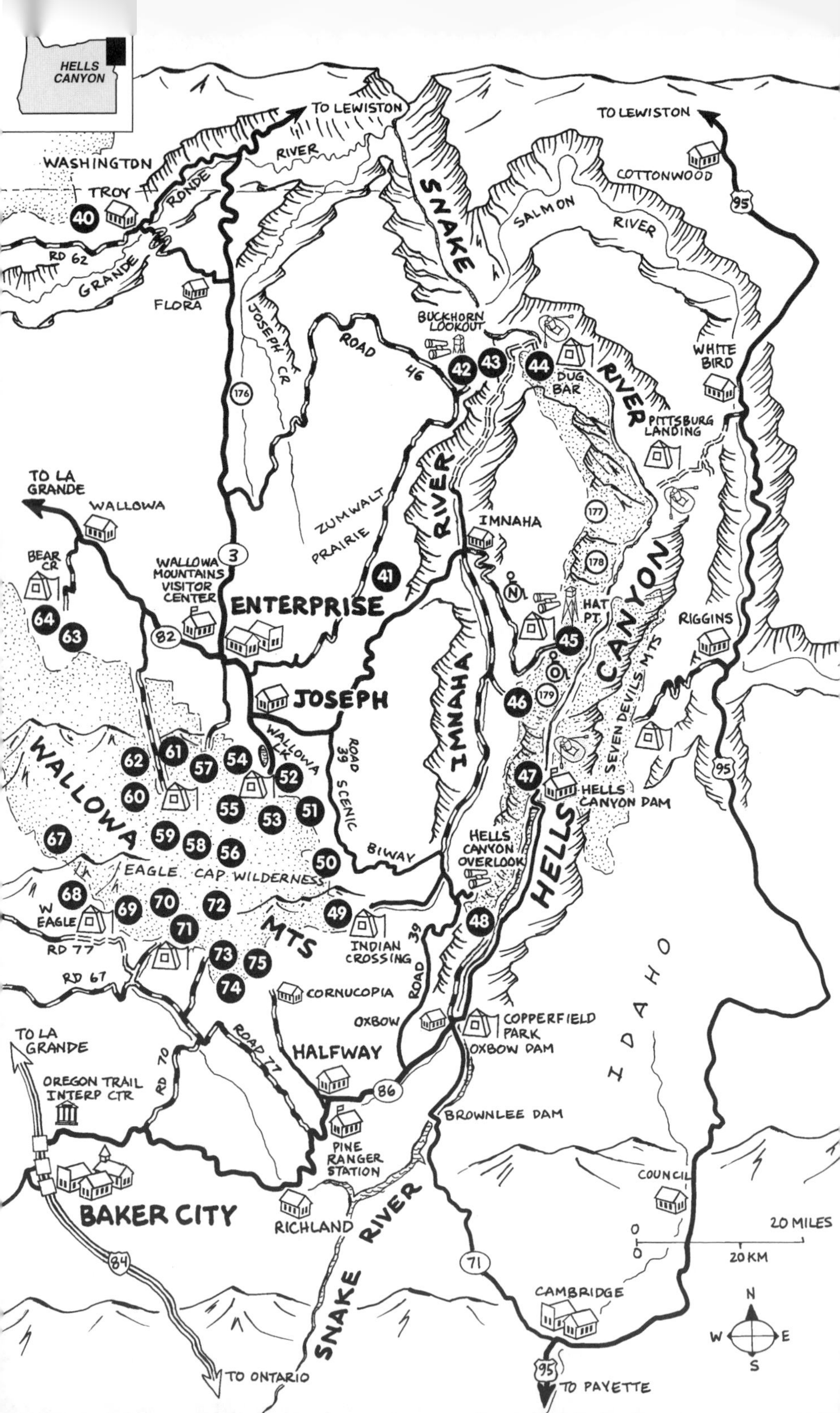
HELLS CANYON
TO LEWISTON
TO LEWISTON
WASHINGTON
TROY
RONDE
RIVER
SNAKE
SALMON
RIVER
COTTONWOOD
95
RD 62
GRANDE
FLORA
JOSEPH CR
BUCKHORN LOOKOUT
ROAD 46
DUG BAR
RIVER
WHITE BIRD
PITTSBURG LANDING
176
TO LA GRANDE
WALLOWA
ZUMWALT PRAIRIE
RIVER
IMNAHA
177
178
BEAR CR
3
WALLOWA MOUNTAINS VISITOR CENTER
ENTERPRISE
HAT PT
CANYON
RIGGINS
82
JOSEPH
179
SEVEN DEVILS MTS
IMNAHA
WALLOWA
WALLOWA LK
ROAD 39 SCENIC BIWAY
HELLS CANYON DAM
95
HELLS CANYON OVERLOOK
HELLS
EAGLE CAP WILDERNESS
W EAGLE
RD 77
MTS
INDIAN CROSSING
ROAD 39
RD 67
CORNUCOPIA
IDAHO
OXBOW
COPPERFIELD PARK
OXBOW DAM
TO LA GRANDE
ROAD 77
RD 70
HALFWAY
OREGON TRAIL INTERP CTR
86
BROWNLEE DAM
PINE RANGER STATION
COUNCIL
BAKER CITY
RICHLAND
RIVER
0
20 MILES
0
20 KM
84
71
SNAKE
CAMBRIDGE
N
W
E
S
TO ONTARIO
95
TO PAYETTE
40
41
42
43
44
45
46
47
48
49
50
51
52
53
54
55
56
57
58
59
60
61
62
63
64
67
68
69
70
71
72
73
74
75

HELLS CANYON

Deeper than the Grand Canyon, this colossal river gorge looks like the ragged edge of a broken planet, with rimrock tiers stacked to the sky. The canyon is so deep that it has two completely different climate zones. Snow drapes the subalpine forested rim from November to June, but shimmering summer heat bakes the desert landscape of the Snake River's rocky banks 6000 feet below.

Hells Canyon Viewpoints

For such a monumental canyon, Hells Canyon has remarkably few convenient viewpoints. At only four places can passenger cars drive to canyon vistas on the Oregon side. At the south end of the gorge, drive a paved road along the Hells Canyon Reservoir and across the **Hells Canyon Dam** to a riverside visitor center, described in Hike #47. For a paved route to the rim's crest, take the Hells Canyon Scenic Byway route north from Halfway toward Joseph and follow signs to the **Hells Canyon Overlook**. For a better view, take a long, steep gravel road up from the town of Imnaha to the **Hat Point lookout tower** (see Hike #45), where observation decks, trails, and a picnic area add to the attraction. Some claim the most attractive panorama of all is at **Buckhorn Lookout** (see Hike #42), a quieter pullout beside an old lookout building north of Joseph.

Snake River whitewater trips

Drifting the Snake River through Hells Canyon is a 2- to 8-day voyage through some of the biggest scenery on earth. From the Hells Canyon Dam launch site it's 32 miles downriver to the boat ramp at Pittsburg Landing, 51 miles to Dug Bar, 79 miles to the mouth of the Grande Ronde River, and 104 miles to Lewiston, Idaho. Be forewarned, however, that the most dangerous rapids are packed into the first 17 miles of the trip. For this thrilling stretch, ranger-issued permits are required from the Friday before Memorial Day through September 10. For reservations call 509-758-1957. Also check with rangers for advice on suitable floatcraft, river levels, weather, and the canyon's strict campfire restrictions. If you need help shuttling a vehicle between your launch and take-out sites, check with Hells Canyon Shuttle in Halfway (800-785-3358 or *www.hellscanyonshuttle.com*).

Guided jet boat tours are a simpler but noisier alternative. Tours leave from the dock at the visitor center just below Hells Canyon Dam. Expect to pay about $60 for a 2-hour tour (leaves at 10am and 2pm Pacific Time), $80 for a tour to Granite Creek (leaves 10am and 2pm), and $172 for a 6-hour, 65-mile tour with lunch (leaves at 10am). Longer trips in rubber rafts are also available. For details and reservations, call 800-422-3568 or check *www.hellscanyonadventures.com.* Several other tour companies offer jet boat trips from Lewiston upriver into Hells Canyon.

Imnaha

Where pavement ends on the road to Hat Point's viewpoint, stop in the village of Imnaha to visit its rustic **tavern/general store.** The establishment features cigar-store Indian statues and an eclectic sampling of wares, but doesn't have gasoline. For a bed & breakfast, drive 5 miles north along the Lower Imnaha Road to the **Imnaha River Inn's** huge log lodge ($130 rooms; 866-601-9214 or *www.imnahariverinn.com*).

41 Zumwalt Prairie

Easy (Wild Rye Trail)
2.4 miles round trip
40 feet elevation gain
Open all year

Moderate (Harsin Butte scramble)
1.6 miles round trip
690 feet elevation gain

Raptors soar above this rolling grassland, between the snowy Wallowa Mountains and the ragged cliffs of Hells Canyon. Zumwalt Prairie has one of the highest concentrations of breeding hawks and eagles in the world—largely because the native bunchgrass prairie here teems with their favorite prey, ground squirrels.

Oregon State University researcher Marcy Houle celebrated the area's rich ecosystem in her 1995 book, *The Prairie Keepers*, and marveled that a century of careful cattle grazing may actually have improved raptor habitat. This intrigued The Nature Conservancy, a nonprofit group that bought 51 square miles here, making this the state's largest private nature preserve.

Most of the preserve is off limits, but you're allowed to stroll to a pond on the Wildrye Trail or scramble up Harsin Butte for a look around. For the best wildflowers, visit between late April and June. Avoid the freezing winds of winter and the heat of August. Pets, horses, fires, vehicles, and camping are banned.

Start by driving Highway 82 east of Enterprise 3.2 miles (or north of Joseph 3 miles). At a pointer for Buckhorn Spring between mileposts 68 and 69, turn north onto paved Crow Creek Road for 1.1 mile to a fork. Veer right to stay on Crow Creek Road for another 3.9 miles to another fork. This time veer right onto Zumwalt Road, which is paved for the first 2.4 miles. Continue on a good gravel road an additional 11.2 miles, turn right on one-lane gravel Duckett Road for half a mile, and park where the road turns right *(GPS location N45°33.563' W116°59.052')*.

Walk straight ahead through a brown metal gate with a small orange Zumwalt

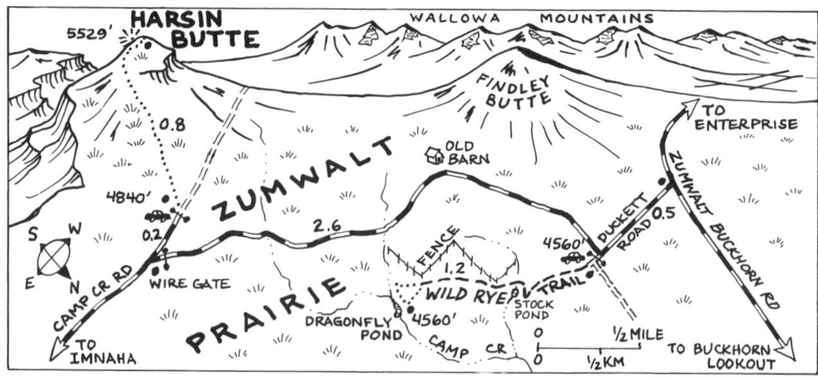

Harsin Butte. Opposite: The Wallowas from Zumwalt Prairie.

Prairie Preserve sign. Then continue straight between two rock cairns, following the Wildrye Trail, a very faint old road that strikes off across the prairie.

The big horizon is empty, save for the humps of Harsin and Findley Buttes. The real view is at your feet, where you'll see six kinds of native grasses, including 5-foot clumps of basin wildrye. Look for the blooms of yellow bells in April, pink Nootka roses and yellow lupine in May, and pink Clarkia and white mariposa lilies in June. The Nature Conservancy burns this area periodically to boost native plants, including the threatened Spaldings catchfly, an inobtrusive white-petaled flower that can catch flies with its sticky leaves.

The road/trail switchbacks down past a 30-foot stock pond at the half-mile mark and continues 200 yards to the cornerpost of a fenceline. Here the path becomes very faint. Continue straight (due southeast) 0.4 mile to another fence cornerpost. The path may be lost amid the grass, but continue 200 yards to the (possibly dry) swale of Camp Creek, which you can follow left to a teardrop-shaped pond with dragonflies, cattails, and wild mint *(GPS location N45°33.105' W116°57.968')*.

Return to your car as you came. For the second hike, drive Duckett Road south and east another 2.6 miles, open a wire gate (and then close it behind you), and then turn right on gravel Camp Creek Road for 0.2 mile to a cattle guard *(GPS location N45°32.149' W116°57.383')*.

Park beside the road, walk across the cattle guard, and veer left off the road toward Harsin Butte. Although there is no trail up this rounded knoll, it's the only high ground for miles, so there's not much chance of confusion.

The route steepens as it passes a ponderosa pine grove where elk like to bed. The wildflowers bloom later on this butte than on the prairie below, with blue gentians and other alpine favorites. When you puff to the summit you'll find a solar-powered antenna and a 360-degree view. Zumwalt Prairie stretches to the north, a many-fingered mesa bordered by the rimrock-striped canyonlands of the Imnaha River.

Scramble back down to your car. If you have plenty of gas, you might drive back by way of Imnaha, touring a rough but very wild and beautiful canyon. Drive gravel Camp Creek Road east 11 miles to paved Highway 350. Imnaha's quaint store is a mile to your left, and Joseph is 28 miles to your right.

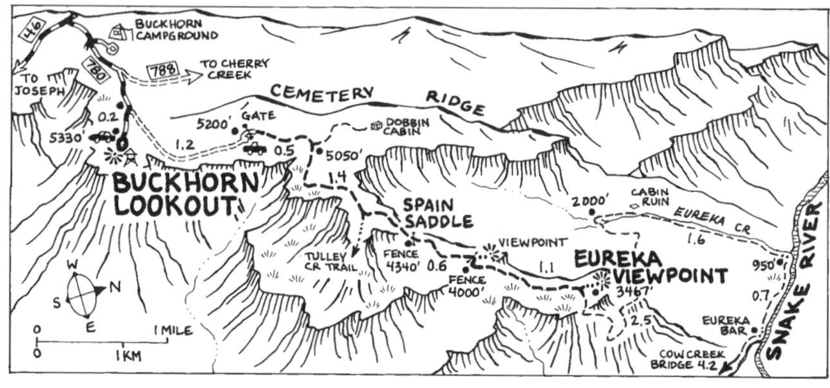

42 Buckhorn Lookout

Moderate (to Eureka Viewpoint)
7.2 miles round trip
1780 feet elevation **loss**
Open June to mid-November
Use: hikers, horses, bicycles

Very Difficult (to Eureka Bar)
15.4 miles round trip
4150 feet elevation **loss**

The panorama is breathtaking from the historic Buckhorn fire lookout, perched on the lip of Hells Canyon's colossal chasm. But the view actually improves the farther you hike from the lookout, following a well-graded trail down across slopes of wildflowers. The danger here is that you'll be tempted to romp too far down this trail into Hells Canyon. Remember that you will have to regain every step of lost elevation (perhaps thousands of feet!) later in the hot afternoon sun.

Start by driving Highway 82 east of Enterprise 3.2 miles (or north of Joseph 3 miles). At a pointer for Buckhorn Spring between mileposts 68 and 69, turn north onto paved Crow Creek Road for 1.1 mile to a fork. Veer right to stay on Crow Creek Road for another 3.9 miles to another fork. This time veer right onto Zumwalt Road, which is paved for the first 2.4 miles. Continue on a good gravel road an additional 30 miles across high, scenic Zumwalt Prairie (see Hike #41). Weathered barns remain from the homesteaders who tried to settle this arid upland—including Henry and Josie Zumwalt, who opened a post office here in 1903.

At a sign for Buckhorn Overlook (9 miles after Zumwalt Road becomes Forest Road 46), turn right on Road 780. After 0.3 mile ignore a rough spur road that descends to the left to the primitive, free, 5-site Buckhorn Campground. Go straight at this junction and then keep right at the next two forks to reach the Buckhorn Lookout parking turnaround *(GPS location N45°45.232′ W116°49.401′).*

The view from Buckhorn Lookout. *Opposite: Buckhorn Lookout.*

The vast canyons of the Imnaha River and its tributaries steal the show at Buckhorn Lookout because the Snake River itself is hidden. Look for Idaho's snow-capped Seven Devils above Hat Point's plateau, and the long white horizon of the Wallowa Mountains above Zumwalt Prairie. With a view like this, the 14-foot-square lookout building never needed a tower, so it sits on the ground. Built in the 1930s, the building is no longer staffed.

The actual trailhead is 1.4 miles from the lookout turnaround, but if you're driving a passenger car, it's probably best to park here. Walk back from the turnaround 0.2 mile to a fork and turn right on a rutted, rocky track for 1.2 miles to a green metal gate marked "Road Closed." If you have a high-clearance vehicle with good tires, park in a gravel pullout just before the gate and start your hike here.

Beyond the gate, the old road becomes a wide trail along a ridge with scattered Douglas firs, wild rose bushes, yellow desert parsley, scarlet gilia, and orange paintbrush. After 0.5 mile, fork to the right in a grassy saddle. The path now traverses a view-packed bunchgrass slope speckled with countless colors of wildflowers from early June to mid-July. After another 1.4 miles the trail crosses a wire fence and enters a partially burned forest at Spain Saddle. Continue at least another 0.6 mile to the next wire fence crossing, where a cliff edge 100 yards to the left offers a first view down to the Snake River.

For an even better view, continue down the trail another 1.1 mile to a rock cairn, where the trail turns sharply right. To the left 50 feet you'll notice a fenceline ending in a small saddle. Leave the main path here and bushwhack left up amid 6-foot lava formations for 300 yards to Eureka Viewpoint, a ridge-end summit where prickly pear cactus blooms *(GPS location N45°48.004' W116°46.825')*. From this eerie vantage point, teetering in the midst of Hells Canyon, you can see the Snake River in three different places.

Most hikers should turn back at Eureka Viewpoint. Beyond this point the trail continues downhill 4.1 miles to the Snake River, and then follows a canyon bottom with bushy poison oak for 0.7 mile to Eureka Bar (see Hike #43).

43 Eureka Bar

Difficult
9.8 miles round trip
350 feet elevation gain
Open all year
Use: hikers, horses, bikes

Where the Imnaha River rages through a jagged rock gorge to Eureka Bar, the scenery looks as though some giant had jackhammered a crack in the earth's crust and inserted a river sideways. Incredibly, a well-built, nearly level trail clings to the cliffs for the river's final 4.2 miles. At trail's end hikers emerge from the gorge to find themselves at the cobble-banked Snake River, amidst the ruins of an improbable mining boomtown, deep in Hells Canyon.

Hikers should be sure to wear long pants because the path is occasionally crowded with blackberry vines and poison oak—obstacles that block nearly all horse, mountain bike, and motorcycle users.

Start by topping off your tank at the gas station in downtown Joseph. Then turn east beside the station at a large "Hells Canyon Scenic Byway" sign and follow signs 29 paved miles to the village of Imnaha. One block past the Imnaha store/ tavern, turn left on Lower Imnaha Road for 6.6 paved miles to Fence Creek.

At this point the Lower Imnaha Road suddenly becomes a rutted, steep one-lane dirt road strewn with rocks. Although most passenger cars can handle it, turn back if you don't like the first 100 yards, because this is perfectly typical of what lies ahead: 15 miles of road so rough it takes a full hour to drive. Three miles beyond the Thorn Creek Guard Station you'll reach the Cow Creek Bridge—which actually spans the Imnaha River near Cow Creek. Just before the bridge turn left on a dirt spur road 100 feet to a small, unmarked turnaround and parking area *(GPS location N45°45.826' W116°44.896')*.

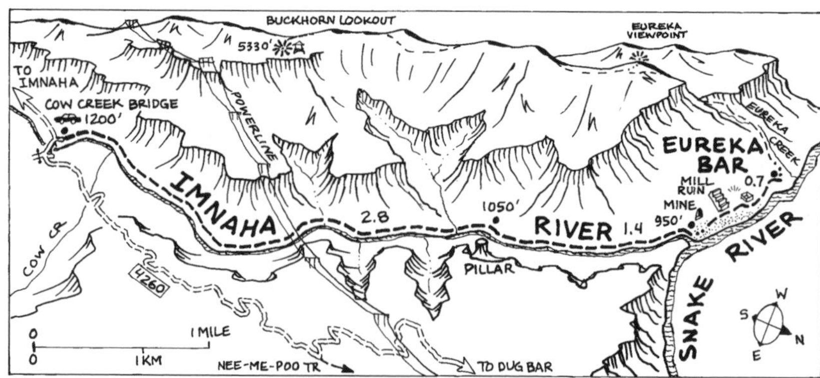

The Imnaha River canyon. *Opposite: Mine at Eureka Bar.*

Set off downstream along the Imnaha River, a 100-foot-wide torrent with car-sized boulders turning up whitewater. Enormous orange cliffs on either hand shoulder out most of the sky, leaving the trail shady even on hot days. Make sure you recognize—and step around—the shiny triple leaflets of poison oak. What look like dwarf palm trees along the trail are actually sumac, a harmless relative of poison oak. Sumac has a 6-foot woody stalk with compound leaves that turn scarlet in September. You're also likely to see ducks starting up from the river, 3-inch crickets hopping out of the path, and countless fluttering butterflies—yellow swallowtails, orange monarchs, and black admirals.

When you reach Eureka Bar's long, gravelly beach, where the Imnaha joins the Snake River, keep left along the base of the cliffs to find a campsite beside an explorable, 30-foot-long mining tunnel *(GPS location N45°49.035′ W116°46.005′).* From the campsite a trail continues past the stonework ruins of a 7-story gold stamp mill and a house. These are the remains of the mining boomtown of Eureka.

In 1899 a group of cagey local miners announced they had found copper ore in the granite of Hells Canyon's inner gorge. They made good money for two or three years, selling shares of stock back East. When investments lagged, the miners claimed the copper ore contained gold. Bedazzled stockholders financed a 125-foot sternwheeler that could claw its way up the Snake River rapids from Lewiston to the new El Dorado. A town of 2000 sprang up on this remote gravel bar to build a huge gold processing mill. But on the day the steamer sailed upriver with the machinery that would finally enable Eureka to begin shipping gold, the ship lost control in the rapids, bridged the canyon, broke in two, and sank. The eastern investors lost their money. And the city of Eureka vanished as swiftly as a stranger who writes bad checks.

Beyond the ruined mill the trail follows a stonework roadbed toward the old steamboat landing. The trail now vanishes near Eureka Creek at a cairn with a signpost—a good turnaround point for your hike.

44 Dug Bar

Easy (to Dug Bar viewpoint)
1.2 miles round trip
480 feet elevation gain
Open all year
Use: hikers, horses

Difficult (to Deep Creek)
8.6 miles round trip
1700 feet elevation gain

When the U.S. Army forced Chief Joseph to leave Oregon in 1877 he led his Nez Perce band through Hells Canyon on a difficult trail that crossed the raging Snake River at Dug Bar. Today that remote crossing site is still a trailhead for paths through colossal canyon scenery. It's also the only place where vehicles can drive to the Oregon shore of the Snake River in the heart of Hells Canyon—but the access road is so long and rough that you're apt to be reminded of Chief Joseph's travails. Passenger cars are not recommended.

Begin by topping off your tank at the gas station in downtown Joseph. Then turn east beside the station at a "Hells Canyon Scenic Byway" sign and follow signs 29 paved miles to the village of Imnaha. One block past the Imnaha store, turn left on Lower Imnaha Road for 6.6 paved miles to Fence Creek.

At this point the Lower Imnaha Road suddenly becomes a rutted, steep one-lane dirt road strewn with rocks. Turn back if you don't like the first 100 yards, because this typifies the 25.4 miles ahead. Vehicles must be driven so slowly on this rugged track that the first 14 miles to the Cow Creek Bridge over the Imnaha River will take you a full hour. Beyond this bridge, the 11.4 miles to Dug Bar are slightly worse, requiring another full hour to drive.

If you're hauling a horse trailer, consider parking at the Cow Creek Bridge and riding horseback to Dug Bar. In that case you'll need to follow the road only for another 2.8 miles. When you reach a rock cairn and a small trail sign, turn right on the Nee-Me-Poo Trail *(GPS location N45°47.451′ W116°44.179′)*. This shortcut is the route traveled in 1877 by the 400 people of Chief Joseph's band. After climbing 1.1 shadeless miles, the faint Nee-Me-Poo Trail passes Lone Pine Saddle's solitary ponderosa and descends for 3 miles to a roadside cairn 0.8 mile from the Dug Bar Campground. The word "Nee-Me-Poo" (or *nimipu*) means "the real people" in the Nez Perce language, and is that tribe's own name for itself. The French term *nez percé* means "pierced nose" and was based on the mistaken assumption that the tribespeople wore ornaments in their noses.

If you're driving the final miles to Dug Bar you'll eventually reach a wire gate. Continue 0.5 mile across the grassy bar, turn left at a ranch house, and go through a metal gate to a fork. Park here beside a restroom *(GPS location N45°48.246′ W116°41.211′)*. The left-hand road leads to a boat ramp, while the right-hand fork peters out in a free camping area without designated sites or tables.

From the restroom, walk back up the road 150 feet and turn left on the Snake River Trail, skirting the ranch's corral. Keep uphill to the right on the main trail

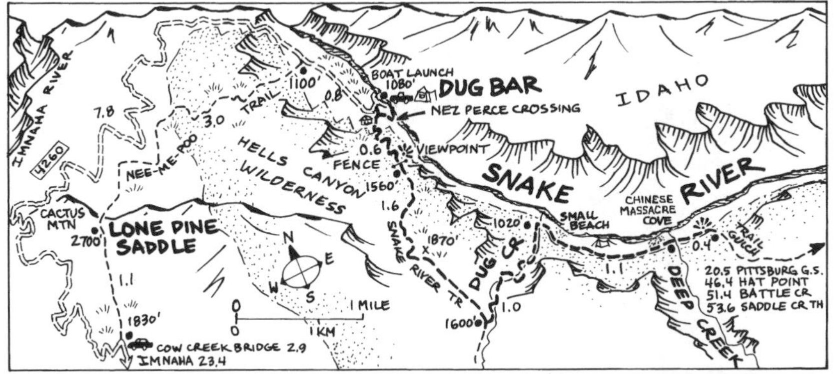

for 0.6 mile to climb to a spectacular viewpoint of Dug Bar just before a wire gate marking the Hells Canyon Wilderness boundary. Cattle graze this entire area from November to May, leaving cow pies and dried hoofprints. Among the cheatgrass you'll also find prickly pear cactus, white mariposa lilies, and yellow balsamroot. Grasshoppers snap out of the trail before you like firecrackers.

If you decide to continue past the viewpoint, you'll amble for 1.6 nearly level miles to a cairn with a trail signpost. Turn left down Dug Creek on a fainter path that repeatedly splashes across the creek and wades through patches of poison oak. Wear good boots and long pants. After a mile the trail finally turns right along the Snake River past sandy coves, swimming holes, and campsites.

The alder grove at Deep Creek's crossing makes a good turnaround point—and has a grim story to tell. In 1886, the 32 Chinese men who had set up a small gold mining operation here were murdered for their gold by seven Idaho cowboys. The shooting was discovered after the cowboys threw the corpses in the river and they washed ashore near Lewiston. The killers buried the gold on the spot. Did they return to get it? Mystery remains, even after a prospector discovered a Chinese vial with $700 of gold dust here in 1902.

Other Options

Backpackers or equestrians who continue past Deep Creek will find that the Snake River Trail climbs away from the river at Trail Gulch on its 51.4-mile route to Battle Creek. The closest trailheads are 46.4 miles away at Hat Point (Hike #45) and 53.6 miles away at the Saddle Creek Trailhead (Hike #46).

Dug Bar from the Snake River Trail. *Opposite: Fence at the Wilderness boundary.*

45

Hat Point

Meadow below Hat Point.

Easy (Granny View and Hat Point)
0.3-mile and 0.4-mile loops
100 feet elevation gain
Open early June to mid-November
Use: hikers

Difficult (to Elk Ridge viewpoint)
10.2 miles round trip
2600 feet elevation **loss**
Use: hikers, horses

Very Difficult (to Snake River)
15.4 miles round trip
5600 feet elevation **loss**

Perhaps the most difficult day hike in Oregon descends 5600 feet from Hat Point to the bottom of Hells Canyon and back. But there are easier trips here too. If you venture just halfway down into the canyon, you can visit a cabin and get a bird's-eye view of the Snake River without such an exhausting climb back to your car. And if you just stroll a few short nature loops you'll see many of Hells Canyon's wildflowers and views without losing any elevation at all. A fire burned some of the trees in the Hat Point area in 2007, but fire fighters saved the lookout tower itself by wrapping it in fireproof Kevlar.

Start by topping off your tank at the gas station in downtown Joseph. Then turn east beside the station at a "Hells Canyon Scenic Byway" sign and follow signs 29 paved miles to the village of Imnaha. Drive straight through Imnaha onto Hat Point Road 4240, which promptly becomes gravel. Although this steep, narrow road has blind curves and washboard, passenger cars do just fine if driven care-

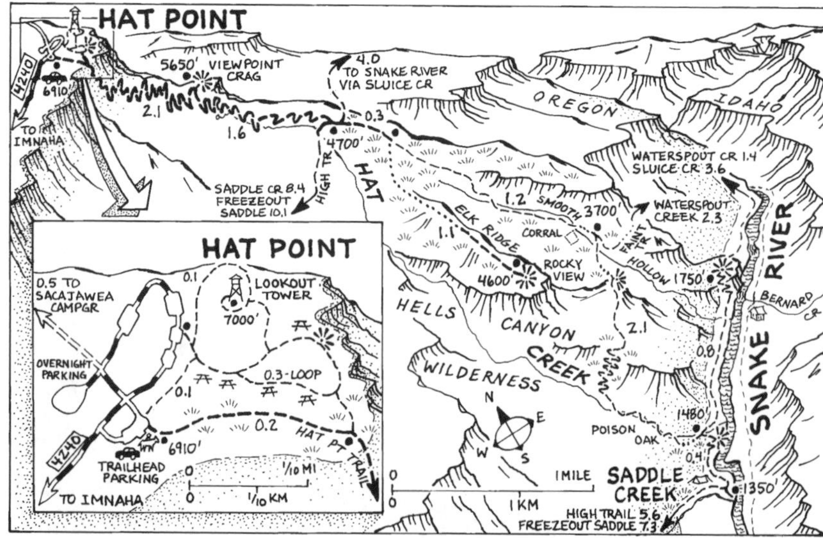

The Snake River at Saddle Creek.

fully. The first 5 miles climb so relentlessly that you may need to pause in the shade to keep your car's engine from overheating. After this the road widens a bit and begins to level out.

Beyond Imnaha 16.6 miles turn right at a sign for Granny View Vista and park by the restroom for this short nature trail. Astonishing views of the vast Imnaha River canyon open up at each turn on a 0.3-mile loop (not shown on map). Expect dense alpine wildflowers in June and July, including red paintbrush, blue penstemon, purple larkspur, and yellow balsamroot.

After a quick walk at Granny View Vista, get back in your car and drive on up the Hat Point Road another 6 miles to a series of parking areas below the Hat Point lookout tower. If you only have time for a short walk, park at a display board nearest the tower, take a gravel 0.3-mile loop to the right through a picnic area to a viewpoint, and then climb up to the lookout tower itself. Public stairs climb 60 feet up the tower to an observation deck. Only lookout staffers are allowed the final 30 feet up to the historic, 8-foot-square cabin.

If you have the energy for a longer hike, park instead at the official "Trailhead and Loading Dock," the first parking lot on your right at Hat Point *(GPS location N45°26.208' W116°33.841')*. The trail traverses left across a meadow of blue lupine, purple larkspur, and scarlet gilia. Soon the path begins switchbacking down through a Douglas fir forest that burned in 2007. After 3.7 miles you'll reach a T-shaped junction in a ponderosa pine flat *(GPS location N45°24.675' W116°37.352')*.

Turn left at the T-shaped trail junction for 100 yards to a fork, and veer right. This path leads across a grassy benchland with views to the snow-capped Seven Devils in Idaho. After 0.3 mile the trail starts to descend into Smooth Hollow, but beware of losing any more elevation, because you will have to regain it all later. Instead consider leaving the trail and veering to the right along a nearly level grassy ridgecrest. An elk path traces this ridge 1.1 mile to its end at a panoramic rocky viewpoint in the midst of Hells Canyon, overlooking the Snake River at Saddle Creek. Declare victory at this knoll and turn back.

If you opt to take the very steep and faint trail down Smooth Hollow to the Snake River, continue 1.2 miles until the path crosses a dry wash beside an old corral and vanishes in the grass. Head for a rock cairn with a signpost just above a half dozen dead cottonwood trees. Here head downhill to the right on a faint path that traverses to a small pass beside a rock knoll. Next the path switchbacks faintly down an extremely steep, rocky slope to Hat Creek, and then follows a rugged canyon bottom through knee-deep patches of poison oak to the Snake River Trail. Turn right on this large, well-built path 0.4 mile to a campable, grassy field at Saddle Creek, where a path descends to a boulder bar beside the Snake River *(GPS location N45°23.501' W116°37.447')*.

Other Options

To return on a loop from Saddle Creek, head north along the Snake River Trail through a particularly dramatic whitewater gorge. Don't attempt to find the virtually abandoned trail up Waterspout Creek. Continue a total of 4.8 miles and turn left up the well-built Sluice Creek Trail 4 miles to the junction below Hat Point. A longer loop option from Saddle Creek heads up Saddle Creek 5.6 miles and turns right on the High Trail for 10.1 miles to the junction.

46 Freezeout Saddle

Moderate (to Freezeout Saddle)
5.6 miles round trip
1950 feet elevation gain
Open early May through November
Use: hikers, horses

Difficult (to Summit Ridge)
11.9-mile loop
3470 feet elevation gain

Left: View west from Freezeout Saddle.

The lowest point on the Oregon rim of Hells Canyon, this surprisingly balmy saddle is usually free of snow a month before Hat Point (Hike #45). As a result, equestrians and backpackers prefer the Saddle Creek Trail through Freezeout Saddle as a more reliable, and better graded, route to the Snake River. For a day hike here, climb to the views at Freezeout Saddle or continue on a difficult loop through the wildflower meadows of Summit Ridge.

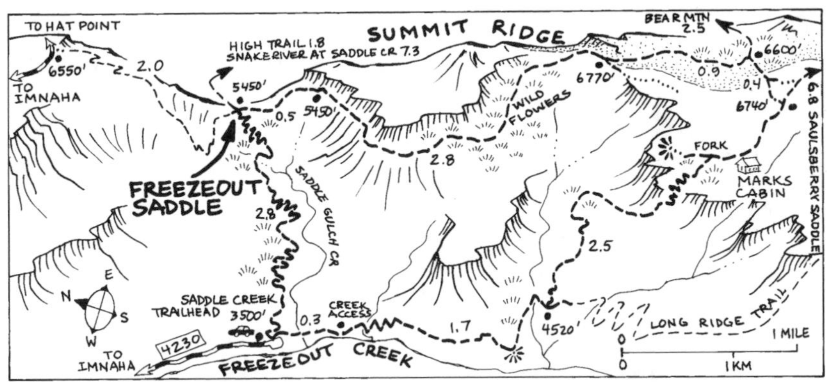

Begin at the gas station in downtown Joseph, where you should top off your tank. Then turn east beside the station at a large "Hells Canyon Scenic Byway" sign and follow signs 29 paved miles to the village of Imnaha. Following a sign for Halfway at the Imnaha store, turn right onto Upper Imnaha Road. Drive this wide gravel road 13 miles to a fork just before a bridge. Veer steeply up to the left on one-lane gravel Road 4230, following a "Saddle Creek Trail" pointer, and drive 2.9 miles to a large gravel parking lot at road's end, where parking permits are required *(GPS location N45°22.535' W116°45.703')*.

The trail starts at a message board and a horse watering trough on the left. The path switchbacks up past old-growth ponderosa pines to a grassy slope with salsify blooms, mulleins, and wild roses. You'll pass a few shady Douglas firs, but the trail mostly stays in the open. Near the pass the wildflowers become profuse. Masses of clarkia line the trail with their pink crosses in June and July. Also expect yellow balsamroot, blue flax, orange paintbrush, and blue lupine.

When you reach Freezeout Saddle's large rock cairn, you'll gain a view down the Saddle Creek canyon to the rugged inner gorge of the Snake River. To the west, a long row of snowy Wallowa Mountains rises above Morgan Ridge and the Imnaha River's chasm. Even if you're not doing the longer loop, you might want to amble to the right on the level trail along the saddle's crest 0.5 mile, enjoying the views and the flowers, before heading back.

If you're continuing on the rugged loop, sally southward another 2.8 miles, climbing through slopes thick with wildflowers, to a junction at the edge of Summit Ridge's plateau. Keep left on the main trail through a young forest regrowing from an old fire. After 0.9 mile you'll reach an ugly meadow junction, where cows and elk have churned a spring to mud. Although this is now in the official Wilderness, set aside by the U.S. Congress for preservation, the Forest Service allowed salvage logging and intensive grazing here after a 1970s fire, leaving blackened stumpfields of cow pies.

At the desolate meadow junction, turn right on an old logging road, keep right at a fork, and follow a cow trail across the crest of a bleak ridge until the path peters out. Continue downhill and slightly left 100 yards to a rock cairn with a signpost at a real trail *(GPS location N45°20.084' W116°43.723')*. Turn right on this path 0.4 mile to Marks Cabin, a private cowboy camp. Continue another 0.2 mile to a fork and veer downhill to the left across a steep meadow. This cattle-drivers' path descends steeply another 1.9 miles through woods to a T-shaped junction with the relatively level Long Ridge Trail. Turn right for 1.7 miles to return to your car.

47 Hells Canyon Dam

Easy (to Stud Creek)
2.4 miles round trip
180 feet elevation gain
Open all year
Use: hikers

Easy (to Deep Creek)
0.4 miles round trip
150 feet elevation gain

Built by the Idaho Power Company in 1956, the 330-foot-tall Hells Canyon Dam flooded 20 miles of the deepest gorge in the United States and led to the demise of the native salmon runs for half of Idaho. Today, surrounded on three sides by the Hells Canyon Wilderness, the colossal concrete structure remains a monument to the threats facing America's most scenic places. But the dam's paved access road also offers hikers a back door into the midst of Hells Canyon's mile-deep chasm. From road's end, an easy trail follows the whitewater Snake River into the canyon's wondrous wilds. At the dam itself, a railed catwalk descends the fearsome cliffs to Deep Creek. There are no easier paths to the spectacular scenery of Hells Canyon.

If you're coming from the west, leave Interstate 84 at exit 302 just north of Baker City, drive Highway 86 east 65 miles to Oxbow, follow signs another 23 miles to Hells Canyon Dam, and continue 1.1 mile to a parking lot by the visitor information center at road's end. If you're coming from the south, leave Interstate 84 at exit 374 in Ontario, drive north 48 miles through Weiser to Cambridge on Highway 95, turn left 40 miles to Oxbow, keep right for 23 miles to the Hells Canyon Dam, and continue 1.1 mile to road's end.

Start by perusing the displays in the visitor center. Then go out the building's back door to the deck and take the stairs down to the boat launch area. Special permits, equipment, and skills are required to pilot rafts down the churning Snake River 32 miles to the next take-out point, Pittsburg Landing. Jet boat tours are also available. At a dock beside the launch site, a private operator offers rides that range from $60 for a two-hour trip to $172 for a six-hour outing with lunch.

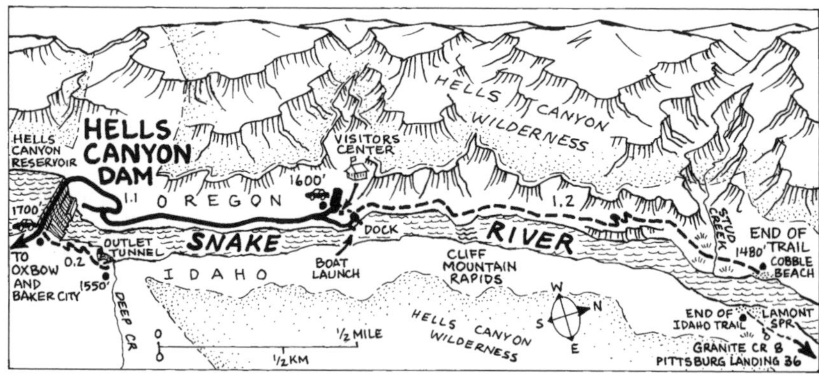

Hells Canyon from Stud Creek. Opposite: The Hells Canyon Dam.

But the quietest and most thorough way to explore this canyon country is on foot. From the boat dock, follow a walkway past a railed archeological site—a prehistoric pit house depression where poles once supported a roof made of reed mats. Continue another 100 yards along the trail and you'll pass a cave-like overhang in the cliffs. Scratches on the cliff face here may be evidence of prehistoric visitors. Today the markings are guarded by a dense stand of poison oak. Take a moment to identify these triple-leafleted plants, so you can avoid them when they occasionally appear along the edges of the trail ahead.

A friendlier plant to spot along the trail is the mock orange, a bushy tree with sweet-smelling white blossoms in June. If you're hiking in fall, you'll probably notice another attractive, bushy tree—the sumac, whose leaflets turn fiery red in autumn.

After a mile the riverside trail enters Stud Creek's outwash plain, a gravelly slope of bunchgrass, mullein stalks, and a few ponderosa pines. Just beyond the creek crossing the path ends at a cobble beach. Ahead, sheer 500-foot cliffs rise directly from the Snake River, blocking further foot travel. And although a rough trail does start on the Idaho shore at this point, the Snake River is far too deep and swift to cross without a boat. So enjoy the view from the beach and then return as you came to your car.

If you'd like to do another short hike nearby, drive back 1.1 mile and park on the shoulder at the far end of the Hells Canyon Dam. A sign here marks the start of the Deep Creek Trail, a perilous-looking series of steel catwalks and railed stairs that descends 0.2 mile down the misty cliffs beside the spillway to a rocky creek near the outlet of the dam's diversion tunnel.

Hells Canyon from the reservoir trail. Below: Swallowtail butterfly.

48 Hells Canyon Reservoir

Easy (to Spring Creek)
5.2 miles round trip
600 feet elevation gain
Open all year
Use: hikers, horses

The Oregon side of the Hells Canyon Reservoir is full of surprises—waterfalls in side canyons, slopes of wildflowers, and clifftop viewpoints where you can watch giant fish idling in the Snake River's still green waters. Perhaps most surprising of all is the solitude. Power boats rarely venture here, and traffic is so light on the highway across the reservoir in Idaho that hours can pass without the sound of a motor. Because occasional patches of poison oak grow beside the shoreline trail, be sure to wear long pants.

To drive here from Baker City, leave Interstate 84 at exit 302 just north of town and follow Highway 86 east 65 miles through Richland and Halfway to Oxbow. Just before reaching the Snake River keep left onto Homestead Road at pointers for Homestead and the Hells Canyon Trail. Follow this increasingly bumpy gravel road 9.2 miles to its end on a grassy slope beside the reservoir. Impromptu campsites and parking places abound. (If you're driving here via Ontario or Boise, take Highway 95 north through Weiser to Cambridge, turn left on Road 71 for 40 miles to Oxbow, and then take Homestead Road to its end.)

Start at a trailhead message board a few feet before road's end, where the track forks three ways. Follow the left-hand road to a colorful rock outwash plain of red, purple, black, green, and white boulders. Hop across Copper Creek to a register box marking the start of the actual trail.

In early summer, wildflowers brighten the slopes of dry bitterbrush above the reservoir. Look for stalks of yellow four-o'clocks, purple asters, white yarrow, yellow salsify, and tiny purple penstemons. The pretty little pink flowers with four elegant, cross-shaped petals are clarkias. The name honors Lewis and Clark, who first identified the flower in 1805-06 when they passed the northern end of Hells Canyon.

The upper Snake River's native salmon runs died when the Hells Canyon Dam impounded this reservoir in the 1950s. The hundreds of brown, 2-foot-long fish you see lazing in the water are unappetizing crappies or catfish, whose O-shaped mouths suck scum from rocks. Look in the shadows near shore to spot dozens of livelier, 8-inch rainbow trout.

After 0.9 mile the path crosses Nelson Creek in a gully, and at the 1.8-mile mark the trail appears to end at the broad, gravel outwash plain of McGraw Creek. In spring this 15-foot-wide stream is deep enough that you may have to wade, but by summer it's possible to cross on rocks or logs. Every few years, flash floods strip this canyon bottom of vegetation and repave the plain with fresh gravel.

For a worthwhile side trip, follow McGraw Creek up the canyon 300 yards and look for a rock cairn on the right. The abandoned McGraw Creek Trail begins here amid small trees and climbs a quarter mile to a clifftop viewpoint of a 15-foot waterfall in a canyon of house-sized boulders. Keep an eye out for the triple-leafletted poison oak crowding this path. Beyond the falls, flood washouts have eliminated this old trail, so turn back to the reservoir.

If you're continuing on the reservoir's shoreline trail beyond the mouth of McGraw Creek, be prepared to make short detours where patches of poison oak have overgrown the trail. After 0.6 mile keep right at a signed junction with the 32-Point Trail. Then continue another 0.2 mile down to Spring Creek, a braided stream in an outwash plain of willows and alders. Plan to turn back here. Although the Hells Canyon Trail once continued 1.9 miles to Leep Creek, the final portion has become so faint and overgrown that it's only suitable for adventurous pathfinders.

Other Options

Explorers can extend this hike by taking the 32-Point Trail up Spring Creek's canyon. The trail soon forks. To the right, a faint path follows Spring Creek up the canyon. To the left, a new trail switchbacks steeply up to a high bench crossed by the old trail to McGraw Creek Cabin.

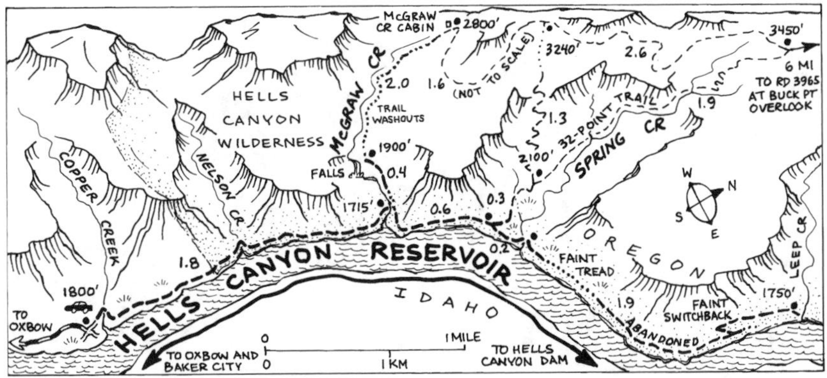

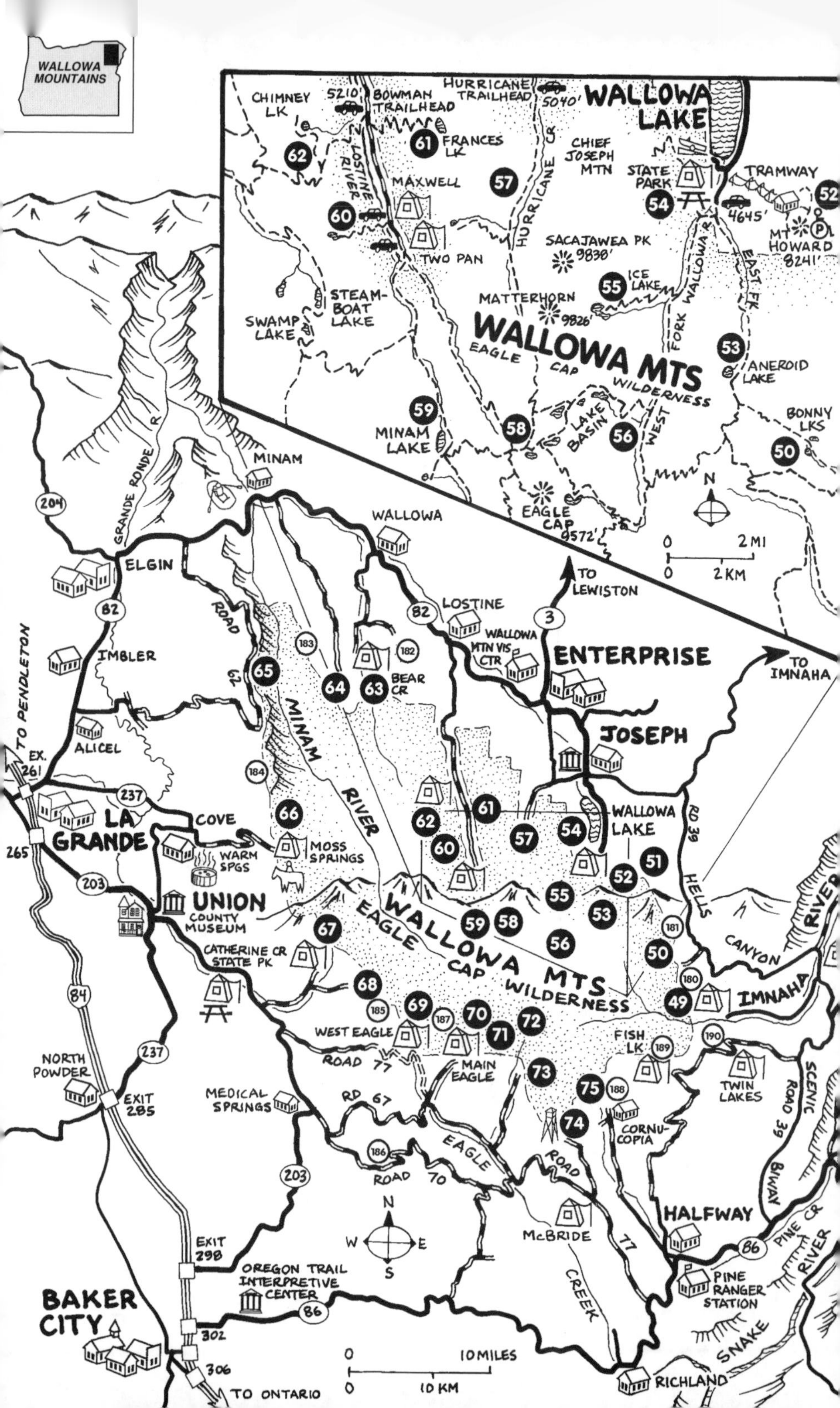

WALLOWA MOUNTAINS
CHIMNEY LK
5210'
BOWMAN TRAILHEAD
HURRICANE TRAILHEAD
5040'
WALLOWA LAKE
FRANCES LK
CHIEF JOSEPH MTN
LOSTINE RIVER
MAXWELL
HURRICANE CR
STATE PARK
TRAMWAY
4645'
MT HOWARD 8241'
TWO PAN
SACAJAWEA PK 9838'
ICE LAKE
MATTERHORN 9826'
WEST FORK WALLOWA R
EAST FK
STEAMBOAT LAKE
SWAMP LAKE
WALLOWA MTS
EAGLE CAP WILDERNESS
ANEROID LAKE
LAKE BASIN
WEST
BONNY LKS
MINAM LAKE
EAGLE CAP 9572'
N
0 2 MI
0 2 KM
TO LEWISTON
MINAM
GRANDE RONDE R
WALLOWA
204
ELGIN
ROAD 62
82
LOSTINE
3
WALLOWA MTN VIS CTR
ENTERPRISE
TO IMNAHA
IMBLER
183
182
BEAR CR
JOSEPH
TO PENDLETON
ALICEL
MINAM RIVER
EX. 261
184
237
LA GRANDE
COVE
WARM SPGS
MOSS SPRINGS
WALLOWA LAKE
RD 39
265
203
UNION
COUNTY MUSEUM
WALLOWA MTS
EAGLE CAP WILDERNESS
HELLS CANYON
RIVER
181
CATHERINE CR STATE PK
180
IMNAHA
84
185
187
WEST EAGLE
ROAD 77
MAIN EAGLE
FISH LK
189
190
TWIN LAKES
237
NORTH POWDER
EXIT 285
MEDICAL SPRINGS
RD 67
188
CORNUCOPIA
SCENIC BYWAY ROAD 39
186
ROAD 70
EAGLE CREEK ROAD 77
203
N
W E
S
McBRIDE
HALFWAY
EXIT 298
86
PINE CR
OREGON TRAIL INTERPRETIVE CENTER
PINE RANGER STATION
RIVER
BAKER CITY
86
302
SNAKE
306
0 10 MILES
0 10 KM
TO ONTARIO
RICHLAND

Bronze sculpture in downtown Joseph.

ENTERPRISE

The Wallowa Mountains form an alpine backdrop to the country that was home to Chief Joseph's Nez Perce band until 1877. The Forest Service's visitor center here burned in 2010, but stop in Enterprise to see the 1909 **Wallowa County Courthouse,** built of local stone. For dinner, try a buffalo burger and a pint of fresh IPA at **Terminal Gravity Brewing** at the east end of town (803 SE School Street; closed Sunday-Tuesday). Spend the night at the historic 1910 **Enterprise House Bed & Breakfast** at 508 East First South Street ($85-189; 888-448-8825 or *www.enterprisehousebnb.com*).

Joseph

Monumental **bronze sculptures** line Joseph's scenic main street, the work of local foundries and artists (also represented in this charming little town's many art galleries). The **Wallowa County Museum**, in a 1888 bank building at 110 S. Main in the middle of downtown, includes a Nez Perce room with a tepee and is open daily 10am-4pm from late May to mid-September. Admission is $4, with kids under 7 free. If you're hungry, try a calzone and microbrew on **The Embers'** spacious deck (206 Main St.). For a place to stay, head for **Chandlers' Inn**, a 12-room bed & breakfast with a raised hot tub deck overlooking the mountains at 700 S. Main Street ($80-160; 541-432-9765, *www.josephbedandbreakfast.com*).

Wallowa Lake

Wedged against spectacular alpine peaks, this beautifully blue, 3-mile long lake fills the footprint of a vanished glacier. As you drive here from Joseph, stop at the lake's near end to see the **grave of Old Chief Joseph,** moved here in 1925. At the far end of the lake, **Wallowa Lake State Park** features a picnic area, marina, boat ramp (motors OK), chilly swimming beach, and popular 210-site campground with $38 yurts (reservations recommended, 800-452-5687). Near the park entrance, the rustic yet elegant **Wallowa Lake Lodge** offers 22 rooms ($80-185) in the grand style of National Park lodges and 8 cabins ($155-275) as well as affordable dining (541-432-9821, *www.wallowalake.com*). Beyond the park entrance 0.3 mile, the gondolas of the **Wallowa Lake Tramway** zoom visitors up 3700 feet of elevation in 15 minutes to panoramic views atop Mt. Howard (see Hike #52). The tramway is open 10am-4:45pm daily from late May to early October, and costs about $26 for adults, $21 for kids age 12-17, and $17 for kids age 4-11.

Halfway

In this scenic hamlet on the quieter, southern side of the Wallowas, the **Pine Valley Lodge** has converted three houses and an 1891 church into a lodge, spa, and restaurant. Rooms run $65-180, double occupancy (541-742-2027, *www.pvlodge.com*). Nearby, the Forest Service rents the rustic 1959 **Two Color Guard Station** (which sleeps 12) for $80 in summer and $60 in fall. Reservations are at *www.recreation.gov.*

Cove and Union

At the western foot of the Wallowa Mountains (14 miles east of La Grande on Highway 203), the quaint little town of Union preserves its early 1900s charm. Visit the **Union County Museum's** excellent exhibit on cowboys (333 N. Main). Hours are 10-4:30 Tue-Sat from May through October. Admission is $4 for adults and $2 for students. For a room, book at the surprisingly grand 1921 **Union Hotel** (16 rooms at $39-109; 541-562-6135, *www.theunionhotel.com*). Then drive 9 miles north to the even smaller town of Cove. By the white-steepled church, turn right on French Street and follow "swimming pool" pointers 0.4 mile to **Forest Cove Warm Springs,** an old-timey bathhouse and 9-foot-deep concrete pool built over a bubbling 86° F spring. Admission is $6 for adults, $5 for seniors and students, and $2.50 for kids. It's open 1-4pm Monday to Saturday in summer.

Eagle Cap Excursion Train

A passenger train travels 79 miles along the roadless Grande Ronde and Wallowa Rivers on most Saturdays from late June to mid-October, departing from Elgin at 10am. Adults are $75, seniors $65, and kids 3-16 $35. Trips for fishermen run in February and March. Check *www.eaglecaptrain.com* or call 800-323-7330.

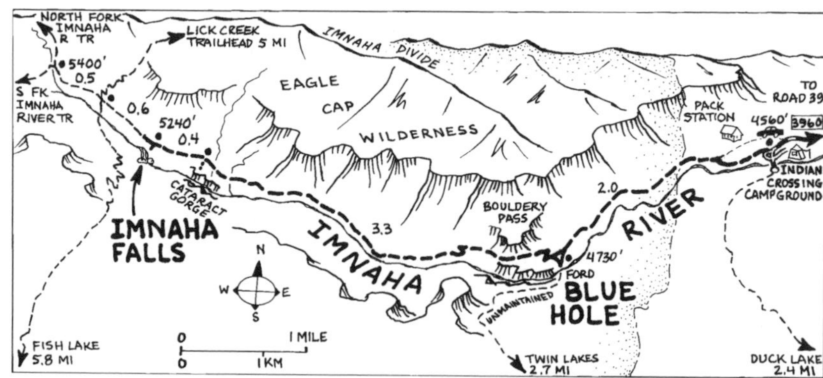

49 Imnaha Falls

Easy (to Blue Hole)
4 miles round trip
200 feet elevation gain
Open mid-May to mid-November
Use: hikers, horses

Difficult (to Imnaha Falls)
11.4 miles round trip
800 feet elevation gain

Refer to map on previous page.

Blue Hole.

The Imnaha River roars out of the Eagle Cap Wilderness 40 feet wide, but upstream it squeezes through spectacular, 10-foot rock slots at Blue Hole and Imnaha Falls. Children do well on the easy 2-mile walk to Blue Hole, where the riverbank is full of skipping rocks. For a longer hike, continue to Imnaha Falls.

From the gas station in downtown Joseph, turn east on the Hells Canyon Byway, follow Imnaha Road 8.3 miles to a sign for Halfway, and turn right onto paved Wallowa Mountain Road 39 for 32 miles. A mile beyond Blackhorse Campground turn right on paved Road 3960. After 9 miles, at the entrance sign for Indian Crossing Campground, park by a restroom on the right. *Do not* drive across a bridge to the end of the road, where a different trail begins.

If you're driving here from Baker City, leave Interstate 84 at exit 302 just north of town and follow Highway 86 east for 58 miles through Richland and Halfway. At a pointer for Joseph between mileposts 63 and 64, turn left onto paved Road 39 for 23.7 miles. Just beyond Ollokot Campground, turn left on paved Road 3960 for 9 miles to Indian Crossing Campground. Parking permits are required.

The trail sets off near the river through an open forest of grand fir, Douglas fir, and lodgepole pine. After 0.8 mile you'll enter a 1996 fire zone with the blooms of pink fireweed, pearly everlasting, and white yarrow among the snags. You're almost certain to see red-shafted flickers, the robin-sized woodpeckers that swoop from tree to tree, flashing reddish-brown wings. With luck you'll also spot a pileated woodpecker, a foot-tall bird with a bright red head.

When the trail forks at the 2-mile mark, detour left 200 yards to visit Blue Hole, where the Imnaha River emerges from a narrow rock gorge to a beach of white marble pebbles. The straight, 50-foot-deep slot follows a geologic fault.

If Imnaha Falls is your goal, return to the main trail and continue upriver into unburned forest. Notice that the exposed bedrock and bluffs along the way have been rounded by the glacier that filled this valley during the Ice Age. The trail does not pass within sight of Imnaha Falls, so listen for the roar of rushing water. The first such roar you'll hear, beyond Blue Hole 3.3 miles, is made by Cataract Gorge. If you follow the sound and bushwhack 200 feet to the left you'll find a 100-yard-long river chasm, but no waterfall. To find Imnaha Falls, continue on the main trail 0.4 mile to the next roar. Here, 0.6 mile before the trail reaches a marked 4-way junction, look for a short path to the left. This path leads to an 8-foot falls where the river squirts into a blue pool with the shadows of fish.

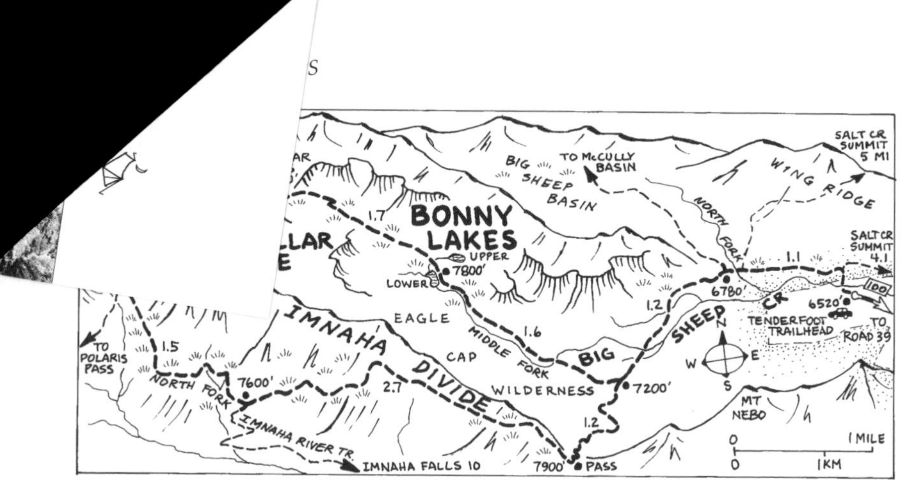

50 Bonny Lakes

Moderate (to Bonny Lakes)
7.8 miles round trip
1300 feet elevation gain
Open mid-July through October
Use: hikers, horses

Difficult (to Dollar Lake)
11.8 miles round trip
2000 feet elevation gain

Difficult (around Imnaha Divide)
16.3-mile loop
3000 feet elevation gain

The crowds struggling up the steep, dusty trail from Wallowa Lake to the gorgeous alpine country above Aneroid Lake obviously don't know about this easier, much quieter route. If you park at the little-used Tenderfoot Trailhead, you can trim a mile and nearly 2000 feet of elevation gain from the hike to dramatic Dollar Lake. Along the way you'll climb through wildflower fields at the Bonny Lakes, a good goal in itself. And because the trail really is less steep, you may have enough energy to continue on a grand loop around the Imnaha Divide.

Group size is limited to six. Campsites must be at least 100 feet from lakeshores, tethered horses must be at least 200 feet from lakes, and campfires are strongly discouraged. The use of snags for firewood is banned.

From the gas station in downtown Joseph, turn east on the Hells Canyon Byway, follow Imnaha Road 8.3 miles to a sign for Salt Creek Summit, and turn right onto paved Wallowa Mountain Loop Road 39 for 13 miles. Beyond the Salt Creek Recreation Site 3 miles, where the road crosses a creek on a concrete bridge, turn right onto gravel Road 100 for 3.2 miles to the Tenderfoot Trailhead, a large gravel parking area at road's end. Parking permits are not required.

The trail sets off through a lodgepole pine forest that burned in a 1989 fire. Young pines are regrowing amid the spires of dead trees. Grass, white yarrow blooms, pearly everlasting, pink fireweed, and chipmunks have helped refill the woods. After 200 yards the path fords Big Sheep Creek, but look for a nearby log that allows you to cross dry-footed.

Keep left at the next couple of junctions, following the main trail as it leaves the burned area and climbs through occasional sagebrush meadows. At the 2.3-mile mark you'll reach a fork—the start of the long loop around the Imnaha Divide. Veer right, following an "East Fork Wallowa River" pointer. This path follows a creek up amid a parade of colorful wildflowers. Look for blue lupine, white bugbane, red paintbrush, purple asters, and tall stalks of purple monkshood. A special treat are the delicate mariposa lilies, whose three large, creamy petals each have a lavender dot.

At the 3.9-mile mark the trail passes between the two Bonny Lakes, shallow pools fed by meandering marshy meadows that harbor mosquitoes during the last weeks of July. For the best view of the lakes, continue across their connecting creek 200 yards to a marble outcrop.

For a better mountain panorama, continue up the trail another 1.7 miles to Dollar Pass, a grassy alpine saddle where domestic sheep sometimes graze. Ahead is the craggy white crest of Bonneville Mountain, with the rounded tops of the Matterhorn and Sacajawea looming beyond. Allow enough time in the Dollar Pass area for an easy cross-country detour to Dollar Lake. Leave the trail at Dollar Pass and amble 0.3 mile to the left (due south), through a level ridgecrest meadow toward a cliffy peak with snowfields. At the peak's base you'll discover a dramatic blue lake, round as a dollar coin.

Dollar Lake is an excellent spot to declare victory and head back the way you came. But backpackers (or athletic day-hikers) may want to return on a longer loop. Go back to Dollar Pass, follow the trail left 0.9 mile to a junction by a creek fork, and turn left again. If you keep turning left at every junction for the next 6.9 miles, you'll climb across scenic Tenderfoot Pass, traverse fabulous wildflower meadows along the Imnaha Divide, cross another pass, and descend to a junction at the end of the loop, near Big Sheep Creek. From there on you'll have to keep right at junctions for the final 2.3 miles back to your car.

Upper Bonny Lake. *Opposite: Dollar Lake.*

51 McCully Basin

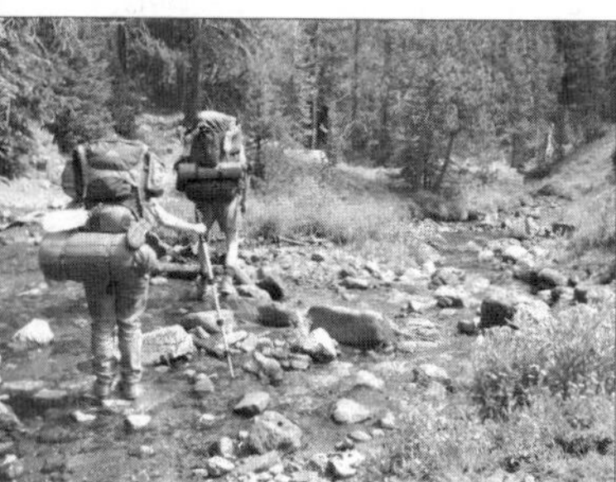

Moderate (to creek crossing)
9.2 miles round trip
1910 feet elevation gain
Open mid-July through October
Use: hikers, horses

Difficult (to McCully Basin)
11.6 miles round trip
2260 feet elevation gain

Difficult (to pass)
12.8 miles round trip
3160 feet elevation gain

Question: Why is this delightful trail, just 10 miles from Joseph, virtually unused? Answer: McCully Basin doesn't have a lake. So if you can't live without fishing or swimming, forget McCully Basin. Come here if you love alpine brooks, meadows, and high country where you can roam all day without seeing another human. It's also the best base camp for a non-technical climb of Aneroid Mountain, Oregon's ninth tallest peak. Parking permits are required and group size is limited to 12.

From the gas station on Main Street in downtown Joseph, turn east on Wallowa Avenue at a sign for Ferguson Ridge. After 5.4 miles, turn right onto Tucker Down Road for 3.1 miles of pavement and another 0.6 miles of good gravel to a ski area parking area. Then continue 1.4 miles on rough gravel (keeping right at junctions) to a trailhead turnaround at road's end *(GPS location N45°16.631′ W117°08.155′)*.

The trail starts beside an outhouse and soon joins a (gated) service road that climbs to the tramway atop Mount Howard—a popular loop route for mountain bikers who have taken their bikes up the tram. After 0.7 mile the service road turns right, but fork to the left on an old roadbed that becomes the trail up McCully Creek. The forest here is mostly lodgepole pine, with Engelmann spruce, Douglas fir, scrub alder, red huckleberry, and blue lupine. You'll also find some pink

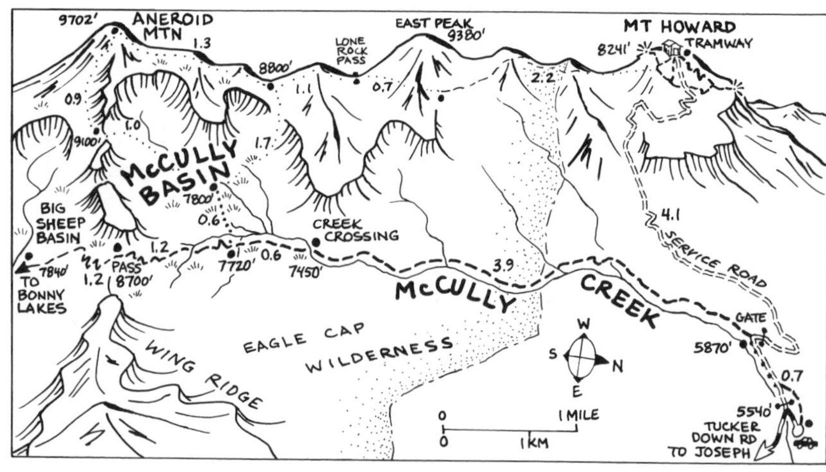

Aneroid Mountain from McCully Basin. *Opposite: The creek crossing after 4.6 miles.*

fireweed, because fires have burned a few patches in these woods.

At the 4.6-mile point the trail crosses 12-foot-wide McCully Creek, a ford that's usually passable dry-footed on rocks. Beyond is the hike's first big meadow. This is a possible turnaround point for day hikers.

If you're still going strong, continue 0.6 mile, crossing two small side creeks along the way, to another meadow where you face a choice. Both choices require a sense of adventure. Ahead, the trail suddenly begins to climb. If you charge on ahead for 1.2 miles you'll climb on an increasingly faint trail through increasingly spectacular meadows until you puff to a high pass overlooking Big Sheep Basin and a fair share of the high Wallowas. This is a very nice goal.

If, however, you want to see McCully Basin's main meadows, you'll have to leave the trail and bushwhack a bit. Where the trail suddenly steepens *(GPS location N45°1.03' W117°08.72')*, strike off to the right across a meadow 200 feet, cross a creek, scramble up a sandy slope 60 feet, and continue 200 more feet to the first of McCully Basin's three large meadows *(GPS location N45°13.00' W117°08.92')*. From here, Aneroid Mountain is but one blip in a wall of stripey red-brown cliffs ringing the horizon. A creek burbles out from the meadow amid purple aster, blue gentian, and white grass of parnassus.

The meadows here are heavenly, and even if you come in August you might well be the first visitor of the season. Where else in the Wallowas can you say that?

Other Options

McCully Basin is the best base camp for a climb of 9702-foot Aneroid Mountain. Because there are two non-technical routes to the summit from this side, it's possible to hike there from McCully Basin's main meadow on a 4.9-mile loop that gains only 1900 feet. The map shows these routes, but attempt them only with contour maps and a guide with off-trail experience. Even so, you'll have to use your hands, and there is a danger of rockfall, so helmets are a good idea. Turn back if you're in doubt or if the weather is iffy. At the top an ammo can holds a summit register, but no camera can hold the view.

Mount Howard

Easy (summit tour)
1.9-mile loop
300 feet elevation gain
Open July through September
Use: hikers

Moderate (to East Peak springs)
5.5 miles round trip
1140 feet elevation gain

For a quick sample of the Wallowa Mountain's high country, ride a tramway's gondola up from Wallowa Lake to Mt. Howard. Crowds of tourists follow an easy loop trail from the tramway station to Mt. Howard's summit, where the panorama includes a jagged horizon of snowpeaks. For a more adventurous outing, continue on a faint ridgecrest path to East Peak's wildflower meadows.

From Interstate 84 at La Grande, take exit 261 and follow Wallowa Lake signs on Highway 82 through Enterprise and Joseph a total of 78 miles. At the far end of Wallowa Lake, at milepost 6 where the main road veers right into Wallowa Lake State Park, turn left for 0.3 mile and park on the left at the Wallowa Lake Tramway station. The tramway is open 10am-4:45pm daily from late May to early October. The ride up gains 3700 feet of elevation in 15 minutes and costs about $26 ($21 for children age 12-17 and $17 for kids age 4-11). Expect impressive views north to 3-mile-long, cucumber-shaped Wallowa Lake. An Ice Age glacier left the curving moraine hill of sandy debris that rims the lake.

At tramway's top you'll step out onto the patio of the Summit Grill, a cafe that serves sandwiches and hamburgers for about $8. After exclaiming at the view from the patio, most people remark on the fat Columbia ground squirrels begging for handouts. These native squirrels were getting so many french fries and other unhealthy leftovers that the tramway operators began selling packages of "squirrel food." Unfortunately, this only encouraged the begging. Before long,

The view from Mt. Howard. Above: The Wallowa Lake Tramway.

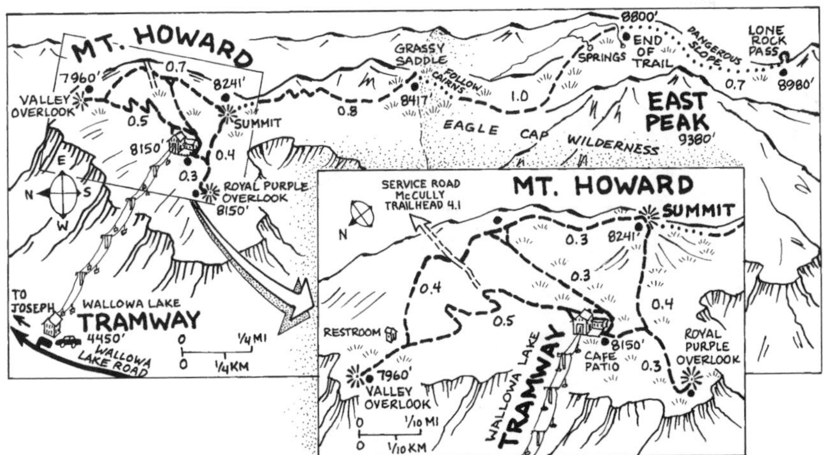

the mountain's chipmunks, squawking Clark's nutcrackers, and golden-mantled ground squirrels were pestering people too. Please don't feed any of these wild animals. They are truly healthier and happier on their own, gathering the plentiful grass and wildflower seeds that grow nearby.

The best way to see all three of the viewpoints on the edges of Mt. Howard's broad top is to set off from the patio and keep right at all trail junctions. The path leads past storm-bent limber pines, fields of pink heather, and yellow desert parsley. After 0.3 mile you'll climb a rocky knoll to the Royal Purple Overlook. The snowy peak in the distance is Eagle Cap. Somewhat closer to the right is a taller summit, the 9826-foot Matterhorn, capped with white marble.

Turn around at the Royal Purple Overlook and continue keeping to the right for 0.4 mile to reach Mt. Howard's summit. The view stretches east across distant Hells Canyon to the jagged blue horizon of Idaho's Seven Devils Mountains.

If you simply continue on the well-marked loop trail from the summit, keeping right at junctions, you'll visit the Valley Overlook and return to the Tramway station in 1.2 miles. Adventurers who yearn to escape Mt. Howard's crowds, however, can leave the main trail at the mountain summit and bushwhack 0.2 mile south (to the right) down to a pass with a faint, old trail. This path climbs steeply up a ridge and then suddenly contours to the right around a peak for half a mile to a grassy saddle. Here the trail temporarily peters out, but follow rock cairns straight up the grassy slope to the right toward East Peak. After climbing 0.2 mile, look for the continuation of the trail—a lovely path that contours 0.7 mile to the left around East Peak. The trail finally ends by a spring on a grassy bench where yellow monkeyflowers, blue gentians, and white grass-of-parnassus bloom. This is a pleasant spot to rest before turning back to Mt. Howard—but don't rest too long, because the last gondola leaves at 5:45pm.

Other Options

The trail ends at East Peak's meadows, but sure-footed pathfinders can scramble onward 0.7 mile, across a dangerously steep talus slope, to Lone Rock Pass. Ahead is a tempting view of Aneroid Lake, 2.2 miles away and 1500 feet down. The route is not easy, but explorers sometimes bushwhack there and hike down the East Fork Wallowa Trail (see Hike #53) to the bottom of the tramway.

53 Aneroid Lake

Moderate (to waterfall)
3.8 miles round trip
1150 feet elevation gain
Open June through October
Use: hikers, horses

Difficult (to Aneroid Lake)
12 miles round trip
2950 feet elevation gain
Open mid-July through October

Admittedly, the trail to Aneroid Lake is long and steep. Granted, the path is dusty from countless boot soles and horse hooves. But if you're staying at Wallowa Lake State Park, this is the shortest route to one of the Wallowa high country's famous alpine lakes. The trail's final miles traverse gorgeous wildflower meadows backed by snowy 9000-foot peaks. If you decide to turn back before the lake, there's a consolation prize: a stop at a cool, cascading waterfall.

Note that group size is limited to 12. Tents must be at least 100 feet from the lakeshore, horse grazing is banned within 200 feet of the lake, and campfires are strongly discouraged. Firewood cutting from standing trees or snags is banned.

From Interstate 84 at La Grande, take exit 261 and follow Wallowa Lake signs on Highway 82 through Enterprise and Joseph a total of 78 miles. At the far end of Wallowa Lake, at milepost 6 where the main road veers right into Wallowa Lake State Park, turn left for a mile to road's end at the Wallowa Lake Trailhead. On the right is a state park picnic area. The trail itself begins on the left, beside a message board and wilderness registration box.

Up the trail 50 yards, a dusty path joins from nearby horse rental corrals. A few yards later, veer left onto the East Fork Wallowa River Trail. This path climbs up amid a mixed forest of Douglas fir, grand fir, and larch, with an understory of golden currant and thimbleberry. Ignore a gravel service road that joins from the left. You'll also want to ignore a dusty side trail that heads down to the right at the 0.8-mile mark—a return loop for the rental horse tours. After the fourth

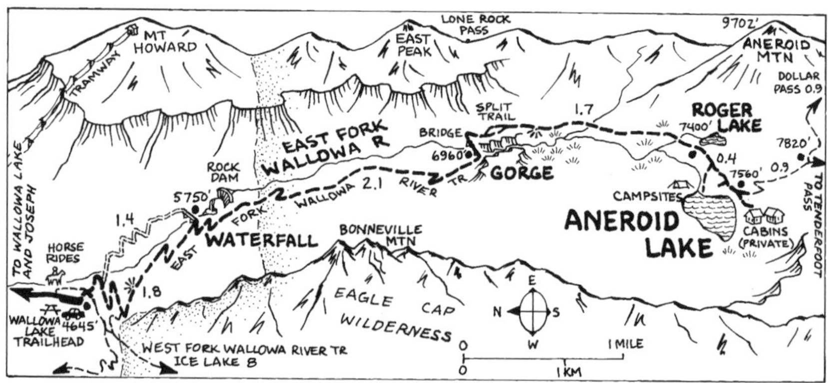

Bonneville Mountain from Aneroid Lake. *Opposite: Cabin at Aneroid Lake.*

switchback, when the trail crosses a rockslide with a view across Wallowa Lake, pause to listen to the flutter of quaking aspen leaves and the cheeping of pikas, the little round-eared "rock rabbits" that live under the boulders.

After 1.8 miles the path reaches a river bridge at the upper end of the old service road. Continue up the trail for two more quick switchbacks to the base of a 100-foot waterfall, a pleasant turnaround point for a moderate hike.

Above the waterfall the trail passes an old rock dam that diverts water through a flume to generate electricity. Then the path leaves the river, climbs steadily for 2 miles, recrosses the river on a footbridge below a dramatic gorge, and ambles up past two large meadows. Mosquitoes are a problem here in July.

The first lake you see, through the trees to the left, is Roger Lake. Continue 0.4 mile on the main trail, passing two side trails to camping areas, to a bench overlooking Aneroid Lake. The deep, blue-green lake, with its dramatic backdrop of Bonneville Mountain's white crags, was named by a fish surveyor who brought an aneroid ("liquid-free") barometer here in 1897 to measure elevation.

Just beyond the bench viewpoint, the trail forks. If you turn right, past a sign "Camp Halton; Private Property; Please Respect," you'll find a collection of eight log cabins that began as a 1920s silver mining camp. By the 1950s a colorful character named Charley Seeber had turned one of the rickety cabins into a store, supplying thirsty hikers with cold cans of soda pop—at prices nearly as steep as the trail from Wallowa Lake. Since then the property has changed hands several times and the rustic store has closed, but the cabins remain. Since the 1990s the owners have employed a caretaker who welcomes respectful visitors.

Other Options

If you've backpacked into the Aneroid Lake area, you might spend the next day exploring the high country with a day pack. One option is to continue up the main trail 0.9 mile and fork left for 0.9 mile to Dollar Pass, where you can bushwhack 0.3 mile to Dollar Lake (see Hike #50).

BC Falls. Below: Wallowa Lake from the viewpoint near BC Falls.

54 Wallowa Lake

Easy (to BC Falls)
2.6 miles round trip
680 feet elevation gain
Open June to mid-November
Use: hikers

Moderate (from campground)
4.9-mile loop
1050 feet elevation gain

Wallowa Lake State Park is one of Eastern Oregon's most popular recreation destinations, so it's surprising how few easy trails start here. Perhaps the best short family hike crosses a river gorge footbridge to a viewpoint beside BC Falls. If you don't mind a little scrambling, you can do the hike as a loop.

From Interstate 84 at La Grande, take exit 261 and follow Wallowa Lake signs on Highway 82 through Enterprise and Joseph a total of 78 miles. At the far end of Wallowa Lake, at milepost 6 where the main road veers right into Wallowa Lake State Park, turn left for a mile to road's end at the Wallowa Lake Trailhead. On the right is a picnic area. The trail itself begins on the left, beside a message board.

Up the trail 50 yards, a dusty path joins from nearby horse rental corrals. A few yards later the trail forks. Keep right on the West Fork Wallowa River Trail. After another 0.3 mile, fork to the right again—this time on the Chief Joseph Trail. This path heads up the gorge of the West Fork Wallowa River (ignore scramble paths to the right). The trail crosses the river on a footbridge, switchbacks uphill, and traverses through the woods to a sudden drop at BC Falls, a nice spot for lunch.

This 50-foot corkscrewed cascade gets so wild in winter that it washed out the footbridge here twice. The Forest Service gave up on replacing the bridge and no longer maintains the trail beyond this point.

Would you rather start your hike at the campground? If you're willing to scramble just a little, you can hike to BC Falls on a loop. When you drive into the entrance of Wallowa Lake's campground, keep straight for a quarter mile and curve right toward the boat ramp until you're almost to the lake. Then turn left 200 yards and park by a fish-cleaning log shelter on the left. Walk another 200 feet along the road toward the docks to find the trail, which climbs left into the woods just beyond a brown concrete block shed. Follow this nature trail 0.1 mile to an X-shaped junction and turn uphill to the right on a small steep path.

The rough path here follows the wooden pipe of an old water line on power company property, so access could someday be revoked. Expect to step over some roots and push a few branches aside. After 0.4 mile you'll switchback up through a steep meadow to a junction with the abandoned Chief Joseph Mountain Trail. Turn left for 1.2 miles to the waterfall at BC Creek. Although the bridge is gone, it's usually not hard to cross dry-footed on shaky poles and rocks. Then continue on the trail, keeping right at junctions for a mile to a marked junction with the West Fork Wallowa River Trail. Then turn left and keep left for 0.3 mile down to the Wallowa Lake Trailhead.

To complete the loop, you'll have to walk down along the road 0.5 mile. Then turn left on Bailey Lane, cross the river on a bridge, and take the next street to the right—a lane that takes you back to the campground and lakeshore.

Other Options

A shorter loop back from BC Falls follows a spectacular gorge to a 20-foot waterfall on the West Fork Wallowa River. This unofficial trail is too rough for children, and the route crosses power company land leased by the Boy Scouts, so access may be denied at any time. To find the route, hike 0.5 mile from BC Falls toward the Wallowa Lake Trailhead. When you reach a relatively level, grassy patch of pine woods, turn left on an unmarked side trail. This rough, steep path drops 0.3 mile to the waterfall. Then pass a Boy Scout campfire area and turn right on a dirt road past old camp buildings. The flash flood that destroyed BC Creek's footbridge in 2001 also devastated this camp. When you reach residential roads, turn right and keep right.

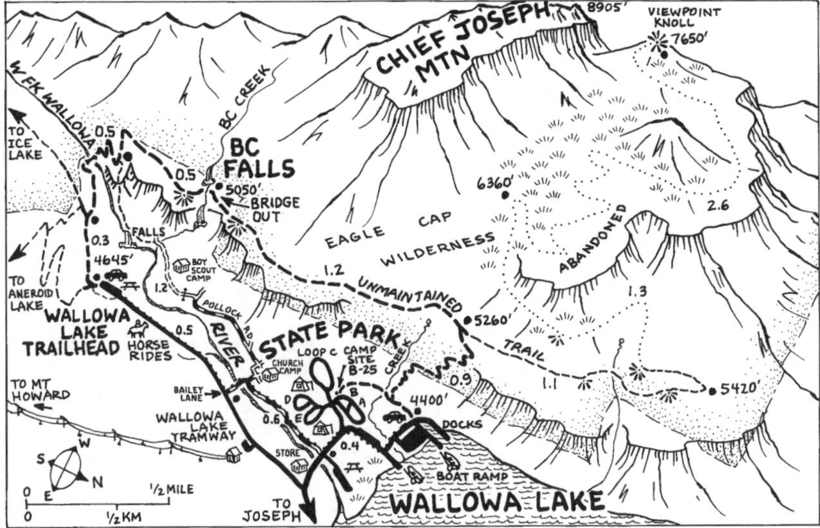

55 Ice Lake

Difficult
15 miles round trip
3300 feet elevation gain
Open mid-July through October
Use: hikers, horses

Backed by the two tallest peaks in Eastern Oregon, Ice Lake belongs to an alpine world halfway to the sky. You'll feel like you've climbed to the sky, too, after hiking up the seemingly endless switchbacks from the Wallowa Lake Trailhead. Although the round-trip distance is 15 miles, the scenery is so great that this is one of the most popular hikes in the Eagle Cap Wilderness.

Note that group size is limited to 12. To protect the fragile lakeshore, tents must be kept 100 feet away, grazing horses must be kept 200 feet from shore, and campfires are not allowed within a quarter mile.

From Interstate 84 at La Grande, take exit 261 and follow Wallowa Lake signs on Highway 82 through Enterprise and Joseph a total of 78 miles. At the far end of Wallowa Lake, at milepost 6 where the main road veers right into Wallowa Lake State Park, turn left for a mile to road's end at the Wallowa Lake Trailhead. On the right is a state park picnic area. The trail itself begins on the left, beside a message board and wilderness registration box.

Up the trail 50 yards, a dusty path joins from nearby horse rental corrals. A few yards later the trail forks. Keep right on the West Fork Wallowa River Trail for 0.3 mile to another fork. Go left for 50 steps and then keep straight, ignoring a dusty loop trail on the left used as a return route for rental horse tours.

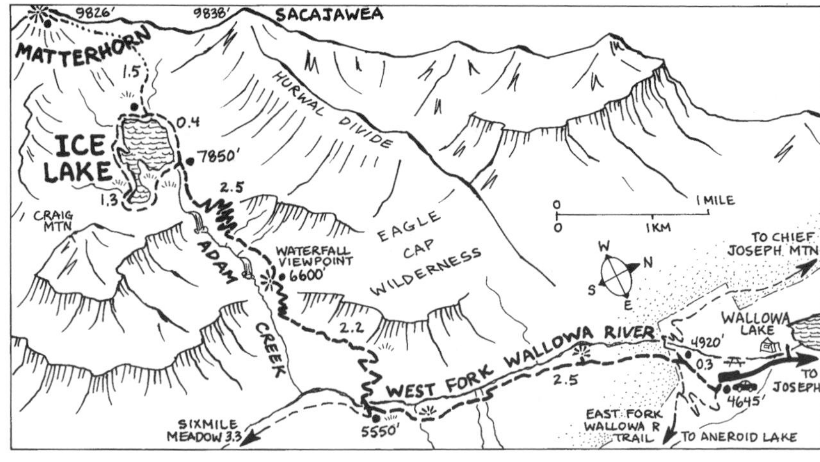

The Matterhorn from Ice Lake. Opposite: Gentians.

For the next 2.5 miles the West Fork Wallowa Trail climbs steadily through the woods, with occasional viewpoints down into the churning river's whitewater gorge. Then turn right at a fork, following an "Ice Lake" pointer. This trail promptly crosses the river and begins to switchback uphill.

Winter avalanches on these slopes have cleared stripes of steep meadow where you'll find purple aster, red paintbrush, and white pearly everlasting. Don't touch the stinging nettles, identified by their serrated leaves on tall stalks beside the trail.

After half a dozen switchbacks the path traverses nearly a mile to an overlook of cascading Adam Creek. There the path launches up a second set of switchbacks to a viewpoint of several spectacular waterfalls. The third and longest set of switchbacks brings the trail to a bridge across Ice Lake's outlet, the hike's goal. If you're backpacking, take the 1.7-mile loop around Ice Lake to find quiet campsites hidden away from the lake's fragile shore.

Other Options

The 9826-foot Matterhorn is a non-technical climb from Ice Lake. Keep right around the lakeshore trail 0.4 mile to an inlet creek at the far end of the lake. From there a sometimes faint path climbs steeply 1.5 miles up a broad ridge to the summit. The only requirements for scaling this relatively gentle, eastern face of the Matterhorn are stamina, strong knees, and excellent weather – turn back if lightning or clouds threaten. The mountain earns its name for the startling, 3000-foot white marble cliff on its far side, to the west.

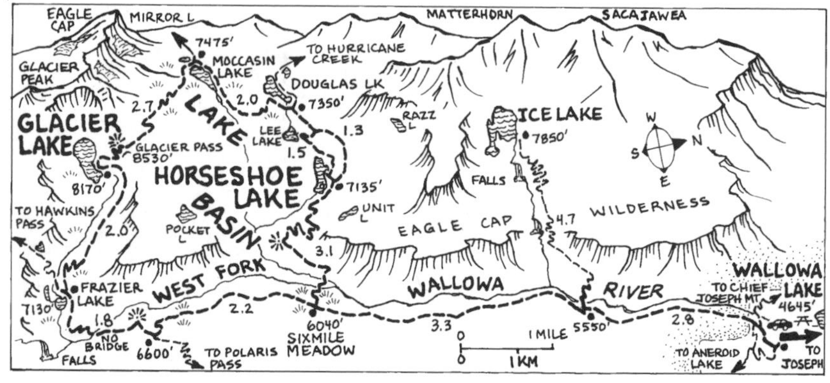

56 Horseshoe and Glacier Lakes

Difficult (to Horseshoe Lake)
18.4 miles round trip
2500 feet elevation gain
Open mid-July through October
Use: hikers, horses

Difficult (to Glacier Lake)
27.3-mile loop
4000 feet elevation gain

In the high Wallowas' wondrous Lake Basin, a dozen alpine lakes shimmer among wildflower meadows and polished granite outcrops, while ragged peaks rim the horizon. The price of admission here, however, is steep indeed: a dusty, 9-mile trudge up one of the most heavily used paths in the Eagle Cap Wilderness. As a result, only backpackers and equestrians can tour the miraculous high country between Horseshoe Lake and Glacier Lake.

The area's popularity has led to some restrictions. Group size is limited to 12 on trails and six in camps in the Lake Basin. Tents must be kept at least 100 feet from lakeshores and grazing horses must be at least 200 feet from lakes. Campfires are banned within a quarter mile of lakes, so bring a stove to cook.

Start by driving Interstate 84 to La Grande exit 261. Then follow Wallowa Lake signs on Highway 82 through Enterprise and Joseph a total of 78 miles. At the far end of Wallowa Lake, at milepost 6 where the main road veers right into Wallowa Lake State Park, turn left for a mile to road's end at the Wallowa Lake Trailhead. The trail begins on the left, beside a message board.

Up the trail 50 yards, a dusty path joins from the horse rental corrals on the left. A few feet later the trail forks. Keep right on the West Fork Wallowa River Trail for 0.3 mile to another fork. This time go left, and then ignore a dusty loop trail that peels off to the left 50 steps later—a return route for rental horse tours.

The West Fork Wallowa Trail climbs steadily through mixed woods of Douglas fir and lodgepole pine, with occasional viewpoints into the churning river's whitewater gorge. Near the Ice Lake junction at the 2.8-mile mark, you'll start traversing small meadows of pearly everlasting, thimbleberry, white cow parsnip, and purple aster. Watch out for stinging nettles—the serrated leaves on tall stalks beside the trail.

After 6.1 miles you'll reach a junction beside Sixmile Meadow, a broad field heavily used by backpackers. If you have to stay in this crowded area, pack used toilet paper out in a plastic bag rather than attempting to burn or bury it. To hike onward, turn right beside Sixmile Meadow to a horse ford at the swift, 30-foot-wide river. The hiker footbridge is gone, but logs usually allow you to cross dry-footed. Beyond the river the trail climbs a hot slope 3.1 miles to Horseshoe Lake, a pool with a small island and a huge reflection of a 1000-foot-tall white granite ridge. Horseshoe Lake is a common goal, but it would be a shame to turn back here. Much of the lake's shore is roped off for restoration, and the prettiest scenery lies ahead, on the grand loop to Glacier Lake. So sally onward if you can.

The trail forks beside Horseshoe Lake. Go right, although the two routes rejoin in about a mile. Beyond that point, follow "Glacier Pass" pointers. These will aim you to the left on a trail that skirts Douglas Lake. The path crosses 2 more miles of glorious alpine country to Moccasin Lake, and a close-up view of Eagle Cap. The meadows here blaze with giant blue gentian, delicate pink heather, and the aromatic, ball-shaped purple flowers of wild onion.

At a junction beside Moccasin Lake, turn left across a scenic isthmus between the lake's two parts. Next the loop trail climbs steeply over Glacier Pass to Glacier Lake. Until recently this spectacularly stark, rocky cirque was home to the Benson Glacier, the last in Eastern Oregon. From Glacier Lake, simply follow the trail downstream 6 miles to complete the loop to Sixmile Meadow. Along the way you'll pass grass-rimmed Frazier Lake, a 100-foot waterfall on the canyon cliffs, and a tricky, bridgeless river crossing on stepping stones.

Eagle Cap from Glacier Lake. *Opposite: Reflection in Horseshoe Lake.*

57 Hurricane Creek

Easy (to Falls Creek Falls)
0.6 miles round trip
200 feet elevation gain
Open May to mid-November
Use: hikers, horses

Moderate (to Slick Rock gorge)
6.2 miles round trip
750 feet elevation gain
Open mid-June through October

Difficult (to Echo Lake)
15.4 miles round trip
3400 feet elevation gain
Open late July through October

Pioneers named Hurricane Creek because they thought the broken trees in this otherwise picturesque valley must be the work of violent windstorms. In fact the valley is not particularly windy, but its sides are so steep that snow avalanches crash down through the forests in winter. In summer the avalanche clearings provide views up the valley to the startling, 3000-foot white marble face of the Matterhorn, second highest peak in the Wallowas.

For a quick sample of the valley's scenery, take a short walk to Falls Creek Falls, in a side canyon stripped by flash floods. For a longer hike, continue 3 miles up Hurricane Creek to a slot-like gorge with a pair of waterfalls. For an athletic challenge, tackle the steep trail up to Echo Lake's snowy cirque.

From Interstate 84, take La Grande exit 261 and follow Wallowa Lake signs 65 miles on Highway 82 to downtown Enterprise. Beyond the county courthouse 0.3 mile, where the highway jogs left toward Joseph, follow a "Hurricane Creek" pointer right onto Hurricane Creek Road 8205. After 5.2 miles this paved road forks to the right and becomes one-lane. Continue another 3.9 miles to the Hurricane Trailhead at road's end, where parking permits are required.

The trail sets off through an oddly mixed stand of quaking aspen, lodgepole pine, Douglas fir, and juniper. After just 150 yards a sign marks the side trail to Falls

Echo Lake. Above: The Matterhorn from Hurricane Creek.

Creek Falls on the right. Don't miss this quick side trip to see a 60-foot waterfall in a rock canyon stripped by winter floods. It's just 0.2 mile up to the best viewpoint, where the trail switchbacks up to the right.

Then return to the main trail and continue up alongside Hurricane Creek. This route occasionally emerges from the forest to cross barren boulder fields where avalanches or mudflows have roared out of side canyons. At the 3-mile mark you'll switchback up beside a 200-foot-deep rock slot where Hurricane Creek churns through a series of waterfalls. At the top of the gorge, the path crosses Slick Rock Creek, a side stream barreling down a bedrock chute.

If you're getting tired, this is a good place to have lunch before turning back. Take a moment to notice the bluebells, red paintbrush, and white yarrow blooming here amid sagebrush and subalpine fir. Also note two kinds of purple flowers: penstemon (shaped like trumpets) and aster (shaped like daisies).

If you're headed for Echo Lake, continue another 1.6 miles to a large rock cairn with the junction sign. But before you turn right on the Echo Lake Trail, you might want to continue straight 300 yards to a gorgeous meadow where the Hurricane Creek Trail fords its namesake stream. There is no bridge.

Then return to the Echo Lake Trail and follow this extremely steep, infrequently maintained track straight up the canyon wall. After 1.9 miles you'll crest what appears to be a summit. It's actually the lip of a basin with a pond. Here the trail briefly peters out in a meadow crowded with blue gentian blooms. Continue straight toward the lowest point on the horizon to find the continuation of the tread. Another 1.1 mile of climbing brings you to deep, blue Echo Lake. Listen here for the cheep of pikas, the little "rock rabbits" on the far shore's rockslide. If you're backpacking, remember to tent at least 100 feet from the lake.

Other Options

If you wade across the Hurricane Creek Trail's ford you can continue up the valley 5.3 miles to a junction in the Wallowas' popular Lake Basin. From there, one trail goes left to Douglas Lake and the Wallowa Lake Trailhead (see Hike #54), while another goes right to Mirror Lake and the Two Pan Trailhead (Hike #58). Both routes make good trips for backpackers who can arrange a car shuttle.

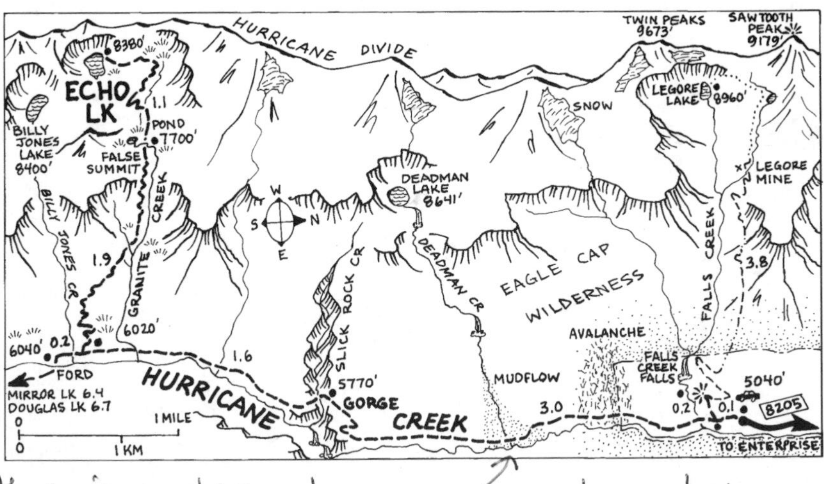

58 Mirror Lake and Eagle Cap

Moderate (to meadow crossing)
10.2 miles round trip
1500 feet elevation gain
Open mid-July through October
Use: hikers, horses

Difficult (to Mirror Lake)
14.8 miles round trip
2020 feet elevation gain

Difficult (to Eagle Cap)
19.6 miles round trip
4000 feet elevation gain
Open late July through October

Eight valleys radiate from 9572-foot Eagle Cap, the rock hub of the Wallowa Mountains. Although Eagle Cap is not quite the tallest peak in this range, its 360-degree view is unmatched, and a surprisingly well-graded trail climbs to the summit from the East Lostine River's meadows. If your goal's the summit, plan on a two-day trip. If you're out for a day hike, settle for a view of the cliff-edged peak from the Lostine meadows or Mirror Lake.

Note that group size is limited to 12 on trails and 6 in camps. Tents must be at least 100 feet from lakeshores, grazing horses must be at least 200 feet from lakes, and campfires are banned within a quarter mile of Mirror Lake.

Drive Interstate 84 to La Grande exit 261 and follow Wallowa Lake signs 55 miles on Highway 82 to Lostine. In the center of town, where the highway turns left, go straight on Lostine River Road, following a pointer for "Lostine River Campgrounds." This route is a two-lane paved road for the first 12.2 miles to the Lostine Guard Station. Then continue on a rougher, one-lane gravel road another 6.1 miles to road's end at the Two Pan Trailhead. Parking permits are required.

At the trailhead you'll find a large parking area for horse trailers on the left. Continue down to the right another 0.1 mile to a smaller parking area at the actual trailhead with a registration box. Start here and hike onward 0.1 mile to a

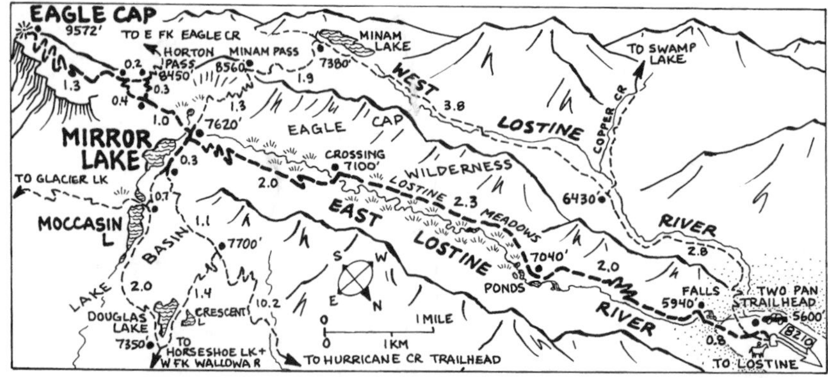

Eagle Cap from Mirror Lake. Opposite: Mirror Lake from Eagle Cap.

major fork. Veer left on the East Fork Lostine River Trail. This path climbs through a mixed forest of fir, lodgepole pine, and spruce for 0.8 mile to a footbridge across the river, just above an 8-foot waterfall. Beyond this the trail steepens and climbs up 11 switchbacks in 2 miles. As you pass rockslides listen for the cheep of pikas, the "rock rabbits" that gather grass to store in their rockslide burrows.

Finally the path levels off beside several ponds at the start of a long, beautiful meadow. Here at last is a grand view ahead to Eagle Cap. During the Ice Age, a glacier from Eagle Cap filled this high valley, sculpting it into a long U-shaped trough. When the glacier melted, it left a shallow lake that filled with sediment to become a meadow traced with the river's looping meanders. Ground squirrels scurry across the fields and then stand on their hind legs like prairie dogs to watch you pass. The trail along this meadow is nearly level for 2.3 miles to a stream crossing at the far end—a good turnaround point for a moderate hike.

If you're continuing, hop across the stream at a collapsed bridge. Beyond, the trail climbs 2 miles to a rock cairn at a junction within sight of Mirror Lake. Here the old glacier has left patches of bare, polished granite amid fields of brilliant alpine wildflowers—especially the thumb-sized blue blooms of gentian.

If you have time, detour left to see Mirror Lake's reflection of Eagle Cap's snowy cliffs. Then return to the rock cairn and keep left at all trail junctions. After a mile the trail forks at a signless post. Horton Pass is to the right, but the left-hand path is a shorter, if snowier, route. The two trails rejoin on a ridgecrest and climb left 1.3 miles to Eagle Cap's summit, a wind-swept knoll where only a mat of tortured whitebark pines and fuzzy alpine dandelions survive. A green ammunition can holds the summit climbers' register. Peer over a cliff to the east for a breathtaking look down at barren Glacier Lake. To the left, blue-green lakes dot the forested Lake Basin beneath the white cliffs of the Matterhorn. Still farther left, meadows roll down the barrel-shaped East Lostine River valley toward the Two Pan Trailhead where you began.

Other Options

Several backpacking loops return from the Mirror Lake area. If you can arrange a car shuttle, hike east through the Lake Basin and down the West Fork Wallowa River (see Hike #56) to the Wallowa Lake Trailhead for a total of 20.6 miles. If you don't have a shuttle, hike west to Minam Lake (see Hike #59) and down the West Lostine River for a total of 16.9 miles.

59 Minam Lake

Difficult (to Minam Lake)
11.6 miles round trip
1800 feet elevation gain
Open mid-July through October
Use: hikers, horses

Difficult (to Blue Lake)
15 miles round trip
2150 feet elevation gain

A range of white sawtooth crags looms above the wildflower meadows where Minam Lake spills into the West Lostine River. The scene is just pretty enough to help you forget the long, steep, dusty trail you've just hiked from the heavily used Two Pan Trailhead. To make the most of your time in this glorious high country, consider continuing around Minam Lake and up another 0.9 mile to Blue Lake, a smaller pool in a cirque ringed with snowy cliffs.

Start by driving Interstate 84 to La Grande exit 261 and following Wallowa Lake signs 55 miles on Highway 82 to the village of Lostine. In the center of town, where the highway turns left, go straight on Lostine River Road, following a pointer for "Lostine River Campgrounds." This route is a two-lane paved road for the first 12.2 miles to the Lostine Guard Station, a log cabin visitor information center. Stop here to fill your water bottles from the valley's only tested water supply, an outdoor drinking fountain. Then continue on a rougher, one-lane gravel road another 6.1 miles to road's end at the Two Pan Trailhead. Parking permits are required.

At the trailhead you'll find a large parking area for horse trailers on the left. Continue down to the right another 0.1 mile to a smaller parking area at the actual trailhead with a registration box. Start here and hike onward 0.1 mile to a major fork. Veer right on the West Fork Lostine River Trail. This path crosses a fork of the river on a concrete footbridge and climbs through a forest of Douglas fir, lodgepole pine, and grand fir. Views of the river or the mountains are rare at first. After 2.8 miles, turn left at a junction marked by a signpost in a rock cairn, and follow the path uphill

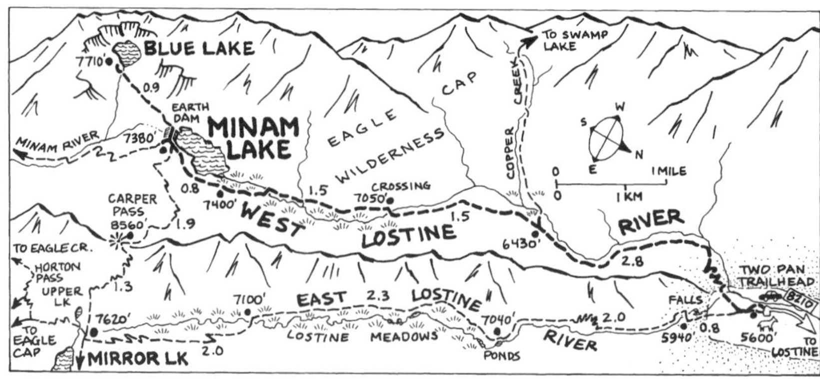

The West Lostine River. Opposite: Minam Lake.

across a rockslide of white boulders. Another 1.5 dusty miles brings you to an easy crossing of the 30-foot-wide West Lostine River on stepping stones.

The final 1.5 miles from this river crossing to Minam Lake are a delight, following the meandering river through meadows of blue gentian, red paintbrush, pink heather, and purple aster. At the lake itself, remember that campsites are banned within 100 feet of the shore and horse grazing is not allowed within 200 feet. Campfires are strongly discouraged. Group size is limited to 12.

Minam Lake used to be the headwaters of the Minam River, not the Lostine. If you continue 0.8 mile to the far end of the lake you'll discover an old, grassy dam built by early Wallowa County irrigators. This earth dike is only 15 feet tall, but it sufficed to send the lake spilling north instead of south. If you're headed for Blue Lake, walk across the dam and continue 0.9 mile to trail's end.

Other Options

If you're out for a 2- or 3-day backpack, try the spectacular 16.9-mile loop that returns from Minam Lake via Mirror Lake and the East Lostine River. Hike to the far end of Minam Lake, but just before the dam, switchback up to the left at a "Lake Basin" pointer. This path climbs 3.2 miles over scenic Minam Pass to a pair of trail junctions 70 yards apart, both marked by large rock cairns. If you turn right at the first one, you'll be headed up Eagle Cap. If you go straight at both, you'll visit Mirror Lake. If you keep left at both, you'll descend the East Lostine River back to your car.

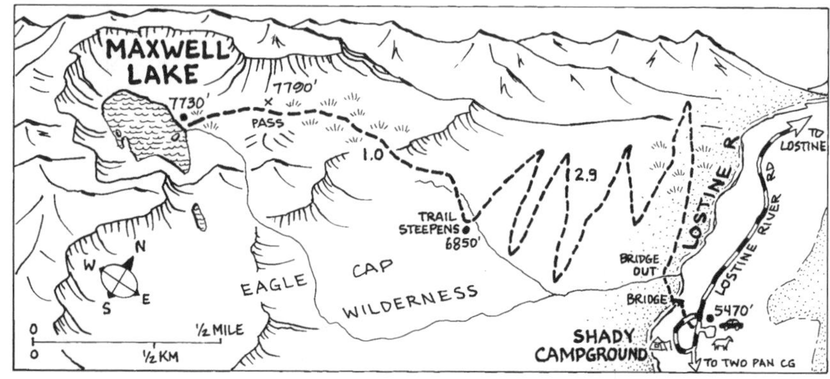

60 Maxwell Lake

Difficult
7.8 miles round trip
2420 feet elevation gain
Open late July through October
Use: hikers, horses

Left: Maxwell Lake. Opposite: Frances Lake.

Most of the Wallowa Mountains' beautiful alpine lakes are simply too far away to visit on a day hike—but not this jewel. Maxwell Lake sits in a glacially carved notch high on the side of the Lostine River canyon, with mountain crags and wildflowers. Just don't expect this trip to be a stroll. Although the trail starts out gently, it steepens later on. Maximum group size is 12.

From Interstate 84, take La Grande exit 261 and follow Wallowa Lake signs 55 miles to Lostine. Where the highway turns left in Lostine, go straight on Lostine River Road at a sign for "Lostine River Campgrounds." Follow this two-lane paved road 12.2 miles to the Lostine Guard Station and continue on rougher gravel another 5.6 miles to the Maxwell Lake Trailhead on the left, where parking permits are required.

The trail immediately crosses the road, passes some Shady Cove Campground sites, and crosses the Lostine River on a bridge. Just beyond is Maxwell Creek, and although the bridge here has washed out, it's usually easy to cross on big granite boulders. Then the path climbs 2.5 miles on seven long switchbacks.

At this point the trail suddenly steepens, scrambles straight up a dusty, rocky slope 0.8 mile to a pass, and ambles 0.2 mile down to its end beside Maxwell Lake. Almost the entire hike is on open slopes with views across the valley to high Wallowa peaks. As you climb higher you'll trade Oregon grape, wild strawberry, and bracken fern for monkshood, pink monkeyflower, and Christmas-tree-sized firs.

The lake itself is a deep blue pool with a cute little island and a backdrop of boulder rockslides below gigantic gray crags. Look for the blue blooms of gentians in the narrow heather meadow along the shore. Tents are banned within 100 feet of the lake, grazing horses must be kept 200 feet from the lake, and campfires are prohibited within a quarter mile.

61 Frances Lake

Difficult
17.8 miles round trip
4235 feet elevation gain
Open late July through October
Use: hikers, horses

Frances is the largest, highest, and most beautiful lake in the Wallowas that most hikers have never seen. That's because the trail here just won't quit. Sure, it's well graded, and it's not particularly difficult mile for mile, but there are simply so many miles and so many switchbacks that the trip becomes an athletic challenge.

From Interstate 84, take La Grande exit 261 and follow Wallowa Lake signs 55 miles on Highway 82 to the village of Lostine. Where the highway turns left in Lostine, go straight on Lostine River Road at a sign for "Lostine River Campgrounds." Follow this two-lane paved road 12.2 miles to the Lostine Guard Station, a visitor information center. Then continue on a rougher, one-lane gravel road another 2.9 miles and turn left into the parking area of the Bowman/Frances Lake Trailhead. Parking permits are required and maximum group size on the trail is 12.

Walk back down to the parking lot's entrance to find a sign marking the Frances Lake Trail on the left. This path briefly parallels the Lostine River Road before climbing through Douglas fir woods with lots of chattering, scolding, black-tailed Douglas squirrels. After 1.1 mile you'll reach the first big switchback, at a corner where you can hear an unseen waterfall.

For the next 2.8 miles the trail climbs past 15 more switchbacks, each progressively

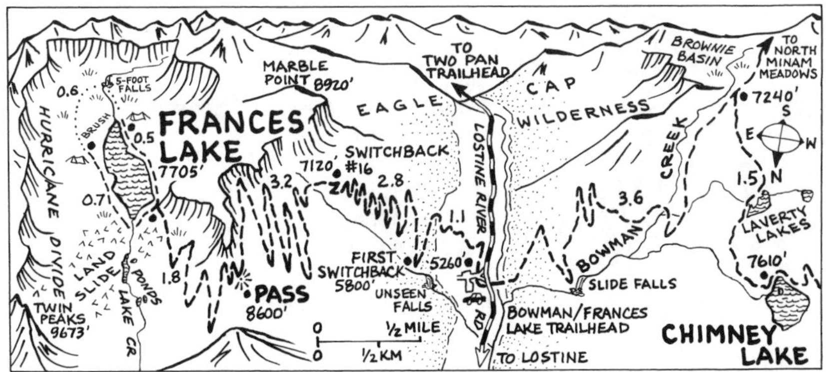

Frances Lake's outlet. Below: Chimney Lake.

shorter. Then you cross an open gully beneath Marble Point's gigantic white cliff and launch into another set of eight big switchbacks. Finally you crest at the trail's highest point, a red shale pass with a sweeping view of Frances Lake's box canyon. Perhaps a century ago a landslide from Twin Peaks dammed and deepened Frances Lake.

If you're planning on pitching a tent, note that the landslide has covered the lake's entire outlet area with an uncampable jumble of red boulders. Good campsites remain in the hummocky granite terrain a quarter mile before you get to the lake itself. Once you're at the lakeshore there are only two large campsites. One of these is 0.7 mile around the lake to the left, on a faint path that crosses the outlet creek. The other campsite is 0.5 mile to the right, on a trail that ends by the lake's fish-filled inlet creek.

While you're here, you could explore downstream to the landslide's swimmable ponds or you could hike around Frances Lake. To connect the trails on the left- and right-hand shores you'll have to bushwhack 0.6 mile, skirting above a patch of marshy brush on the lake's far bank.

62 Chimney and Steamboat Lakes

Difficult (to Chimney Lake)
10.2 miles round trip
2420 feet elevation gain
Open late July through October
Use: hikers, horses

Difficult (to Steamboat Lake)
29.3-mile loop
5920 feet elevation gain

Here are the Wallowa Mountains at their best: heather-rimmed alpine lakes, granite peaks, and wildflower meadows. But this isn't the famous, crowded Lake Basin below Eagle Cap's cliffs. It's a quieter corner of the Eagle Cap Wilderness.

For a strenuous day hike, explore Chimney Lake, in a basin with four other lakes. For a 3-day trip, continue across passes to Steamboat and Swamp Lakes.

Start by dirving to the Bowman/Frances Lake Trailhead described in Hike #61. Parking permits are required, and maximum group size on the trail is 12.

Walk back down to the parking lot's entrance to find a sign marking the Bowman Trail on the right. Follow this path across the road to a footbridge over the Lostine River. Then the trail climbs through a forest of lodgepole pine, fir, and spruce. After 0.8 mile the path switchbacks beside a 100-foot slide waterfall. Continue uphill another 2.8 miles to a trail junction at a rock cairn above Brownie Basin.

For the day hike, turn right at this junction for 1.5 miles to Chimney Lake, a large, swimmable lake with two small islands, set in a huge bowl of white granite rockslides and heather meadows. Campfires are banned within a quarter mile of all lakes in this area. If you have the time and energy, continue up the well-graded trail another 1.2 miles to a high pass with a terrific view across Chimney Lake to the high Wallowas' snowpeaks. From this pass, a 0.4-mile trail climbs up to the left to end at Hobo Lake, in a windy, barren cirque, while a 1.2-mile trail descends through the forest to the right to end at Wood Lake.

However, if you're prepared for the 3-day trek to Steamboat Lake, you might skip the detour to Chimney Lake altogether, and instead camp at less-visited John Henry Lake. To find it from the junction above Brownie Basin, follow a "Wilson Basin" pointer up 1.1 mile to Wilson Pass and continue down the far side of the pass 1.2 miles to the fourth switchback. When the trail turns sharply right, go straight on an unmarked side trail for 0.5 mile. John Henry Lake is shallow, and has mosquitoes until early August, but a low rise north of the lake has good campsites.

For the trip's second day, return to the main trail and continue west 3.7 miles down to a junction at North Minam Meadows. Turn left, following a "Copper Creek" pointer. After climbing 5.3 miles you'll reach Steamboat Lake, a large lake with several sandy coves, set in a granite basin. The few good campsites here may be taken, so consider continuing 1.7 miles to Swamp Lake. This misnamed, gorgeous alpine lake is surrounded by granite hillocks where tents can hide. Shaped

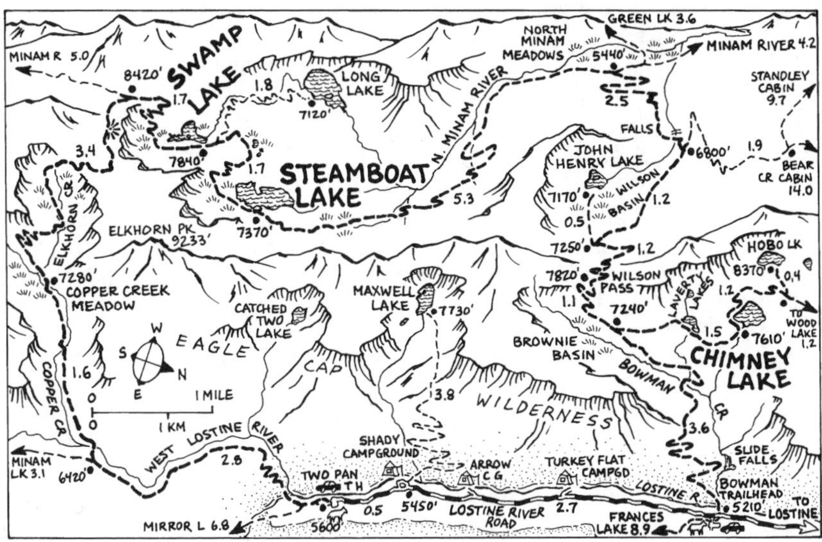

Swamp Lake. Below: Bear Creek at the guard station.

like a silhouette of Bullwinkle the moose, the lake features an island "eye" and "antler" inlets branching into snowmelt meadows. Fish are so scarce that bats skim insects off the surface in the evening. Campfires are banned within a quarter mile of either Swamp or Steamboat Lakes.

On the third day, climb from Swamp Lake to a high, granite upland and keep left at all junctions for 9.5 miles to descend along Copper Creek and the West Lostine River to the Two Pan Trailhead. If you haven't left a shuttle car here, you'll face a 3.2-mile walk down the road to your car at the Bowman Trailhead.

63 Bear Creek

Moderate
10 miles round trip
900 feet elevation gain
Open May through November
Use: hikers, horses

Refer to map on page 156.

The Wallowa Mountains are best known for alpine lakes and high country meadows. But here's another side of the range: a surprisingly low-elevation walk through a creekside forest to a historic log cabin.

To drive here from La Grande, take Interstate 84 exit 261 and follow Wallowa Lake signs 46.5 miles on Highway 82 to the village of Wallowa. Just as you are about to enter the town's city limits, turn right at a sign for North Bear Creek Road. Follow this road (which becomes Bear Creek Road and then Road 8250) for 3.2 paved miles and another 5 miles of good gravel to a fork. Following a "Boundary Campground" pointer, go straight on Road 040. In the next 0.8 mile you'll pass a string of nice campsites (some for equestrians) along 20-foot-wide Bear Creek. The road ends at a large trailhead parking lot. If you don't have a parking permit, you can buy one at a pay box here for $5. Maximum group size on the trail is 12.

The wide, nearly level trail sets off through a fir forest with snowberry and the white blooms of solomonseal. Big cottonwood trees line the bouldery creek. After 0.2 mile you'll cross the creek on a 60-foot bridge beside mossy, 200-foot-tall cliffs. For the next 4 miles the path simply follows the creek, occasionally climbing above it on bluffs. Then the trail crosses a rocky meadow to a trail sign cairn and a bridge across Goat Creek. Some nice, large campsites are in the forest to the right.

To find the log cabin, continue on the main trail 0.7 mile beyond Goat Creek and turn right on a large, unmarked side trail for 200 yards. The early 1900s Bear Creek Guard Station *(GPS location N45°24.648' W117°32.099')* is a masterfully built 18-by-24-foot structure, with carefully hewn log walls and dovetailed corners. Although the building itself is locked and closed to the public, the large porch makes a good place to stop for lunch. Note the telephone wire connectors on the outside wall that once tied this guard station to a network of fire lookouts and outposts such as Standley Cabin (Hike #64). Horse hitchrails and campsites are nearby. A side trail crosses a gravel bar 200 feet to a placid portion of Bear Creek.

Other Options

Backpackers or equestrians can continue into the Eagle Cap Wilderness for days (or weeks!). Beyond the guard station 0.5 mile the main trail forks. To the right, a path fords Bear Creek (which can be crossed dry-footed by August) and climbs along Dobbin Creek toward Standley Cabin. The main path up Bear Creek continues 15.4 miles to Wilson Basin, near John Henry Lake (Hike #62).

64 Standley Cabin

Difficult
10.2 miles round trip
1400 feet elevation gain
Open mid-July through October
Use: hikers, horses

Right: Standley Cabin's meadow.

This backdoor route into the Eagle Cap Wilderness follows a sparsely forested ridgecrest to a wildflower meadow with a spring and an old log cabin.

To drive here from Interstate 84, take La Grande exit 261 and follow Wallowa Lake signs 35 miles on Highway 82. At milepost 35, turn right onto Big Canyon Road 8270 for a slow, hour-long drive to the trailhead. After 10.8 miles on gravel Road 8270, veer left at a fork onto Road 050, a bumpier road that's passable for passengers cars if driven carefully. Take the largest road at junctions for the next 6.9 miles to a parking turnaround and horse ramp at the Bearwallow Trailhead *(GPS location N45°26.992' W117°35.312')*.

The trail starts at a registration box and sets off through a dusty, open forest. The woods here are recovering from an insect infestation that killed many of the lodgepole pines, allowing young subalpine firs and other trees to take hold. After 0.8 mile the path skirts Bald Knob through a meadow of sweet-smelling mint and

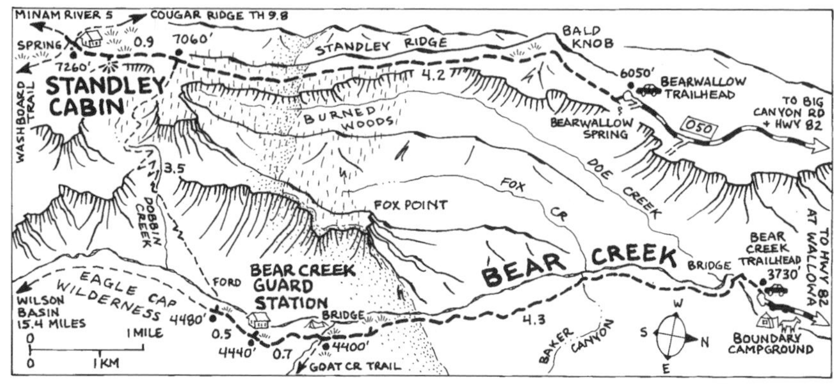

petalless coneflowers. Then the trail traces a breezy little ridgecrest with views.

At the 2.5-mile mark you'll enter a 1990s fire zone of silver snags and pink fireweed that extends 1.6 miles to the Dobbin Creek trail junction. Continue on the main trail 0.9 mile up to Standley Cabin *(GPS location N45°22.922' W117°34.504')*. The 18-by-24-foot log building is locked and closed to the public, but has a nice porch. Beside the cabin, a muddy spring launches a lovely moss-lined creek across a broad, grassy meadow of coneflowers and hellebore (corn lily). Camping is banned within 50 yards of the spring, but there are plenty of sites beyond that limit.

Although this cabin is the logical turnaround point for a day hike, it lacks a view. To find a better vantage point, head back down the trail 0.3 mile to the far end of the meadow and bushwhack up to the right 100 feet to a clifftop rim. From there you can survey the green cirque bowl of Dobbin Basin, the immense gorge of Bear Creek, and the distant summits of high Wallowa peaks, including the Matterhorn's white cliff and Sacajawea's brown pyramid.

The view from Rock Springs Trailhead. *Opposite: Meadow by abandoned lodge.*

65 Minam River via Rock Springs

Difficult
8.4 miles round trip
2500 feet elevation **loss**
Open mid-June through October
Use: hikers, horses

The Minam River gathers its forces high in the Wallowa Mountains and barrels down a 2500-foot-deep rimrock canyon for 40 miles. There are no easy paths to this mighty torrent in the heart of the Eagle Cap Wilderness, but the trail down from Rock Springs is the least difficult. There's plenty of room for camping, too, beside a meadow with the explorable ruins of an old lodge. Just be sure to save some energy for the hike back up to your car on the canyon rim.

From Interstate 84, take La Grande exit 261 and follow Wallowa Lake signs on Highway 82 toward Elgin for 8 miles to the grain elevator silos at Alicel. Turn right on paved Alicel Lane for 0.6 mile to a T-shaped junction, and turn left to keep on Alicel Lane through several zigs and zags for another 3.4 miles. Then turn right on gravel Gray's Corners Road for exactly 1 mile and turn left on an unmarked gravel road that climbs steeply uphill. After 10.2 miles you'll cross a bridge to another T-shaped junction. Turn left on gravel Road 62. After 6.8 miles veer right at an unmarked fork and then continue on Road 62 for another 3 miles to the Rock Springs Trailhead, between mileposts 12 and 13.

At the trailhead you'll see a horse trailer parking area on the left, but the trail itself starts at a sign 200 feet farther along the road on the right, and you may want to park your car on the shoulder there *(GPS location N45°24.319′ W117°42.397′)*. Note that group size on the trail is limited to 12 people and/or 18 head of stock.

The woods along the canyon rim are full of huckleberry bushes, so if you're here during the last three weeks of August, stock up on the blue fruit. The trail marches

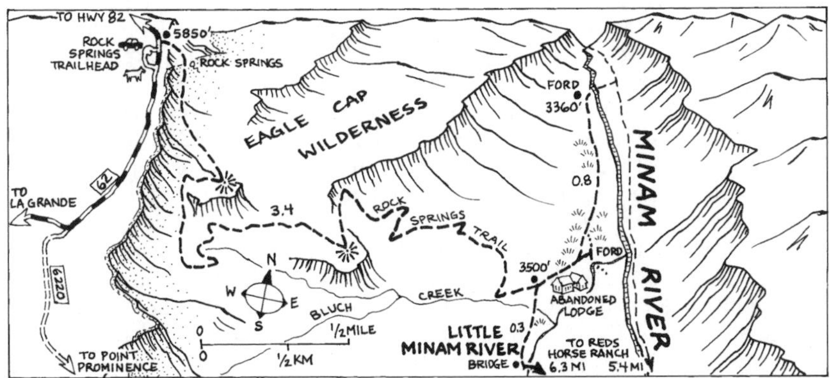

downhill through an open forest of lodgepole pine, subalpine fir, grand fir, and larch. Twice the path emerges from the woods at ridge-end viewpoints where you can look up the Minam River's canyon to the snowy peaks of the high Wallowas.

At the bottom of the trail keep left at a junction to a collection of mostly roofless log cabin ruins from an old lodge *(GPS location N45°24.120' W117°40.393')*. Beyond the cabins the trail traverses a large grassy field. The main trail appears to go right, but it merely ends at the bank of the 20-foot-wide Little Minam River, a popular spot to water horses. To find the larger Minam River you'll need to keep straight (and level) through the meadow. After more than half a mile this path reaches a ford of the boulder-strewn, 80-foot-wide river. Horses can manage this bridgeless crossing, but hikers should plan on turning back here. In early summer the dangerously swift current is waist deep. By late summer it's still knee deep and cold.

Other Options

You don't need to risk fording the Minam River to continue into the Eagle Cap Wilderness. Instead go back to the junction by the ruined lodge and veer left on the trail up the Little Minam River. After 0.3 mile you'll cross the stream on a bridge. Continue another 5.2 miles and you'll reach a trail junction in a pass (see Hike #66). Turn left for 1.1 mile to Reds Horse Ranch (another old lodge), where a bridge crosses the Minam River to the Minam River Trail.

66 Minam River via Moss Springs

Difficult
15.2 miles round trip
2300 feet elevation gain
Open mid-June through October
Use: hikers, horses

Popular with equestrians, the trails radiating from Moss Springs Campground seem long and dusty to hikers. The top goal is Reds Horse Ranch, a closed old lodge by a vast meadow with the only bridge across the Minam River for miles.

Make a special note of Eagle Cap Wilderness rules: Maximum group size on the trail is 12 people and/or 18 head of stock. Horses may not be hitched or tethered to trees at campsites, or within 100 feet of any stream. Any extra horse feed brought along must be certified to be free of weed seeds that might introduce alien plants.

From La Grande, take Interstate 84 exit 261, follow Wallowa Lake signs 1.8 miles to a stop at a major intersection, and go straight on Highway 237 for 14 miles to Cove. In Cove follow the highway as it turns right on Main Street for a block, but then turn left at a white steepled church onto French Street at a sign for Moss Springs Campground. Follow this paved street (which becomes Mill Creek Lane and then Road 6220) for a total of 9.1 miles to the campground. The last 6.9 miles are relentlessly uphill on narrow, washboard gravel. Fork to the right through the campground for 0.3 mile to the trailhead parking area at the far end of a long loop.

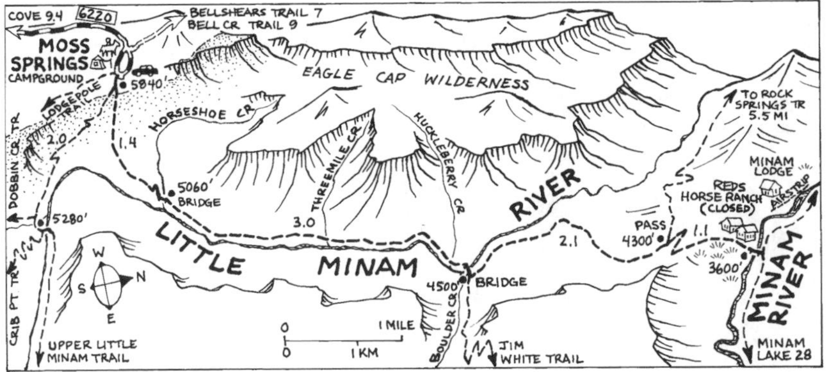

A fee box is provided for purchasing a trailhead parking permit. You don't need a trailhead permit if you're staying in the campground ($5 per site), a horse-friendly area with corrals and hitching rails.

Don't set off on the marked Lodgepole Trail. Start instead at a message board beside the parking area and follow a broad, very dusty track 100 yards to a major fork. Keep left on the Horse Ranch Trail. After descending gradually 1.4 miles through a forest of grand fir, subalpine fir, and larch, you'll cross Horseshoe Creek on a bridge and start following the 15-foot-wide Little Minam River downstream. Blue huckleberries ripen along the trail in August. In another 3 miles you'll cross the river on a bridge, a possible turnaround point for hikers.

Beyond the Little Minam bridge turn left at a junction, traverse 2.1 miles to a pass, and fork to the right for a mile down to the broad grassy field at Reds Horse Ranch. The caretaker who lives here often offers tours. Perhaps the nicest campsites are across the river bridge and to the right along the Minam River Trail—a wilderness thoroughfare that continues 28 miles to the river's head in the high country at Minam Lake (Hike #59).

The Minam River. *Opposite: Blue huckleberries.*

67 Catherine Creek Meadows

Moderate
8.6 miles round trip
1450 feet elevation gain
Open June to mid-November
Use: hikers, horses

A log cabin from the early 1900s sits at the edge of a meadow in this quiet corner of the Eagle Cap Wilderness. The well-graded trail to the meadow follows the North Fork of Catherine Creek up a long, curving valley gouged from the mountains by an Ice Age glacier. Expect to share the meadow with grazing cattle.

If you're driving from La Grande, take Interstate 84 exit 265 and follow Highway 203 for 14 miles to Union. In the center of town, turn left on Beakman Street at a sign for Medical Springs and continue on Highway 203 for 11.4 miles. Between mileposts 11 and 12, turn left on Catherine Creek Lane (Road 7785) for 6.1 gravel miles to the Catherine Creek Trailhead and horse ramp on the right. Parking permits are required. Maximum group size on the trail is 12.

If you're driving from Baker City, take Interstate 84 north 6 miles to exit 298 and follow Highway 203 through Medical Springs a total of 29 miles. Between mileposts 12 and 11, turn right on Catherine Creek Lane for 6.1 gravel miles.

The trail doesn't begin at the official trailhead parking area, but rather 0.2 mile farther up Road 7785, where the road ends at a primitive, free, 6-site campground by the creek. Parking is tight, so only leave your car here if you're planning to camp.

From the campground message board *(GPS location N45°09.245' W117°36.931')*, the trail climbs gradually through a grand fir forest along the river. After 1.3 miles, when the trail crosses the 30-foot-wide creek on a bridge, take a moment to look for water ouzels, the dark, robin-sized birds that whir from boulder to boulder before diving underwater to search for insect larvae on the creek bottom.

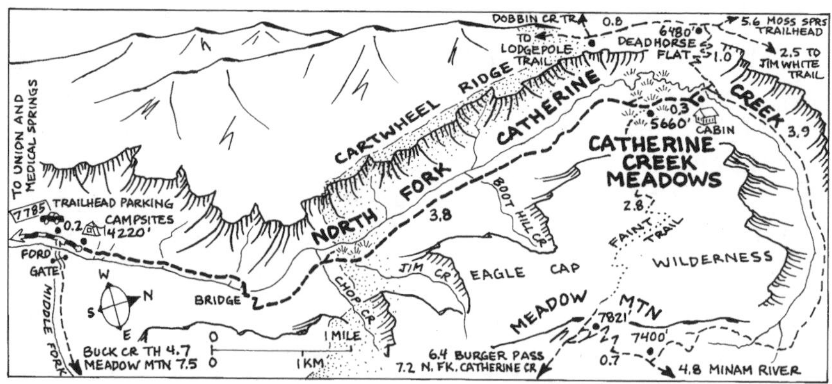

For the next mile the trail climbs through a zone of huckleberry bushes, where hikers can pick ripe blue berries during the latter half of August. Finally the path enters Catherine Creek Meadows, a broad, half-mile-long field. A few dozen cattle crop the grass and wildflowers. Grasshoppers jump out of your path and fat ground squirrels stand on their hind paws to watch you pass. In the midst of the meadow, a rock cairn marks a junction with the faint Meadow Mountain Trail. Continue on the main trail to the end of the meadow and through a spruce grove to a smaller meadow with an unsigned but obvious trail fork.

Veer right at this fork for 200 yards to find the cabin *(GPS location N45°13.221' W117°36.588')*. The 14-by-18-foot log building has a shake roof, two glass windows, four cots, a box stove, and a cupboard. Graffiti on the cupboard and door date to 1944, with comments such as "Dam Mosquitoes" (1994), "10 feet of snow" (December 23), and "Fishing bad, Borbon perfect" (1961).

Other Options

The main trail forks to the left near the cabin and continues deeper into the Wilderness. For a 16.1-mile loop, head up the creek 4.6 miles to the summit of Meadow Mountain, keep left on the China Ridge Trail 1.6 miles, and turn right for 5.9 miles to your car, following Squaw Creek and the Middle Fork of Catherine Creek. The loop ends with 3.3 miles on an old road and a knee-deep wade at a river ford.

Catherine Creek Meadows. *Opposite: Corner of Catherine Creek log cabin.*

68 Burger Pass

Difficult
8.8 miles round trip
2440 feet elevation gain
Open mid-July through October
Use: hikers, horses

Left: China Cap from Burger Pass.

This path through volcanic ash to an alpine viewpoint might be the dustiest trail you've ever hiked. But at Burger Pass, in a quiet corner of the Eagle Cap Wilderness, you can stand on the dividing line of a mountain range with two very different personalities. To the east, the Wallowa Mountains flash white granite snowpeaks in the sun. To the west, the range is a brown basalt tableland.

The dust on this trail is a result of the Wallowas' schizophrenic geologic past. The range began as a string of Pacific Ocean islands nearly a billion years ago. Currents in the Earth's molten mantle gradually "rafted" the islands eastward and scraped them off onto the North American continent. Later additions to Oregon's shore left the Wallowas inland, and erosion wore the islands down to their granite roots.

About 17 million years ago the continent buckled, allowing volcanic eruptions to roar up out of cracks in the ground near the Grande Ronde River. Enormous floods of basalt lava buried most of Eastern Oregon and Washington. But then the Wallowas rose again. During the Ice Age, glaciers wore the basalt off the higher, eastern half of the mountains, exposing the white granite underneath. Today Burger Pass balances between the granite peaks and the basalt tablelands. The dust of the trail is volcanic ash sandwiched in between.

If you're driving here from La Grande, take Interstate 84 exit 265 and follow Highway 203 for 14 miles to Union. In the center of town, turn left on Beakman Street at a sign for Medical Springs and continue on Highway 203 for 11.4 miles. Between mileposts 11 and 12, turn left on Catherine Creek Lane (alias Road 7785)

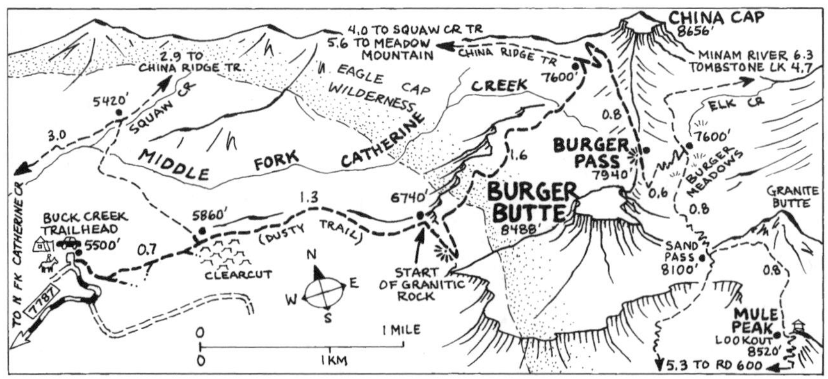

for 4.2 gravel miles, turn right on Road 7787 for 3.9 miles to a fork, and veer left for 0.3 mile to the Buck Creek Trailhead on the right, where parking permits are required *(GPS location N45°08.846' W117°34.259')*.

If you're driving from Baker City, take Interstate 84 north 6 miles to exit 298 and follow Highway 203 through Medical Springs a total of 29 miles. Between mileposts 12 and 11, turn right on Catherine Creek Lane for 4.2 gravel miles, turn right on Road 7787 for 3.9 miles, and fork left for 0.3 mile.

The trail begins at a message board and follows an old logging road a quarter mile. Then fork to the left on a genuine trail that is scheduled for realignment to avoid a shadeless 1990s clearcut. By the 0.9-mile mark you'll be in cooler woods, but the dust is still 2 inches deep, puffing at each step like cocoa powder. It comes as a relief at the 2-mile mark when the trail switchbacks up from the volcanic ash into less dusty granite terrain. Hop across the 4-foot-wide Middle Fork of Catherine Creek and climb to a junction with the China Ridge Trail. Turn right for a 0.8-mile climb through pink heather and spire-shaped subalpine firs to Burger Pass *(GPS location N45°08.640' W117°30.817')*, a good turnaround goal. To the right, remnant lava layers stacked atop Burger Butte resemble a gigantic Big Mac.

Other Options

Beyond Burger Pass the trail dives 0.6 mile down into the white granite canyon of Burger Meadows. For a longer hike, continue to the right on a steep, dusty 0.8-mile path to Sand Pass (in the ashy contact zone between granite and basalt), and traverse another 0.8 mile to the view at the historic Mule Peak fire lookout cabin, now shuttered closed.

69 Tombstone and Traverse Lakes

Difficult (to Traverse Lake)
13.4 miles round trip
2290 feet elevation gain
Open mid-July through October
Use: hikers, horses

Difficult (to Tombstone Lake)
17.8 miles round trip
3550 feet elevation gain

Right: Echo Lake.

Snowy crags surround Tombstone and Traverse Lakes like castle walls, yet within these alpine fortresses are delightful gardens—gentle lakeshore meadows of pink heather and white phlox. Crowds aren't likely, and not just because these lakes lie on the less-visited, southern side of the Wallowa Mountains. The price of admission to tour these castle gardens is a bit steep: long trails with lots of switchbacks.

Because the gardens are so fragile, campsites must be at least 100 feet from any lakeshore, horses may not be grazed within 200 feet of lakes, and fires are banned within a quarter mile of Tombstone or Traverse Lakes. The use of snags for firewood is prohibited, and downed wood is scarce. Group size is limited to 12.

From La Grande, take Interstate 84 exit 265 and follow Highway 203 for 14 miles

Tombstone Lake from the trail's pass. Opposite: Arrow Lake.

to Union. In the center of town, turn left on Beakman Street at a sign for Medical Springs and continue on Highway 203 for 14.2 miles to the highway's summit. At a pointer for "West Eagle" turn left on gravel Road 77 for 15.7 miles to the West Eagle Trailhead parking area on the left (*GPS location N45°04.783′ W117°28.599′*). The final 5.4 miles of this road are so rough that cars creep along at 10 miles per hour.

If you're driving from Baker City, take Interstate 84 north 6 miles to exit 298 and follow Highway 203 for 18 miles to Medical Springs. Following signs for Boulder Park, turn right on Eagle Creek Drive, which soon becomes gravel. After 1.6 miles,

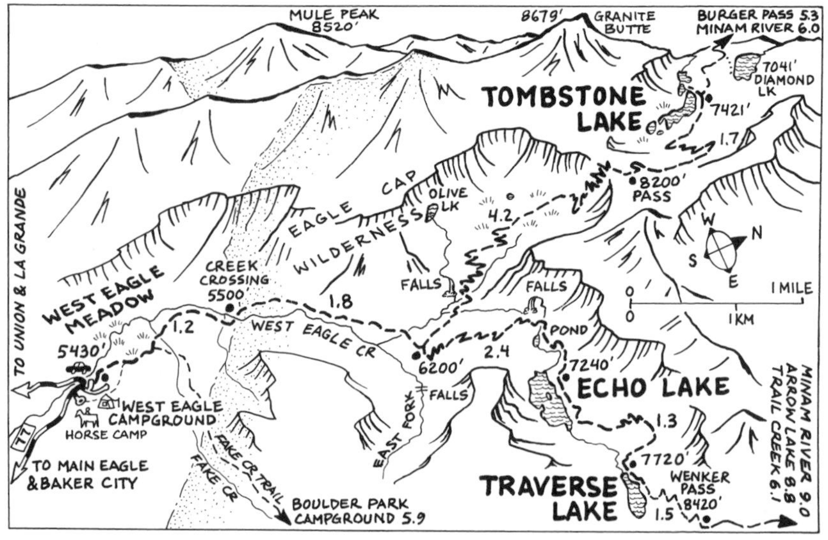

fork left onto gravel, one-lane Big Creek Road 67. In another 14 miles, turn left on Road 77 for 0.7 mile, and then turn left to keep on Road 77 for 4.5 miles to the West Eagle Trailhead. The final 3.2 miles are bumpy and very slow.

The trailhead area has 24 campsites and a large equestrian campground. Look for nice walk-in tent sites where the creek meanders out into West Eagle Meadow, a broad field visited by elk and deer at dusk. Expect to pay $5 per car at a fee box if you don't already have a Northwest Forest Pass.

The trail launches into a forest of grand fir, Douglas fir, Engelmann spruce, and larch. Douglas squirrels scold from the trees and red-shafted flickers swoop from trunk to trunk. After 1.1 mile the path meets 15-foot-wide West Eagle Creek. There is no bridge, but logs and boulders upstream make a dry crossing possible. Then continue 1.8 miles up the scenic canyon to a signpost at a fork.

Here you have to choose between the tough trip to Traverse Lake (to the right) or the even tougher trip to Tombstone Lake (to the left). If you take the left-hand fork toward "Elk Creek" you'll switchback up past falls and meadows 4.2 miles, gaining 2000 feet to a pass with a view of Tombstone Lake—but to actually reach the lakeshore you'll still have to hike another 1.7 miles, losing 780 feet of elevation. Whew! You may be ready for a swim when you get there, and if so, note that the lowest (and farthest) of Tombstone Lake's four connected pools is least icy. Granite boulders around the lake really are as white and smooth as cemetery slabs.

If the trip to Tombstone sounds like a killer, keep right at the trail's fork and switchback up a mere 1040 feet in 2.4 miles to Echo Lake. With echoing cliffs and a little island, this lake would be an excellent destination but for the fact that Traverse Lake, another 1.3 miles up the trail, is an even more spectacular goal.

70 Arrow and Eagle Lakes

Difficult (to Arrow Lake)
10.6 miles round trip
2720 feet elevation gain
Open mid-July through October
Use: hikers

Difficult (to Eagle Lake)
19.1-mile loop
4080 feet elevation gain

Refer to map on page 167.

The Ice Age glaciers that scalloped the southern Wallowa Mountains left granite lake basins around the rim of Eagle Creek's spectacular valley like cupboards in a giant's kitchen. Day hikers only have time to peek in one of those cupboard doors, but backpackers can visit one alpine lake after another on a loop. The difficult route is impassable for horses, making this one of the few hiker-only Wallowa tours.

From Baker City, take Interstate 84 north 6 miles to exit 298 and drive 19 miles on Highway 203 to Medical Springs, an old stagecoach stop. (If you're coming via La Grande, take Interstate 84 exit 265, follow Highway 203 for 14 miles to Union, and turn left to continue on Highway 203 for 21 miles to Medical Springs.) At

Eagle Creek Meadow. *Opposite: Bear Lake.*

Medical Springs turn east on Eagle Creek Drive, following the first of many signs for Boulder Park. The road soon becomes gravel. After 1.6 miles, fork left onto one-lane Big Creek Road 67. After another 14.6 miles, turn left on Road 77 for 0.8 mile and then keep straight on Road 7755 for 3.7 miles to its end at the Main Eagle Trailhead, where parking permits are required. A landslide obliterated the old Boulder Park Resort near here, but the name lives on at the 10-site Boulder Park Campground and horse unloading site just before the trailhead. Maximum group size on the trail is 12 people and/or 18 head of stock. Tents and fires are banned within 100 feet of lakeshores.

The trail sets off across the debris of the landslide, launched from a white scar on the opposite canyon wall. The path crosses 30-foot-wide Eagle Creek on footbridges at the 0.6-mile and 2.5-mile marks. Then you'll hop on rocks across Copper Creek and glimpse the 60-foot fan of Copper Creek Falls to the left. In another 300 yards, look for a sign marking the small Bench Trail that forks uphill to the left.

The Bench Trail begins so steeply that it resembles a bobsled chute. It climbs across slopes of sagebrush and wildflowers for 1.5 miles to a crest. Continue 150 yards downhill to a confusing turn beside Bench Canyon Creek. Instead of going straight to a small campsite, cross the creek to the left on the less-obvious main trail. This path climbs another 0.8 mile to Arrow Lake *(GPS location N45°06.613' W117°23.540')*, in a spectacular granite bowl with pink heather and blue gentians.

To continue on the loop, follow the Bench Trail past Arrow Lake over a pass 0.8 mile, turn right for 1.6 miles to another pass with a panoramic view, and continue 2 miles down to a 4-way trail junction. To the right is Cached Lake (*GPS location N45°07.076' W117°22.140'*), a lovely pool rimmed with alpine wildflower meadows and rockslides. Straight ahead is a clifftop viewpoint and campsite. Turn left, however, to continue the loop route. In another mile, veer left to detour 1.1 mile up to the 20-foot-tall stonework dam that has converted the otherwise immensely scenic Eagle Lake into a reservoir. Fires are banned at Eagle Lake, but the bare rock bluff at its outlet makes a dramatic campsite. To complete the loop from Eagle Lake, return 1.1 mile to the main trail and follow it 6.2 miles back to your car.

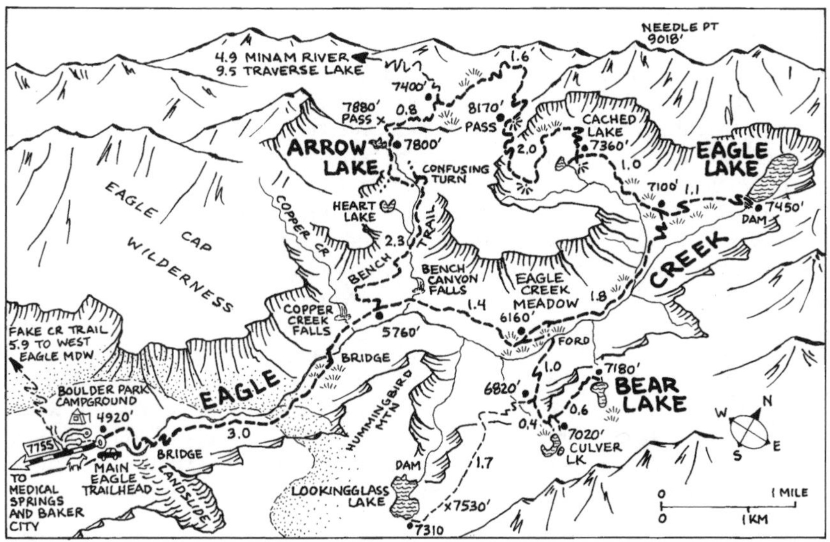

71 Bear Lake

Moderate (to Eagle Creek Meadow)
8.8 miles round trip
1250 feet elevation gain
Open early July through October
Use: hikers, horses

Difficult (to Bear Lake)
12.8 miles round trip
2240 feet elevation gain
Open mid-July through October

Not all of the best goals in the southern Wallowa Mountains are as difficult to reach as Arrow Lake and Eagle Lake (Hike #70). Even families with children can generally manage the trek to Eagle Creek Meadow, a creekside field surrounded by granite canyon walls reminiscent of the Swiss Alps. From there, a side trail climbs the canyon wall 2 miles to beautiful Bear Lake, one of the few large alpine lakes in Northeast Oregon that has never been dammed to serve as an irrigation reservoir.

Start by driving to the Main Eagle Trailhead described in Hike #70, at the end of gravel Road 7755 near the free Boulder Park Campground. Parking permits are required. Remember that group size on the trail is limited to 12 people and/or 18 head of stock. Campsites must be at least 100 feet from any lakeshore, tethered horses must be at least 100 feet from water or campsites, and fires are strongly discouraged. Firewood may only be gathered from downed, dead trees.

The trail begins on the outwash plain of a landslide, whose source is visible as a white scar on the opposite canyon wall. After crossing scenic footbridges over

Eagle Creek at the 0.6-mile and 2.5-mile marks, you'll have to hop on rocks across Copper Creek. Look for the 60-foot fan of Copper Creek Falls to the left. Continue on the main trail past the 8-foot waterfall of Bench Canyon Creek and hike another mile to the start of Eagle Creek Meadow's vast opening. Where the trail enters the clearing you'll cross an exceptionally well preserved example of glacial polish. This valley's Ice Age glaciers smoothed the bedrock granite here as they ground past 6000 years ago, and the shiny finish still gleams as if wet.

At a well-marked fork, veer right on the Bear Lake Trail into the grassy flat of Eagle Creek Meadow. If this is your goal, don't camp in the meadow itself, but rather in the trees at the far end. If you're continuing to Bear Lake, head for the creek, where you'll find a 30-foot-wide ford. By mid-August you may be able to complete this crossing dry-footed. On the far shore the path climbs most of a mile to a fork. To the right a 1.7-mile path climbs over a ridge to Lookingglass Lake, a reservoir. Instead go left 0.4 mile, where two different side paths detour to Culver Lake, backed with a ring of snow and a spectacular amphitheater of cliffs. Keep left for another 0.6 mile to reach Bear Lake *(GPS location N45°06.036′ W117°20.908′).* A substantial fir forest abuts this lake on three sides, but the far end opens onto a large meadow with a colossal backdrop of cliffs. There's plenty of room to camp on the sparsely wooded rise overlooking Eagle Creek's canyon.

72 Hidden Lake

Difficult
16.4 miles round trip
2650 feet elevation gain
Open mid-July through October
Use: hikers, horses

Deep in the Wallowas, this lake seems a hidden Eden. Snowy crags surround a high valley of wildflower meadows, subalpine firs, brooks, and tarns. From rocks beside the still green waters you can dive into the depths or sit and watch fish. The gate protecting this secret glen is distance: 8.2 miles of trail that bar all but backpackers, equestrians, and the most determined of day hikers.

If you venture here, remember that groups cannot be larger than 12. Campsites must be at least 100 feet from any lakeshore, tethered horses must be at least 200 feet from lakes, and campfires are strongly discouraged. Firewood cutting from standing trees or snags is prohibited, and downed wood is scarce.

From Interstate 84 at the north edge of Baker City, take exit 302 and follow Highway 86 east toward Richland 23.2 miles. At a pointer for Sparta just beyond milepost 23, turn uphill to the left on gravel Sparta Lane for 4.9 miles. Then turn left on East Eagle Creek Road for 5.8 miles to a 5-way road junction. Veer right on Empire Gulch Road 7015 for 4.8 miles and cross a bridge to a T-shaped junction. Turn left on Road

77 for 2.8 miles and fork to the right on East Eagle Road 7745 for another 6.4 miles. Only if you're pulling a horse trailer should you heed the "Eagle Creek Trailhead" pointer and turn right into an equestrian staging area. Otherwise, continue straight another 0.8 mile to a parking turnaround loop at the end of the gravel road *(GPS location N45°03.389' W117°19.351')*. Parking permits are not required.

Although there is no official campground near the trailhead, you'll pass plenty of free creekside campsites as you drive in. This area was used in the filming of the 1968 Lee Marvin movie, *Paint Your Wagon*.

Start at an "East Eagle Trail" sign on the left side of the parking loop and hike along a rough dirt extension of Road 7745 for 0.2 mile. Before you reach a gate in the road, fork to the right onto a real trail. This path heads up the canyon past the massive 2400-foot face of Granite Cliff. After 2.5 miles the creek in the gorge below the trail twists through a corkscrew-shaped slot and emerges sideways as a rooster tail of spray. For the next 4 miles the path crosses meadow openings cleared by the avalanches that roar down this canyon's steep walls in winter. Look here for brown coneflower, red paintbrush, fuzzy blue mint, purple aster,

Eagle Cap from Hidden Lake. *Opposite: Corkscrew Falls.*

and quaking aspen.

At the 6.5-mile mark turn left at a large rock cairn, cross the 15-foot-wide East Fork Eagle Creek on boulders, and climb a rocky path 1.4 miles to Moon Lake. A meadow of pink heather and blue gentian fringes this shallow pool. Then continue 0.3 mile over a small pass to the trail's end in a brookside meadow. At this point, Hidden Lake is still hidden. To find it, cross the brook and head cross-country 200 yards over a low rise to the right. The large, deep lake *(GPS location N45°08.500' W117°19.741')* is surrounded by a charming blend of meadows and subalpine groves with discreet campsites. Leave time to explore the lake's basin to find the scenic ponds at the headwaters of the brook.

Other Options

Adventurers with strong knees and stout hearts can use Hidden Lake as a base camp for several large-scale adventures—notably, the 7.4-mile climb to the summit of Eagle Cap or a 17.7-mile loop over three passes to Minam Lake.

73 Crater Lake

Difficult
11.8 miles round trip
2970 feet elevation gain
Open late July through October
Use: hikers, horses

Much smaller and quieter than Oregon's more famous Crater Lake, this pool high in the southern Wallowas is so clear that you can watch fish swim away from their jump-rings. The lake's deep, circular basin is not a volcanic crater, but rather a dimple in an ancient glacier's bed. The trail here is truly an athletic challenge, with nearly 6 miles of unrelenting uphill switchbacks.

Note that maximum group size on the trail is 12, that campsites must be at least 100 feet from the lake, and that horses cannot be grazed within 200 feet of the shore. Campfires are strongly discouraged. Expect a $5 parking fee.

Start at one of the trailheads described for Hidden Lake (see Hike #72)—either the equestrian staging area or the parking loop 0.8 miles farther along Road 7745 at the end of gravel. If you park at the turnaround loop, look for a small wooden sign for the "Little Kettle Creek Trail" on the uphill, right-hand side of the loop. Follow this trail up through a forest of Douglas fir and Engelmann spruce 200 yards to a junction with the path from the equestrian trailhead. Then continue uphill on a route that switchbacks up out of the forest, zigzagging across sagebrush slopes with quaking aspen, yellow balsamroot blooms, and red paintbrush. Views extend across the U-shaped canyon of East Fork Eagle Creek.

After 3.5 miles you'll crest the lip of a hanging valley, but instead of leveling off, the trail crosses a creek (with the first water of the hike) and switchbacks up out

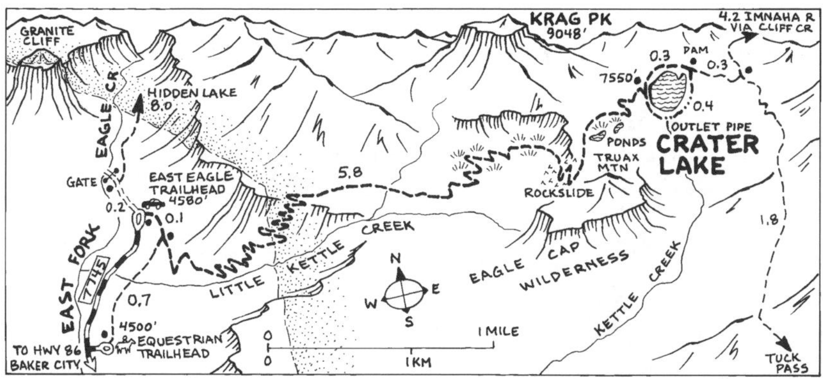

of the valley across a rockslide. The rocks clatter musically underfoot. Listen here for the double-cheep of pikas, the "rock rabbits" who live in this slide.

Finally the path crests at an alpine upland of heather meadows, passes a pair of ponds, and forks at the shore of Crater Lake *(GPS location N45°03.468' W117°16.650')*. The main trail goes left, but circle the lake on a path to the right for the best views. Here you'll also find the tunnel and 16-inch pipe that have converted this lake to a reservoir. Originally the lake drained north to the Imnaha River. Now it leaks south to Kettle Creek each summer, feeding thirsty ranchlands near Richland.

Crater Lake. Opposite: Granite Cliff from the Little Kettle Creek Trail.

74 Summit Point Lookout

Easy (to lookout)
2 miles round trip
550 feet elevation gain
Open late July through October
Use: hikers, horses

Difficult (to Pine Lakes pass)
11.8 miles round trip
2120 feet elevation gain

Difficult (to Pine Lakes)
16.2 miles round trip
2950 feet elevation gain

You'll see timberline meadows and wide-ranging views even at the start of this hike, because the trailhead is one of the highest in the Wallowa Mountains. For a quick trip, climb an ancient roadbed to the Summit Point fire lookout tower. For a more substantial day hike, traverse the length of Little Eagle Meadows to a spectacular, high pass overlooking the Pine Lakes. Backpackers can continue onward to the lakes themselves, although that goal is slightly easier to reach via the Cornucopia Trailhead described in Hike #75.

From Baker City, drive Interstate 84 north 2 miles to exit 302 and follow Highway 86 east toward Halfway 49 miles. Beyond Richland 6 miles (between mileposts 48 and 49), turn left on gravel Road 77, following a green "Summit Pt. L.O." sign. After 11 miles you'll reach a X-shaped intersection. If you're looking for a place to spend the night, you might turn left into the entrance of McBride Campground, a quiet camp with eight sites. Otherwise turn right on one-lane Road 7715 for 4.8 slow, steep miles to the Summit Point Trailhead parking area at road's end.

The trail begins as a steep, rough road that's closed to vehicles but used occasionally by cattle. The sagebrush slope is punctuated by the spires of subalpine firs and a variety of wildflowers: blue lupine, scarlet gilia, fuzzy white mint, and red paintbrush. After 0.7 mile the dusty road forks at a ridgecrest. For the short hike, turn right 0.3 mile to the 14-by-14-foot lookout building, perched on a 20-foot tower atop a summit knoll. The lookout is staffed only in times of

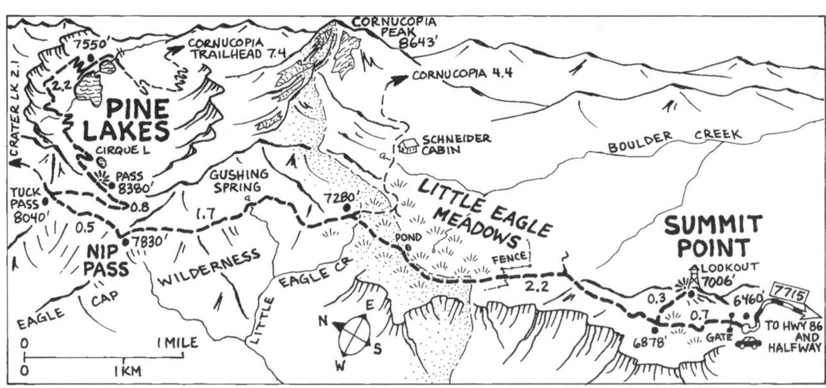

high forest fire danger. The view extends from the craggy Elkhorn Range on the far western horizon to the rumpled brown badlands that roll east toward the Hells Canyon. In the middle distance, the metal rooftops of Halfway glint from a patchwork of ranchfields.

For a more substantial hike, take the other ridgecrest fork and follow a genuine trail 2.2 miles to the far end of Little Eagle Meadows. Backed by the massive white granite face of Cornucopia Peak, the mile-long meadows cover a gorgeous, rolling plateau with grass, lupine, and aster. Expect to see Clark's nutcrackers, blue butterflies, and some cattle. At the far end of the meadows cross a small creek to a trail junction signpost and turn left. In the next 2.2 miles you'll traverse a steep slope past a gushing spring, climb through Nip Pass, and reach a trail junction in Tuck Pass. Switchback up to the right for 0.8 mile to an even higher pass with a breathtaking view of a small cirque lake and the two large, green Pine Lakes in a gigantic granite bowl.

This scenic, unnamed pass makes a good lunch stop—and a wise turnaround point for day hikers. Backpackers can continue on down 2.2 miles to the Pine Lakes, confident that the climb back up to this pass can be left for another day.

Pine Lakes. Opposite: Summit Point lookout.

75 Pine Lakes

Easy (to Chute Falls)
4.2 miles round trip
480 feet elevation gain
Open June through November
Use: hikers, horses

Difficult (to Pine Lakes)
14.8 miles round trip
2720 feet elevation gain
Open late July through October

Difficult (around Cornucopia Mtn)
18.2-mile loop
3700 feet elevation gain

The 1885 boomtown of Cornucopia extracted $15 million of gold from the southern Wallowa Mountains before its mines closed in 1941. Today the town's derelict buildings, with their spookily tilted porches and gaping windows, seem strangely out of place so near the Eagle Cap Wilderness. A trail from the ghost town climbs to the Pine Lakes, a pair of deep green pools in a gorgeous alpine basin of heather, wildflowers, and granite cliffs. For a backpacking trip, continue on a loop around Cornucopia Mountain.

From Baker City, drive Interstate 84 north 2 miles to exit 302 and follow Highway 86 east through Richland a total of 52 miles to the village of Halfway. Turn left on the Halfway Business Loop and keep straight through town on Main Street (which becomes Cornucopia Road 4190) for 7.2 miles of pavement and another 5.1 miles of gravel to a junction at a sign announcing Cornucopia. Most of the ghost town's ruins are half a mile ahead on a very rough road, but to find the trailhead, turn right for half a mile to the Cornucopia Wilderness Pack Station. Most of the land here is private. The pack station often allows hikers to park in their lot, but if you drive 100 yards past the station you'll find a small pullout on the right with public parking.

Pine Lakes. *Above: Pika (rock rabbit).*

From the map board at the pack station's parking area, keep left on the Pine Lakes Trail (an ancient mining road) past the horse corrals and red buildings of the pack station. Soon the route enters meadows of brown coneflower and blue mint beside the creek's big cottonwood trees. To the left the cliffs of Cornucopia Mountain rise 3000 feet, marked by the caverns and white debris fans of old mines.

After 1 mile the trail crosses Pine Creek. The footbridge here replaces an earlier bridge destroyed by an avalanche in 2005. Continue on the old roadbed to a second bridge at the 2.1-mile mark, where the track narrows to a genuine trail. Beyond this second bridge 0.3 mile you'll come to a right-hand switchback where you can hear a waterfall. To find the falls, bushwhack straight 100 feet. The creek plunges 10 feet before sliding through a 30-foot bedrock chute. This makes a good turnaround point for an easy hike.

If you're continuing to Pine Lakes, the trail switchbacks up a mile through a Douglas fir forest and then traverses several miles across hot, shadeless rockslide slopes. You'll see a few quaking aspen and sagebrush, as well as entire fields of red paintbrush and fireweed. Finally the path switchbacks up to a small cement dam that turned the lower Pine Lake into a reservoir. Continue 0.3 mile to the undammed and very beautiful upper lake, rimmed with meadows and white cliffs.

If you're staying overnight, remember that campsites must be at least 100 feet from any lakeshore, tethered horses must be at least 200 feet from lakes, and campfires are strongly discouraged. Firewood cutting from standing trees or snags is prohibited. Maximum group size is 12.

To return on a loop, continue on the trail past the Pine Lakes, switchbacking up through glorious alpine wildflower meadows to a 8380-foot pass. Continue 0.8 mile to Tuck Pass, turn left for 1.7 miles to the start of Little Eagle Meadows, and fork to the left on a faint, confusing route among cowpaths. Don't disturb Schneider Cabin, a cowboy outpost that's still in use. When you reach a rough, rocky road, follow it 0.9 mile down to the center of the Cornucopia ghost town and turn left to return to your car.

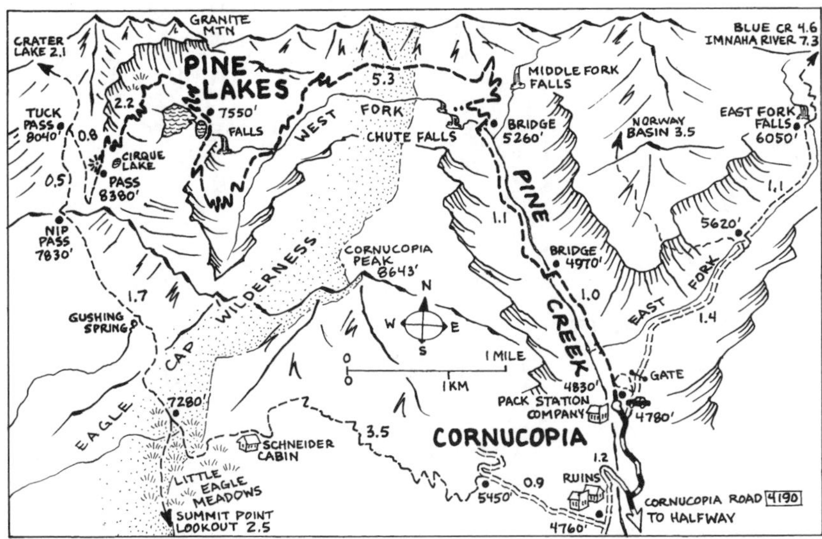

HIGH DESERT
TO SISTERS
TO THE DALLES
BEND
HIGH DESERT MUSEUM
DRY RIVER
6
7
NEWBERRY NAT'L VOLCANIC MONUMENT
8
PAULINA LAKE
9
10
LA PINE
97
BROTHERS
20
HAMPTON
TO EUGENE
58
31
FORT ROCK STATE PARK
76
77
DERRICK CAVE
CRACK IN THE GROUND
LOST FOREST
SAND DUNES
FORT ROCK
CHRISTMAS VALLEY
WAGONTIRE
395
CHEMULT
SILVER LAKE
138
ROAD 76
RD 27
RD 28
HAGER MT
KLAMATH MARSH
SILVER CREEK MARSH
78
YAMSAY MTN
191
FREMONT TRAIL
EAST BAY
WINTER
79
SUMMER LAKE WILDLIFE REFUGE
SUMMER LAKE
HOT SPRINGS
SYCAN MARSH
TO CRATER LAKE
COLLIER STATE PARK
80
RIDGE
RD 30
PAISLEY
ABERT LK
ABERT RIM
HART MTN
NAT'L ANTELOPE REFUGE
91
62
192
GEARHART MTN
194
81
82
193
ROAD
ROAD 33
31
195
87
89
90
CHILOQUIN
UPPER KLAMATH LK
TRAIL
84
WOODS
VALLEY JUNCTION
PLUSH
RD 34
3660
28
88
DRAKE PK
WARNER LKS
HART MTN HOT SPRINGS
BEATTY
140
BLY
83
196
85
KLAMATH FALLS
140
LAKEVIEW
197
CRANE MTN
ADEL
TO WINNEMUC
39
97
OREGON
GOOSE LAKE
198
TULE LAKE
CALIFORNIA
NEVAD
TULE LAKE
TO WEED
LAVA BEDS NAT'L MON
86
139
N
W
E
S
395
0 10 20 30 MIL
0 10 20 30 40 KM
TO ALTURAS
TO ALTURAS

The Homestead Village Museum in Fort Rock.

KLAMATH FALLS

In the rain shadow of the Cascade Range, Oregon's high desert country is strewn with curiosities—lava caves, fault-block mountains, hot springs, and oasis lakes.

Fort Rock

Like an island in a sea of sagebrush, Fort Rock serves as a landmark for travelers heading southeast from Bend into the high desert. Visit the picnic area and loop trail at the rock itself (Hike #76). Next, stop in the nearby hamlet of Fort Rock to see the **Homestead Village Museum** (open Fri-Sun 10-4 in summer), a collection of homes and buildings salvaged from early 1900s dry-land farms. Then tour the rest of Fort Rock's valley, stopping to explore sand dunes, an enormous crack in the ground, and other geologic oddities (Hike #77).

Summer Lake

The marshes of the **Summer Lake Wildlife Area** attract white pelicans, Canada geese, and sandhill cranes in summer, thousands of migratory birds in spring and fall, and bald eagles in winter. To see the birds, walk along a dike (Hike #79), or drive an 8.5-mile gravel road tour of the refuge, following "Wildlife Viewing Loop" signs from Highway 31. The refuge sells required parking permits for $7 day or $22 a year. For more bird info, check Oregon's important bird areas at *www.oregoniba.org*.

The refuge's campgrounds resemble gravel parking lots, but you can book a room or cabin across from refuge headquarters (near milepost 70 of Highway 31) at the **Lodge at Summer Lake** (866-943-3993), which prides itself on a dinner menu of 1-pound steaks.

Looking for an artistic retreat? Consider **Playa**, a posh center for artists, writers, scientists, and naturalists 12 miles south on Highway 31, between mileposts 80 and 81. Playa rents 6 elegant cabins on Summer Lake's shore from May 19 to August 12, but only if you book at least 6 nights ($720 for one person, $900 for two). The rest of the year, the center awards one- and two-month fellowships to deserving artists and authors for free. Check *www.playasummerlake.org* or call 541-943-3983 for details.

For a swim, drive 11 miles south to **Summer Lake Hot Springs** (near milepost 92), a rustic 1928 bathhouse with a 102° F pool, open 9am-7pm daily for a $10 fee. Geothermally heated cabins rent for $85-165, and camping is $15 per person (541-943-3931, *www.summerlakehotsprings.com*).

Downtown Klamath Falls

Linkville modernized its name to Klamath Falls in 1893, but the city's downtown preserves an old-time charm. For a walking tour, pick up a brochure at the tourism office at 507 Main. The walk begins, however, at the **Klamath County Museum** at 1451 Main Street. Originally built as an armory, this 1935 art deco building features displays of Klamath tribal history and Klamath Lake wildlife. It's open Tue-Sat 9-5 for a $5 admission. Then head west on Main Street past the 1927 Balsiger Ford Building (with Egyptian revival palm motifs), and the **Baldwin Hotel Museum** at 31 Main Street, a 1906 brick building with displays of Klamath history, open Wed-Sat 10-4 from June through Sept for $10. After a mile, turn back on the far side of the Link River at the **Favell Museum,** a private collection of Western theme art and Indian artifacts, including 60,000 arrowheads, open Tue-Sat 10-5 for a $8 admission ($5 for children age 6-16). See also Hike #85.

Collier State Park and Logging Museum

A welcome stop on the drive from Bend to Klamath Falls, this park features an outdoor museum of logging equipment (steam donkey engines, giant circular saws, and railroad logging cars), a "pioneer village" of half a dozen relocated log cabins, two streamside picnic areas, and a 68-site campground. Drive Highway 97 north of Klamath Falls 30 miles (or north of Chiloquin 5 miles).

Lakeview

Billing itself as the "Tallest Town in Oregon," 4800-foot-high Lakeview advertises its ranching heritage with giant cowboy-shaped signs. Taste that tradition at the **Willow Springs Guest Ranch** (541-947-5499), a remote 2500-acre working ranch north of town 30 miles, where dinner is often cooked on a campfire. Cabins for two run $115 and include breakfast (*www.willowspringsguestranch.com*).

Hart Mountain

Pronghorn antelope, bighorn sheep, and mule deer roam the 430-square-mile **Hart Mountain National Antelope Refuge** (see Hikes #89-91). The area's only campground is a treasure, with streamside sites near a free, natural hot springs pool. To the west, below a 2000-foot fault scarp cliff, the marsh-rimmed alkali Warner Lakes offer canoe routes through bird habitat.

Fort Klamath Museum

South of Crater Lake on Highway 62, this free, historic Army fort includes the graves of four Modoc tribal leaders. Open 10-6 Thurs-Mon, June to late Sept.

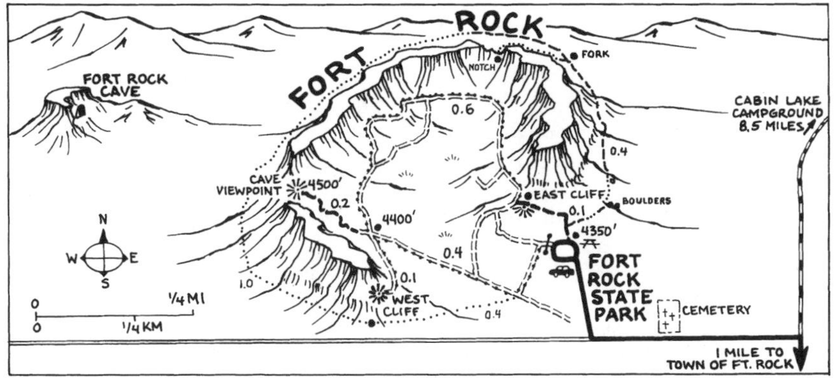

76 Fort Rock

Easy (around the inside)
1.7-mile loop
250 feet elevation gain
Open all year
Use: hikers, horses, bicycles

Moderate (around the outside)
1.9-mile loop
200 feet elevation gain

Right: Fort Rock from the notch.

An easy stroll explores the inside of this fortress-shaped outcropping in the arid bed of a vanished Ice Age lake. A rougher route loops around the outside of ring's cliff. Near here, in a cave overlooking what is now the sagebrush country of arid Fort Rock Valley, archeologists in 1938 unearthed a 9000-year-old cache of more than 70 sandals woven from sagebrush bark.

Originally, Fort Rock did not have cliff edges at all, but rather the gently sloping sides of a *maar*—a volcanic explosion crater. When Ice Age rainstorms filled the valley with a vast, 250-foot-deep lake 13,000 years ago, Fort Rock became an island, battered by storm waves from the south winds. The surf wore the outer slopes back to steep cliffs and then breached the crater's south wall.

Amidst Fort Rock's sagebrush you'll find brilliant red paintbrush in June, yellow clumps of sunflower-like Oregon sunshine in summer, and yellow-tipped rabbit brush in fall. Cliff swallows swoop from mud nests high on the guano-stained rock walls, watched by prairie falcons. Avoid the heat of July and August. Winter months are windy and very cold.

From Bend, drive 29 miles south on Highway 97. Beyond LaPine, turn left at a "Silver Lake" pointer for 29.2 miles on Highway 31, and then turn left at a "Fort Rock" sign for 6.5 miles. Turn left again just beyond the Fort Rock store, following signs 1.7 paved miles to Fort Rock State Natural Area.

For the easy tour around the inside of Fort Rock, take a paved path from the far end of the picnic area's parking lot for 100 feet and continue uphill on a rougher trail 200 yards to a viewpoint beside Fort Rock's east cliff. Notice the 10-foot-tall notch in the cliffs, carved by the vanished lake's surf. Then keep right at all junctions, following a broad trail around the inside of Fort Rock 0.6 mile to a 4-way junction. Take two viewpoint detours from here. First climb to the right on a faint path 0.2 mile to a cliff-edge notch overlooking the historic sandal cave (a dark spot on a knoll a mile away). Then return to the 4-way junction and turn right 0.1 mile to Fort Rock's west cliff. Finally return to the 4-way junction and turn right for 0.4 mile to your car.

If you've already seen the inside of Fort Rock and you're ready for a wilder exploration, try bushwhacking around the outside of the rock instead. Long pants are essential. From the parking lot, walk 100 feet up the paved path to a plaque commemorating Reub Long and turn right for 50 feet to a turnstile in a wire fence. A faint, braided path climbs past several boulders, becomes a real trail for 0.3 mile, and then forks. To the left is a scramble route that deadends at a viewpoint notch high on Fort Rock's rim. So keep to the right. This route squeezes past a wire fence and scrambles across a slope of rocks. Then the trail mostly vanishes, but it's easy to walk through the sagebrush around the spectacular cliffs of Fort Rock's outer wall. It's a mile to the west cliff viewpoint, and another 0.4 mile across a sagebrush flat to your car.

77 Fort Rock Valley

Easy (4 short hikes)
0.4 to 1.4 miles each, round-trip
50 to 170 feet elevation gain
Open all year
Use: hikers only

Four short desert walks explore this area's geologic oddities: sand dunes, a "lost" forest, a gigantic crack in the ground, and a lava cave with a natural skylight. Because you'll need to drive from site to site, you may not have time to visit all four attractions in one day. If you're staying overnight, note that the area's only public campground is 9 miles due north of Fort Rock at Cabin Lake. The village of Fort Rock has an RV park and Christmas Valley has motels.

During the Ice Age, rains filled the Fort Rock Valley with a 1500-square-mile lake. That lake has vanished, but desert winds have corralled its former beaches into 60-foot dunes. To drive to the dunes, take Highway 97 south of Bend 29 miles, turn left at a "Silver Lake" pointer on Highway 31 for 29.2 miles, turn left 6.5 miles to the village of Fort Rock, and follow signs east another 27 miles to the town of Christmas Valley. Check your gas gauge here. Then continue straight 8 miles to a 4-way junction. Following "Sand Dunes" pointers, turn left on paved Road 5-14D for 8 miles to a T-shaped junction and turn right on gravel Road 5-14E for 3.3 miles. The main road turns left

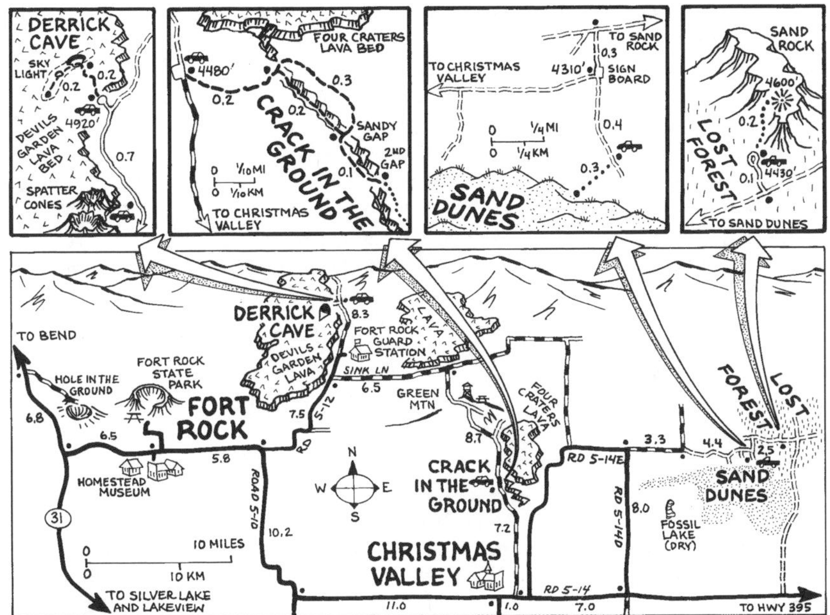

here, but go straight, passing a "Rough Road Ahead" sign. In fact, this narrow, sandy track can be impassable in wet weather. If it's dry, keep straight for 4.4 miles until you reach a wood rail fence and message board at a T-shaped junction.

Turn right and drive the rough, sandy road 0.4 mile to the trailhead parking area. There is no trail, but you can see the dunes clearly. Walk 0.3 mile southwest across the open desert to them. Tracks remain for months from passing deer and coyotes—and from all-terrain vehicles, a notable nuisance on summer weekends. Explore the dunes as far as you like, but be sure you can find your way back to your car.

Next, get back in the car and bump up the sandy road to the Lost Forest. Drive 0.4 mile back to the Sand Dunes' T-shaped junction, continue straight (to the north) for 0.3 mile to another T-shaped junction, and turn right for 2.2 miles on a very

Crack in the Ground. Opposite: Derrick Cave.

rough, sandy road until you approach a large, orange rock bluff. A rough spur to the left leads 200 yards to a turnaround at the rock's base. Park here and scramble up the trailless knoll 0.2 mile to a viewpoint of the forest.

The five-square-mile Lost Forest survives on a mere nine inches of annual rainfall, half of what ponderosa pines usually require. Here the pines' taproots have found an underground water source. The buried hardpan of Fort Rock's ancient lakebed collects rainfall that might otherwise sink into the subsoil.

To continue to Crack in the Ground, first return to Christmas Valley. At the eastern edge of this sprawling desert town, turn north off the main paved road at a "Crack in the Ground" pointer. Follow a good gravel road 7.2 miles to a signed parking area. A wide trail leads 0.2 mile to the 70-foot-deep lava slot. The rock chasm is so narrow that boulders hang wedged overhead, and snow sometimes lingers in the shade until May. Walk 0.2 mile along the bottom of this slot to a sandy gap. Beyond this point a ladder makes possible only a few hundred more yards of scrambling before the crack is blocked by boulders, but explorers can follow the crack's upper rim another mile.

Crack in the Ground appeared a few thousand years ago when four cinder cones erupted nearby, emptying an underground magma chamber. As the ground settled, a crack formed along the edge of a broad depression.

To find the fourth geologic curiosity in this area, Derrick Cave, you could drive on gravel backroads over Green Mountain (see map), but many people find it simpler to start from the paved road at Fort Rock. From the town of Fort Rock, drive east 5.8 miles toward Christmas Valley. At a sharp curve to the right, go straight on Derricks Cave Road 5-12. Stick to this paved, zigzagging road for 9.1 miles to the Fort Rock Guard Station entrance, and continue straight on gravel 6.8 miles to Derrick Cave's parking area. Hike a rough road 0.2 mile to the cave entrance. When you hike down into the entrance pit, you'll see that the cave extends both left and right. If you explore to the right you'll find the cave quickly ends where Civil Defense authorities set up a bomb shelter in the 1960s.

In the other direction (downhill), Derrick Cave extends nearly a quarter mile. The first hundred yards are lit by two natural skylights: jagged holes in the ceiling. Beyond this you'll need a flashlight or lantern. You'll want a warm coat, too. In winter, dripping water from the ceiling forms three-foot-tall ice stalagmites. Look along the walls for stripes in the rock, the "high water marks" of the lava river that formed the cave. At cave's end the rock river is frozen in place, puddled up on the floor like freshly poured cake batter.

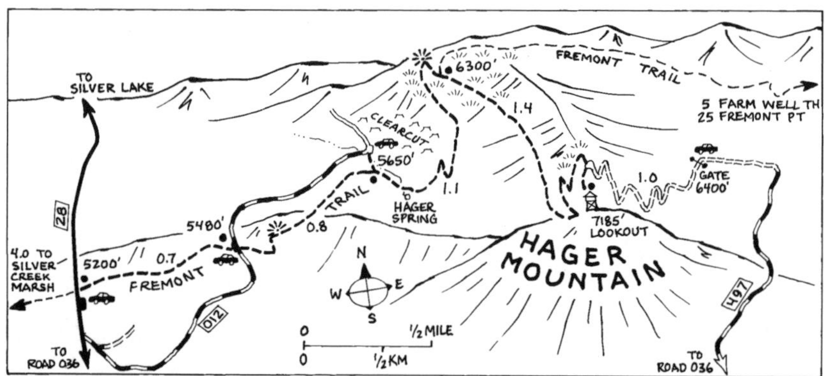

78 Hager Mountain

Hager Mountain's lookout.

Easy (from gate)
2 miles round trip
785 feet elevation gain
Open June to early November
Use: hikers, horses, bicycles

Moderate (from Road 012)
6.6 miles round trip
1710 feet elevation gain

Difficult (from Road 28)
8 miles round trip
1990 feet elevation gain

Refer to map on previous page.

Like its more famous cousin Black Butte, Hager Mountain is a charming little volcano with a summit trail that climbs through wildflowers to a panoramic fire lookout. But because Black Butte lies in a heavily trafficked area near Bend, its trail draws as many as a hundred people a day, while hardly a dozen people a week make their way to Hager Mountain's scenic summit.

From Bend, drive Highway 97 south 29 miles and turn left on Highway 31 for 47 miles to Silver Lake. Near milepost 47 (just after the Silver Lake Ranger Station), turn right on paved Road 28 for 9.3 miles to the Hager Mountain Trailhead, a parking pullout on the left. Although this is the official trailhead, there are *three* other possible trailheads—all of them involving easier hikes. If you're determined to park here, you'll have to walk back on the road 100 yards to find the actual trail, and then climb 4 miles to the summit.

If you're short on time, you might opt instead for the shortest possible route to the top: Hager Mountain's lookout service road. To find it, drive past the official trailhead on Road 28 another 1.9 miles, turn left on gravel Road 036 for 3.9 miles, and turn left on Road 497 for 2.6 miles to a locked gate. The last 0.2 mile are steep and rough. From the gate, simply walk up the service road 0.9 mile to the lookout staff's parking area, 200 yards below the summit building.

The prettiest route to the top begins at a less obvious trailhead. From the official trailhead on Road 28, drive another 0.2 mile, turn left on faint dirt Road 012, and keep right for 1.2 miles to a small, easy-to-miss trail sign and blue diamond marker on the right *(GPS location N43°00.475′ W121°03.536′)*. Parking is tight on the shoulder here. From this quiet trailhead, the path climbs through a forest that has been thinned and intentionally burned, leaving stately ponderosa pines and masses of yellow balsamroot and orange paintbrush wildflowers.

After hiking 0.8 mile along a scenic ridge, turn right at a junction near yet another possible trailhead. You'll pass fenced Hager Spring, switchback up past a 1990s clearcut, and traverse a meadowed slope of wildflowers. Views here extend from Mt. Shasta (above Thompson Reservoir) to Mt. Thielsen and even Mt. Jefferson. Then keep straight at a trail junction for 1.4 miles to the summit's lookout building, staffed each year from June until early October. Snowshoers or skiers willing to make the trek from Road 28 can rent the lookout for $40 a night from November 15 to May 15 by calling 877-444-6777 (*www.recreation.gov*).

79 Summer Lake

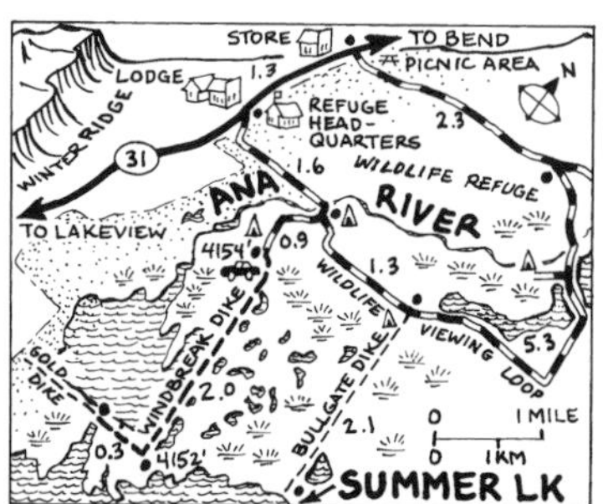

Easy
4.6 miles round trip
No elevation gain
Open all year
Use: hikers, horses, bicycles

When explorer John C. Fremont struck south from The Dalles to California in 1843, he crested a snowy ridge on December 16, saw this sunny alkali lake 2700 feet below, and named the features Summer Lake and Winter Ridge. Since 1944 the Oregon Department of Fish and Wildlife has bought 18,380 acres of marshland as a wildlife preserve where the Ana River meanders into the landlocked lake. Great flocks of birds arrive here in March and April, en route to the arctic from Central America. White pelicans, Canada geese, and ducks linger through summer. Bald eagles and swans remain in the winter. Herons, egrets, and terns are common.

From Bend, take Highway 97 south 29 miles and turn left at a "Silver Lake" pointer on Highway 31 for 70 miles. Near milepost 70, opposite the Lodge at Summer Lake, turn left through the wildlife area headquarters compound, following "Wildlife Viewing Area" pointers onto a gravel road. At a T-shaped junction after 1.6 miles, turn right for 0.9 mile to the Windbreak Campground, which consists of a gravel parking lot with outhouses and garbage cans. Parking permits are required here, and cost $7 a day or $22 a year.

From the parking lot, hike onward along a dike-top road that's cabled closed to motor vehicles most of the year (March 15 to August 15 and early October to late January). On either hand are large patches of open water surrounded by reeds and cattails. Redwing blackbirds, mallards, avocets, black-necked stilts, and long-billed curlews are everywhere. Ignore short side dikes that deadend to left and right.

After 2 miles the dike road turns right alongside a wave-lapped lake rimmed with rounded cobbles. Continue 0.3 mile to three large culverts that release the Ana River to Summer Lake. This makes a good turnaround point. White pelicans start up reluctantly with a few flaps. To the south, alkali duststorms dim the horizon across the lake. Ahead, the dike road ends at a private ranch.

Summer Lake and Winter Rim. *Opposite: Ponderosa pine on Winter Ridge.*

80 Winter Ridge

Easy (to Currier Spring)
5.4 miles round trip
320 feet elevation gain
Open late May to mid-November
Use: hikers, horses, bicycles

Moderate (to landslide viewpoint)
9.6 miles round trip
580 feet elevation gain

The long, fault-block mountain that Captain John Fremont dubbed Winter Ridge is known by the locals as Winter *Rim,* perhaps because the rimrock exposed in its dramatic, 3000-foot-tall eastern cliff really does resemble the rim of a giant, broken bowl. Tracing this monumental crest is the Fremont Trail, a 147-mile route that traverses the entire Fremont National Forest. Much of the Fremont Trail is best toured on horseback, but day hikers and mountain bikers do well on the scenic section along the rim north of Government Harvey Pass.

Wildflowers bloom amidst the sagebrush and ponderosa pines here throughout June. Of course, June is also when mosquitoes swarm across the Fremont National Forest. Fortunately, a reliable ridgecrest breeze helps keep the bugs at bay. Expect to meet grazing cattle along the route in August and September.

Drive Highway 97 south of Bend 29 miles and turn left at a "Silver Lake" pointer on Highway 31 for 87 miles. At milepost 87 (northwest of Paisley 12 miles), turn right on gravel Road 29 at a sign for Government Harvey Pass and drive 9.5 miles up to a T-shaped junction at the pass. Turn right on Road 2901, driving slowly for just 0.1 mile until you spot a tiny trail marker on a pine tree to the right. Park on the shoulder here *(GPS location N42°42.183′ W120°47.910′)* and hike up to the right.

The ponderosa pines along the trail are two feet in diameter, but grow only 60 feet tall before they're trimmed by winds. Fires have left patches of snags. Four-foot stumps recall older trees, skidded out on winter snow in the 1920s. Swallowtail butterflies abound. Flowers include red paintbrush, purple penstemon, blue lupine,

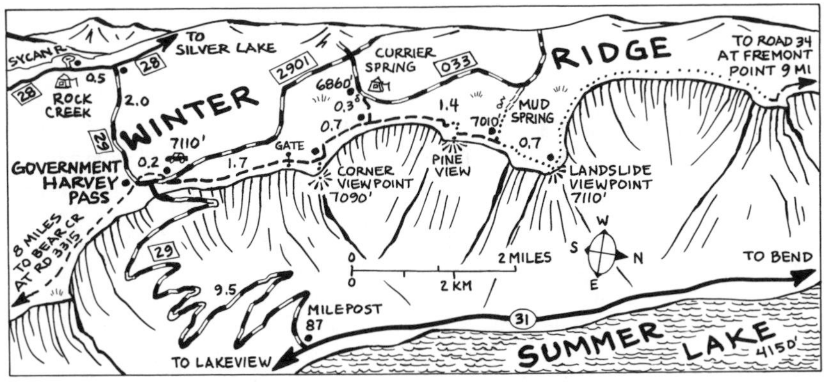

Summer Lake from Winter Ridge. *Opposite: Campbell Lake from Campbell Rim.*

white yarrow, and arrowleaf balsamroot (a wild yellow sunflower).

After 1.5 mile you'll pass a gate. A few hundred yards later, when the trail turns downhill to the left at a sharp corner, you might bushwhack up to the right 200 feet to a viewpoint on a rimrock promontory. Far below, dust devils swirl along the alkali shore of Summer Lake.

Then continue on the main trail 0.7 mile to a big signpost marking a side path to Currier Spring. It's worth detouring downhill 0.3 mile to see the spring. The trail cuts through a lovely aspen grove with hellebore (corn lily) and purple larkspur on its way to Road 033. Across the road is a horse camp, while the spring is in a fenced area to the left. Mosquitoes can be fierce here, so you might turn back to the main trail on the breezy rim before settling down for lunch.

If you're not yet ready to return to your car, and if you're good at route finding, you might continue north along the rim another 2.1 miles to a viewpoint overlooking a vast landslide. After 1.2 miles the Fremont Trail in this direction grows faint, and after another half mile it's all but unfindable. Still it's hard to get lost when you're following the rim of such a gigantic cliff, and the open terrain makes for fairly easy walking.

Turn back at a rimrock edge *(GPS location N42°45.412' W120°48.686')* beyond the rim's highest point 100 yards. The viewpoint here overlooks a two-mile-wide bite taken out of Winter Ridge's rising fault scarp by a giant landslide, leaving lakelets in hummocky terrain all the way to Summer Lake.

81 Campbell and Dead Horse Lakes

Moderate (to Campbell Rim)
4.9-mile loop
810 feet elevation gain
Open mid-July through October
Use: hikers, horses, bicycles

Moderate (to Dead Horse Rim)
7.4-mile loop
1170 feet elevation gain

Although this mountain lake basin is as high as the alpine lakes of the Cascades or Wallowas, the dense lodgepole pine forest here limits views. For a look around, take a loop trail up from Campbell Lake to a cliff—the headwall of the vanished Ice Age glacier that scooped out this basin. Anglers rush to Campbell and Dead Horse Lakes as the snow is melting in early June. If you're not fishing, plan your visit later, when the mosquitoes are gone and the rim trail clears of snow.

If you're coming from Bend, drive Highway 97 south 29 miles and turn left on Highway 31 for 47 miles to Silver Lake. Near milepost 47 (after the Silver Lake Ranger Station), turn right toward East Bay Campground on paved Road 28. Follow Road 28 for 18 miles to a stop sign at a T-shaped junction. Then turn left to keep on Road 28 for another 34 miles (paved all the way), turn right on gravel Road 033 for 1.9 miles, turn left into the Campbell Lake Campground entrance, and drive 0.5 mile (past nice, free campsites) to a trailhead parking pullout and restroom on the left.

If you're coming from the south, drive Highway 140 between Lakeview and Klamath Falls to a summit near milepost 67, turn north on paved Road 3660 for 14 miles, turn right on paved Road 34 for 10.4 miles to a T-shaped junction, turn left on paved Road 28 for 6.2 miles, turn left on gravel Road 033 for 1.9 miles, and turn left into the Campbell Lake Campground 0.5 mile.

Set off on the Lakes Loop Trail past a pond with ribbeting Cascade toads. After 0.2 mile, fork left on a path that climbs 1.3 mile to a viewpoint on Campbell Rim. To

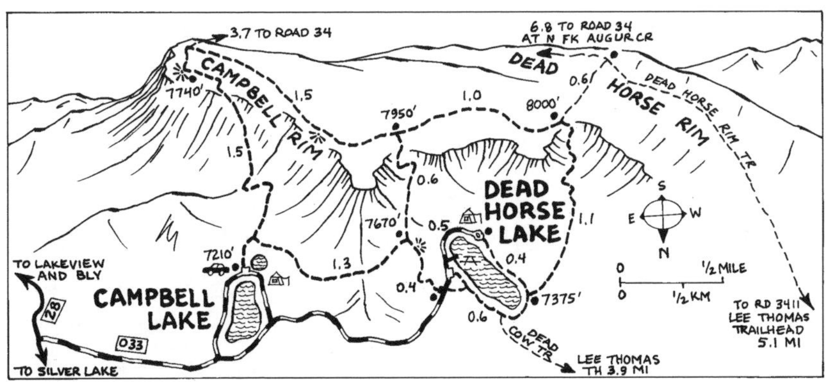

the east, fault-block mountains form a series of horizons, with Winter Rim closest, followed by Abert Rim, Hart Mountain, and faint Steens Mountain.

Next the loop trail traverses a lodgepole pine plateau. The tread is faint, so follow blazes. The path stays near the rim edge for a mile to a viewpoint of Campbell Lake. Then the trail descends nearly half a mile to a marked junction. For the short loop, turn right and follow signs back to the Campbell Lake trailhead. If you'd like more exercise, veer left for a viewless mile through the woods to another marked junction in a saddle. Turn right on a steepish 1.1-mile path, turn left on a wide trail around Dead Horse Lake 0.6 mile, and head uphill to the left on a poorly marked path toward Campbell Lake. If you miss this junction, simply go left when you see a picnic area's steps and follow the road left 200 yards to a trailhead pullout. Then follow trail signs back 1.7 miles to Campbell Lake.

82 Gearhart Mountain

Difficult (to The Notch)
12 miles round trip
1920 feet elevation gain
Open mid-July through October
Use: hikers, horses

The centerpiece of the Gearhart Mountain Wilderness is a 8370-foot-tall ridge of strangely layered lava outcrops. The trail here winds through The Palisades, a rock garden of 30-foot pillars arrayed like an army of gnomes. Later the path crosses two scenic passes snuggled below the mountain's summit cliffs. For the best view, bushwhack to the summit itself. Note that group size in the Wilderness is limited to ten "heartbeats", counting people and animals.

From Klamath Falls, drive east on Highway 140 toward Lakeview for 55 miles. Beyond the town of Bly 1.4 miles, turn left on Campbell Road for 0.6 mile, and then turn right onto paved Road 34 for 15.3 miles. At a sign for Corral Creek Camp-

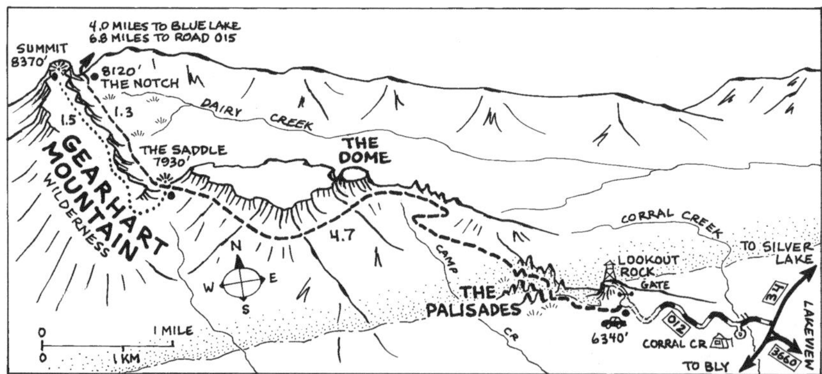

Gearhart Mountain's summit. Opposite: The Palisades.

ground, turn left on gravel Road 012 for 1.5 miles to the trailhead at road's end *(GPS location N42°27.834' W120°48.367')*. The final half mile of this road is rough and steep. If you need a place to camp nearby, the free Corral Creek Campground 1.2 miles before the trailhead has six nice sites with horse stalls.

If you're coming from Bend, drive Highway 97 south 29 miles and turn left on Highway 31 for 47 miles toward Silver Lake. Just beyond the Silver Lake Ranger Station, turn right toward East Bay Campground on paved Road 28 for 18 miles to a stop sign at a T-shaped junction. Then turn left to keep on Road 28 for another 40 miles (paved all the way), turn right on Road 34 for 10.4 miles to a pointer for the Corral Creek Campground, and turn right on gravel Road 012 for 1.5 miles to road's end. The final half mile is rough and steep.

At the trailhead, a road to the right with a locked green gate leads up 0.2 mile to Lookout Rock's fire tower, a possible side trip. The trail to Gearhart Mountain, however, starts at a message board on the left side of the trailhead turnaround. This path sets off through a forest of 3-foot-thick ponderosa pines and white firs. After 0.7 mile you'll enter The Palisades, where stratified andesite has weathered into pinnacles. Growing among the outcrops are orange paintbrush, lavender phlox, and the bushes of snowberry and pinemat manzanita.

Beyond The Palisades the trail returns to the forest for a long climb with occasional looks at other rock formations. At the 4.7-mile mark you'll reach a high saddle with wind-stunted whitebark pines *(GPS location N42°28.937' W120°51.945')*. Ahead is a colossal view of Gearhart Mountain's summit and the alpine meadows at the head of Dairy Creek. This would make a satisfactory turnaround point for a day hike, except that the next 1.3 miles are the prettiest of all, crossing those alpine openings below the mountain's cliffs to an even better viewpoint at a pass called The Notch. Mosquitoes are a problem in July.

Other Options

To bushwhack to Gearhart Mountain's summit, set out from the saddle at the trail's 4.7-mile mark and scramble up to the left 0.2 mile to the mountain's long summit ridgecrest. You'll need to look for a break in the cliffs, and you may have to use your hands. Once atop the ridge, however, simply amble north through open woods 1.3 nearly level miles to the top *(GPS location N42°29.761' W120°52.641')*, where views extend from Mt. Shasta to faint Mt. Jefferson.

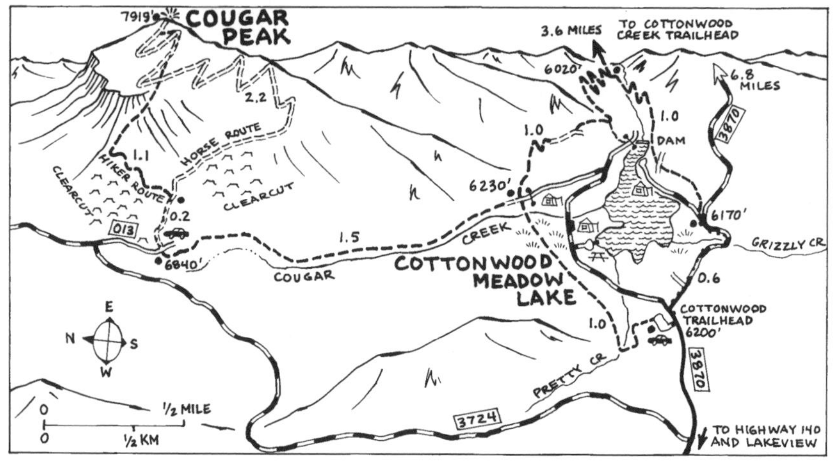

83 Cougar Peak

Easy (around lake)
3.6-mile loop
380 feet elevation gain
Open early May through November
Use: hikers, horses, bicycles

Moderate (to Cougar Peak)
7.6 miles round trip
1820 feet elevation gain
Open June to mid-November

Left: Cougar Peak.

Hidden in the forested mountains between Klamath Falls and Lakeview, Cottonwood Meadow Lake is a pleasant little reservoir among the pines, with free campgrounds, picnic sites, and trails. Expect mosquitoes in June. For an easy 3.6-mile loop, circle the lake. For a more challenging trip, climb nearby Cougar Peak to a lookout site with views from Mt. Shasta to Lakeview.

Start by driving Highway 140 east of Klamath Falls 74 miles (or west of Lakeview 17 miles). At a "Cottonwood Meadow" pointer near milepost 74, turn north on Road 3870 for 6.1 miles to the end of pavement. Campground areas are ahead and to the right, but for the hike, turn left into the Cottonwood Trailhead parking lot.

The trail climbs amid ponderosa pine and white fir, crosses a mountain stream, traverses an open pine grassland, and hops across 4-foot-wide Cougar Creek. On the far shore you'll meet an abandoned road and face a choice: Would you rather circle the lake or climb to Cougar Peak?

To continue around the lake, cross the old road and take an uphill path. This trail ambles a mile to the lake's outlet stream, Cottonwood Creek, where you'll cross a roadbed that's been converted to a trail. Continue straight another mile to the end of the lakeshore trail, and walk 0.6 mile along Road 3870 back to your car.

If you'd rather climb Cougar Peak, turn left beside Cougar Creek on the abandoned road, now designated as a trail. After 1.5 miles you'll cross dirt Road 013 at a rough, small upper trailhead. It's possible to shorten the climb by starting here. To drive here from the main Cottonwood Trailhead, drive back 0.9 mile on paved Road 3870, turn right on gravel Road 3724 for 3.4 miles to a T-shaped junction, and turn right on rough dirt Road 013 for 0.2 mile to the trail.

From the upper trailhead, go uphill alongside a clearcut on an old roadbed—the original lookout access road. Horses should follow this track 2.4 miles to the summit, but hikers can follow the road 0.2 mile and turn left on a genuine trail. This path climbs steeply 0.7 mile, crosses the lookout road once, briefly follows the old road to a switchback, and then angles up to the summit viewpoint. The vanished lookout's stone foundation makes a nice place to spread out lunch.

84 OC&E Railroad

Easy (Switchback Trailhead tour)
2.8 miles round trip
80 feet elevation gain
Open all year
Use: hikers, horses, bicycles

Easy (to Brown Cemetery)
4.8-mile loop
130 feet elevation gain

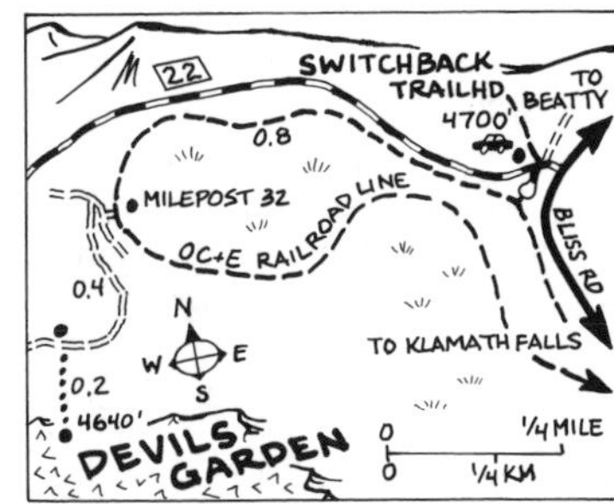

The state's longest and narrowest park consists of a hundred miles of railroad grades east of Klamath Falls. Open to hikers, bicyclists, and equestrians, the OC&E Woods Line State Trail follows an abandoned logging railroad from Klamath Falls over a mountain to the Sprague River. There the path forks, with one branch continuing upriver to Bly and another spur climbing to Sycan Marsh.

The railroad's story begins in 1917, when Klamath Falls entrepreneurs dreamed of building east to connect with railroad lines in Lakeview and Burns. Although the tracks stopped in Bly in 1929, the steam locomotives of the Oregon, California, & Eastern Railroad kept busy by hauling away Klamath County's forests. Up to a million board feet of ponderosa pine rode the steel rails to Klamath Falls each day. When the big trees were gone the line fell into disuse. In 1992 the route became a linear park as part of the "Rails to Trails" movement.

Only the first 7 miles of the old railbed have been paved, on the outskirts of Klamath Falls. The remainder is a smooth gravel route that slices straight across ranch fields and curves through pine woods. Perhaps the most interesting sections for day trips are at a mountain switchback where trains backed over a pass, and at Beatty where the railroad forks beside the Sprague River. If you have time, you can do both in one day.

Start by driving Highway 140 east of Klamath Falls toward Lakeview 17 miles. At the Yonna Valley Store, turn left on Bliss Road for 12 miles to a forested pass, turn left on Road 22, and immediately pull into the Switchback Trailhead parking area on the left *(GPS location N42°24.897' W121°33.014')*. Trains crossing this steep little pass used to loop around a switchback, stop on a deadend spur, and then back over the summit. Just beyond the switchback is the Devils Garden, a mile-wide patch of weird lava formations filling the caldera of an ancient volcano.

Hike to the right down the railroad grade 0.8 mile to the switchback. There is no trail to the Devils Garden, but if you're feeling adventurous (and especially if you have a GPS device), you can bushwhack there through the sagebrush and ponderosa pines. Near a milepost labeled "32" at the far end of the switchback loop, turn right a hundred yards on a faint dirt road. Then turn left on another dirt road for 0.4 mile, and finally strike off cross-country to the left (due south) across a small gully for 0.2 mile to the Devils Garden *(GPS location N42°24.66' W121°33.84')*. Ash from Crater Lake's eruption has left this lava field riddled with sandy openings that make for easy walking, but it's easy to get confused. Note your route so you can find your way back!

For the hike near Beatty, drive Bliss Road north 4 miles from the Switchback Trailhead, turn right on the Sprague River Highway 10 miles, and turn left on Highway 140 for 5 miles to Beatty (pronounced BAY-tee). Beside the Beatty Store turn north on paved Godowa Springs Road for 0.6 mile. When the road dips to cross a slough, look for a green metal gate on the right with signs banning motor vehicles and hunting. This is the railroad trail, but there's only enough space for one car to park here without blocking the gate. If your vehicle won't fit, drive back 0.6 mile to a shoulder pullout just before Highway 140 and walk back to the trail.

The trail sets off alongside a pond with cattails, redwing blackbirds, and snowy egrets. After 0.3 mile the glassy, 80-foot-wide Sprague River meanders up beside the path. After crossing Spring Creek on a bridge, the line forks. Keep straight for 0.6 mile, crossing the river on a low, 250-foot-long trestle.

Two roads join from the left at a river narrows called Beatty Gap. Turn left on the larger, uphill road for 0.3 mile. Then detour to the right 0.2 mile on a spur road to Brown Cemetery, a panoramic final resting place for Modoc families.

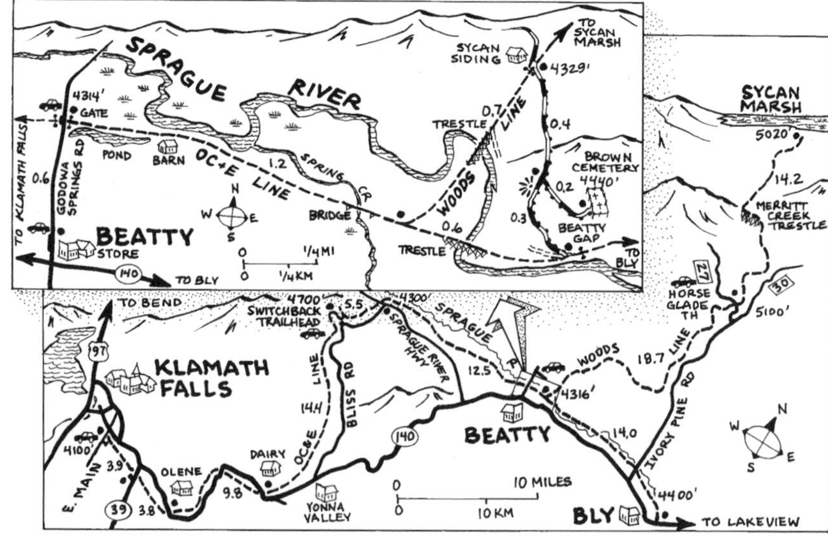

Sprague River trestle. *Below: Klamath Falls' Link River.*

After exploring the Indian cemetery, return to the main road for another 0.4 mile to Sycan Siding, an abandoned railyard. At a ranch house by the siding, turn left through a green metal gate onto a red cinder road that becomes the railroad trail and crosses another river trestle to complete the loop.

Other Options

Other top attractions on the OC&E Woods Line Trail include an 1898 steel railroad bridge in Klamath Falls (between Washburn Way and Highway 39), Five Mile Creek (where the tracks cross a stream 3 miles south of Horse Glade Trailhead), and the 400-foot Merritt Creek Trestle (8 miles north of Horse Glade Trailhead).

85 Klamath Falls

Easy
4.8 miles round trip
60 feet elevation gain
Open all year
Use: hikers

A seemingly magic resource allowed the Klamath tribe to live like kings—a waterfall at the outlet of Upper Klamath Lake, where salmon returned year after year. *Tiwishkeni*, or the "rush-of-falling-waters-place," has not been entirely lost amidst the city of Klamath Falls. Along the Link River trail from Upper Klamath Lake you can still expect to see pelicans and ruddy ducks. And although the path passes a freeway, a walk here still seems sheltered by wildness and magic.

Drive Highway 97 a mile north of downtown Klamath Falls, take the Lakeshore Drive exit, and follow signs toward Lakeshore Drive (which starts out as Nevada Avenue) for 0.8 mile. Immediately after crossing the Link River on a bridge, turn left into a paved parking lot for the Link River Nature Trail.

The wide gravel trail starts at a pedestrian turnstile with a "Pets On Leash Only"

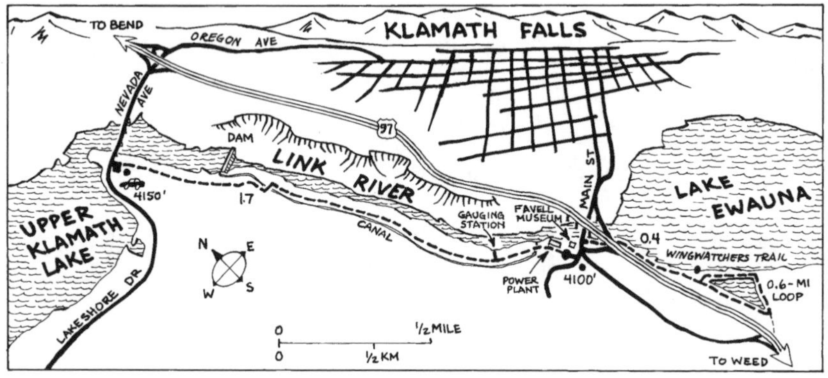

sign. The Link River here has been dammed to create a lake popular with birdlife. Giant white pelicans glide past, lanky black cormorants line up on the dam's boom logs, seagulls squawk, and blackbirds warble. Hikers who venture off trail may find stinging nettles among the willows and juniper of the shore, so stay on the main path. The trail passes the dam, bridges a 30-foot canal, and then follows the green canal along the edge of a remarkably wild river canyon. If you'd like to get down to the actual shore of the Link River, wait for the 1.4-mile mark and climb down a steel staircase to a small gauging station in jungly riverbank woods. This makes a good turnaround point for hikers with children.

If you continue on the main trail you'll soon pass a power station and a parking turnaround. Turn left on Main Street a few feet to the Favell Museum, a private collection of Western theme art and Indian artifacts (see page 178). In front of the museum, carefully cross busy Main Street to a gravel parking lot with a small brick building beside the Link River. Then continue on the gravel Klamath Wingwatchers Nature Trail to Lake Ewauna, ducking underneath three freeway bridges. After 0.4 mile turn left on a dike beside a cattail slough. Then keep right along the dike to circle the slough and start heading back to your car.

86 Modoc Lava Beds

Easy (Stronghold and Mushpot Cave)
0.9-mile total (for both short hikes)
100 feet elevation gain
Open all year
Use: hikers

Moderate (3 other interesting trails)
6.4 miles total
770 feet elevation gain

Left: Catacombs Cave entrance.

Riddled with lava caves, this volcanic landscape in Northern California was the setting for one of the West's most famous battles, where a defiant band of 52 Modoc men held off up to a thousand US Army troops for five months in 1872-73.

Today hiking trails tour the Lava Beds National Monument's geologic and historic sites. If you're short on time, hike the 0.7-mile loop to Captain Jack's Stronghold and explore the visitor center's Mushpot Cave. Otherwise spend the night at the campground and hike three slightly longer trails. Pets are banned on trails.

To drive here from Klamath Falls, follow signs for Reno. You'll end up on Highway 39, which turns into Highway 139 at the California border. Turn right 8.3 miles beyond the border and follow signs for the Lava Beds headquarters. After 11.4 miles, park in a large pullout on the left for Captain Jack's Stronghold.

An interpretive trail here winds through a lava moonscape where pressure ridges, outcrops, and caves served as a natural fortress for Keintpoos ("Captain Jack") and his Modoc warriors. The Modocs had been forced to leave their homeland here in 1864 to join their enemies the Klamaths on an Oregon reservation. After more than 600 of the Modocs returned, the US Army arrived in November, 1872 to take them to the reservation by force. Keintpoos stymied the troops and killed General Canby in a parley—the first US general to die in an Indian war. After Keintpoos' surrender on June 1, 1873, he and three other Modoc leaders were hanged.

At the 0.5-mile mark you'll reach a T-shaped trail junction. Turn right to complete a short loop back to your car, or turn left for a longer loop tour.

After hiking through Captain Jack's Stronghold, drive onward another 12.9 paved miles to the visitor center at the park's headquarters. Park here to tour the center's indoor displays. Then look for the entrance to Mushpot Cave, a railed pit with a steel staircase in the middle of the parking lot. This is the only lava tube in the national monument that is lighted inside. The lights go off at 5pm in winter and 6pm in summer. The 400-foot-long cave features *lavacicles* (where superheated gas remelted the rock walls), *cauliflower lava* (a chunky lava flow that puddled up on the floor), and a *mushpot*, where liquid rock bubbled up from a lower cave. Like all lava tubes, Mushpot Cave formed when a liquid basalt lava flow formed a crust but the hotter lava underneath kept on flowing, draining tube-shaped caves.

If Mushpot Cave catches your fancy, you can explore two dozen other lava tubes nearby. Simply drive the 1.3-mile paved loop road from the visitor center and stop

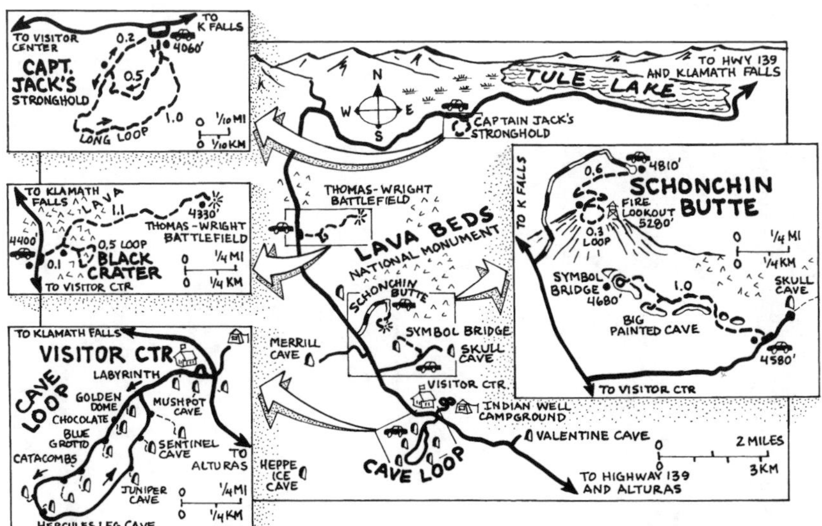

Schonchin Butte from the Cave Loop.

at one of the many parking pullouts. For these less developed caverns you'll need to remember some safety rules. Bring battery-powered flashlights (available for free at the visitor center). Never explore alone. Wear warm coats because the caves are cold even on hot days. Wear a helmet because many caves have low ceilings. Fires and gas lanterns are banned. Remember that several hours may be needed to explore a single cave. Also note that Labyrinth Cave, Hercules Leg - Juniper Cave, and Sentinel Cave have more than one entrance.

If you're staying overnight, head for the Indian Well Campground across the road from the visitor center. On your second day, consider hiking three other interesting trails. For the first of these recommended hikes, drive 1.6 miles north from the visitor center toward Klamath Falls. At a sign for Skull Cave, turn right for a mile to a pullout on the left for Symbol Bridge. This 1-mile path follows a partly collapsed lava tube to a natural arch with prehistoric petroglyphs.

For the next hike, return to the main road, drive another 0.7 mile north, and turn right toward Schonchin Butte for a mile. From here a trail climbs 0.6 mile up the cinder cone to its crater. A 0.3-mile loop around the rim visits a fire lookout tower (staffed in late summer) with a view from Mt. Shasta to Mt. McLoughlin.

For the final recommended hike, return to the main road and drive another 2.5 miles north to the Black Crater parking pullout. This path sets off across a sagebrush prairie with penstemon, larkspur, and other wildflowers in May and June. After 150 yards, fork to the right for a half-mile loop tour of Black Crater, a giant

Lake Abert from Abert Rim.

spatter cone with contorted, red-and-black lava outcroppings along its walls. Then return to the main trail and hike another 1.1 mile to trail's end at an overlook of the Thomas-Wright battlefield, where Captain Jack's warriors wiped out most of a 64-man Army patrol on April 26, 1873.

87 Abert Rim

Difficult
3.6 miles round trip
2010 feet elevation gain
Open: May through November
Use: hikers

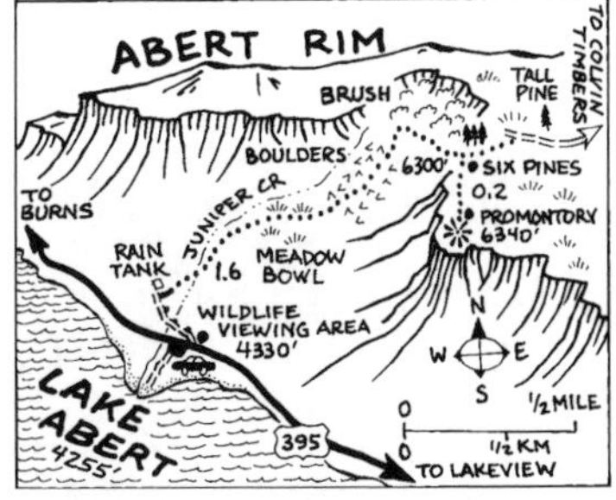

At first glance, Abert Rim's stark, 2000-foot cliff looks unclimbable, but a little known scramble route from Highway 395 takes hikers right to the top. The trip is both an athletic challenge and a panoramic tour through a high desert landscape, from the alkali shores of giant Lake Abert to the rimrock wildflowers of a 6340-foot promontory.

Start by driving 30 miles north of Lakeview on Highway 395. Between mileposts 85 and 84 (2 miles after the highway starts following Lake Abert's shore), park in a large gravel pullout on the left marked "Wildlife Viewing Area" *(GPS location N42°32.810' W120°12.866')*. An interpretive sign here explains that Lake Abert is the salty remnant of ancient Lake Chewaucan, which extended 40 miles to Summer Lake during the rainier climate of the Ice Age.

To see the lake's wildlife up close, you might want to drive (or walk) a rough dirt track from this parking pullout down 300 yards to the lake's sandy shore. Although there are no camp facilities here, picnicking and camping are permitted. Sandpiper-like plovers run along the lake's beach and giant white pelicans sail on white-capped waves. The birds throng here to feast on brine shrimp, which thrive in the alkali water. Because the shrimp are so hardy—capable of surviving freezes, drought, and even transport by desert wind to other lakes—they have also been successfully marketed as mail-order aquarium pets under the name "sea monkeys."

For the hike up Abert Rim, cross the highway from the parking pullout, bushwhack up through the sagebrush 80 feet, and turn left on an old roadbed for 0.1 mile to a metal rainfall collector that provides water for bighorn sheep. Then set off cross-country again, hiking uphill through the broad canyon of (often dry) Juniper Creek. The sagebrush is slightly less dense on the right-hand side of the creek wash, but you'll still want to be wearing long pants.

Continuing uphill, you'll cross a meadow bowl of bunchgrass, yellow balsam-root, orange paintbrush, and pale yellow locoweed. Then climb up a steep, bouldery slope—a rough pitch that requires nimble feet. At the top of the boulder field you'll find an upper basin filled with dense mountain mahogany brush. There is no easy way through. Crash upward through the brush, keeping right toward the closest part of the rimrock. After a final scramble up a rockslide you'll crest Abert Rim near a cluster of half a dozen ponderosa pine trees *(GPS location N42°32.060′ W120°12.305′)*. For the best view, keep right along the rim edge 0.2 mile to a spectacular rock promontory *(GPS location N42°32.050′ W120°12.543′)*. Directly below you 2000 feet, your car appears as a speck beside the vast, pale green sheet of Lake Abert.

88 Crooked Creek

Moderate
6.9 miles one way
2100 feet elevation **loss**
Open early June to mid-November
Use: hikers, horses, bicycles

The three completed segments of the Fremont Trail ramble more than 100 miles across south-central Oregon, through sagebrush desert, ponderosa pine forests, and high mountain meadows. Sample the trail's variety with a day trip along Crooked Creek, in the quiet Drake Peak area northeast of Lakeview. If you can arrange a car shuttle, the trip's all downhill. If you lack a shuttle, you can still explore either the upper or the lower end of Crooked Creek's canyon.

Start with a visit to the lower trailhead. From Lakeview, drive Highway 395 north 11 miles. Just after milepost 132, where the highway curves left, veer right at a "Mill Trailhead" sign onto a gravel road. After 0.2 mile, continue straight across a yellow cattle guard, and then keep straight for another 1.3 miles to the trailhead at road's end, avoiding left-hand forks that lead to a private ranch.

Ponderosa pines surround the turnaround at this lower trailhead *(GPS location*

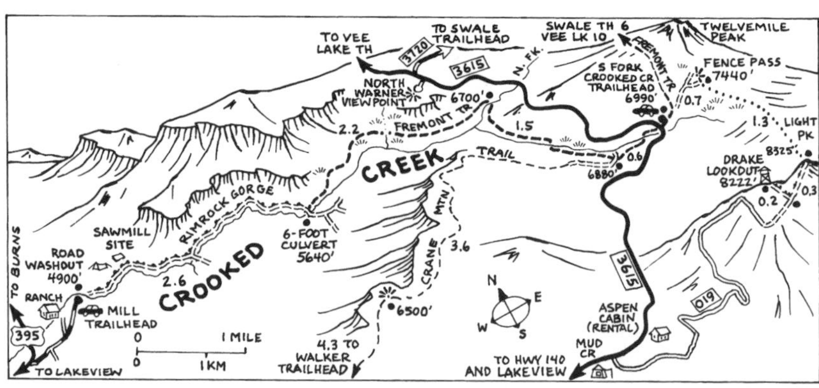

Light Peak from Fence Pass. *Opposite: South Fork Crooked Creek.*

N42°20.235′ W120°16.282′). This part of the canyon is usually snow-free from April through November. The trailhead used to be farther upstream near the foundations of an old sawmill, but floods washed out a road culvert. As it is, hikers will have to look for logs or rocks to cross the creek, and then continue up the abandoned roadbed through a scenic rimrock gorge.

If you plan to hike the trail downhill, leave a shuttle car at the Mill Trailhead and then drive a second car around to the South Fork Crooked Creek Trailhead. To find this upper trailhead, drive back on Highway 395 toward Lakeview 6 miles, turn left on Highway 140 toward Winnemucca 8.5 miles, and then turn left on narrow, paved North Warner Road 3615 for 10.6 miles to the South Fork Crooked Creek Trailhead on the right *(GPS location N42°19.001′ W120°10.068′).*

Walk across the paved road to find the faint start of the Fremont Trail opposite the parking lot entrance. The path ambles through a quaking aspen grove and soon enters a dense forest of lodgepole pine and white fir. After 0.6 mile the path crosses an abandoned road that serves as the Crane Mountain Trail. Continue straight on the Fremont Trail another 1.5 miles, hopping across first the South Fork and then the North Fork of Crooked Creek. Expect some cattle in July and August. For the next 2.2 miles the Fremont Trail descends across slopes with meadow openings where the tread can be a little faint. The path follows the 15-foot-wide creek down to an old road. Walk to the right along the old road for 2.6 scenic miles through a canyon to a bridgeless creek crossing at the lower trailhead.

Other Options

For a better view of the Drake Peak area's high country, hike uphill from the South Fork Crooked Creek Trailhead. After 0.1 mile the path forks. To the left is a new portion of the Fremont Trail, angling up around Twelvemile Peak. If you keep to the right, however, you'll follow an abandoned road uphill 0.6 mile through sagebrush meadows to Fence Pass, a windy gap with high desert wildflowers and far-ranging views. From there, explorers can follow an open sagebrush ridge south 1.3 miles, climbing to Light Peak, where a dirt road leads 0.5 mile to the panoramic view at the Drake Peak Lookout. The historic lookout cabin, also accessible by road (see map), is available for overnight rental from June 15 to October 15 for $40. Call 877-444-6777 or *www.recreation.gov* for reservations. The same rate and reservation system applies to Aspen Cabin, a small log cabin nearby on Road 3615.

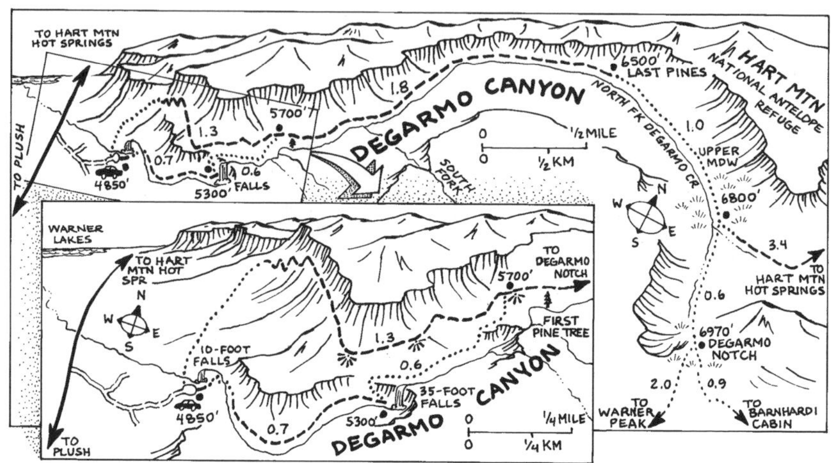

89 DeGarmo Canyon

Easy (to 35-foot falls)
1.4 miles round trip
450 feet elevation gain
Open late April through November
Use: hikers

Moderate (to first pine tree)
2.6-mile loop
850 feet elevation gain

Difficult (to DeGarmo Notch)
9.4 miles round trip
2120 feet elevation gain
Open June to mid-November

Like a secret door in a 2000-foot-tall wall, DeGarmo Canyon's spectacular slot offers adventurers a route from the Warner Lakes' valley into the high desert country of the Hart Mountain National Antelope Refuge. For a quick look at the canyon, follow a 0.7-mile trail to an oasis-like grotto at the base of a 35-foot waterfall. If you don't mind some steepish scrambling, you can return on a 2.6-mile loop trail with far-ranging views. If you want to explore the trailless upper end of the canyon, hike or backpack 5.7 miles to DeGarmo Notch.

Drive Highway 395 north of Lakeview 5 miles and turn east on Highway 140 toward Winnemucca for 16 miles to a fork. Following a pointer for Plush, veer left onto paved Road 3-13 for almost 20 miles to Plush's store/cafe/tavern/gas station. Continue straight through town 0.8 mile and turn right on paved Road 3-12 toward the Hart Mountain Refuge for 9.2 miles to a "DeGarmo Canyon" pointer. There is no side road here, but if you back up 100 yards you'll find a rough dirt road to the right marked "No Camping." Follow this track 0.5 mile uphill, keeping right at the 0.2-mile mark and left at the 0.3-mile mark, to a parking area at road's end *(GPS location N42°28.733' W119°47.379')*. The trail climbs immediately into the canyon's mouth, a red rock chasm with tall sagebrush and a tangle of quaking aspen. After just 100 yards the trail meets rushing DeGarmo Creek at a dangerous ford just above a 10-foot waterfall. Don't cross here. Instead follow rock ledges along the right-hand bank of the creek another 50 yards to an easier creek crossing. On the far side, scramble a few feet up to a clear trail. This path follows the creek upstream 0.6 mile to a cliff-lined grotto with a 35-foot waterfall. Listen here for the *zeet!* of water ouzels, dark, robin-sized birds that dive underwater in search of insects.

The trail ends at this waterfall, but adventurers can continue up the canyon by backtracking 100 feet to a steep scramble route that climbs around the end of the waterfall's cliffs. Then bushwhack half a mile upstream to another lava layer cliff that chokes the canyon. Detour around this one the same way, on a steep scramble route to the left. But then keep angling up the canyon's side 500 feet until you meet a well-built, relatively level trail at a viewpoint overlooking the canyon's first ponderosa pine tree. You may hear or even see a rattlesnake in this part of the canyon. If you do, stop a moment to let it retreat to safety.

The upper trail is an old cattle drive route from the days when the refuge allowed grazing. To return to your car on a loop, follow the trail left, traversing high above DeGarmo Canyon's rugged inner gorge. Dramatic views extend out the canyon mouth to Hart Lake. After 0.9 mile the trail suddenly dives down a sagebrush slope with a confusion of steep switchbacks. The path peters out at the slope's base *(GPS location N42°29.005' W119°47.327')*. At this point, however, you can see your car at the canyon mouth, so it's easy enough to bushwhack through the sagebrush and scramble across the creek to the trailhead.

If you'd like to explore the upper canyon, turn right when you first meet the old cattle trail. This part of the path has a few faint spots, but is generally easy to follow for 1.8 miles, passing groves of quaking aspen and big ponderosa pines. The trail ends when you pass the last pines, but the treeless upper canyon makes for easy walking. A range fire in the late 1990s replaced most sagebrush with the blooms of orange paintbrush. A mile past the last pines the canyon forks at a grassy meadow of corn lilies (hellebore). If you veer left, you can follow a faint old road 3.4 miles to the Hart Mountain Hot Springs campground. If you keep right you'll hike past a quaking aspen grove to the canyon's end at DeGarmo Notch. Both routes are described in Hike #90. If you're backpacking, you'll need a self-issued backcountry permit, available free at all hours at the refuge's headquarters, 15 miles up the main road from the DeGarmo Canyon turnoff.

Hart Lake from DeGarmo Canyon. *Opposite: The 35-foot waterfall.*

90 Hart Mountain Hot Springs

Tortoiseshell butterfly.

Moderate (to Barnhardi Cabin)
5.3-mile loop
750 feet elevation gain
Open late May to mid-November
Use: hikers, horses

Difficult (to DeGarmo Notch)
7.4-mile loop
1600 feet elevation gain
Open June to mid-November

Difficult (to Warner Peak)
11.1 miles round trip
2320 feet elevation gain

At this hot springs in the high desert country of the Hart Mountain National Antelope Refuge, you can soak in a free, natural 102° F rock pool, watching bubbles rise from the rocks below while songbirds zoom overhead. Plenty of free campsites are nearby, scattered along grassy streambanks amid groves of silver-leaved quaking aspen.

Most visitors here take a dip in the hot springs, camp, and then drive on. But to see the refuge's wildlife and mountain scenery up close, use the campground as a base for some exploration afoot. Although the only trails are animal paths, bushwhacking is easy through the high desert's sagebrush meadows. For a moderate loop, hike along Rock Creek to an old sheepherder's cabin at Barnhardi Basin. For a longer loop, continue through a high pass to DeGarmo Canyon. For an even tougher day hike, bushwhack to the area's highest viewpoint, 8017-foot Warner Peak.

From Lakeview, drive 5 miles north on Highway 395 and turn east on Highway 140 toward Winnemucca for 16 miles to a fork. Following signs for the Hart Mountain Refuge, veer left onto paved Road 3-13 for almost 20 miles to Plush.

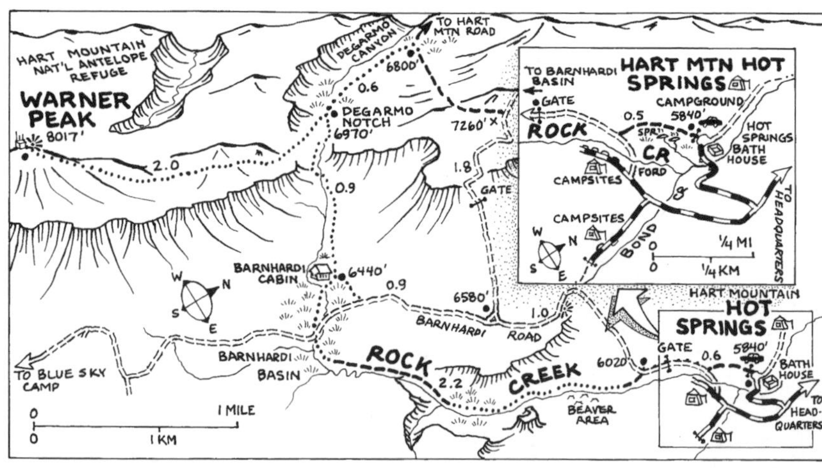

A rustic ranching hamlet, Plush has a combination store/cafe/tavern/gas station. Check your gas gauge here. Then continue straight through town 0.8 mile and turn right on Road 3-12 for 24 miles (the last 10 miles on good gravel) to the refuge headquarters. A visitor room here, always open, has displays, brochures, restrooms, and the free, self-issuing backcountry permits required for overnighting anywhere except at Hot Springs Campground.

Beyond the refuge headquarters, keep right at road forks for 4.5 miles to a parking area at the hot springs bath house, where a rock-faced wall surrounds a natural 8-by-10-foot rock pool. Signs note the pool rules: No glass containers. No soap. No more than six people. Maximum stay 20 minutes if others are waiting.

For the hike, cross the parking area from the bath house and walk along a closed old road that curves left through a meadow with several undeveloped hot springs. After 0.2 mile, turn right on Barnhardi Road for 0.3 mile to a silver gate (locked to vehicles December 1 to August 1). Continue another 150 yards, but when the road curves to the right away from the creek, fork left on a faint track with a "No Motor Vehicles" sign. This track soon peters out. Simply continue up Rock Creek for 2.2 miles to Barnhardi Basin, keeping right along the creek's main branch.

Wear long pants to protect your legs from the sagebrush. Expect to scramble a bit when you pass an aspen grove with trees felled by beaver. When you reach the broad meadow bowl of Barnhardi Basin, you'll have to cross Barnhardi Road to reach the cabin, a dilapidated 10-by-16-foot plank shack in a grove of giant aspens *(GPS location N42°28.790' W119°43.200')*. If the cabin is your goal, you can return on a loop by following Barnhardi Road back to your car. If you'd like a longer hike, skirt the boggy area directly behind the cabin and follow a little creek up through aspen groves 0.9 mile to DeGarmo Notch, a broad, grassy saddle *(GPS location N42°29.094' W119°43.917')*.

For a loop route back from DeGarmo Notch, continue straight 0.6 mile down the sagebrush meadows and aspen groves of DeGarmo Canyon. Where the canyon forks, turn right on a faint old roadbed up a side valley. After climbing 0.7 mile to a windy ridgecrest, turn right on a larger dirt road that descends 1.1 mile to the Barnhardi Road and the route back to your car.

A detour to Warner Peak's summit adds 4 trailless miles to your trip, but it's mostly easy walking along an open alpine ridge. From DeGarmo Notch, traverse uphill to the south, angling below an outcrop of cliffs, to a bare ridge shoulder

Warner Peak from Rock Creek.

above a grove of mountain mahogany trees. Then simply continue south along the ridge. Soon you'll see your goal: a small concrete building and radio towers on the summit *(GPS location N42°27.579′ W119°44.474′)*, where views extend from Steens Mountain to California's South Warner Mountains.

Other Options

Those who arrange a car shuttle can connect Hikes #90 and #89 into a single 9.4-mile trek from Hart Mountain Hot Springs through DeGarmo Notch and down the length of DeGarmo Canyon.

91 Petroglyph Lake

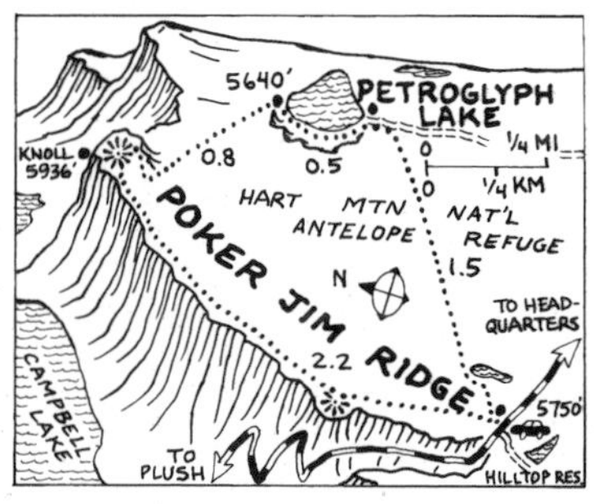

Moderate
5-mile loop
320 feet elevation gain
Open early May to mid-November
Use: hikers, horses

Little is known about the people who painted red spirals and animalistic figures on Oregon's desert cliffs thousands of years ago. Because modern Oregon tribes have no similar painting traditions or legends, the petroglyphs may well be the work of a different people—a mysterious, earlier culture that hoped to communicate with the spirit world through symbolic messages at sacred sites. One of those sacred places must have been this small lake on the vast desert plateau atop Poker Jim Ridge. In what is now the Hart Mountain National Antelope Refuge, nearly 100 drawings decorate the black basalt ledge ringing Petroglyph Lake's western shore.

An interesting 5-mile tour of this trailless landscape skirts the spectacular rim of Poker Jim Ridge's 1300-foot cliff before returning via Petroglyph Lake. To be sure, this is no hike for the disrespectful, nor for the ill prepared. Even the touch

Ancient art at Petroglyph Lake.

EAGLE CAP (Hike #58), at the center of the Wallowa Mountains, reflects in a pond above Mirror Lake.

THE PINE LAKES (Hike #75) fill an alpine basin in the Southern Wallowas above the ghost town of Cornucopia.

DOUGLAS LAKE lies in the heavily used Lak (Hike #56) south of Joseph and Wallowa Lake

TRAVERSE LAKE (Hike #69) is one of many heavily visited lakes in the Southern Wallowa

Pika

THE WALLOWAS

EAGLE CAP'S summit (Hike #58).

RONZE SCULPTURES line the streets of Joseph, with the Wallowa Mountains behind.

HELLS CANYON sign.

Chief Joseph and the Nez Perce

yo-tailed
allowtail.

Among the most peaceable of Northwest tribes, the Nez Perce caught salmon at the outlet of Wallowa Lake and bred prized Appaloosa ponies on the plains below. When the US Army ordered the 400-member Wallowa band to move to a small Idaho reservation in May 1877, Chief Joseph led his people across Hells Canyon, crossing the Snake River at flood stage. A shootout just short of the reservation, however, sent the tribe on a 4-month tactical retreat, ending with defeat just 30 miles short of political sanctuary in Canada. The tribe was exiled to distant reservations where Joseph died of what his doctor called "a broken heart." In 1997 the federal government granted the tribe 10,000 acres of Wallowa County land as compensation for broken treaties. Since then the tribe has held an annual summer friendship powwow along the lower Wallowa River.

Signs mark the tribe's 1877 route.

A MONUMENT beside Wallowa Lake, on Highway 82 just south of Joseph, contains the bones of Chief Joseph's father.

AT DUG BAR (Hike #44) Chief Joseph led his tribe across the Snake River.

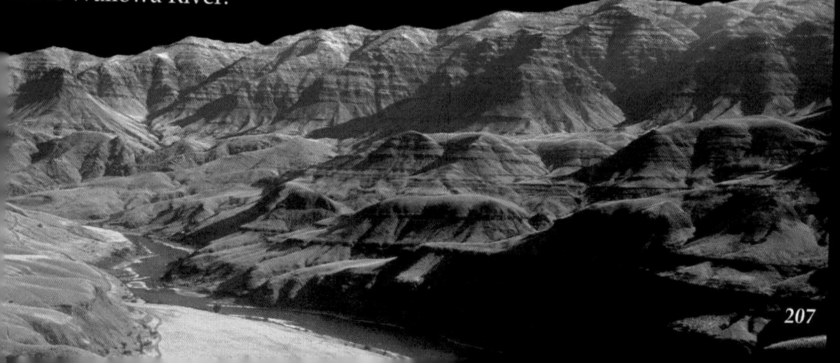

FORT ROCK (Hike #76), looming like a castle in the desert, was once an island in a giant Ice Age lake.

CRACK IN THE GROUND (Hike #77) is a 2-mile-long lot through the high desert country near Fort Rock.

DERRICK CAVE (Hike #77), is a lava tube near Fort Rock with natural skylights.

THE WARNER LAKES (see page 178) flood the desert below Hart Mountain in wet years, a haven for birds.

Mountain Wildlife

BIGHORN SHEEP. Herds of a dozen or more graze cliffy slopes and alpine meadows at Strawberry Mountain, Hells Canyon, and Steens Mountain. Males butt heads at up to 20 miles per hour.

ELK. Bull elk can weigh 1000 pounds, collecting "harems" of up to 60 females and bugling to declare their territory. They're not seen a lot because they graze at night and bed in thickets by day.

MOUNTAIN GOAT. Rare in the Wallowas but common in the Elkhorn Range, mountain goats sometimes descend from their cliff ledges to nibble an unwatched backpack for salt.

STEENS MOUNTAIN looms snowy and sudden a mile above Oregon's driest point, the stark Alvord Desert.

Steens Mountain

KIGER GORGE (Hike #92) is one of seven giant canyons carved into Steens Mountain by Ice Age glaciers.

FRENCHGLEN'S HOTEL (see page 216), a center for Steens Mountain explorations, has been restored by the Oregon State Parks.

LESLIE GULCH (Hike #98), east of Steens Mountain, features canyons of colored "honeycomb" formations.

WILDHORSE LAKE (Hike #92) is a nice goal for a hike from Steens Mountain's summit.

BORAX HOT SPRINGS (Hike #96), protected by The Nature Conservancy for its rare fish, is unswimmable.

HART MOUNTAIN hot springs (Hike #90) has a free campground nearby.

SUMMER LAKE hot springs' bathhouse dates to 1928 (see page 177).

THE ALVORD DESERT and Steens Mountain's snowy rim serve as a backdrop to Alvord Hot Springs (page 217).

MICKEY HOT SPRINGS (see page 217) has dangerous boiling pools and one small pool cool enough for a swim.

ALVORD HOT SPRINGS (see page 217) is on private land, so be prepared to pay a small fee.

BORAX HOT SPRINGS (Hike #96) has weird algae (right) and vats (below) from its 20-mule team borax mining days.

AT THREE FORKS (Hike #100), in the extreme southeastern corner of Oregon, cliffs reflect the Owyhee River.

The Warner Lakes and Poker Jim Ridge.

of a finger can damage the ancient paintings. And the desert in all directions is a rock-strewn flat of matted sagebrush with few landmarks. Antelope and deer race past with apparent ease, but hikers here will need long pants, good boots, strong ankles, and routefinding skills.

From Lakeview, drive 5 miles north on Highway 395 and turn east on Highway 140 toward Winnemucca for 16 miles to a fork. Following signs for the Hart Mountain Refuge, veer left onto paved Road 3-13 for almost 20 miles to Plush's combination store/cafe/tavern/gas station. Check your gas gauge here. Then continue straight through town 0.8 mile and turn right on Road 3-12 for 21.6 miles, the final 7.6 miles on gravel. At the crest of a long, steep uphill grade (2.4 miles before reaching the refuge headquarters), park beside a "Hilltop Reservoir" pointer at the junction of a small road to the right *(GPS location N42°33.833' W119°41.643')*. Vehicles are not allowed farther than one car-length off the road here, or anywhere on refuge land.

Walk across the gravel road from the signpost and strike off north across the desert, heading uphill. Sagebrush forms a 6-inch mat, interspersed with bunchgrass, desert parsley, and the white plumes of death camas. If you don't reach the rim of Poker Jim Ridge's colossal cliff within a mile, bear left until you do. The cliff overlooks the Warner Lakes—a dozen vaguely oval alkali seas interspersed with thousands of sinuous lakes and waterways. Hike north along the rim another 1.2 miles up to a juniper knoll with an even better view *(GPS location N42°35.479' W119°40.999')*.

From the knoll you'll be able to look east across Poker Jim Ridge's plateau to two relatively nearby lakes. Petroglyph Lake is the one on the right. To hike there you'll first have to detour a bit to the right around a bouldery cliff. When you've scrambled down around the cliff you won't be able to see the lake anymore, so simply head straight toward the refuge headquarters, a distant cluster of buildings with a tree. On this southeast bearing you'll cross 0.8 mile of desert to the 20-foot basalt cliff embracing Petroglyph Lake. Thousands of years ago the lake was much higher, but today's drier climate has left it ringed with an alkali beach. Walk the length of the cliff's base to see the ancient paintings, but *touch nothing!*

At the far right-hand end of the lakeside cliff, follow a road 200 yards up a wash that once served as the lake's outlet *(GPS location N42°34.538' W119°40.446')*. Leave the dirt road at a "Road Closed" post and strike off to the right, southwest across the desert. Head straight for the giant cliff of Warner Peak's west face, the steepest landform in sight. After a mile you'll see your car ahead, a dot beside the road.

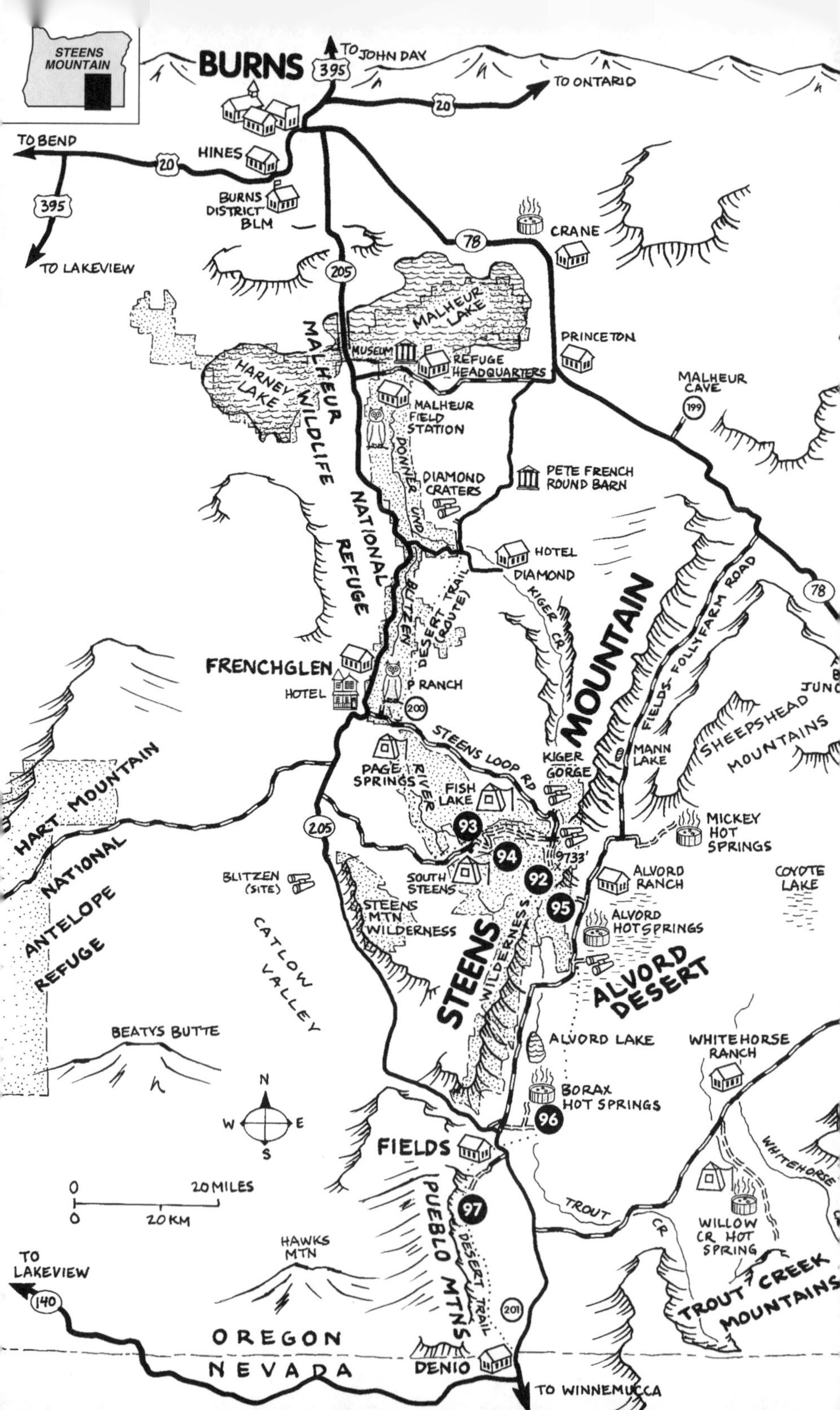

STEENS MOUNTAIN
BURNS
TO JOHN DAY
395
TO ONTARIO
20
TO BEND
HINES
BURNS DISTRICT BLM
TO LAKEVIEW
CRANE
78
205
MALHEUR LAKE
MUSEUM
REFUGE HEADQUARTERS
PRINCETON
MALHEUR CAVE
199
HARNEY LAKE
MALHEUR WILDLIFE NATIONAL REFUGE
MALHEUR FIELD STATION
DONNER UND
DIAMOND CRATERS
PETE FRENCH ROUND BARN
HOTEL
DIAMOND
KIGER CR
BLITZEN
DESERT TRAIL (ROUTE)
FIELDS-FOLLYFARM ROAD
MOUNTAIN
FRENCHGLEN
HOTEL
P RANCH
200
STEENS LOOP RD
PAGE SPRINGS
RIVER
FISH LAKE
KIGER GORGE
MANN LAKE
SHEEPSHEAD MOUNTAINS
HART MOUNTAIN NATIONAL ANTELOPE REFUGE
93
94
92
95
9733'
MICKEY HOT SPRINGS
BLITZEN (SITE)
SOUTH STEENS
ALVORD RANCH
COYOTE LAKE
STEENS MTN WILDERNESS
ALVORD HOTSPRINGS
CATLOW VALLEY
STEENS
WILDERNESS
ALVORD DESERT
BEATYS BUTTE
ALVORD LAKE
WHITEHORSE RANCH
BORAX HOT SPRINGS
96
N
W
E
S
FIELDS
WHITEHORSE
0
20 MILES
0
20 KM
TROUT
CR
97
WILLOW CR HOT SPRING
HAWKS MTN
PUEBLO MTNS
DESERT TRAIL
TO LAKEVIEW
140
201
TROUT CREEK MOUNTAINS
OREGON
NEVADA
DENIO
TO WINNEMUCCA

The Frenchglen Hotel.

BURNS

Landmark for all of southeast Oregon, 50-mile-long Steens Mountain looms a vertical mile above the Alvord Desert's stark alkali flats. Nights are crisp and starry in this quiet corner of Oregon. Days are pungent with the scent of sage.

Burns, the area's commercial center, is about ten times smaller than Bend. Rooms run $95-125 in the town's quaintest retreat, the **Sage Country Inn Bed & Breakfast** (541-573-7243, *www.sagecountryinn.com*), a 1907 Georgian-Colonial home at 351½ W. Monroe, on the corner of Highway 20 (W. Monroe Street) and S. Court Avenue.

Steens Mountain

Congress protected much of this 9733-foot-tall fault-block mountain with the 174,573-acre **Steens Mountain Wilderness** in 2000. Most visitors begin in Frenchglen (see below) and drive the **Steens Mountain Loop Road,** a 65-mile gravel circuit that slices through the Wilderness almost to the mountain's summit. Because this is the highest road in Oregon, cresting at 9550 feet, snow gates close the upper part of the loop from November through June, depending on snow levels. Even when the gates are open, many visitors drive only the northern part of the loop to avoid the Rooster Comb, a very rough, steep 6-mile road section not suitable for trailers, RVs, or low-clearance vehicles.

Highlights along the Steens Mountain Loop Road, clockwise from Frenchglen, include the **Page Springs Campground** (open all year, $8 per site), the **Fish Lake Campground** (open mid-July through October, $8 per site, no motorboats allowed on lake), the **Jackman Park Campground** (open July 1 to October 31, $6 per site), the **Kiger Gorge and East Rim viewpoints** (see Hike #92), the Rooster Comb, and the **South Steens Campground** (open May through November, $6 per site, see Hikes #93 and #94). Expect to see wild horses, deer, and antelope.

Malheur Wildlife Refuge

Most of Steens Mountain's winter snow melts into creeks that flow westward down gigantic U-shaped gorges to the marshlands of the Malheur National Wildlife Refuge. Huge flocks of migrating birds stop here from March through May: sandhill cranes, snow geese, egrets, swans, grebes, herons, pelicans, songbirds, and many kinds of ducks. Bring binoculars or a spotting scope to watch birds from your car without disturbing them. From Burns, drive east 1.7 miles on Highway 78, turn right toward Frenchglen on Highway 205 for 23.2 miles, and turn left 6 miles to the Malheur Refuge Headquarters. A worthwhile museum here (open dawn to dusk) has some 200 mounted specimens of birds. A nearby visitor center offers road tour maps, brochures, and tips on recent bird sightings. For more bird info, check Oregon's important bird areas at *www.oregoniba.org*.

Frenchglen

An hour south of Burns, this frontier hamlet consists of a few dozen buildings. The 1916 **Frenchglen Hotel** (open March 15 to November 1), restored by the Oregon State Parks, still has no public telephone or television. Rooms run $70 for a double with a shared bath and $90 with a private bath. For meals, guests pack family-style around two large tables. Typical dinner fare is herb-baked chicken with garlic roast potatoes and marionberry pie for about $14. Reservations are required, but drop-ins are welcome for lunch and breakfast (about $6). Closed November 1 to March 15. Call 541-493-2825.

P Ranch Headquarters

The P Ranch and Frenchglen were named for Peter French, sent to Oregon in 1872 by ranching mogul James Glenn. French ruthlessly amassed ranchland, including much of the present Malheur Wildlife Refuge. In 1897 French was shot dead by a homesteader, but a local jury acquitted the murderer. To see the ranch headquarters, drive the Steens Mountain Loop Road west of Frenchglen 1.5 miles, turn left on a gravel road 0.2 mile, and turn left to a parking area beside the Donner und Blitzen River. First walk the left-hand road 0.1 mile to a 200-foot-long horse barn built with juniper trunks. A square winch outside hoisted slaughtered cattle. Then stroll along the glassy river to spot redwing blackbirds and ducks.

Diamond

Less well known than Frenchglen, the village of Diamond is dominated by the **Hotel Diamond,** a rambling old white clapboard building with a cafe and eight hotel rooms ($74-97; open April through October, 541-493-1898, *www.central-oregon.com/hoteldiamond*). Drive Highway 205 south of Burns 44 miles (or north of Frenchglen 17 miles), and turn east for 13 paved miles to Diamond.

Nearby **Diamond Craters** is a 2500-year-old lava field strewn with volcanic craters, domes, and cracks. Drive west of Diamond 6 miles, turn right on paved Lava Beds Road toward Highway 78 for 3.2 miles, and turn left to the craters on a 4.7-mile cinder road suitable only for high-clearance vehicles. Next continue north toward Highway 78 on the paved road another 9 miles to a sign for **Peter French's Round Barn,** a 100-foot-diameter building with a circular stone corral inside. French built the unusual barn about 1880 to train horses.

Crystal Crane Hot Springs

Commercialized but practical, this resort 25 miles southeast of Burns on Highway 78 offers a hot pool for $3.50, private hot tubs for $7.50, tent sites for $15, and five simple cabins for $45-60. Call 541-493-2312 or check *www.cranehotsprings.com*.

Alvord Desert and hot springs

For a spectacular drive along the base of Steens Mountain's abrupt eastern cliff, follow the excellent gravel Fields-Follyfarm road to hot springs and desert viewpoints. Start at the rustic cafe/store/gas station that is **Fields,** where you'll want to stop for one of their famous milkshakes. Take the paved road 1.3 miles north toward Frenchglen and keep right onto the wide gravel Fields-Follyfarm road toward Highway 78. (This junction is also the turnoff for **Borax Hot Springs,** Hike #96). Drive north 19.6 miles to the turnoff for the **Alvord Desert** on the right. Look for this unmarked side road 1.4 miles after your first view of the Alvord Desert's 9-mile-long dry alkali lakebed. A rough dirt spur descends 0.5 mile to the alkali flat, which is open to hiking or driving except on the rare occasions when the playa actually fills with water. Annual precipitation here is just 6 inches.

From the Alvord Desert turnoff, continue north on the main road another 2.6 miles to the unmarked **Alvord Hot Springs.** Just beyond a cattle guard, look for a tin shed 200 yards to the right of the road. Privately owned, but open to the public for $5, the springs fill two 8-by-8-foot concrete pools at about 102°F.

North of Alvord Hot Springs 2 miles the road passes Pike Creek (Hike #95). To find **Mickey Hot Springs,** continue another 8.5 miles, passing the Alvord Ranch and two 90° highway curves. At a green cattle guard immediately after the road has curved sharply to the left, turn right on an unmarked gravel side road. Follow this washboard track through several zigzags. After 2.6 miles, keep left at a fork. After another 3.9 miles, park at a railed turnaround on the right. Very dangerous for children or pets, the moonscape at Mickey Hot Springs features boiling pools, steam jets, mudpots, and the scalding, 30-foot-deep turquoise Morning Glory Pool. All pools are far too hot for humans, with the possible exception of a single bathtub-sized basin carved into the ground by frustrated bathers.

Steens Mountain's summit in April.

92 Steens Summit

Easy (to three viewpoints)
1 mile total
250 feet elevation gain
Open mid-July to late October

Moderate (to Wildhorse Lake)
2.4 miles round trip
1100 feet elevation **loss**

The windswept cliffs at the summit of Steens Mountain seem perched on the edge of the planet. More than a vertical mile below, the Alvord Desert shimmers faintly, a mirage in the void. At 9733 feet, this is the eighth tallest mountain in Oregon, and the easiest to climb. In fact, after strolling through an otherworldly landscape half a mile to the top, you're likely to have enough energy left over to scramble down into a hanging valley of wildflowers at Wildhorse Lake.

Fill your car's gas tank before leaving Burns. Then drive 1.7 miles east on Highway 78 toward Crane and turn right on paved Highway 205 for 61 miles to Frenchglen. Just beyond the Frenchglen Hotel, fork left onto the gravel Steens Mountain Loop Road for 2.9 miles to the Page Springs Campground entrance. Keep left, past a snow gate that's closed from about mid-November until Memorial Day.

Driving up Steens Mountain is like climbing a 20-mile ramp. A tilted mesa with an active fault on its steep, eastern side, this fault-block mountain has risen up in the past five to seven million years. During the Ice Age, seven large glaciers gouged 2000-foot-deep, U-shaped canyons into the western slope.

After driving 13.2 miles up from the gate, detour to the right into the Fish Lake Recreation Site. Mountain lakes are rare in southeast Oregon and this pool's a beauty, with a campground and picnic area among silvery-leaved quaking aspen. Then continue up the main road another 5.7 miles, passing a snow gate that's closed from about November 1 until July 1, depending on snow levels. At a pointer for the Kiger Gorge Viewpoint, detour 0.4 mile to the left and walk 100 yards to a cliff-edge panorama of Kiger Creek's gorge. This colossal trough breaches the mountain's crest, leaving a gap called Kiger Notch.

Wildhorse Lake. Above: Steens Mountain's East Rim Viewpoint.

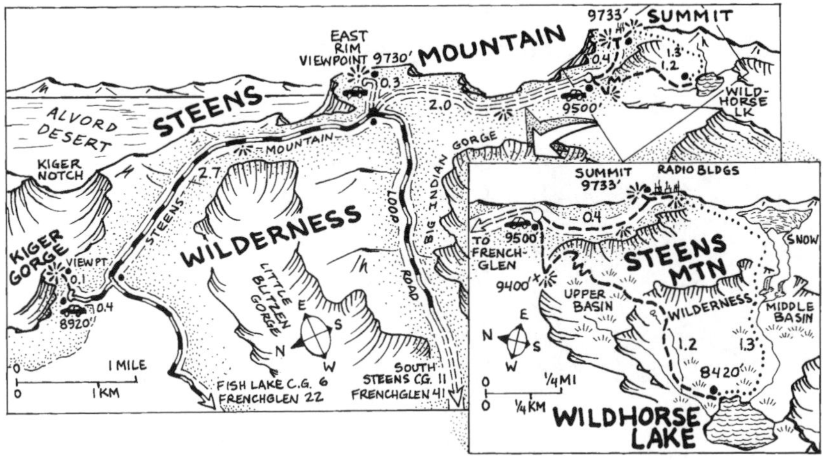

From the Kiger Gorge Viewpoint, return to the main gravel road and continue 2.7 miles to a 4-way junction. First turn left for a 0.3-mile side trip up to the East Rim Viewpoint and a dizzying look down to the Alvord Desert. Then return to the 4-way junction and follow a "Wildhorse Lake" pointer left on a rough dirt road for 2 miles to a parking lot at road's end. The sparse blooms of white yarrow, pink desert buckwheat, and white phlox struggle here in a field of lava rocks encrusted with black, green, and orange lichens.

Two trails start from this parking lot. If you're headed for Steens Mountain's summit, simply hike up a barricaded, steep, rocky roadbed 0.4 mile to a crest. The actual summit is 100 feet to the left. To the right, you'll find a different viewpoint just beyond five small radio buildings.

If you have a little more time and energy, however, try the other trail from the parking lot. This path heads downhill past a hiker registration box for 0.2 mile to a rimrock cliff overlooking Wildhorse Lake. Here the trail suddenly turns left, traversing down a precariously steep rocky slope. Soon the path begins following a brook through increasingly lush meadows, ablaze with pink monkeyflower, orange paintbrush, and yellow Oregon sunshine. At the 1.2-mile mark, the narrow sand beach of Wildhorse Lake makes a good turnaround point. If you're backpacking, camp well away from the fragile shore and bring a cookstove, because fires are not allowed.

Other Options

Adventurers who don't want to backtrack can return from Wildhorse Lake on a loop through trailless but open alpine country. When you first reach the lakeshore, having followed an inlet creek down from the rimrock, walk to the left around the beach 150 yards to a different 3-foot inlet creek, and follow this stream uphill. After climbing above the waterfalls at a meadowed middle basin, head straight for the radio towers on Steens Mountain's summit. At the top, simply walk the wide, 0.4-mile trail down to your car.

If you have a passenger car, it's safest to drive back to Frenchglen the way you came. If your vehicle has high clearance, however, drive back 2 miles to the 4-way junction and turn left on the continuation of the Steens Mountain Loop Road. This longer route to Frenchglen includes a rough, 6-mile stretch of steep, rocky road.

93 Little Blitzen River

Easy (to Donner und Blitzen River)
5.6 miles round trip
400 feet elevation **loss**
Open late May to late November
Use: hikers, horses

Moderate (to 4-Mile Camp)
8.2 miles round trip
900 feet elevation gain
Open June to mid-November
Map: Fish Lake (USGS)

Riddle me this: How many bachelor cowboys does it take to create a historic ranch district? The answer is three, if we're talking about the Riddle Brothers Ranch along the Little Blitzen River. Three brothers—Fred, Ben, and Walt Riddle—built plank-and-log ranchhouses on Steens Mountain in the early 1900s. The trio died childless, and the Bureau of Land Management later bought the area. The partially restored ranches recall a simpler, Old West lifestyle, with kerosene lamps, woodstoves, and barns full of horse gear.

The ranch area also serves as a starting point for hikers exploring trails along the Little Blitzen River. An easy 1.5-mile path downstream from Fred Riddle's cabin is popular with fly fishermen and hikers with children. A longer route up Little Blitzen Gorge prowls the rugged high country of Steens Mountain.

The Riddle brothers were the third generation of the pioneer family that founded the town of Riddle, south of Roseburg. Fred, Ben, and Walt raised mules, herded them south to the rail line at Winnemucca, and sold them to the US Army cavalry. They raised cattle and irrigated hayfields. They brewed moonshine, read books, played records on a Victrola, and complained about who had to do the cooking. Fred kept 40 cats, feeding them six gallons of milk a day.

Fill your car's gas tank before setting out from Burns. Then take Highway 78 east toward Crane for 1.7 miles, turn right on Highway 205 for 61 miles to Frenchglen, continue towards Fields another 10 paved miles, and then turn left onto the gravel Steens Mountain Loop Road, closed by a gate from about Thanksgiving to late May. Drive 19.2 miles to a sign for Riddle Ranch (0.3 mile before South Steens Campground), and turn left on a dirt road for 1.3 miles to a parking area by a gate.

The road ahead is too rough for passenger cars, so you may need to park here and walk the next 1.3 miles to road's end. High-clearance vehicles can continue when the gate's unlocked, Thursday through Sunday from mid-June to October.

From road's end, cross a footbridge over the Little Blitzen River to tour Fred Riddle's ranch house. Then return to road's end and go up a steep little trail near an outhouse. This path heads downriver past a corral of woven willow branches, forks briefly, rejoins, and ends at a meadow by the Donner und Blitzen River. This is a lovely spot to lie in the grass and watch the glassy rivers merge. Butterflies flit past. Trout dart in the water. It's easy to see why the Riddles liked the place.

For a longer hike up Little Blitzen Gorge, drive back to the Steens Mountain Loop Road and turn left 0.8 mile. Beyond South Steens Campground half a mile pull into the Little Blitzen Trailhead on the right (*GPS location N42°39.663' W118°43.303'*).

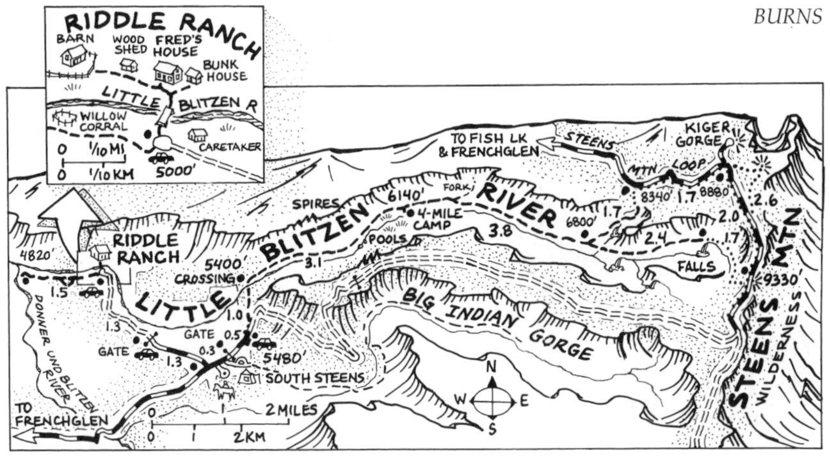

The trail itself starts 100 yards farther up the road on the left and descends a mile to a bridgeless crossing of the Little Blitzen, which you can usually manage dry-footed on wobbly logs. Then turn right on a fainter, brushier route that enters a spectacular canyon lined with 1000-foot cliffs. Wear long pants and boots! At the 3-mile mark you'll pass two deep little pools in the river and enter a broad meadow with wildflowers among the sage. A mile upriver is 4-Mile Camp, with a ruined corral and big cottonwood trees (*GPS location N42°41.569′ W118°40.435′)*.

Other Options

Four-Mile Camp makes a good day-hike goal, but if you backpack there you can explore the rest of Little Blitzen Gorge the next day. It's 3.8 increasingly rough miles up to a fork at a rimrock knoll that divides the canyon. To the left a steep, rough path climbs to the Steens Mountain Loop Road. To the right the trail continues faintly upriver 2.4 miles to a 20-foot waterfall at the lip of the valley's bowl-shaped cirque, filled with alpine flowers and rimmed with headwall cliffs. Climbing out of this mile-wide bowl is tricky and requires the use of your hands, even at the easiest spot, alongside a cascade to the right.

Little Blitzen Gorge near 4-Mile Camp. *Opposite: Fred Riddle's ranch house.*

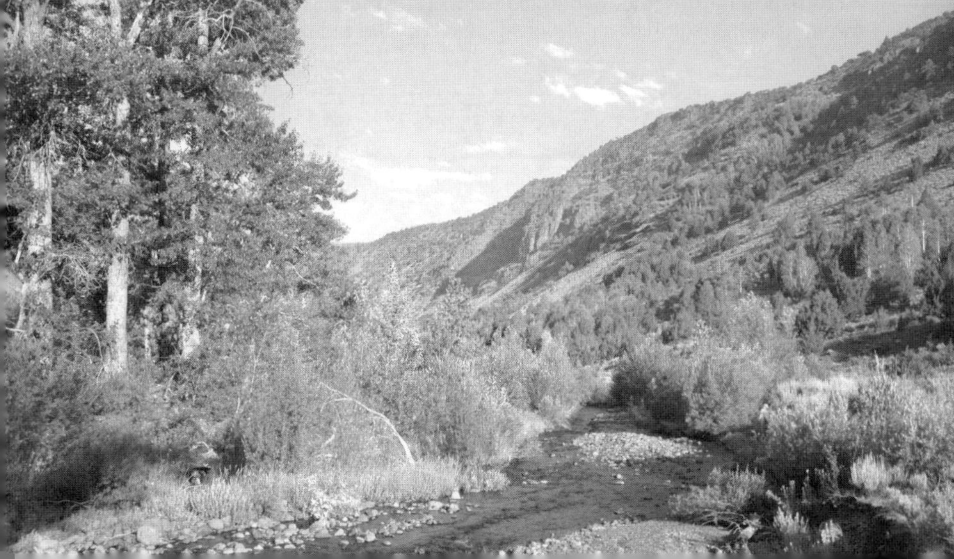

94 Big Indian Gorge

Moderate (to boulder)
8.2 miles round trip
960 feet elevation gain
Open June to mid-November
Use: hikers, horses

Difficult (to cottonwood camp)
13 miles round trip
1270 feet elevation gain

Snow fell so heavily on Steens Mountain during the Ice Age 10,000 years ago that glaciers crept 10 miles down the western slopes. The rivers of ice gouged seven colossal 2000-foot-deep gorges, each with the U-shaped cross section typical of glacial valleys. Because the climate has become relatively dry since then, the canyons still have their elegant curving silhouette, and not the V-shape of valleys cut by rivers.

One of the most accessible of these scenic canyons, Big Indian Gorge, has a modern campground at its mouth. To be sure, you'll still have to trudge along an old road for the first 1.9 miles, and then negotiate three creek crossings, but that's the price of admission to this quiet world of quaking aspen groves and wildflowers in the Steens Mountain Wilderness.

Fill your car's gas tank before leaving Burns. Then drive 1.7 miles east on Highway 78 toward Crane and turn right on paved Highway 205 for 61 miles to Frenchglen. Continue on the paved highway towards Fields for another 10 miles and turn left onto the gravel Steens Mountain Loop Road for 19.5 miles to the South Steens Campground on the right. The first campground entrance is for equestrians. The second entrance has family campsites amidst junipers and sagebrush. Cold drinking water is available from a spigot on a well house. The trail begins at the far end of this camp loop at a gate marking the wilderness boundary.

From the gate, hike the abandoned roadbed 1.9 miles to road's end at a ford of Big Indian Creek. Usually it's possible to cross dry-footed on a log just downstream.

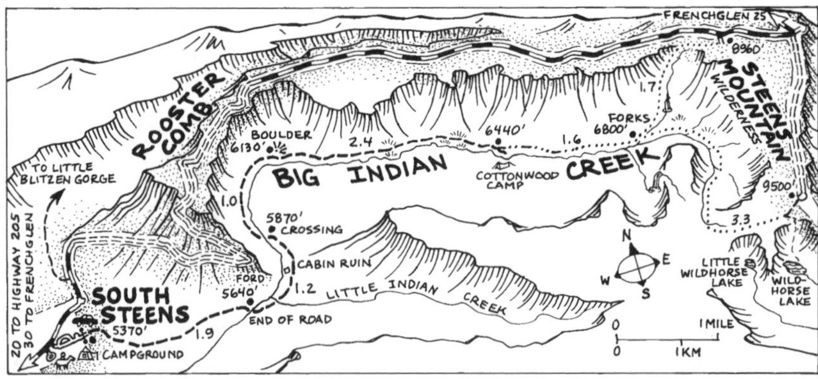

Big Indian Gorge. *Opposite: Mariposa lily.*

A trail leads up the canyon on the far shore. In 0.2 mile you'll reach a crossing of Little Indian Creek, a 15-foot-wide stream that skillful hoppers can cross on rocks. In another 0.4 mile you might notice a ruined log cabin on the left, and in another 0.6 mile you'll reach a final, awkward crossing of Big Indian Creek. Either scramble across on logs downstream or look upstream for stepping stones.

Sagebrush crowds the path beyond this last creek crossing, so you'll want to be wearing long pants. After a mile the trail curves around a bend in the canyon to a 5-foot boulder where weary hikers can declare victory and turn back. This is the first viewpoint of the canyon's distant headwall, where snow patches cling to the cliffs of Steens Mountain's summit ridge. The canyon's flora changes here too. Junipers have begun to yield to white-barked quaking aspen and tall cottonwoods. Flowers among the sagebrush include yellow senecio, blue lupine, and the beautiful, 3-petaled lavender blooms of mariposa lily.

If you're up for a longer hike, continue 2.4 miles through grassier meadows to a campsite near the gravelly 15-foot-wide creek in a cottonwood grove. Beyond this point the increasingly faint trail is easy to lose. Adventurers who continue 1.6 miles will reach a fork in the creek below a castle-shaped outcrop in the canyon wall, with several waterfalls in view. Tempted to continue still farther? Stamina, balance, and route-finding skills are required to climb out of this steep-walled canyon to the road more than 2000 feet above, following either the left- or right-hand fork of the creek.

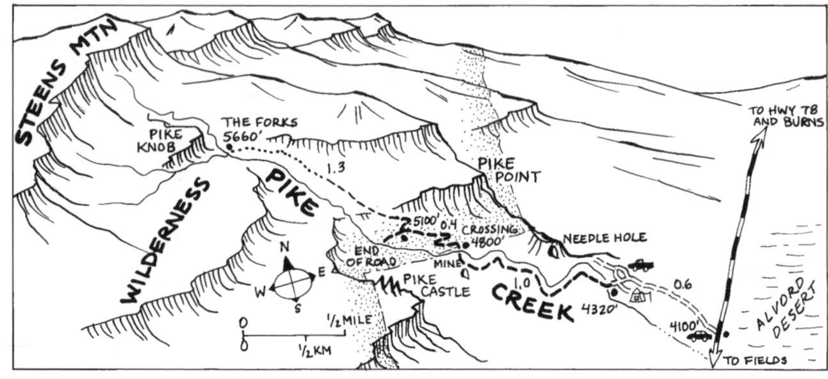

95

Pike Creek

Easy (to end of road)
2.8 miles round trip
850 feet elevation gain
Open late April through November
Use: hikers, horses

Difficult (to forks)
5.4 miles round trip
1400 feet elevation gain

At first glance, it hardly seems possible for a hiking route to be hiding on Steens Mountain's east face, a mile-high cliff that juts from the Alvord Desert's alkali flats to a sky full of snow-streaked crags. At Pike Creek, however, an ancient mining road gives hikers a secret entryway into a spectacular box canyon of colorful rock formations and wildflowers.

Drive here via the Fields-Follyfarm road, a wide gravel route with some of the best scenery in Oregon. Just be sure to top off your gas tank before leaving civilization behind. From Burns, drive east through Crane on Highway 78 for 65 miles. At a pointer for Fields near milepost 65, turn right onto a broad gravel road for 40 miles to the unmarked Pike Creek road. To find this unsigned turnoff, set your car's trip odometer to zero when you pass a sign for the Alvord Ranch. After another 3.7 miles, turn right across a yellow cattle guard onto the dirt Pike Creek road *(GPS location N42°34.275' W118°31.26')*.

If you're coming from Fields instead, you'll want to take the paved road 1.3 miles north toward Frenchglen and keep right onto the wide gravel Fields-Follyfarm road toward Highway 78 for 24 miles. Beyond Alvord Hot Springs' unmarked tin shed 2 miles, turn left across a yellow cattle guard.

If you have a passenger car, it's safest to park by the yellow cattle guard. If your vehicle has high clearance, however, bump up the rough road 0.6 mile and park at a fork. To the left and right are about a dozen shady campsites in the cottonwoods along Pike Creek. Avoid the campsites downstream to the left, because they are on unmarked private land.

Hop across the creek at a public campsite straight ahead, by a house-sized boulder. Then follow the old mining road up the far bank through the sagebrush. Wildflower patches along the way include sunflower-shaped balsamroot, yellow lupine, purple penstemon, and red paintbrush. As you climb, you'll gain a view back through a small hole in the cliffs toward the Alvord Desert. At the 0.9-mile mark you'll pass the collapsed entrance of an unsuccessful uranium prospect. The path then traverses a cottonwood grove, crosses the 8-foot-wide creek, and switchbacks up a hill. Just 100 feet before the crest of the old roadbed, you'll see fist-sized, red rock nodules on the slope. Rockhounds have cracked many of these open in search of quartz crystals or the colorful jasper of thundereggs.

At the crest of the old road, 1.3 miles from your car, you'll face a choice. For an easy hike, simply continue on the old road 100 yards down to its end at a shady creekside cliff—a nice spot for lunch before turning back. If you're ready for some trailless exploration, however, leave the old road at its high point and follow rock cairns steeply up through the sagebrush on a faint trail. For the next 1.3 miles, occasional cairns and bits of path mark a route that traverses the canyon slope above Pike Creek's right bank. Views keep improving of Steens Mountain's snow-streaked summit cliffs ahead. Finally scramble down to the forks of Pike Creek, where two 3-foot-wide streams join at the base of Pike Knob, a red tower that splits the canyon into two gigantic amphitheaters. Explorers can continue as far as they like, but this makes a satisfying turnaround point.

Steens Mountain from Pike Creek Canyon. *Opposite: Forks of Pike Creek.*

96 Borax Hot Springs

Easy
3 miles round trip
60 feet elevation gain
Open all year
Use: hikers

At Borax Lake, fish thrive in warm alkaline water. Steam rises from boiling turquoise pools. Curlews with curling bills swoop through the sagebrush, screaming. In the distance, the snowy crest of Steens Mountain shimmers above the desert like a mirage.

The strange desert hot springs at Borax Lake are fired by the same active fault system that hoisted Steens Mountain more than a vertical mile above the surrounding plains. Here, groundwater seeps into the planet's crustal cracks and boils back to the surface through deep, trumpet-shaped pools.

During the wetter climate of the Ice Age, a gigantic lake filled this valley hundreds of feet deep, spilling north to the Snake River. As the rains lessened, the lake evaporated, leaving an alkali playa at the Alvord Desert. Incredibly, not all of the fish perished. At Borax Lake, one minnow-like species evolved to suit the increasingly warm, alkaline water. Today the Borax Lake chub lives in 600-foot-wide Borax Lake, and nowhere else on earth. Arsenic levels in the lake are 25 times higher than the limit considered fatal for humans, but the diehard chubs don't seem to mind.

Borax Lake fell into private hands in the late 1800s, when entrepreneurs hired Chinese laborers to collect sodium borate crusts and dissolve them in huge vats to

Steens Mountain from Borax Hot Springs. *Above: Hot springs pool.*

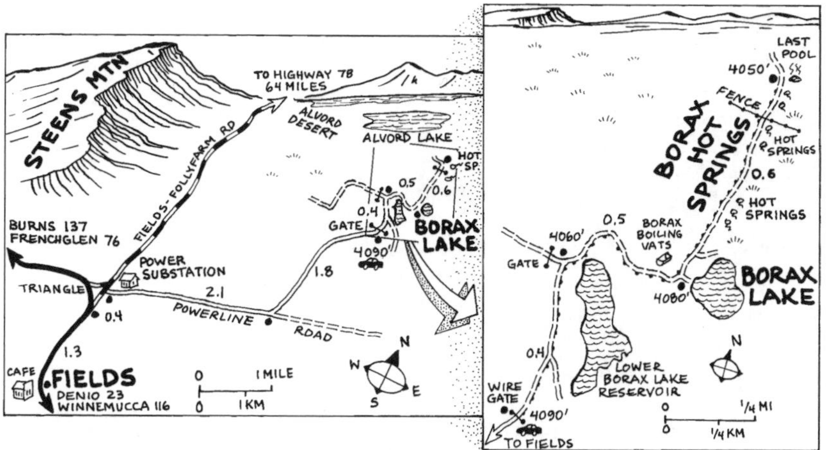

produce borax. Mule-drawn wagon caravans hauled the chalky borax more than a hundred miles to the railroad in Winnemucca. To preserve the area's fragile ecosystem, the non-profit Nature Conservancy bought the lake in the 1990s. Today hikers pass the rusted remains of the old vats beside the lake.

To visit this unusual hot springs, first drive to Fields, a remote roadside settlement that consists of a combination cafe, store, motel, garage, and gas station. A wall chart records annual sales of the cafe's famous hamburgers and milkshakes since the 1980s. The milkshakes are winning. To find Fields from Burns, drive east 1.7 miles toward Crane on Highway 78, turn right on Highway 205 for 59 miles to Frenchglen, and continue another 50 miles on the paved road toward Winnemucca.

Check your gas gauge in Fields. Then drive back toward Frenchglen 1.3 miles, heading north on the paved road. When you reach a junction, go straight onto a broad gravel road, following a pointer for Highway 78. After 0.4 mile, turn right beside a power substation onto a dirt road that follows a large powerline. At the first fork, after 2.1 miles, veer left away from the powerline for 1.8 miles and park beside a closed wire gate with the sign, "Danger! Hot Springs. Scalding Water. Ground May Collapse. Control Children and Pets." In fact, dogs and other pets are banned to protect the area's birdlife. Fishing and boating are not allowed either.

Heeding those cautions, hike onward along the road. Ignore a side road to the right after 0.2 mile and another road to the left after 0.4 mile. You'll pass a lower reservoir and the old boiling vats before climbing up to Borax Lake. An erosion resistant rock layer has left the lake perched 20 feet above the surrounding flats.

Dozens of smaller hot springs, strung out in a line to the north for 0.6 mile, are visible from here as wisps of steam rising from the grass. For a closer look, walk back 100 feet toward the vats, turn right on a faint road, and keep straight toward distant Steens Mountain. The pools are to the right of the road, but be careful if you leave the track, because these deep, sheer-sided springs are dangerously hot at 180°F. After 0.5 mile a wire fence crosses the road. Beyond the fence 200 yards, where the road veers left, turn back at two large, final hot spring pools on the right. The Nature Conservancy prohibits visitors from attempting to swim in any of the area's pools, not only because of the obvious danger, but also to protect the fragile ecology of this eerie place.

97 Pueblo Mountains

Difficult
7.2 miles round trip
2200 feet elevation gain
Open mid-July to mid-November
Use: hikers, horses

Most Oregonians have never heard of the Pueblo Mountains, a commanding fault-block range between Steens Mountain and the Nevada border. The Pueblo crest hiking route described here has no trees, no water sources, and no trail tread. But the starkness of this remote desert range conceals charms that can haunt adventurers' souls: silent top-of-the-world viewpoints, herds of antelope, huge blue skies, and unexpected wildflowers.

Although views extend for 50 miles in all directions throughout much of this cross-country route, the only man-made artifacts visible are 15 rock cairns. These 4-foot stacks have been spaced at roughly quarter-mile intervals to mark the general course of the Desert Trail. The trail's planners envision a 2000-mile-long hiking corridor from Mexico to Canada. More than 100 miles of the route in Oregon have already been mapped, from the Nevada border north beyond Steens Mountain. Because hikers are left to find their own route through the sagebrush from one cairn to the next, however, it is important to bring a topographic map that shows precise cairn locations. You can pick up a copy of the $5 map for this area, the "Pueblo Mountains Desert Trail Guide," at the Book Parlor at 181 N. Broadway in Burns, or you can order it from the Desert Trail Association, P.O. Box 34, Madras, OR 97741 (*www.madras.net/~dta/trail_guide.htm*).

To drive here from Burns, take Highway 78 east toward Crane 1.7 miles, turn right on Highway 205 for 59 miles to Frenchglen, and continue south on the paved road toward Winnemucca another 50 miles to the tiny settlement of Fields. Check

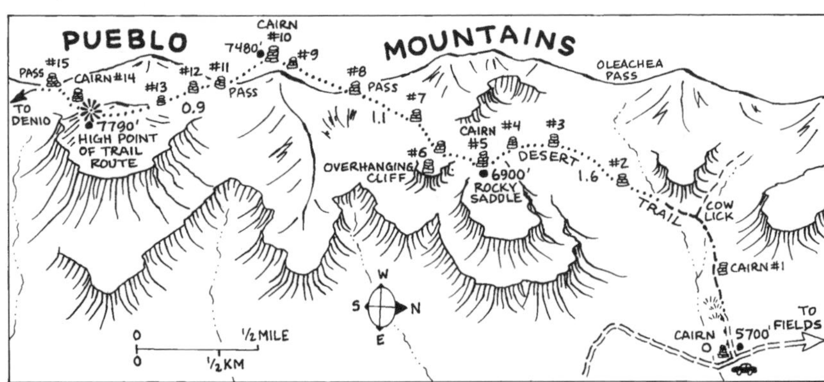

your gas gauge here. Then, carefully watching the mileage on your car's odometer, continue south on the paved road 3.1 miles. At a pointer for Domingo Pass, turn right across a yellow cattle guard onto a one-lane gravel road for 3.8 miles. At a fork, veer up to the right on the larger branch—now an increasingly rough dirt track with sharp gravel. After another 0.5 mile, veer left at a faint fork, again staying on the largest road. In another 0.2 mile you'll cross a yellow cattle guard and reach a third fork. This time veer left, and then keep straight. In 0.9 mile the road bends 90° to the left around a fence corner. Turn the corner and continue exactly 1.25 miles. Just after the road's high point, park by a rock cairn marking a very faint side road to the right *(GPS location N42°10.67′ W118°43.25′)*.

Hike up this faint side road 0.6 mile through the sagebrush to a barren area (an old cow lick) and veer left, heading cross-country up the leftmost branch of the valley. Scramble up past a grove of shrub-sized mountain mahogany trees to find cairn #3 on a rise at the 1.3-mile mark. Climb steeply up 0.3 mile to cairn #5, atop a 12-foot rock in a saddle *(GPS location N42°9.73′ W118°44.05′)*. Views here extend from Steens Mountain's snowy crest in the north to the Pine Forest Range in Nevada. Traverse 0.4 mile onward (and less steeply upward) to cairn #6, perched atop an overhanging cliff. In another 0.3 mile, cross a pass to the western side of the Pueblo Mountains' crest. Contour 0.4 mile to cairn #10 *(GPS location N42°8.96′ W118°44.45′)*. Continue contouring 0.2 mile to a shaley pass with cairn #11, and then follow the mountains' crest up 0.7 mile to the trail route's highest point, a bare viewpoint knoll just above cairn #14 *(GPS location N42°8.275′ W118°44.20′)*.

This viewpoint makes a satisfying turnaround point for day hikers after the trip's wearying elevation gain and cross-country scrambling. Determined backpackers can continue downhill past a pass, following the Desert Trail's rock cairns through alpine basins and cattle meadows along the western face of the Pueblo Mountains for 13 miles to Denio.

The Pueblo Mountains from cairn #14. *Opposite: Lupine leaves.*

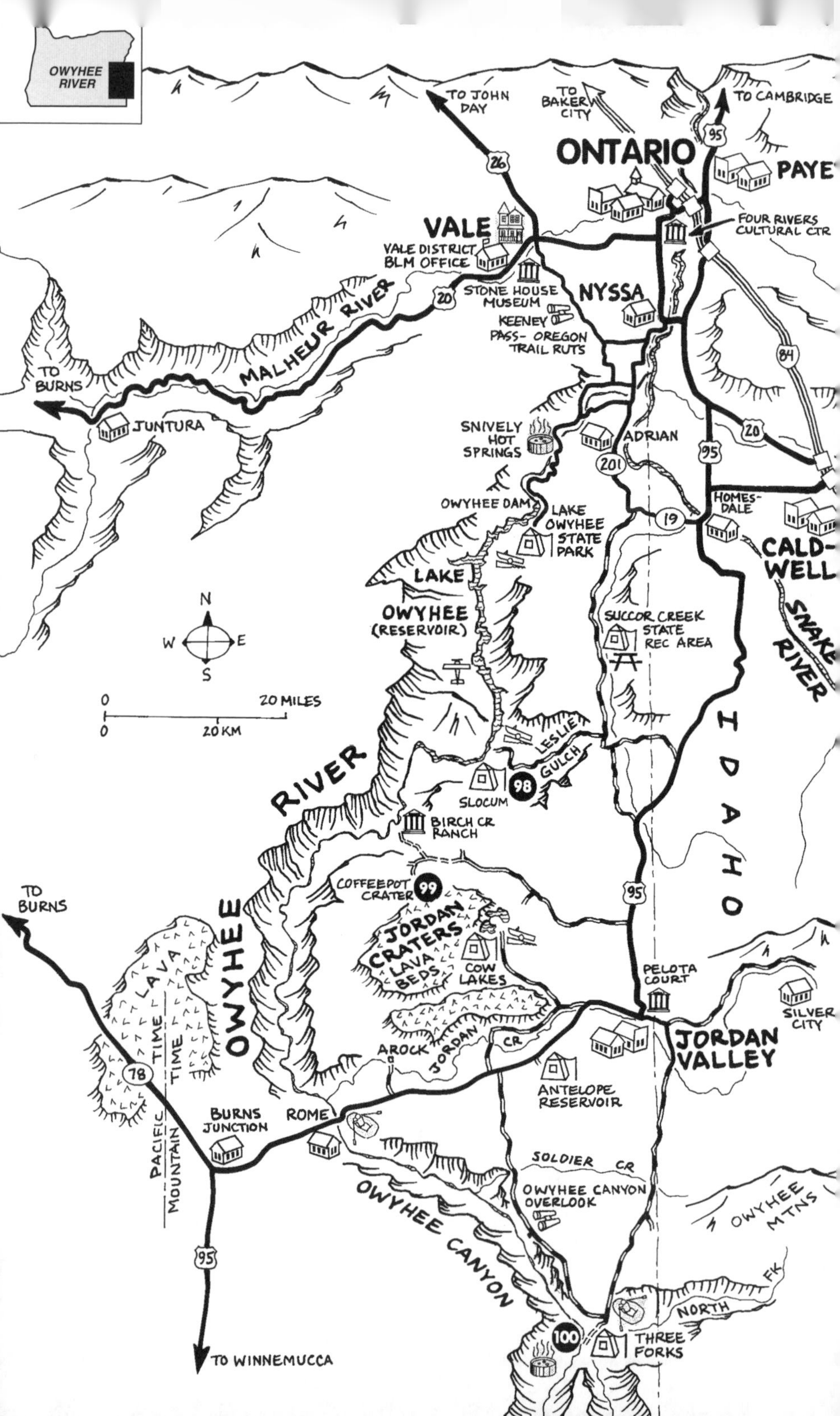

OWYHEE RIVER
TO JOHN DAY
TO BAKER CITY
TO CAMBRIDGE
ONTARIO
PAYE
VALE
VALE DISTRICT BLM OFFICE
FOUR RIVERS CULTURAL CTR
STONE HOUSE MUSEUM
NYSSA
KEENEY PASS- OREGON TRAIL RUTS
MALHEUR RIVER
TO BURNS
JUNTURA
SNIVELY HOT SPRINGS
ADRIAN
OWYHEE DAM
LAKE OWYHEE STATE PARK
HOMES-DALE
CALD-WELL
LAKE OWYHEE (RESERVOIR)
SUCCOR CREEK STATE REC AREA
SNAKE RIVER
N
W
E
S
0
20 MILES
0
20 KM
LESLIE GULCH
98
SLOCUM
RIVER
BIRCH CR RANCH
IDAHO
COFFEEPOT CRATER
99
TO BURNS
JORDAN CRATERS LAVA BEDS
COW LAKES
OWYHEE
LAVA
PELOTA COURT
SILVER CITY
TIME
TIME
AROCK
JORDAN CR
JORDAN VALLEY
ANTELOPE RESERVOIR
BURNS JUNCTION
ROME
PACIFIC
MOUNTAIN
SOLDIER CR
OWYHEE CANYON OVERLOOK
OWYHEE MTNS
OWYHEE CANYON
NORTH FK
100
THREE FORKS
TO WINNEMUCCA
26
95
20
84
201
19
78

ONTARIO

The Owyhee and Malheur Rivers wind through spectacular desert canyons to the green farmlands surrounding Southeast Oregon's commercial center, Ontario. When in town, stop by the **Four Rivers Cultural Center & Museum,** a first-rate interpretive center describing the region's Native American, Basque, and other cultures. At 676 SW 5th Avenue, the museum is open 10-5 Mon-Sat and noon-4 Sun. Admission runs $4 for adults and $3 for children and seniors.

Vale

Once an Oregon Trail campsite at a Malheur River ford, Vale now boasts a historic downtown decorated with more than two dozen murals. In an 1872 stagecoach inn, the free **Rinehart Stone House Museum at** 255 Main (open 12:30-4 Tue-Sat, Mar-Oct) features Oregon Trail artifacts and historic photos. Almost as interesting are the antique saddles, rifles, and Indian goods at the **U2 Saddle Shop and Dry Goods** at 192 A Street East. For the night, visit the turreted **Oregon Trail Inn** at 484 N. 10th (541-473-3030, *www.searshomebb.com*), a house that was actually ordered from a Sears catalog in 1900. Then drive Glen Street south 6 miles toward Lake Owyhee to see the **Oregon Trail ruts at Keeney Pass.**

Lake Owyhee

The Owyhee River's reservoir twists 53 miles through colorful desert canyons. **Lake Owyhee State Park** (open mid-April through October) has 65 campsites, showers, a boat ramp, and a nearby resort with boat rentals. For a free hot soak, drive the paved road 15 miles back from the campground toward Ontario to a sign for **Snively Hot Springs,** a natural riverside pool by a cottonwood grove on a spur road.

Succor Creek and Leslie Gulch

A 34-mile gravel road winds through a colorful rock canyon from Highway 201 (south of Ontario 34 miles) to Highway 95 (north of Jordan Valley 19 miles). The drive passes **Succor Creek State NaturalArea,** a free, primitive camp (with 18 walk-in campsites and no drinking water) open March to November. Don't miss the 14-mile side trip down the spectacularly narrow canyon of **Leslie Gulch** (Hike #98).

Jordan Valley

Two-thirds of the residents are of Basque descent in this ranching town, where a restored 1916 stone **Pelota Court** is used for Basque handball games. From here, drive the 79-mile **Soldier Creek Watchable Wildlife Loop Road**, a mostly dirt route (impassable in wet weather) to a breathtaking overlook of the **Owyhee River Canyon** and the primitive riverside camping area at **Three Forks** (Hike #100). From Jordan Valley, drive Highway 95 west 16 miles, turn left on the dirt road toward Three Forks for 29 miles, and keep left for 33 miles back to Jordan Valley.

Owyhee River

Only experienced boaters should drift or kayak the **Owyhee River,** usually runnable from March through early June. The 39-mile section from Three Forks to Highway 95 at Rome includes half a dozen dangerous rapids, among them Widowmaker Rapids' 10-foot drop. The 55-mile stretch from Rome to Lake Owyhee includes three difficult rapids. The routes pass cliffs, caves, and hot springs.

98 Leslie Gulch

Easy (Juniper Gulch)
1.6 miles round trip
400 feet elevation gain
Open except in wet weather
Use: hikers

Easy (Dago Gulch)
1.6 miles round trip
190 feet elevation gain

Moderate (Timber Gulch)
1.2 miles round trip
350 feet elevation gain

Most travelers view the slot-like canyons, rock pinnacles, and colorful desert badlands of Leslie Gulch through the windows of their cars. But after driving all the way to Oregon's extreme eastern border, why not explore this spectacular scenery up close by hiking up a few of Leslie Gulch's five interesting side canyons.

The rock formations here date back 15 million years, when a volcano blasted out a 10-mile-wide caldera that filled with volcanic ash 1000 feet deep. Minerals colored the ash as it solidified to rock.When the land rose, flash floods carved narrow gulches lined with orange, yellow, purple, and red cliffs. Soft spots in the rock weathered into niches and small caves known as "honeycombs."

Leslie Gulch won its name when an 1882 lightning strike killed pioneer cattleman Hiram Leslie. Today the gulch is valued not only for its scenery, but also for several species of rare plants and a herd of bighorn sheep.

To drive here from Interstate 84 at Ontario, follow signs south 14 miles to Nyssa. In Nyssa, turn right at a pointer for Adrian onto Highway 201 for 20.6 miles. Then turn right on gravel Succor Creek Road for 15 miles to Succor Creek State Recreation Area, continue 10 miles to a sign for Leslie Gulch, and turn right on a gravel road down this canyon 14.5 miles to its end at the Owyhee Reservoir boat ramp.

If you're driving here from Jordan Valley (140 miles southeast of Burns), take Highway 95 north for 27 miles and turn left at a sign for Succor Creek for 8.4 gravel miles. At a T-shaped junction, turn left toward Succor Creek another 1.8 miles, and then turn left on the gravel Leslie Gulch road for 14.5 miles to road's

Dago Gulch. Above: Honeycomb formations in Timber Gulch.

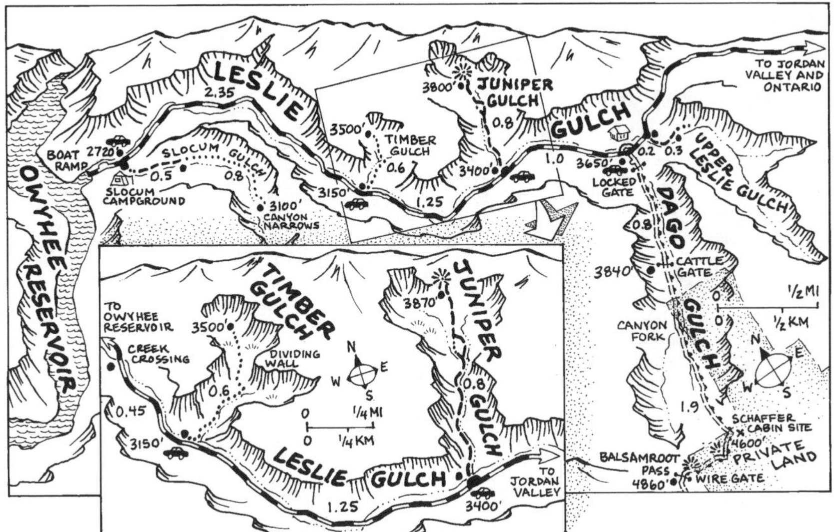

end at the reservoir boat ramp.

Camping in Leslie Gulch is permitted only at Slocum Campground, a barren gravel flat 0.2 mile up the road from the boat ramp. This free camp has eight picnic tables, but no shade or water. Horses are not allowed anywhere in Leslie Gulch.

If you have time for only one hike, choose Juniper Gulch. From Slocum Campground, drive back up Leslie Gulch 3.6 miles to the marked Juniper Gulch parking pullout on the left. The trail hops across Leslie Creek and follows a narrow sandy wash up past gigantic, overhanging cliffs. After 0.6 mile keep right at a fork. Then follow the path up a ridge to its end at an orange cliff of "honeycomb" rock. Turn back here, because steep and slippery slopes lie ahead.

For another easy hike nearby, head for Dago Gulch. From Juniper Gulch, drive up the Leslie Gulch road 1 mile, turn right at a sign for Dago Gulch, and park in 0.2 mile at a turnaround just before a locked green gate. Then walk up the closed road 0.8 mile, past cliffs with columns and fluted green ash. Turn back at a cattle gate because the road ahead crosses patches of unmarked private land.

The prettiest gulch to explore, Timber Gulch, isn't marked with a sign. To find it, drive down the Leslie Gulch road exactly 1.25 miles from the Juniper Gulch sign (or 2.35 miles up from Slocum Campground) and park at a one-car pullout on the north beside some wild roses *(GPS location N43°18.29' W117°17.37')*. Walk up the (usually dry) bed of Leslie Creek about 100 feet and veer left up a dry sandy wash toward giant orange rock formations. There is no trail in this narrow, sagebrush-choked canyon, so you'll want to be wearing long pants. After 0.3 mile, where the canyon splits at a 200-foot-tall rock wall, turn left for 0.3 mile to the canyon's end at an amphitheater of sheer, pinnacled cliffs.

Leslie Gulch has two other explorable side canyons. From Slocum Campground, a faint trail goes up the left side of Slocum Gulch 0.5 mile before petering out; bushwhackers can continue another 0.8 mile before the canyon becomes too narrow and brushy. If you drive up Leslie Gulch's road from the campground 4.8 miles (past Dago Gulch 0.2 mile), you can park at an "Upper Leslie Gulch" sign and follow a trail 0.3 mile until it vanishes amid tall sagebrush.

99 Coffeepot Crater

Easy
1.1-mile loop
140 feet elevation gain
Open except in wet weather
Use: hikers

At the Jordan Craters lava beds, a row of spatter cones rises from one of Oregon's most remote sagebrush landscapes. The easy hiking trail that circles Coffeepot Crater here is open all year, but you won't want to attempt this trip in just any weather. January temperatures may cower below freezing all day. The blazing August sun can bake the desert at 120°F. During rare rainstorms, the final miles of the dirt access road can become a quagmire of mud ruts and giant puddles. Perhaps the friendliest month is June, when the desert here greets visitors with giant pink bitterroot blooms.

The Jordan Craters lava beds are one result of North America's shearing collision with the North Pacific seafloor plate. That collision has stretched Oregon diagonally, allowing lava to leak up along a 200-mile swarm of fractures that extend west to the Newberry National Volcanic Monument near Bend. Eruptions at Jordan Craters began less than 9000 years ago when lava spattered to the surface in a 300-yard-long row of cones. An explosion blasted Coffeepot Crater at the lower end of the string. Then vents unleashed a flow of soupy *pahoehoe* basalt lava that inundated 27 square miles of desert.

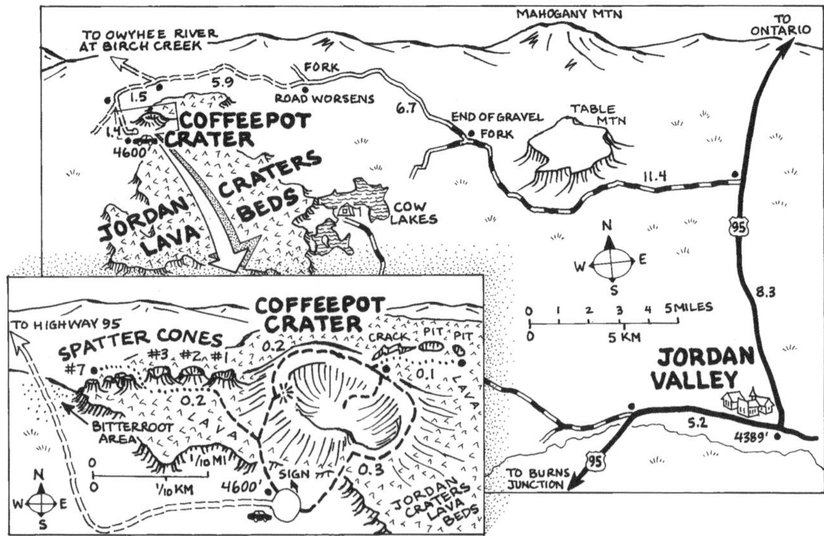

Spatter cone at Coffeepot Crater. *Opposite: Bitterroot.*

Locals have been known to boast that the Jordan Craters lava beds are so fresh you can find cowboy bootprints in them. That puffery won unexpected credence when geologists discovered an 18-acre portion of the lava field that is in fact geologically recent.

Start your visit by filling your gas tank in the remote Highway 95 town of Jordan Valley, east of Burns 139 miles. Drive north on Highway 95 from Jordan Valley for 8.3 miles to a "Jordan Craters" pointer and turn left on a good gravel road. After 11.4 miles, keep right at a fork and leave the gravel behind. At a fork in another 6.7 miles, veer left onto what becomes a rough dirt road, best suited for high-clearance vehicles. In another 5.9 miles, keep left at another fork. And after another 1.5 miles, fork left once again for 1.4 miles to a parking area at road's end *(GPS location N43°8.77' W117°27.54')*.

Hike a trail to the left around the black cinder rim of Coffeepot Crater for 0.2 mile. On the crater's far side, you'll pass a 4-foot rock trench that snakes down into the lava fields. This is one of the original sources of the lava flow. Detour down along the trench 100 yards to see where it becomes a lava tube and tunnels into two large pits, where the cave's roof collapsed. Next return to the crater rim trail to find a different detour—a slippery red cinder path that descends 150 yards to the bottom of Coffeepot Crater. Then complete the loop around the crater rim back to your car.

Before driving home, take a trail across the lava 100 yards to the first spatter cone, a 30-foot shell plastered with lava globs. Explore cross-country another 100 yards to see the other six spatter cones in this row. Then return to your car. But as you leave, pause where the road passes above the spatter cones. In May and June the barren desert gravel here erupts with the seemingly leafless, 2-inch-wide, creamy white blooms of *Lewisia rediviva*, the bitterroot flower.

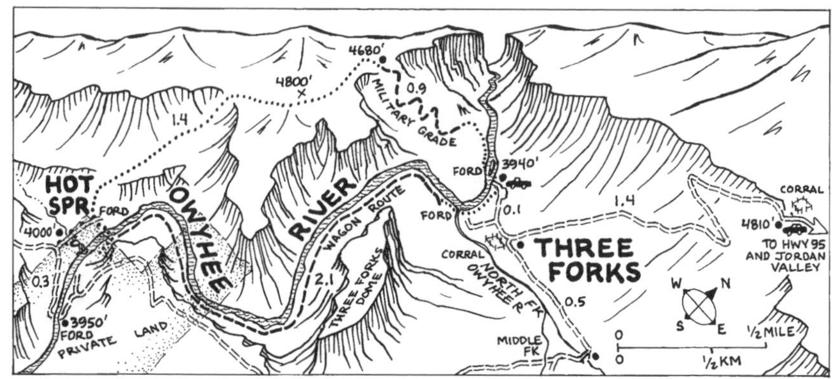

100 Three Forks

Moderate
4.2 miles round trip
50 feet elevation gain
Open except after rains
Use: hikers

Difficult
4.4-mile loop
900 feet elevation gain

Hot springs pools perch between waterfalls on the bank of the Owyhee River, deep in a spectacular desert canyon of red rock cliffs. At the oasis-like confluence of three river canyons, Three Forks is one of the most remote places in Oregon, wedged against the borders of Idaho and Nevada.

Surprisingly, the area was more heavily trafficked in the 1800s. "Owyhee" was a common 19th-century spelling for Hawaii. The river won its name when two Hawaiians, hired by the Hudson's Bay Company as beaver trappers, were killed near the river by Indians in 1819. Despite the Indian danger, thousands of gold miners and ore wagons passed through Three Forks on their way from Silver City, Idaho to the railroad in Winnemucca, Nevada in the late 1860s. After the Bannock Indian War of 1878, the Army built an outpost at Three Forks to keep an eye on the local Paiutes. Today fragments of the area's 19th-century wagon roads help hikers make their way through the canyonlands, but it's still best to come prepared for cross-country routefinding and knee-deep river fords.

To drive here from Burns, take Highway 78 east through Crane 93 miles to Burns Junction and turn left on Highway 95 for 30.5 miles. Near milepost 36 (west of Jordan Valley 16 miles), follow a pointer for Three Forks south onto a dirt road that serves as part of the Soldier Creek Watchable Wildlife Loop. Be warned that the long, lonely dirt road from Highway 95 to Three Forks can become an undrivable trough of slick goo after rainstorms. Fortunately, this area only sees 11 inches of precipitation each year, so the road is usually fine, as long as you don't run out of gas.

After 27.6 miles on the dirt road, you'll reach a signed junction. Ignore the loop route that heads left toward Jordan Valley, and instead turn right toward Three Forks. In 2.7 miles you'll reach a corral at the edge of the Owyhee canyon rim. If you're driving a passenger car, it's best to park here and add 3 miles to your hike. If you're driving a high-clearance vehicle, continue down what suddenly becomes a very steep, rocky track. After 1.4 miles, fork to the right at a boater registration signboard and keep right for 300 yards to a parking area just before a boat launch site *(GPS location N42°32.78' W117°10.04')*.

From the boat ramp, walk left (upstream) through tall sagebrush along the riverbank. After 300 yards, wade the North Fork Owyhee River (usually 6 inches deep in summer) and continue up the main branch of the river on what soon becomes a clear trail with stonework embankments from the historic wagon route.

After 2 miles along the riverbank, the tread peters out where cliffs pinch the trail against the stream. Wade the river here (in summer, a pleasantly cool, knee-deep crossing) to a faint roadbed on the far shore. The largest hot springs pools, usually about 96° F, are to the left along this road 200 yards, just above the 10-foot waterfall of a side creek *(GPS location N42°31.82' W117°11.03')*. Note, however, that the hot springs and the entire riverbank for the next half mile upstream are on unmarked private land. Although hikers have been allowed to visit the hot springs for years, there is no guarantee this will always be so. If you proceed, carry out any litter you find and do not camp.

Adventurous pathfinders can return from the hot springs area on a loop that climbs to better viewpoints. After crossing the river to the roadbed just before the hot springs, bushwhack steeply uphill through grass and sagebrush. Traverse to the right as you climb, heading directly away from the hot springs, and in 0.7 mile you'll reach the rim of a grassy plateau. Cross the plateau to the north for 0.5 mile and then turn right toward Three Forks. Look atop the end of a bluff for a cairn and some stonework marking the start of an old military road *(GPS location N42°32.78' W117°10.66')*. Then follow this switchbacking grade down 0.9 mile to the Owyhee River and wade across to your car.

The Owyhee River at Three Forks. *Opposite: The hot springs' waterfall.*

Barrier-Free Trails of Eastern Oregon

People with limited physical abilities need not miss the fun of exploring new trails. Here are paved, graveled, or hard-packed paths accessible even to those with a stroller, walker, or wheelchair. All have accessible restrooms nearby.

COLUMBIA PLATEAU (map on page 14)

A. Columbia Gorge Discovery Center. Paved paths loop 0.2 mile behind this museum and extend 3 miles east along the Columbia River almost to The Dalles' downtown, passing ponds along the way. Drive Interstate 84 to exit 84 and follow museum signs.

B. Leaf Hill Trail. An 0.1-mile path in the John Day Fossil Beds Nat'l Monument leads to a hill where scientists discovered thousands of fossils. See Hike #15.

C. Story in Stone Trail. Touchable replicas of rhinoceros and horse fossils line this 0.3-mile loop amid the colorful badlands of the John Day Fossil Beds Nat'l Monument. Half of the loop is paved. Drive to the Blue Basin area of Hike #15 and continue north on Hwy 19 about 3 miles. Near milepost 118, turn into a trailhead and picnic area.

CENTRAL OREGON (map on page 24)

D. Lava Lands Visitor Center. Two paved, interpretive loops start from the back patio of this interpretive center, 8 miles south of Bend on Hwy 97. The Trail of the Molten Lands loops 0.8 mile across lava, steeply in places. The easier, 0.3-mile Trail of the Whispering Pines skirts a lava flow edge. Parking fee required.

E. Lava Cast Forest. A paved 1-mile trail loops through a recent lava flow that inundated a forest, leaving trunk-shaped molds in the rock. Steep in spots. Drive 11 miles south of Bend on Hwy 97 to milepost 153 and turn left for 9 gravel miles. Parking fee required. Open May to November.

OCHOCO MOUNTAINS (map on page 38)

F. Sugar Creek Trail. The Sugar Creek Campground (open May-Nov) has 17 mostly accessible campsites ($8 fee), a free all-accessible picnic area, and a 0.4-mile gravel path that loops along the glassy stream beneath ponderosa pines, crossing two bridges. Drive 60 mi east of Prineville to Paulina, continue 3.7 mi, turn left on S Beaver Cr Rd, and follow signs toward Rager Ranger Station 9 miles.

STRAWBERRY MOUNTAIN (map on page 54)

G. Magone Lake. This popular fishing lake in the pine woods north of John Day was created by a landslide in the 1860s. Now a 2-mile packed dirt trail (usable by wheelchairs in dry weather) circles the lake from an all-accessible campground. From John Day take Hwy 26 east 9.5 miles, turn left up Bear Creek on Road 18 for 13 paved miles, turn left on Road 3620 for 1.2 miles, and turn right on Road 3618 for 1.5 miles.

H. Stump Dodger Railroad. Challengingly steep for wheelchairs, this paved, 0.2-mile interpretive loop explores a woodsy portion of the abandoned narrow-gauge railroad that linked Prairie City with Baker City from 1910-1947. From Prairie City, drive Hwy 26 east 8 miles to milepost 184.

BLUE MOUNTAINS - SOUTH (map on page 78)

I. Oregon Trail Interpretive Center. At this world-class museum near Baker City (see Page 79), a 0-5 mile paved loop circles the building, and a more challenging 1.5-mile paved path descends to a bench by the Oregon Trail's actual route. Open all year.

J. Powder River. A mile below Phillips Lake's dam (16 miles south of Baker City on Highway 7), paved riverside trails visit an all-accessible picnic area and fishing dock. About half of the 1-mile path system is accessible.

Stump Dodger Railroad loop.

K. Anthony Lake. High in the Elkhorn Range, a graveled path loops 1 mile around this alpine lake. See Hike #28.

BLUE MOUNTAINS - NORTH (map on pg 98)

L. Jubilee Lake. Only half a mile is paved of the 2.5-mile path around this lake in the Blue Mountains, but adventurous wheelchair users can make it all the way around. See Hike #38.

M. Oregon Trail Interpretive Park. See Oregon Trail wagon ruts and excellent outdoor interpretive displays on a paved 0.5-mile loop in the Blue Mountain forest. Between La Grande and Pendleton, take I-84 exit 248, follow signs 3.3 miles. Open May to October; $5 fee.

HELLS CANYON (map on page 108)

N. Granny View Vista. Incredible views of the vast Imnaha River canyon open up at each turn on this 0.3-mile loop. Along the wide gravel path, expect dense alpine wildflowers in June and July, including paintbrush, penstemon, larkspur, and balsamroot. All-accessible restroom. Drive as to Hat Point (Hike #45), but only drive 17.4 miles up the steep gravel road from Imnaha.

O. Hat Point. Perched on the edge of 6000-foot-deep Hells Canyon, a paved 0.3-mile path loops through a picnic area to a viewpoint that burned in 2007. A separate 0.1-mile paved path spirals up to the base of the Hat Point fire lookout tower itself. See Hike #45.

WALLOWA MOUNTAINS (map on page 126)

P. Mount Howard. The gondolas of the Wallowa Lake Tramway are wheelchair accessible, allowing everyone to ride up the mountain. although the broad dirt paths on top are not maintained expressly for wheelchairs. See Hike #52.

HIGH DESERT (map on page 176)

Q. Klamath Falls railroad. The OC&E Woods Line State Trail is paved for 0.6 mile from Klamath Falls' East Main St to Washburn Way, and then for another 3.3 miles from Washburn Way in Klamath Falls to Highway 39. The route features a historic 1898 railroad bridge and nice trailheads. See Hike #84.

R. Link River in Klamath Falls. The Link River Trail is blocked by turnstiles at either end, but the gravel Wingwatchers' Trail is passable for wheelchairs from Main Street for 0.4 mile to the cattail slough. See Hike #85.

101 More Hikes in Eastern Oregon

Adventurous hikers can explore lots of additional paths in Eastern Oregon. Many of the trails listed below are rough or unmarked, and descriptions are brief, so be sure to bring appropriate maps. Unless noted, mileages given are one-way, not round-trip. Symbols after each entry identify trails suitable for children, winter use, backpackers, equestrians, and mountain bikers.

For more information, check with the trail's administrative agency, abbreviated as follows: (BE)-Bend-Fort Rock Ranger District, (BLM-L)-BLM Lakeview District, (BLM-P)-BLM Prineville District, (BLM-V)-BLM Vale District, (BL)-Bly Ranger District, (BM)-Blue Mountain Ranger District, (E)-Eagle Cap Ranger District, (HC)-Hells Canyon National Recreation Area, (HE)-Heppner Ranger District, (LA)-Lakeview Ranger District, (LG)-La Grande Ranger District, (LM)-Lookout Mountain Ranger District, (N)-North Fork John Day Ranger District, (O)-Oregon State Parks, (PA)-Paulina Ranger District, (PC)-Prairie City Ranger District, (PO)-Pomeroy Ranger District, (PY)-Paisley Ranger District, (WA)-Wallowa Valley Ranger District, (WH)-Whitman Ranger District, (WW)-Walla Walla Ranger District. Phone numbers for agencies are on page 13.

Easy | Moderate | Difficult

COLUMBIA PLATEAU (map on page 14)

101. Deschutes River to Macks Canyon. Hikable section of abandoned railroad grade along Deschutes River extends 23 miles upstream from state park (see Hike #2) to Macks Canyon CG. To find the upper TH from The Dalles, take Hwy 97 S to milepost 34 in Tygh Valley, turn E on Hwy 216 for 8.4 mi; just beyond Sherar Falls, turn L at a "Deschutes River Rec. Lands" pointer 17 rough dirt miles to CG entrance. (BLM-P)

102. White River Falls. This colossal 3-part waterfall in the desert is hidden at an unassuming state park wayside. Drive Hwy 197 between The Dalles and Maupin to milepost 34 in Tygh Valley and turn E onto Hwy 216 for 4 miles. A park path descends 200 ft in 0.2 mi to an abandoned powerhouse near the middle falls. A rougher route (with poison oak) continues a mile

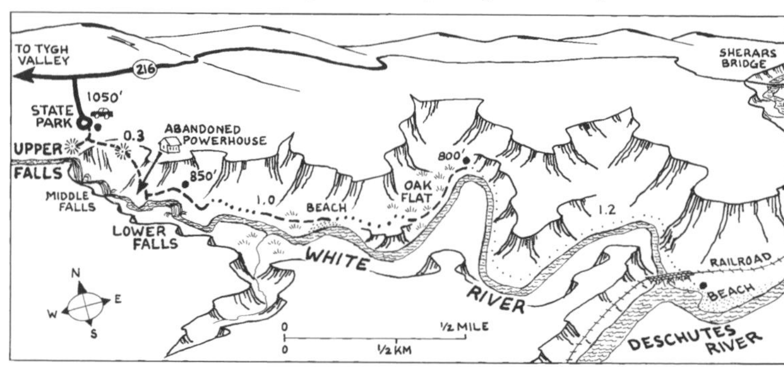

down the White River. Bushwhackers can scramble another 1.2 miles to the Deschutes River confluence. (O)

● **103. Cottonwood Canyon.** A ranch in a desert canyon on the lower John Day River is being converted to a large state park with a network of trails. The park opens in 2013, but hikers can explore part of the area already. See page 16. (O)

CENTRAL OREGON (map on page 24)

●● **104. Otter Bench Trail.** Excellent new 6-mi trail system in scenic Crooked R gorge has two paths down to river and a loop with rimrock views. Best in spring or fall. From Hwy 97 just N of Terrebonne, turn W on Lower Br Way 2.1 mi, turn R on 43rd St 1.8 mi, turn L on Chinook Dr for 5 mi, go straight on Horny Hollow Tr 1.8 to pavement's end. (BLM-P)

● **105. Scout Camp Trail.** Spectacular 3-mi loop in Deschutes canyon dips 600 ft to river, cliffs, ash formations, caves, flowers at confluence with Whychus Cr. From Hwy 97 just N of Terrebonne, turn W on Lower Br Way 2.1 mi, turn R on 43rd St. 1.8 mi, turn L on Chinook Dr 2.4 mi, turn L on Mustang Rd 1.1 mi, turn R on Shad Rd 1.4 mi, turn R on Peninsula Dr 3.3 mi, turn L on Meadow Rd 0.6 mi, turn R on Scout Camp Tr 0.2. (BLM-P)

Cave on the Scout Camp Trail.

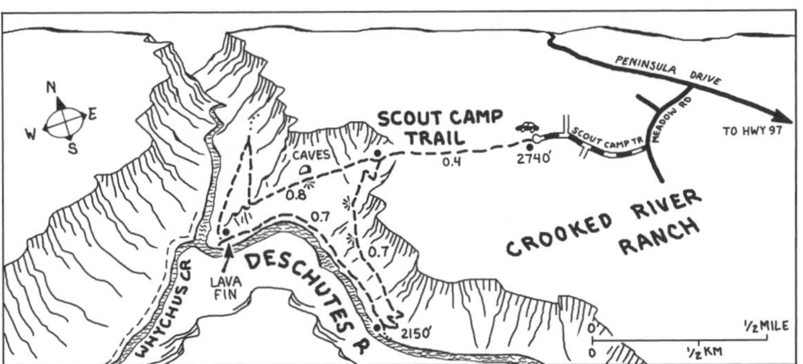

● **106. Steelhead Falls.** Spectacular 3-mi loop in Deschutes canyon dips 600 ft to river, cliffs, ash formations, caves, flowers at confluence with Whychus Creek. See map on page 242. From Hwy 97 just N of Terrebonne, turn W on Lower Br Way 2.1 mi, turn R on 43rd St. 1.8 mi, turn L on Chinook Dr 2.4 mi, turn L on Mustang Rd 1.1 mi, turn R on Shad Rd 1.4 mi, turn R on Peninsula Dr 3.3 mi, turn L on Meadow Rd 0.6 mi, turn R on Scout Camp Tr 0.2. (BLM-P)

Steelhead Falls.

Easy
Moderate
Difficult

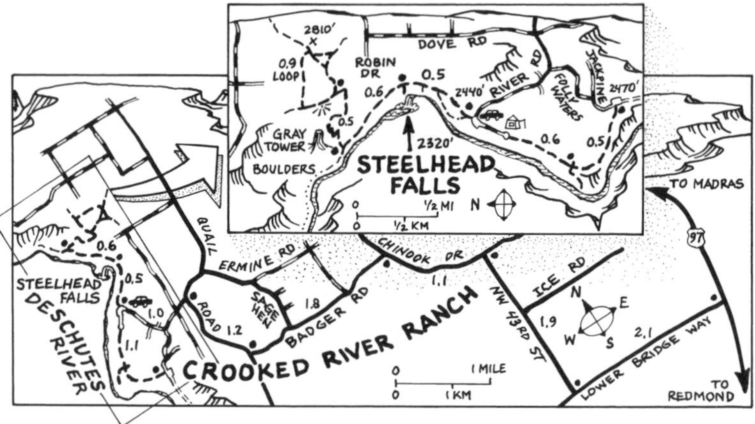

107. Smith Rock. In this state park, the Crooked River loops past giant orange cliffs popular with rock climbers. A spectacular 4-mile trail also loops through the park. See map below, and driving directions on page 27. (O)

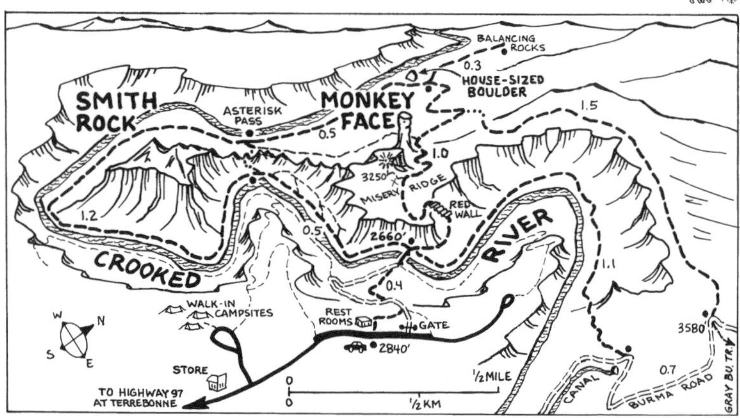

108. Boyd Cave. Bring a flashlight and coat to explore this lava tube. Drive 4 mi S of Bend on Hwy 97 to Ponderosa St and turn L on China Hat Rd 18. After 9 paved miles (just before a "Pavement Ends" sign), turn left onto gravel Road 242 for 0.4 mi to road's end *(GPS location N43°56.523' W121°11.884')*. Descend a metal staircase and hike 0.2 mi to the cave's end. Two other nearby lava tubes, Skeleton Cave and Wind Cave, are permanently gated to protect bats and deter vandals. (BE)

109. Lava River Cave. Longest lava tube in Oregon, this 1.1-mi cave extends under Hwy 97. Drive S of Bend 11 mi on Hwy 97. Open May 2 to Oct 14. Northwest Forest Pass req'd at trailhead; lantern rentals $4. (BE)

110. Newberry Caldera Rim. 21-mi loop traces wooded rim of gigantic, collapsed volcano in Newberry Nat'l Volcanic Monument, passing views at N Paulina Pk, Cinder Hill, Paulina Pk (Hike #10). (BE)

111. Cinder Hill. Climb to view on Newberry Caldera rim, gaining 1000 ft in 2.9 mi. Drive to Hike #10, continue 4.6 paved mi, keep L through Cinder Hill CG to far end of overflow loop. Hike 1.8 mi to rim, turn R for 1.1 mi. (BE)

OCHOCO MOUNTAINS (map on page 38)

112. Wildcat Trail via White Rock. Expect blowdown on this rarely maintained path. Trace the wooded rim of Mill Cr Wilderness 2.9 mi, turn L on Belknap Trail 2.8 mi down through 1995 fire zone, turn L along Mill Cr 2.9 mi to Wildcat CG (Hike #13). The 8.6-mi route loses 1630 ft. Drive Hwy 26 E of Prineville 24 mi, turn L at a sign for Wildcat Mtn for 6 mi on gravel Rd 3350, turn R on Rd 300 for 2 mi to primitive White Rock CG. (LM)

113. Wildcat Trail via Whistler Spring. Follow a wooded ridge (with blowdown) into Mill Cr Wilderness, losing 1000 ft and gaining 560 ft in 7.4 mi. Then either turn R on the Belknap Tr to Wildcat CG (5.7 mi) or go str on Wildcat Tr 2.9 mi to White Rock CG (Hike #112). Drive past upper Twin Pillar TH (Hike #13), continue 3.2 mi on dirt Rd 27 to Whistler Spr CG. (LM)

114. Lookout Mountain via Ochoco Ranger Station. Longer route to Lookout Mtn's summit than Hike #14 gains 2930 ft in 7.3 mi, but offers 2 other turnaround points—woodsy Duncan Butte (2.9 mi and 1600 ft up) and North Point's rimrock viewpoint (6.1 mi and 2600 ft up). Start at a highway pullout 200 yds E of the closed Ochoco Ranger Station. (LM)

115. Lookout Mountain's South Point. Backdoor route to Lookout Mtn's prairie, the Line Butte Tr gains 1000 ft in 3.9 mi (keep R at jcts) to South Pt's rimrock viewpt. Side trail ambles 2.3 mi to Lookout Mtn summit (Hike #14). Drive as to Hike #14 but continue str on Rd 42 an extra 7 mi to Big Summit Prairie, turn R on Rd 4215 for 9 mi, turn R on Rd 4220 for 1 mi, turn L on Rd 257 a mi to Fawn Cr TH. (LM)

116. Round Mountain via Road 42. June wildflowers spangle the summit mdws of this 6755-ft peak. From the lower TH for Hike #14, take Round Mtn Tr across Rd 42 for 4.1 mi, turn L on an old rd 0.3 mi to top, gaining 1350 ft in all. Connect with Hikes #114, #14, and #117 for a 19.7-mi route from the Ochoco Ranger Sta to Walton Lk. (LM)

117. Walton Lake and Round Mountain. Easy 0.8-mi loop circles Walton Lk, a camping and fishing getaway. Turn off the loop onto Round Mtn Tr to climb 4.6 mi to an old rd, turn R on it 0.3 mi to summit, gaining 1600 ft in all. Drive Hwy 26 E of Prineville 17 mi, fork R at Ochoco Cr for 8.3 mi, veer L on paved Rd 22 for 7 mi to Walton Lk. (LM)

118. North Point. The Bridge Cr Wilderness' only trail, a 1.2-mi abandoned road gains 400 ft to a breathtaking rimrock viewpt on the Ochoco Crest. Drive as to Walton Lk (Hike #117), but keep str past lk on Rd 22 an extra 2 mi, turn L on Rd 150 for 0.7 mi, keep R on Rd 2630 for 6 mi (the last 1.8 mi past Thompson Spr are rough) to TH on L. (LM)

119. Black Canyon via Wolf Mountain. A slightly longer route into the Black Canyon Wilderness than via Boeing Field (Hike #17), this tr starts near historic 107-ft Wolf Mtn lookout tower, built 1947 and still staffed June-Oct. Drive as to Hike #17, continue 1.5 mi on Rd 5810, turn L on rough Rd 5840 for 2.2 mi to a jct. Tower is left 0.3 mi; TH is straight 0.2 mi. Trail loses 1450 ft in 3.5 mi to Black Cayon Cr crossing. (PA)

120. Black Canyon via South Prong. South Prong Tr contours 3 mi through woods to Crowbar Spring, then dives down 1750 ft in 2.6 mi to Big Ford, a bridgeless crossing in heart of Black Canyon Wilderness. Drive 1 mi E of Prineville, turn R on the Paulina Hwy 59.5 mi, turn L to Rager Ranger Sta 11 mi, continue on Rd 58 another 4.4 mi, turn L on Rd 5840 for 7 mi, and

Easy Moderate Difficult

turn R on Rd 400 to the NE corner of Mud Spring Campgd (PA)

121. Cottonwood Creek. In unprotected roadless area N of Black Canyon Wilderness, the Cottonwood Tr drops 1500 ft in 3 mi to forks of Cottonwood Cr, continues downstream 0.8 mi to pvt land. Drive to TH for Hike #17, continue str on Rd 38 an extra 3.1 mile to a 4-way jct, go str on Rd 38 for 11.2 mi to a trailhead at the jct of spur Rd 700 on L. (PA)

122. Aldrich Mountain Cedar Grove. Hike a 1-mile trail to a botanical oddity: 60 acres of Alaska cedars growing on an Eastern Oregon mountainside, 130 miles from other Alaska cedar stands. Drive Hwy 26 E of Dayville 13 mi (or W of John Day 18 mi), turn S on paved Fields Cr Rd 10 mi to a pass, turn R on gravel Rd 2150 for 6 mi. (BM)

STRAWBERRY MOUNTAIN (map on page 54)

123. Nipple Butte. 3-mi ridgecrest tr to craggy viewpoint N of John Day gains only about 500 ft but is, alas, open to motorcycles. Drive Hwy 26 E of John Day 9.5 mi, turn L up Bear Cr on Rd 18 for 13 paved miles and 3 miles of gravel, turn L on Rd 279 for 0.7 mi. (BM)

124. Magone Lake and Magone Slide. Circle this fishing lake on a 2-mi loop through pine woods from a CG, then cross road, climb 0.7 mi to landslide that created the lake in 1860s. Drive Hwy 26 E of John Day 9.5 mi, turn L up Bear Cr on Rd 18 for 13 paved miles, turn L on gravel Rd 3620 for 1.2 mi, turn R on Rd 3618 for 1.5 mi. (BM)

125. Arch Rock. Climb 0.3 mi to a natural arch in a cliff of welded ash. Drive Hwy 26 E of John Day 9.5 mi, turn L up Bear Cr on Rd 18 for 10 paved miles, turn R on gravel Rd 36 for 9 mi, turn R on Rd 3650 for 0.7 mi. (BM)

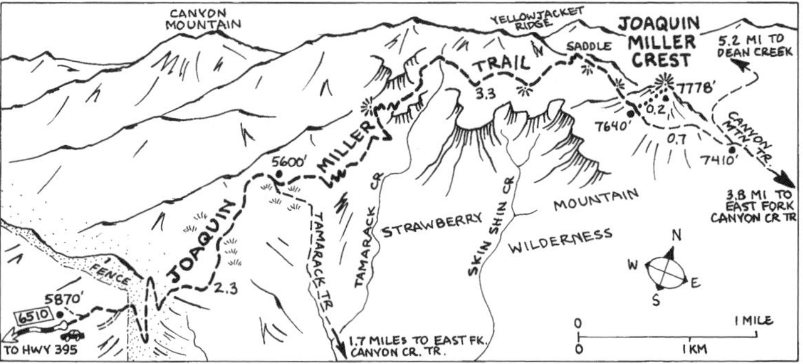

126. Joaquin Miller Trail. A quiet 5.2-mile hike in the Strawberry Mtn Wilderness climbs through pondereosa pine woods to a rocky knoll with a panoramic view, gaining 3250 feet. Drive Hwy 395 south from John Day 9.7 miles to a pointer for "USFS Rt. 15; Wickiup CG 8", turn left on County Rd 65 for 2.9 paved miles, turn left on gravel Rd 6510 at a sign for Alder Gulch, and keep left on Rd 6510 for 5 miles to its end. The start of the trail is confused by cowpaths, but climb 0.3 mile to a wire fence at a hilltop where the tread becomes clear. (BM)

127. Table Mountain Trail. Climb a wooded ridgecrest into the Strawberry Mtn Wilderness. Gain 1500 ft in 3.7 mi to a viewpt knoll, continue level 2.3 mi to a jct with the 3.7-mi loop around Indian Cr Butte in Hike #20.

Easy Moderate Difficult

Drive S on Hwy 395 from John Day 9.7 mi, turn L on paved Rd 65 for 7.2 mi, turn L on gravel Rd 651 for 3 mi. (BM)

128. Buckhorn Meadow Trail. Climb to Wildcat Basin in the Strawberry Mtn Wilderness on a 2.4-mi trail that gains 1000 ft. Shorter than route in Hike #21. Drive Hwy 26 S of John Day 9.7 mi, turn L on paved Rd 65 for 8.9 mi, turn L on gravel Rd 1520 for 4 mi to Canyon Mdw CG, continue 3 rough mi to road's end. (BM)

129. Onion Creek to Strawberry Mountain. Steep, less-used route to Strawberry Mtn Wilderness' highest peak gains 4000 ft in 4.9 mi. Drive as to Hike #23, but park 1.2 mi before Strawberry CG. (PC)

130. High Lake via Lake Creek. This route to High Lake is longer than Hike #22, gaining 1600 ft in 3.7 mi, but is snow-free a month earlier. Drive Hwy 26 S of John Day 9.7 mi, turn L on paved Rd 65 for 13.6 mi, turn L on Rd 16 for 6.5 mi to Logan Valley, turn L on gravel Rd 924 (past Murray CG) for 5.3 mi to rd's end. The last mile is rough. (PC)

131. Mud Lake. This small lake high in the Strawberry Mtn Wilderness is prettier than it sounds. Hike up the Meadow Fork Tr 3 mi, gaining 1300 ft to a jct. Then either go L for 0.2 mi to Mud Lk, or continue 1.5 mi up to the pass between Slide and High Lks (see Hike #22). Drive as to Hike #130, but at Murray CG turn R on Rd 1648 for 0.5 mi, turn L on Rd 021 for 1.4 mi, and turn L on rough Rd 039 for 1.6 mi. (PC)

132. Big Riner Basin. Climb Big Creek's wooded canyon 5.8 mi to a Wilderness viewpt at head of glacial cirque. Gain 2150 ft. Strawberry Lk is 4 mi beyond. Drive as to Hike #130, but at Murray CG turn R on Rd 1648 for 0.5 mi, turn L on Rd 021 for 2.5 mi to its end. (PC)

133. Skyline Trail. Part of a 37.1-mi route tracing the crest of the Strawberry Mtn Wilderness, this faint trail follows a dry, forested ridge 10 mi (gaining 2000 ft) to Big Riner Basin (Hike #132). From Prairie City go 19.5 mi S on paved Rd 62, turn R 1.4 mi on Rd 101. (PC)

134. Delintment Creek. A 3.2-mi loop from Delintment Lake CG descends a creek's grassy swale, returns through ponderosa pines. From Prineville, drive Paulina Hwy SE 59 mi. Beyond Paulina 3.7 mi, fork R on Rd 112 for 16 mi, turn R on paved Weberg Rd 8 mi, continue on gravel Rd 41 for 10.5 mi to TH on right. From Burns, take Hwy 20 west 3 mi, turn R on Burns-Izee Rd 127 for 12 mi, turn L on Rd 41 for 26.5 mi to an X-jct, turn L for 5 mi. (Snow Mtn Ranger Dist, 541- 573-4300)

135. Myrtle Creek. In a ponderosa pine canyon bordering the high desert, this trail ambles down along Myrtle Cr 2.1 mi to a jct. There you either climb R up W Myrtle Cr 2.7 mi to Rd 440, or continue down the main cr 6 mi to pvt land. Drive Hwy 395 N of Burns 18 mi, turn L on Rd 31 for 14 paved mi to cr crossing. (Burns RD, 541-573-4300)

136. Swick Creek Old Growth. Paved, all-accessible interpretive trail loops 0.7 mi through ponderosa pine woods. Drive Hwy 395 S of John Day 16 mi to signed parking area on left. (BM)

137. North Fork Malheur River. For a short hike, follow this river from its start as a mountain brook 2.8 mi down to confluence of Crane Cr (Hike #138). Or continue 8.4 mi downriver through canyon to pvt land, losing 850 ft in all. From Prairie City, take Rd 62 SE for 8 mi, turn left on Rd 13 for 16.2 miles, turn R on paved Rd 16 for 2.2 mi, turn R on rough Rd 1675

Easy Moderate Difficult

for 3 mi to North Fk CG, continue 1 mi to TH. (PC)

138. Crane Creek. 6.3-mi trail down Crane Cr's forested valley to N Fk Malheur River (see Hike #137) begins as abandoned road, loses 1100 ft. From Prairie City, drive paved Rd 62 south 23 mi to Summit Prairie, keep L on paved Rd 16 for 4.5 mi, turn R on gravel Rd 1663 for 1 mi to Crane Cr, fork L to green metal gate at start of trail. (PC)

139. Little Baldy via Lookout Mountain. Stroll 3.6 mi along panoramic ridge to viewpt of John Day Valley. ATVs allowed. From Prairie City, drive S on paved Rd 62 for 20.2 mi, turn L on gravel Rd 1665 for 4 mi, turn L on very rough dirt Rd 548 past Sheep Mtn a total of 6 mi to rd closure at Lookout Mtn. Walk out abandoned roadbed 2.5 mi, continue on a ridgecrest tr 1.1 mi to Little Baldy. Nearly level. (PC)

140. Lookout Mtn via Sheep Creek. Gain 2400 ft in 5.2 mi through open woods along (often dry) Sheep Cr to Rd 548 at Lookout Mtn (Hike #139). From Prairie City, take Rd 62 SE for 8 mi, turn left on paved Rd 13 for 14.9 miles to cattle guard and "Sheep Cr Tr" sign on R. (PC)

141. Reynolds Creek. Stroll 1.4 miles up a forest creek, then scramble 0.2 miles NE up to a rock arch and petroglyphs at a basalt cliff *(GPS location N44°25.449′ W118°29.082′)*. From Prairie City, turn S past Depot Park on paved Rd 62 for 7.5 mi, turn L on gravel Rd 2635 for 4.3 mi. (PC)

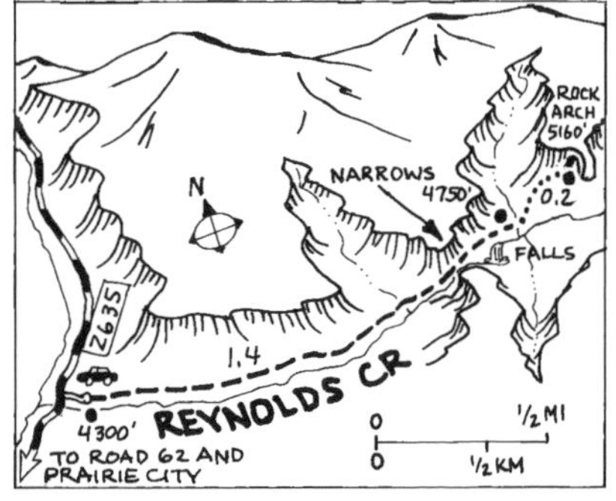

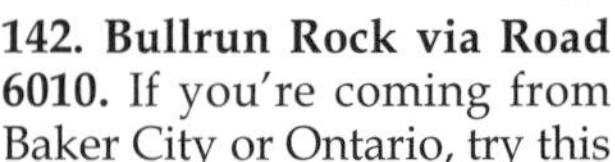

142. Bullrun Rock via Road 6010. If you're coming from Baker City or Ontario, try this route into Monument Rock Wilderness instead of Hike #26. Take Hwy 26 to Unity, turn west onto Rd 600 for 4.2 paved mi and another 3 mi on gravel, turn L on Rd 6010 for 5.2 mi. Tr 1973 gains 1300 ft in 4.3 mi to gate beside Bullrun Rk. (WH)

143. Davis Creek Trail. Woodsy 7.8-mi path contours around Dixie Butte, crossing 3 creeks to Rd 2050. For day hike, go 3.8 mi to Deerhorn Cr, gaining 400 ft. From Hwy 26 at Austin Jct, drive 0.2 mi toward John Day, turn R on gravel Rd 2614 for 2 mi to trailhead on L. (BM)

BLUE MOUNTAINS - SOUTH (map on page 78)

144. Van Patten Lake. Climb to a gorgeous alpine lake in a granite cirque. From I-84 at N Powder exit 285, follow Anthony Lk signs 18.4 mi, turn L on Rd 130 for 0.2 mi, and park. Walk up steep dirt road to left 1 mi, continue 0.5 mi on trail to lk, gaining 970 ft in all. (WH)

145. Dutch Flat. A shorter route to Dutch Flat Lake is described in Hike #29, but you can also ascend a valley with pines, meadows, old mines, and cows 5.7 mi to Dutch Flat and continue 1.3 mi to the lake, gaining 2400 ft in all. From I-84 at N Powder exit 285, follow Anthony Lk signs 13 mi, turn L on Rd 7307 for 1.4 mi. (WH)

146. The Lakes Lookout. Climb 0.7 mile amid granite crags to a former

lookout site above Anthony Lake (see Hike #28) with a panoramic view of the Elkhorn Range. The trail gains 680 feet. From Anthony Lk, drive Rd 73 west 4 mi to a pass near milepost 13, turn L on rough dirt Rd 210 for 1.6 miles, keep R at a pass for 0.3 mi, and turn L to the trailhead *(GPS location N44°57.085′ W118°14.708′)*. (WH)

147. Peavy Trail to Cracker Saddle. Repeated fires have left snags along this faint 3.6-mi trail from the rentable, historic Peavy Cabin to an alpine pass and the Elkhorn Crest Tr. Gains 1700 ft. From Anthony Lk (Hike #28), drive 12 mi east on Rd 73, turn L on rough Rd 380 for 3 mi to its end. (WH)

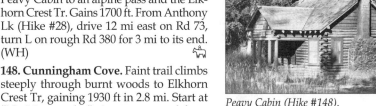

148. Cunningham Cove. Faint trail climbs steeply through burnt woods to Elkhorn Crest Tr, gaining 1930 ft in 2.8 mi. Start at "No Motorcycles" sign across road from the rentable 1934 Peavy Cabin ($45/night, sleeps 4, open July 1 to October 31, call 877-444-6777 or *www.recreation.gov*). From Anthony Lk, drive Rd 73 east 12 mi, turn L on rough Rd 380 for 2.9 mi. (WH)

Peavy Cabin (Hike #148).

149. Summit Lake. This 22-acre subalpine lake (described in Hike #29) can also be accessed by a 1.2-mi trail that gains 1000 ft, but the access road is horrible. From Haines, drive 4 mi toward Anthony Lk, follow signs L through Muddy Cr and Bulger Flats 6 mi, turn L on N Powder River Rd 7301 7 mi. (WH)

150. Red Mountain Lake. Steep trail gains 1100 ft in 1.3 mi to alpine lake ringed by cliffs, but the road to the trailhead is horrible. Drive as to Hike #149 but go only 6 mi on Rd 7301. (WH)

151. Killamacue Lake. Trail follows Killamacue Cr to a lake basin high in the Elkhorn Range's crags, gaining 1800 ft in 3.2 mi. From Haines, drive W on Rock Cr Rd 6 mi to Rock Creek, continue straight 4.5 mi on increasingly miserable road to trailhead. (WH)

152. Rock Creek Lake. This stunning cirque lake, banked with snow and backed by the Elkhorns' tallest pk, would be a popular goal except that the access road is miserable. The 3.5-mi trail gains 2400 ft. From Haines, drive west on Rock Cr Rd 6 mi to Rock Creek, continue straight on increasingly impossible road 6 mi. (WH)

153. Pine Creek Reservoir. Hike an undrivable road past a scenic alpine reservoir into mtn goat habitat. Drive Hwy 30 north of Baker City 4 mi, turn left 2 mi to Wingville, continue on Rd 646 up Pine Creek 5 mi on pavement, then road worsens fast. It's 5.4 steep mi to the reservoir, but expect to walk 1 to 4.4 miles, depending on your car. (WH)

154. Phillips Reservoir. Paths through open pine woods along this reservoir's shore are best for mtn bikers or equestrians, and only then if the reservoir is full. From the popular Union Cr CG (west of Baker City 19 mi on Hwy 7), take the North Shore Trail 4 mi west or 1.7 mi east. The South Shore Trail extends 6 mi from the S end of Mason Dam to SW Shore CG. (WHA)

155. Indian Rock Trail. Open to motorcycles, this 1.6-mi tr climbs 600 ft to a viewpoint of Phillips Reservoir. Start across Hwy 7 from the Union

Easy Moderate Difficult

Cr Campground entrance. (WH)

156. South Fork Desolation Creek. Two trails now start at this quiet trailhead, making possible a 15-mile loop into the Greenhorn Range. First hike up the creek's forested valley 7 mi to the Portland Mine, continue 0.8 mi on old rd to Dupratt Spr Saddle (see Hike #35), gaining 2200 ft. Then keep left at junctions to return via Saddle Camp. Drive as to Hike #35, but continue past Olive Lk 6-mi on Rd 10, turn L on Rd 45 for 1 mi. (N)

157. Indian Rock and Princess Trail. Through burned woods atop the rounded Greenhorn Range, a 3.1-mi trail gains 800 ft to a jct near Head O'Boulder Camp. To the R, climb 0.8 mi to Indian Rock Lookout bldg (on an ancient rd), or go str on Princess Trail 6 faint mi to Dupratt Spring Pass. Drive as to Hike #35, but continue 6 mi past Olive Lk on Rd 10, turn L on Rd 45 for 4.5 mi to a pass. (N)

158. Lake Creek. From the Greenhorn Mtns at Saddle Camp (see Hike #35) hike 4.7 mi south down Saddle Ridge to a crossing of Rd. 10 (east of Olive Lake 4.1 mi at pole fence gates), continue 7.5 mi to Granite Creek in North Fork John Day Wilderness (see Hike #34). (N)

159. Lower North Fork John Day River. Long, rough road accesses the west end of the 26.7-mi North Fork John Day River Trail (see also Hikes #34 and #33). Drive Hwy 395 south of Ukiah 14 mi (or north of Dale 1 mi), turn east on gravel Rd 55 for 5.5 mi, go straight on Rd 5506 for 6.5 mi of gravel and 6 mi of terrible dirt to road's end. (N)

160. Winom Creek. For a 10.2-mi loop in the N Fk John Day Wilderness canyonlands, start at Winom CG, descend Winom Cr Trail 4 mi, turn L up Big Cr Trail 4.5 mi, turn L on tie trail 1.2 mi, and follow CG road 0.5 mi L to your car. Cumulative elev gain: 1700 ft. From Ukiah, drive paved Blue Mtn Byway (Rd 52) SE 23 mi, turn R on Rd 440 a mile. (N)

161. Tower Mountain. Start at Winom CG (Hike #160), but take Upper Winom Tr up 4.4 mi, turn R on ridgecrest Cable Cr Trail 3 mi, turn R on dirt Rd 5226 for 0.8 mi to staffed Tower Mtn lookout, gaining 2400 ft. To complete a 16-mi loop, descend Tr 3156 to Big Cr Mdws, turn R on tie trail to CG. (N)

162. Silver Butte. From Ukiah, drive paved Blue Mtn Byway (Rd 52) SE for 25 mi, turn R on Rd 5225 for 5 mi of gravel and 4.5 mi of dirt. Hike Silver Butte Tr along ridge in Wilderness 3.3 mi to fork and viewpoint of river canyon. Optional 4.6-mi loop continues steeply down to N Fk John Day R (see Granite Cr Hike #34). (N)

BLUE MOUNTAINS - NORTH (map on page 98)

163. Columbia River Railroad. Converted to a hiker/biker path, this abandoned, 4.8-mile gravel railroad grade along the scenic, windy Columbia River shore begins at McNary Beach Park, ends at Hat Rock State Park (picnic area, lake, historic rock). From I-82 in Umatilla, take Hwy 730 east 1.2 mi and follow McNary Beach signs left. (O)

164. Buck Creek and Buck Mountain. Two other Wilderness trails begin at the trailhead for Ninemile Ridge (Hike #37). The well-built Buck Creek Trail goes upstream 3 mi to a ford and climbs a ridge 3 mi to an upper TH. The faint, rough Buck Mtn Tr zooms up 2100 ft in 2.2 mi, contours along rim 5.7 mi (crossing clearcuts and log roads) to Buck Cr Trail's upper TH, making a 13.9-mi loop possible. (WW)

Easy Moderate Difficult

165. South Fork Umatilla River. Trail ascends creek 1.8 mi before petering out in brush. Drive as to Hike #36, but continue 3 mi on Rd 32 to TH on left. (WW)

166. Lick Creek Trail. Steep Wilderness path climbs creek canyon 2.3 mi (gaining 1800 ft) to grassy ridgecrest. Either turn R on main trail 1 mi to upper TH, or turn L on faint ridgetop path 1.6 mi to Grouse Mtn viewpoint. The lower TH is on north side of Rd 32, 1 mi west of the TH for Hike #36. For upper TH, drive E of Weston on Hwy 204 for 15.3 mi, turn R on McDougall Camp Rd 3715 for 3.4 mi to its end. (WW)

167. Bobsled Ridge. This path starts with a deep ford of the Umatilla River, then rockets uphill, gaining 1700 ft in 2 mi, and then ambles along a grassy crest 2.9 mi to remote Rd 3128. Start on the south side of Rd 32, 1 mi west of the TH for Hike #36. (WW)

168. Bear Creek. Long abandoned trail descends 4.8 mi through cool, old-growth woods to log cabin ruin (losing 2000 ft), ascends N Fk Meacham Cr 2.3 mi to grassy campsite at Pot Cr, and climbs 2.5 mi to flat-topped Thimbleberry Mtn, gaining 2600 ft. From I-84 take Kamela exit 243, drive E on Rd. 31 for 13 mi,turn left 1 mi on Rd 3113 to trailhead, opposite Summit Guard Station. (WW)

169. Lookingglass Creek. From Woodland Campground (4 mi E of Tollgate on Hwy 204), take Eagle Ridge Tr across Rd 3725 and down a ridge 4.9 mi to a footridge over Lookingglass Creek, losing 1200 ft. (WW)

170. Wenaha River via Hoodoo Trail. Wilderness trail switchbacks down 1400 ft in 3 mi to thigh-deep river ford and Wenaha River Trail (2.2 mi W of Crooked Cr bridge). From Troy, drive toward Elk Flats on gravel Rd 62 for 13 mi, turn R on Rd 6214 for 5 mi. (PO)

171. Wenaha River via Cross Canyon Trail. Wilderness trail switchbacks down 1760 ft in 2.7 mi to thigh-deep river ford and Wenaha R Tr (7.9 mi W of Crooked Cr bridge). From Troy, drive toward Elk Flats on gravel Rd 62 for 17 mi, turn R on Rd 6217 for 3 mi. (PO)

172. Wenaha River via Elk Flats. Woodsy 4.6-mi Wilderness trail loses 2100 ft to knee-deep ford at Wenaha Forks. From Troy, follow Elk Flats signs on Rd 62 for 21 mi, turn R on Rd 290 for 0.7 mi. (PO)

173. Round Butte. Follow an open, relatively level ridgecrest from Indian CG into Wenaha-Tucannon Wilderness 3.1 mi to a saddle. Either bushwhack left 0.3 mi to Round Butte's viewpt (gain 300 ft) or continue 6 mi to Wenaha Forks, losing 2800 ft. From Walla Walla, drive E on paved road up Mill Creek 12 mi to Kooskooskie, continue on what becomes gravel Rd 65 for 16 mi, turn L on Rd 64 for 5.5 mi. (PO)

174. Bull Prairie Lake. Start at 28-site campground with 3 fishing piers, hike 1.1 mi around lake stocked with trout. From Heppner, drive Hwy 207 south toward Spray 44 mi, turn L on Rd 2039 for 3 mi. (H)

175. Madison Butte. Climb 3.7 mi through dry lodgepole / ponderosa pine woods to Madison Butte lookout bldg, gaining 1600 ft. If you like, return via Alder Cr for 10.2-mi loop. From Heppner, drive south toward Spray 26 mi on Hwy 207 to Wright Park, turn left up Rock Cr on Rd 670 (alias Rd 22) for 3.5 mi, turn L on Rd 2119 for 3.5 mi, turn L on Rd 21 for 6 mi, turn

L on Rd 140 for 0.5 mi, and turn L on Rd 146 for 0.6 mi. Hike up Skookum Trail 2.1 mi to a ridgetop junction. Either go left 1.6 mi to Madison Butte, or keep right at all junctions for 5.5 mi for the Alder Cr loop. The loop's final mile is along a road. (H)

HELLS CANYON (map on page 108)

176. Davis and Swamp Creeks. Descend 1 mile through lovely, old-growth ponderosa pine woods to Davis Creek (losing 900 ft), then cross Starvation Ridge 2.3 mi to Swamp Cr (gaining 700 ft and losing 1250 ft). Intensive cattle grazing lessens the area's charm. From Enterprise, drive Hwy 3 north 21 mi. Between mileposts 23 and 22, turn R on Rd 174 and keep L for 0.3 mi to Chico TH. (Wallowa Valley Ranger Dist, 541-426-4978)

177. Summit Ridge. Follow Hells Canyon's rim to Somers Pt, a spectacular, rarely visited viewpoint a vertical mile above Pittsburg Landing. From Hat Pt (Hike #45) drive 1.5 mi back toward Imnaha, turn R on rough dirt Rd 315 for 4.5 mi, and park at Warnock Corrals. Hike a nearly level, ancient road along rim 9.2 mi, veer R on trail toward Pittsburg 2.5 mi, turn L along rim 1 mi to Somers Pt. (HC)

178. Temperance Creek. From Hells Canyon's rim at Warnock Corrals (see Hike #177), trace this creek 9.9 miles down through Wilderness and burned woods to the Snake River Trail (losing 5250 feet!), turn north through scenic gorge for 9.2 nearly level miles to Pittsburg Guard Station. (HC)

179. High Trail. Traverse the Hells Canyon Wilderness on a zigzagging trail along a grassy benchland halfway between the Oregon rim and the Snake River. From the Saddle Cr TH (Hike #46), hike 4.6 mi across Freeze-out Saddle, and turn L on the High Trail. From there it's 10.1 mi to the Hat Creek cabin and 39.8 mi to Pittsburg Guard Sta. (HC)

WALLOWA MOUNTAINS (map on page 126)

180. Lick Creek. Backdoor route to Imnaha Falls (Hike #49) climbs 2.8 mi up Lick Creek to Imnaha Divide (gaining 800 ft), descends 2.2 mi to Imnaha River, losing 1660 ft in Eagle Cap Wilderness. Drive as to Hike #50, but continue S on paved Rd 39 an extra 3 mi to the Lick Cr CG, turn R on gravel Rd 3925 for 0.2 mi, turn R on Rd 015 for 2.2 mi. (HC)

181. Wing Ridge. More popular in winter than summer, this 10.1-mile loop from a sno-park gains 1300 feet in 2.5 miles through burned woods to Wing Ridge, descends 2.5 miles to Big Sheep Creek (see Hike #50 map), and turns left to return on the Tenderfoot Wagon Road. The loop passes two Nordic ski camp bases that can be rented from Wing Ridge Ski Tours (*www.wingski.com*, 541-398-1980). Drive as to Hike #50, but stop at Salt Cr Summit Sno-park. (WV)

Wing Ridge in winter.

182. Huckleberry Mountain. A panoramic view awaits at this former lookout site on an alpine ridge at the northern edge of the Eagle Cap Wilderness. The switchbacking 1.9-mi trail gains 1950 ft. Drive Hwy 82 to Wallowa, turn south on North Bear Creek Rd 8250 for 3.2 paved miles

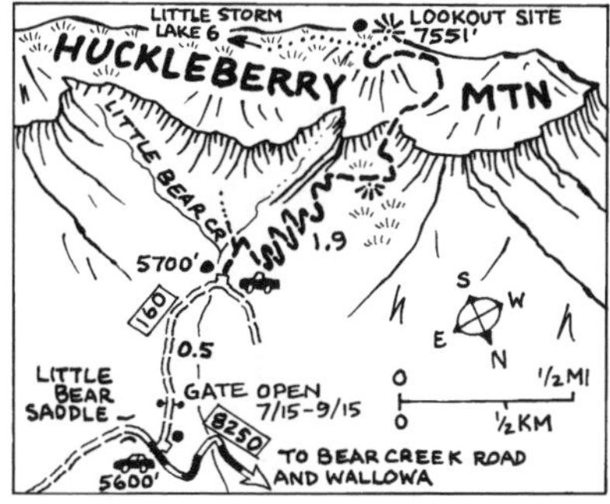

and another 5 mi of good gravel, then fork left on rougher gravel 7.4 mi, keeping uphill on the largest road at junctions to a parking area in Little Bear Saddle. Then walk the gated old road to the right half a mile to the old trailhead, just beyond Little Bear Cr *(GPS location N45°25.81′ W117°28.80′)*. (E)

183. Cougar Ridge. This faint, alternative 9.6-mi route to Standley Cabin (Hike #64) gradually gains 1600 ft along a dry, wooded ridge in Eagle Cap Wilderness. Drive as to Hike #64, but after 10.8 mi on Big Canyon Rd, keep R to continue on Rd 8270 for 5.3 rough miles. (E)

184. Point Prominence and Mount Fanny. Two peaks with classic views are accessible by rough dirt roads popular with ORVs. For Pt Prominence, drive as to Hike #65, but just before Rock Spr TH, follow "Pt. Prominence" sign to R on Rd 6220 for 2 mi to Harris ORV camp, ride L up Rd 800 for 0.3 mi to staffed lookout. For Mt. Fanny, park at Moss Spr CG (Hike #66), follow Bellshears Trail signs 7 mi, keep left 1 mi to summit. The 2 peaks can be connected with a 16.1-mile loop on roads, the Bellshears Tr, and Bell Tr. (LG)

185. Mule Peak Lookout. Steep, faint trails make possible a grueling 11.4-mi loop to Mule Pk's abandoned lookout bldg (see Hike #68 map), gaining 3710 ft. From Union, drive Hwy 203 south 14.2 mi, turn L on gravel Rd 77 for 10 mi to a 5-way jct, turn L on Rd 600 for 4 mi to S Fk Catherine Cr. Hike 3.1 mi upstream, fork L 2.2 mi to Sand Pass, keep R past Mule Pk to return on loop. (LG)

186. Sawtooth Crater. Climb to a viewpoint atop a rock knoll in the center of a giant, forested bowl, gaining 500 ft in 0.8 mi. From Hwy 203 at Medical Springs, take E Eagle Cr Drive 1.6 mi, fork right onto Collins Rd 70 for 5.6 mi to trail sign on spur Rd 740 to left. (LG)

187. Fake Creek. Nearly abandoned 6-mi trail climbs 2000 ft over scenic pa6ss, connecting W Eagle TH (Hike #69) with Main Eagle TH (Hike #70), making possible a grand 3- or 4-day loop past Traverse Lk. (E)

188. East Fork Falls. Park at Cornucopia TH (see Hike #75). Keep to R at pack station parking area, walk up abandoned road 1.4 mi to E Fk Pine Cr ford and hiker bridge, follow trail upstream 1.1 mi to lovely 12-ft E Fk Falls, gaining 1200 ft in all. If you like, continue 4.6 mi to Blue Cr or 7.2 mi to the S Fk Imnaha R. (E)

189. Deadman Canyon. Near Fish Lk Campground, climb 1.8 mi through open forest and high mdws heavily grazed by cattle to the Sugarloaf Trail. Jog left 0.3 mi, then continue R on Deadman Canyon Tr 0.5 mi to a pass, gaining 650 ft in all. If you like, continue down Deadman Canyon into Eagle Cap Wilderness 3.5 mi to the S Fk Imnaha R near Imnaha Falls (Hike #49). Drive to downtown Halfway, continue str on Main St 0.6 mi, turn R and follow signs for Fish Lk 19.3 mi. Just beyond the Fish Lk CG entrance, turn L on Rd 410 for 0.6 mi. (WH)

Easy / Moderate / Difficult

190. Twin Lakes. From a lake with a 6-site campground, a faint 3.1-mi trail descends 1800 feet through burned woods to a S Fk Imnaha R ford at Blue Hole (see Hike #49). Drive as to Hike #189, but continue past Fish Lk 4.5 mi on Rd 66. (E)

HIGH DESERT (map on page 176)

191. Silver Creek & Yamsay Mountain. Overswept by fire, this northern portion of the Fremont Trail has become faint. Drive Hwy 31 west of the Silver Lk Ranger Station 0.3 mi, turn L on paved Rd 27 for 9.4 mi, turn R on gravel Rd 2804 mi for 2.6 mi, and fork L on Rd 7645 to a T-shaped jct. Turn L on Rd 036 and then keep R at junctions for 2.2 mi to the Antler Trailhead's 5-site campground. Hike the Fremont Tr either down 8 mi along Silver Cr to Rd 27 or up 8.6 mi to Yamsay Mtn, gaining 2100 ft. (Silver Lk RD 541-576-2107)

192. Blue Lake. Perhaps the most popular hike in the Gearhart Mtn Wilderness gains 700 ft in 2.4 mi through pine/fir woods to Blue Lake. An 0.8-mi loop circles the lake. If you like, continue 4 mi to The Notch (see Hike #82). Drive paved Rd 28 as to Dead Horse Lk (Hike #81), but go 2.2 mi farther N on Rd 28, turn W on gravel Rd 3411 for 6 mi, turn L on Rd 3372 for 2 mi, and turn R on Rd 015 for 1.5 mi to the North Fork Trailhd. (BL)

193. Deming Creek to Boulder Spring. A backdoor route into the Gearhart Mtn Wilderness follows Deming Cr, gaining 2600 ft in 6 mi to the Gearhart Tr. Continue right 0.8 mi to viewpoint at The Notch (see Hike #82). From Bly, drive Hwy 140 east 1.4 mi, turn L on Campbell Rd for 0.6 mi, turn R on paved Rd 34 for 4 mi, turn L on gravel Rd 335 for 1.5 mi, turn R on Rd 018 up Deming Cr 3 mi to road's end. (BL)

194. Dead Cow Trail to Dead Horse Lake. Popular with equestrians, a trail network through dense lodgepole pine woods allows a 10.7-mi loop from Lee Thomas Trailhead to Dead Horse Lk (see Hike #81). From Dead Horse Lk, return to paved Rd 28, follow it N 2.2 mi, turn L on gravel Rd 3411 for 4.4 mi to trailhead on left. (PY)

195. Abert Rim via Poison Creek. Fenced private land blocks the start of the 1-mi scramble trail up Poison Creek to Abert Rim—otherwise an easier route to the rim than via Juniper Cr (Hike #87). Drive Hwy 395 to milepost 83, hike 0.5 mi around fence to trail. (L-BLM)

196. Walker Trailhead to Crooked Creek. Best on horseback or bicycle, this fairly level, 7.9-mi section of the Crane Mtn Tr skirts Bull Prairie through some clearcuts, largely on old roads, from the Fremont Tr at the S Fk of Crooked Cr (see Hike #88) to the Walker TH, 4.1 mi north of Hwy 140 on paved Rd 3615. (LA)

197. Rogger Meadow. Follow the Crane Mtn Tr from a quaking aspen mdw along a ridgecrest with views from Goose Lake to Hart Mtn. From Lakeview, drive Hwy 140 east up to Warner Canyon ski area, veer R toward Camas Prairie 2.5 mi, and turn R on paved Rd 3915 for 3.5 mi to the Crane Mtn Tr crossing at Rogger Mdw. To the R, the trail climbs along a scenic crest 10.5 mi to Crane Mtn (Hike #198). To the L, the trail ambles 3 mi north and follows paved backroads 6 mi to the Walker TH (Hike #196). (LA)

198. Crane Mountain. Motor vehicles can drive to the fire lookout and panoramic viewpoint atop 8347-ft Crane Mtn, but the road is so steep and awful that you might rather walk, gaining 1400 ft in 2.7 mi. The Crane Mtn Tr that crosses the road just below the summit extends south 8.3 mi to California (open to motorcycles) and north past Rogger Mdw (Hike #197). Drive as to Hike #197, continue on gravel Rd 3915 for 7 mi, turn R on Rd 4011 for 3 mi. (LA)

STEENS MOUNTAIN (map on page 214)

199. Malheur Cave. This privately owned, half-mile long lava tube cave is used for Masonic ceremonies and is not open to the public. From Burns, drive Highway 78 east toward Jordan Valley 52 miles. Between mileposts 51 and 52, turn north on gravel Norman Rinch Rd for 3 miles. After a cattle guard turn left through a green metal gate for 0.4 mile on a dirt road.

Donner und Blitzen River.

200. Donner und Blitzen River. Two trails begin at the far end of the Page Springs Campground, 3 mi east of Frenchglen on the Steens Mountain Loop Rd. The 1.4-mi Nature Trail climbs 200 feet to a rimrock viewpoint. A very rough, faint path also follows the Donner und Blitzen River upstream 0.8 mile. Adventurers can bushwhack onwards amid brush and rocks. (B-BLM)

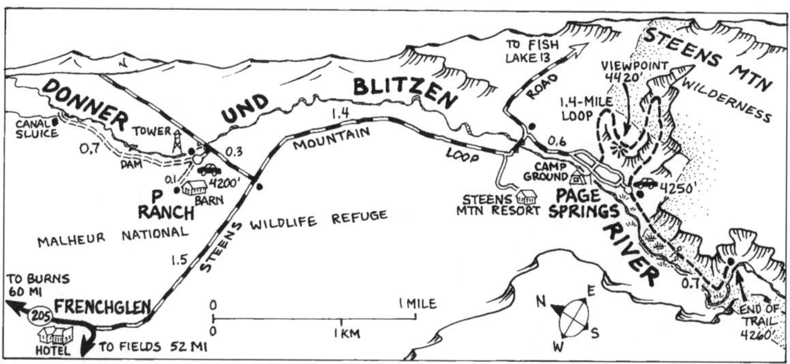

201. Van Horn Creek. Bushwhack up a desert canyon to meadows high in the Pueblo Mtns, gaining 1500 ft in 3.6 mi. From the Nevada border near Denio, drive the paved road N toward Fields (and Burns) for 4 miles to the Van Horn Cr crossing. Park here and follow deer trails up the narrow canyon 2.3 mi to a cabin site amid cottonwoods. Continue scrambling upstream 1.3 mi to Van Horn Basin, a cattle mdw bordering the Desert Trail's route. (B-BLM)

Index

Panorama of Kiger Gorge on Steens Mountain (Hike #92).

NEZ PERCE (NEE-ME-POO) TRAIL
NATIONAL HISTORIC TRAIL

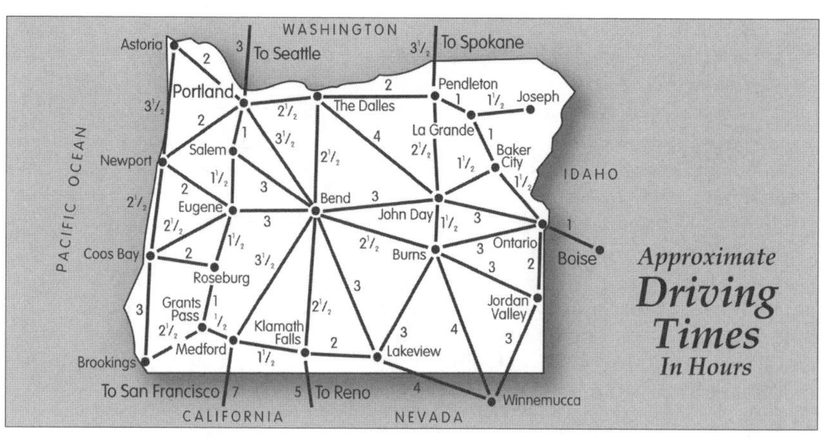
WASHINGTON
To Seattle
To Spokane
Astoria
Portland
The Dalles
Pendleton
Joseph
La Grande
Baker City
Newport
Salem
PACIFIC OCEAN
IDAHO
Eugene
Bend
John Day
Coos Bay
Burns
Ontario
Boise
Roseburg
Grants Pass
Medford
Klamath Falls
Lakeview
Jordan Valley
Brookings
To San Francisco
To Reno
Winnemucca
CALIFORNIA
NEVADA
Approximate
Driving
Times
In Hours

About the Author

William L. Sullivan is the author of a dozen books and numerous articles about Oregon, including a monthly "Oregon Trails" column for the Eugene *Register-Guard* and the Salem *Statesman-Journal.* A fifth-generation Oregonian, Sullivan began hiking at the age of five and has been exploring new trails ever since. After receiving an English degree from Cornell University and studying at Germany's Heidelberg University, he completed an M.A. in German at the University of Oregon.

In 1985 Sullivan set out to investigate Oregon's wilderness on a 1,361-mile solo backpacking trek from the state's westernmost shore at Cape Blanco to Oregon's easternmost point in Hells Canyon. His journal of that two-month adventure, published as *Listening for Coyote,* was chosen by the Oregon Cultural Heritage Commission as one of Oregon's "100 Books."

Information about Sullivan's speaking schedule, his books, and his favorite adventures is available online at *www.oregonhiking.com.* He and his wife Janell live in Eugene, but spend summers at the log cabin they built by hand on a remote, roadless river in Oregon's Coast Range. Sullivan's memoir, *Cabin Fever,* chronicles the adventure of building that cabin retreat.